HERBERT CROLY OF

THE NEW REPUBLIC

HERBERT CROLY OF

THE NEW REPUBLIC

The Life and Thought of an
American Progressive

By David W. Levy

PRINCETON UNIVERSITY PRESS

PRINCETON, NEW JERSEY

Copyright © 1985 by Princeton University Press
Published by Princeton University Press, 41 William Street,
Princeton, New Jersey 08540
In the United Kingdom: Princeton University Press,
Guildford, Surrey

ISBN 0-691-04725-1

Publication of this book has been aided by the
Louis A. Robb Fund of Princeton University Press

This book has been composed in Linotron Bembo

Printed in the United States of America by
Princeton University Press
Princeton, New Jersey

For Lynne

semper amica mihi, semper et uxor eris.
Propertius, ii, 6

CONTENTS

Illustrations ix

Preface xi

1. "Jenny June" and "The Great Suggester" 3

2. Harvard College versus David Croly 43

3. The Blank Years, 1888–1909 72

4. *The Promise of American Life* 96

5. "Taking on the Form of the Sun God" 132

6. *Progressive Democracy* 162

7. A Journal of Opinion 185

8. Years of "Rare Opportunity," 1914–1918 218

9. Years of Despair, 1919–1930 263

10. Conclusion 301

Selected Bibliography 309

Index 327

ILLUSTRATIONS

(between pp. 184 and 185)

1. Herbert Croly (1869–1930)
2. Jane Cunningham Croly (1829–1901)
3. David Goodman Croly (1829–1889)
4. Learned Hand (1872–1961)
5. Felix Frankfurter (1882–1965)
6. Willard and Dorothy Straight
7. Walter Lippmann (1889–1974)
8. Walter Weyl (1873–1919)
9. Francis Hackett (1883–1962)
10. Randolph Bourne (1886–1918)
11. Edmund Wilson (1895–1972)
12. Bruce Bliven (1889–1977)

PREFACE

WHAT follows in these pages is the story of an American intellectual. Herbert Croly fought in no wars. He ran for no public office. He explored no dark lands and left behind no ingenious inventions. His life, as far as I am able to tell, was never put at serious risk. And when he died there were many who hated what he stood for, but no one, I believe, who hated *him*. The simplest truth about him is that he was a man of ideas. What Perry Miller once wrote about Jonathan Edwards is true also of Croly: his real life was the life of his mind.[1] "Temperate, judiciously temperate in all other things," one friend wrote, "he could not let thought alone. A day passed without reflection left him restless."[2]

He was not restless very often. For four decades he resolutely directed his best powers to an analysis of American life, and the results of that long inquiry were so clear-headed, so persuasive and illuminating, they came to be regarded as distinctly helpful by a generation of Americans groping for understanding in the midst of a confusing time. "If I were attempting anything like an appraisal of Herbert Croly," Walter Lippmann declared, "I should say, I think, that he was the first important political philosopher who appeared in America in the twentieth century."[3] That judgment has endured, and with it, a second judgment—that the course of American political thought in our century has been deeply affected by the days he spent in laborious reflection.

His was the sort of mind that probed deeply, and his special talent was the ability to put passing events into large contexts. It was never sufficient for him merely to describe some trend or to outline the contours of some debate or to delineate the character of some politician. He was adroit enough at such description. But he was not content until the trend had been connected to other trends and revealed as part of a general movement of history—thus, for example, the growth of corporations was, for him, part of the sudden rise of specialized activity which characterized the modern world. Nor could

[1] Perry Miller, *Jonathan Edwards* (New York, 1949), iv.

[2] Philip Littell, "As a Friend," *The New Republic*, 63 (July 16, 1930): 243 (hereafter cited as *NR*).

[3] Walter Lippmann, "Notes for a Biography," *NR*, 63 (July 16, 1930): 250.

he rest easy until today's debate was traced backward to its historical genesis—the quarrels of the progressive era were, to him, extensions of the ideological divisions of the federalist period. And no politician was fully delineated—not Bryan, nor Hanna, nor Roosevelt, nor Wilson, nor any of them—until Croly had somehow linked him with some persistent tradition in American life or, even better, with some persistent proclivity in the human spirit. This was what Felix Frankfurter meant when he asserted that "Croly's thinking cut below episodes and incidents. . . . [F]or him, politics floated in the stream of history and was significant only in so far as it fulfilled the possibilities of man's nature."[4] It was also what another friend was trying to express when she wrote that "to talk to him was to see life in all its flow and movement—to see it with meaning, and with a sense of sequence and continuity."[5]

Biographers almost always overestimate the achievements and the influence of their subjects, and our evaluations should be appropriately discounted. But it seems to me that it is not extravagant to suggest that anyone who wants to understand the assumptions that have grounded our politics, the ideas that have defined the limits of our political discourse, must give respectful attention to Herbert Croly's work: his penetrating analysis of American history; his bold critique of progressive reform; his redefinition of liberalism's responsibilities; his enduring contribution to serious journalism.

It would be pleasant to be able to report that Croly combined his intellectual force with a special personal magnetism, that he was a sparkling conversationalist whose ready wit and easy charm caused men and women to travel long distances to bask in his light. Unfortunately nobody ever talked about him that way. According to Edmund Wilson, who admired him greatly, "one's first encounters with Herbert Croly were likely to be rather baffling. It was never easy for him to deal with people, and if the visitor himself were at all diffident, he would be likely to find the conversation subsiding into a discontinuous series of remarks more and more haltingly delivered by himself, to which Croly would mutter responses more and more fragmentary and more and more imperfectly audible. At last the visitor would lose heart and stop, and a terrible silence would ensue: the atmosphere would become taut with panic." In desperation, the visitor would be driven to break the silence with some absurd remark

[4] Felix Frankfurter, "Herbert Croly and American Political Opinion," *NR*, 63 (July 16, 1930): 247.

[5] Dorothy Straight Elmhirst, "Herbert Croly," *NR*, 63 (July 16, 1930): 243.

and Croly, "his eyes dropped on his hands, which would be clasped in his lap," would make an equally absurd reply. Naturally the visitor would slink off, concluding that "the interview was over and that, brief as it had been, he had already stayed too long."[6]

While the chief characteristic of his mind was its venturesome assertiveness, the chief trait of his personality was its shyness. Everyday social intercourse was difficult for him throughout his life and small talk was an ordeal. One co-worker remembered his way of "settling like a stone crab in the middle of a lively company," and another, his "profound, often anguished seriousness."[7] T. S. Matthews, when a young man, appeared before Croly to interview for a job at *The New Republic*. Matthews, who soon became devoted to Croly, never forgot the "excrutiating silence" of that initial meeting: "He just sat in his office. It seemed like an hour; it might have been only five minutes: he didn't say a word and I didn't say a word, and finally he said, 'Well, I'd better introduce you to our Managing Editor.' "[8] The very thought of speaking before a public audience so agonized Croly that he almost never submitted himself to the torture.

Yet there was another side to this strangely reserved and pensive man. Among those with whom he felt secure, he relaxed, joked, opened himself. Puffing on one of the cigars he always carried with him; talking for hours with some intimate friend whom the years had shown to be intelligent, stimulating, and decent; bustling around the office (cigarette dangling, shirt-sleeves rolled, a fistful of copy), Herbert Croly was as capable of warmth and wit as anybody else. With his closest friends, thought Edmund Wilson, there would be an occasion when "contact would be made. Something said would reach below the level on which ordinary conversation is conducted—a level at which it was almost impossible for him to carry on conversation at all—and he would respond with an earnestness which, with a minimum of emphasis, carried a maximum of conviction. He would lift his gaze and meet you directly: his eyes were clear, firm and green, and his gaze was one of the straightest I have ever known."[9]

He liked that sort of intellectual intimacy. It was his favorite recreation. No doubt it was the chance of encountering it, the prospect

[6] Edmund Wilson, "H. C.," *NR*, 63 (July 16, 1930): 266; reprinted in his *Shores of Light: A Literary Chronicle of the Twenties and Thirties* (New York, 1952), 476.

[7] Francis Hackett, *I Chose Denmark* (New York, 1940), 15; and Alvin S. Johnson, *Pioneer's Progress, An Autobiography* (New York, 1952), 241.

[8] T. S. Matthews, *Name and Address, An Autobiography* (New York, 1960), 186; and Matthews, "Oral History," Columbia University Oral History Project, 3.

[9] Wilson, "H. C.," 266.

of widening his small circle of companionship, which kept him struggling against his bashful nature. To the end he denied himself the life of a recluse and, with a determination that resembled physical courage, he kept sallying forth into the social world. He cultivated men and women of power and ideas, he resolutely gave dinners and resolutely dined out. He liked wine and travel and detective stories and the drama. And in the presence of his friends he unfolded himself. They, in turn, admired his intelligence, respected his personal integrity, and for the sake of his thoughtfulness, made allowances for his idiosyncracies.

But they could scarcely have mistaken his priorities. Croly did not live for his recreations; he indulged in them because he discovered that they helped refresh him for the main purpose of his life. "His relaxations, great as was the pleasure he took in them," wrote his friend Philip Littell, "existed in order to keep him fit, to make possible those hours of lonely and original thinking in which he reached and formulated the main conclusions of his political philosophy."[10] Everything always came back to that for him—he was an intellectual, and he had a serious and important mission. "The chief service of his life," Robert Morss Lovett summed it up, was "giving politics the status of an intellectual pursuit. . . ."[11]

Like any intellectual who comments on practical affairs, Croly tried to apply a set of ideas to a set of social conditions. These two elements—the ideas and the world to which they are applied—have an annoying tendency to undergo change, and therein lies the challenge to the intellectual historian.

In this particular case, we have learned a good deal about the social conditions: the America upon which Herbert Croly fixed his straight gaze was a nation encountering bewildering change. When he was born the country had thirty-eight million people and was worrying about how to bring the southern states back into the Union; when he died America's population had tripled and the effects of the Great Depression were already making themselves felt. The United States experienced a tremendous transformation during those sixty years, and literally no aspect of our national life escaped without fundamental modification. The growth of huge industries and of huge cities, the flood of immigration, the emergence of mass culture and machine politics, the rude appearance of international problems and opportu-

[10] Littell, "As a Friend," 243.
[11] Robert Morss Lovett, "Herbert Croly's Contribution to American Life," *NR*, 63 (July 16, 1930): 245.

nities, the rise of the spirit of modern reform—it was to the work of surveying that shifting landscape of change and of suggesting new ways of thinking about its attendant dislocations that Croly devoted his entire life.

The ideas he brought forward to explain and instruct had a remarkable lineage. They came from several places, but the heart of them Croly took from his father, who, in turn, had borrowed them from the French philosopher Auguste Comte. This circumstance will require a brief exploration of this intellectual ancestry. But it will illustrate, I hope, one of the crucially important lessons in the study of social ideas: the impact of this kind of thought must await the arrival of propitious conditions. Croly's reputation as a thinker rested, in part, on the fact that he skillfully applied ideas already two generations old to a world that, at last, had developed in such a way as to make them seem sensible and promising.

Society and ideas about society are tied together in such tangled webs of cause and effect that it is probably impossible to invent a formula to describe their interaction. Of course Herbert Croly exerted influence upon his era and upon our own—we have the testimony of too many of his contemporaries and the accounts of too many historians to doubt it. Of course the complex time through which he passed influenced his thought—philosophers, no matter how reserved and isolated they may appear, do not operate without reference to the questions raised by their place and time. It seems sufficient, therefore, to illustrate, through Croly's example, these interwoven relationships between ideas and the world, hazarding now and then some cautious guesses about how they touched and affected one another. Hardier spirits, if they like, may try to explain their interplay with greater precision.

In the meantime, I agree with Lytton Strachey: "Human beings are too important to be treated as mere symptoms of the past. They have a value which is independent of any temporal processes—which is eternal, and must be felt for its own sake."[12] In the case of Herbert Croly, how should that value be felt? In the end, he was a man who devoted himself to trying to understand his country. And he wanted to understand so that he might instruct his countrymen and lead them to more humane and appropriate social arrangements. To those who can feel the drama of ideas, the quiet heroism of the lonely devotion to the life of the intellect, such a pursuit—despite the absence of bat-

---

[12] Lytton Strachey, *Eminent Victorians* (New York, 1918), viii.

tles and elections, inventions and risk—will arouse, I hope, its own kind of excitement.

I HAVE accumulated many scholarly debts while working on this book, and it is a great satisfaction to acknowledge some of them here.

Charles Forcey encouraged this study in its earliest phases by generously letting me work through the notes he had taken while researching his own book, *The Crossroads of Liberalism*; many years later he gave the completed manuscript a most thorough and valuable reading, saving me from several errors and leading me to reconsider several arguments. My friend Joseph Logsdon pored over the earliest drafts with laborious and painstaking scrutiny; there is scarcely a sentence in the first five chapters that does not bear his imprint.

Some excellent critics have taken the trouble to read parts or even all of this book, and in every case their suggestions have contributed to the final product. I would like particularly to thank Paul Abrahams, Paul Bourke, Russell D. Buhite, Joseph Conlin, Hamilton Cravens, Michael Curran, H. Wayne Morgan, Henry D. Shapiro, Jack Tager, Eugene Trani, William Savage, and Mary Young. Paul Glad, Arthur S. Link, and Robert E. Shalhope read the final version with marvelous care and made many extremely valuable suggestions. It would have been impossible to have enjoyed a long scholarly association with Melvin I. Urofsky without having one's understanding of twentieth-century America constantly sharpened and tested. Conversations with Gary B. Cohen and Robert A. Nye (which they have no doubt forgotten, but which I have not) have also played a part in shaping this study. All of these colleagues and friends have exemplified, over the years, that support and helpfulness which adds so much pleasure to the scholarly enterprise. I have not felt able to follow their advice in every case, but I have followed it in a great many; and I have compiled an obligation to them that I can never fully repay.

My principal intellectual debt, however, is to Merle Curti. As my teacher, he was almost the very first reader of this manuscript; and, as my friend, almost the very last. And entirely aside from the notable aid he rendered in this particular project, the example of his own devotion to the life of the mind has served for me (and for so many others) as a noble, if quite unattainable standard.

The Research Foundation and the Faculty Research Committee of the University of Oklahoma provided timely financial support. Dozens of librarians and archivists—at Columbia, Cornell, Harvard, the Library of Congress, the Newberry Library, the New York Public

Library, the Ohio State University, Princeton, the University of Louisville, the University of Oklahoma, the University of Wisconsin, and Yale—have rendered incalculable service to this work. I regret that they are too numerous to mention by name, but their help is keenly felt and gratefully acknowledged. Gail Filion Ullman of the Princeton University Press has been a source of sympathetic and wise advice; and Kathleen Hyde's meticulous reading greatly improved the readability of the entire work. Martha Penisten has typed several versions of this manuscript with wonderful efficiency and astonishing good humor.

I was "wed" to Herbert Croly long before I married my wife, Lynne, and she has accepted this *ménage à trois* with remarkable grace. What I owe to her and to my children for their tolerance and understanding cannot be expressed in words.

Norman, Oklahoma
November, 1983

HERBERT CROLY OF

THE NEW REPUBLIC

ONE

"Jenny June" and
"The Great Suggester"

HERBERT DAVID CROLY was born on January 23, 1869, in New York City. He once confided (mistakenly) to Edmund Wilson that he had been the very first child in the United States to be "christened" into the Religion of Humanity, Auguste Comte's curious attempt to apply the principles of science to the religious needs of mankind. The outmoded deity of western religion, Comte had argued, was no longer credible; the only proper object of worship was the Goddess Humanity, a female symbol representing all the people of the earth—those already dead, those now living, those yet to be born. The first "sacrament" of the Religion of Humanity was called "Presentation," and Herbert Croly, probably sometime during the first year of his life, received it.[1]

In the ceremony of Presentation, "the mother and the father of the new scion of Humanity come to present it to the priesthood, which receives from them a solemn engagement to prepare the child properly for the service of the Goddess."[2] The parents, the child's two sponsors, the congregation of witnesses gather to affirm that "private

[1] Edmund Wilson, "H. C.," NR, 63 (July 16, 1930): 268; reprinted in his Shores of Light: A Literary Chronicle of the Twenties and Thirties (New York, 1952), 476–84. Wilson has misled later scholars in this matter, but he was merely repeating HC's own opinion. In a brief, unpublished autobiographical fragment written in the mid-1920s (hereafter cited as "Fragment"), HC mentioned the incident: "I was, so I have been told, the only child of any professing Positivist who was officially initiated as a member of the sect by the holy rite of baptism. It may not be an important educational birthmark, but ill-favored as it is, it is unmistakably mine own." "Fragment," 6. The only copy of this "Fragment," a forty-four-page typescript with editorial notes in HC's own hand, may be found in the Felix Frankfurter mss., Library of Congress, Container 215. Frankfurter had expressed a desire, never fulfilled, to write HC's biography, and no doubt HC's widow had sent him the document for that purpose. For an earlier case of "Presentation," however, see Richmond L. Hawkins, Positivism in the United States (1853–1861) (Cambridge, Mass., 1938), 150.

[2] Auguste Comte, The Catechism of Positive Religion, trans. by Richard Congreve (London, 1891), 90. For what became a standard Presentation service, see Congreve, The Sacraments of the Religion of Humanity as Administered at the Church of Humanity (London, 1901), 5–12.

3

life is in the normal conception subordinate to the public," and to promise that the child will be instructed to undertake a life of unselfish service to the human community.[3] Suitable addresses are made and suitable hymns sung:

> How many souls of strongest powers
> To selfish solitude consign'd
> Have whiled in idleness their hours,
> Nor nobly sought to serve mankind.
>
> Unhappy, who, himself to please
> Forsakes the path where duty lies,
> Either in love of selfish ease
> Or in contempt of human ties.[4]

Properly consecrated, then, to the heavy task of serving Humanity all of the days of his life, Herbert David Croly was carried back to his home at 119 Bank Street. Not that any average New Yorker who happened to witness that novel ceremony could have doubted it, but the home to which "the new scion of Humanity" returned was one of the most interesting and unusual in the United States.

I

Herbert's mother, Jane Cunningham Croly, was among the best known women in the country.[5] She had been born in 1829, the fourth child of Joseph H. Cunningham, the Unitarian minister at Market Harborough, Leicestershire. In 1841, when Jane was eleven, the family came to America and settled in Poughkeepsie and finally in New York City. Miss Cunningham was sent to Southbridge, Massachu-

---

[3] Auguste Comte, *The System of Positive Polity*, trans. by J. H. Bridges and others (London, 1875–1877), 4: 90.

[4] *Hymns and Anthems for Use in the Church of Humanity* (Liverpool, 1901), Hymn 91.

[5] The principal source for her life is the memorial book, Caroline M. Morse, ed., *Memories of Jane Cunningham Croly, "Jenny June"* (New York, 1904). Also helpful are Elizabeth B. Schlesinger, "The Nineteenth Century Woman's Dilemma and Jennie June," *New York History*, 42 (October 1961): 365–79; Muriel Shaver, "Jane Cunningham Croly," *The Dictionary of American Biography* (New York, 1928–1937), 4: 560–61; M. James Bolquerin, "An Investigation of the Contributions of David, Jane, and Herbert Croly to American Life—With Emphasis on the Influence of the Father on the Son" (Unpublished Master's thesis: University of Missouri, 1948), 106–23; Ishbel Ross, *Ladies of the Press: The Story of Women in Journalism by an Insider* (New York, 1936), 43–46; Karen J. Blair, *The Clubwoman as Feminist: True Womanhood Redefined, 1868–1914* (New York, 1980), 15–44; *Book News*, 10 (December 1891): 161–62; and her obituary in the *New York Times*, December 24, 1901.

setts, to live with her brother John, now a Unitarian minister himself. "Here it was," John reported, "that her remarkable capacity for journalism first developed itself." She and a co-worker prepared a semimonthly newspaper which was read aloud in the church.

In 1855, when she was twenty-six, Jane Cunningham felt ready to venture into that restless center for aspiring journalists, New York City. She was a delicate girl, small in stature and slight in figure. Despite her lips, which were a trifle too thin and a trifle too wide, she was not without a certain attractiveness. She had deep-brown hair and sparkling blue eyes, and an inner energy which imparted vivacity in her youth and a reservoir for endless work in her later years. She spoke low, in a sweet voice, but she was tough.[6]

Her first New York article was accepted by the great Charles A. Dana, then assistant editor of the *Tribune*.[7] She quickly gained a position with the *Sunday Times and Noah's Weekly Messenger*, and—like the proper Victorian she would always be—she modestly disguised her identity with the pseudonym "Jenny June."[8] Her marriage to David Croly, a young reporter for the *Herald*, rather than ending it, quickened her career. Encouraged by her husband's rapid rise, and by a series of editors anxious to attract the ever-increasing numbers of female readers, Jane Croly, always writing as Jenny June and always devoting herself entirely to subjects of interest to women, advanced to the front rank of American women in journalism.

Her output over the next forty years was simply prodigious. In 1860 she became the editor of *Demorest's Illustrated Monthly*, a position she held for twenty-seven years.[9] She was also connected from time

[6] For portraits of Jane Cunningham Croly, see Morse, ed., *Memories*, 186 (at age 18), 16 (at age 40); frontispiece (at age 61). Also *Book News*, 10: 161; *American Monthly Review of Reviews*, 25 (February 1902): 154; *The Critic*, 44 (March 1904): 238 (at age 21); *Harper's Bazaar*, 33 (March 1900): cover (at age 71). For verbal descriptions, see John Cunningham, "A Brother's Memories," Morse, ed., *Memories*, 3; "Address by Charlotte B. Wilbour," ibid., 18–19; "Tribute from Izora Chandler," ibid., 192; "Tribute from Margaret Ravenhill," ibid., 208; "Tribute from Caroline M. Morse," ibid., 226.

[7] Schlesinger, "Nineteenth Century Woman's Dilemma," 366.

[8] How she chose this particular pen name is described in "Tribute from S. A. Lattimore in the New York *Tribune*," reprinted in Morse, ed., *Memories*, 201–203. Choosing alliterative pen names, however, was the fashion among women columnists: Sara Willis Parton was "Fanny Fern," Sara Jane Clarke Lippincott became "Grace Greenwood," and Anna Johnson Miller, "Minnie Myrtle." Schlesinger, "Nineteenth Century Woman's Dilemma," 365. See also Ann D. Wood, " 'The Scribbling Women' and Fanny Fern: Why Women Wrote," *American Quarterly*, 23 (Spring 1971): 3–24.

[9] *Demorest's* was primarily a women's fashion magazine, with household hints, advice on etiquette, and sheet music. Jenny June's column was entitled "Talks on Women's Topics." In the August 1865 issue, the editors announced the "confident expec-

to time with *Godey's Lady's Book* and *The Home-Maker*. She created *Cycle*, the clubwoman's magazine, and she owned it. When that journal was merged with *The Home-Maker*, she became the sole editor. She wrote the fashion department of *Graham's Magazine* and for Frank Leslie's *Weekly* and *Monthly*. She contributed to *The Democratic Review* and was an associate editor of the *Messenger* and of the *Weekly Times* (where she did the dramatic and literary departments and one-third of the editorial page). In New York she worked for the *World*, the *Times*, the *Messenger*, and the *Daily Graphic*. She is generally credited with being the first writer to syndicate columns, and for over thirty years she sent her letters to a collection of from twenty to twenty-five journals. Between 1869 and 1898, she wrote or compiled nine books.

In 1891 one reporter described Herbert Croly's mother as "the best known writer on fashions and social topics of any in the country." He estimated that "she has had millions of readers every month for over thirty years." Her brother thought that she had "affected the social life of more women, perhaps, than any other single controlling factor in the same period," and T. C. Evans, in the *New York Times*, contended that her pseudonym was "a beloved household word throughout the land, perhaps more widely known than that of any lady journalist." Her friend Margaret Ravenhill thought that "probably no woman of her generation has done more or better work"; and Cynthia Westover Alden, a fellow clubwoman, regarded her as "one of the greatest benefactors of women in literature."[10]

If the first preoccupation of Herbert's mother was journalism, her second was the woman's club. In 1856, the first year of her marriage, she called the first Woman's Congress, an organization that met annually to discuss the changing role of women in society. In 1868, when Charles Dickens re-visited the United States and all the women were summarily excluded from his reception dinner, Mrs. Croly promptly responded by forming Sorosis, the first important woman's club in America. The idea of women's clubs for self-improvement and sisterhood, for education and community service, spread rapidly. In 1889, when Mrs. Croly called for a "general federation" to commemorate the twenty-first birthday of Sorosis, ninety-seven clubs were in existence. By 1896 there were over fourteen hundred and by 1901, 800,000 women belonged to the General Federation of Women's Clubs. In the same year that she organized the General

---

tation" of circulating 100,000 copies by January 1866. See Ishbel Ross's chatty *Crusades and Crinolines: The Life and Times of Ellen Curtis Demorest and William Jennings Demorest* (New York, 1963).

[10] *Book News*, 10: 161; and Morse, ed., *Memories*, 3, 34–35, 207, 209.

Federation (the year, incidentally, of her husband's death), Mrs. Croly also founded the Woman's Press Club of New York, serving as its president or honorary president until the day she died. Finally, encouraged by the success of the General Federation, she organized a New York State Federation in 1894. The last ten years of her life were devoted to her twelve-hundred-page *History of the Woman's Club Movement in America*.[11]

Nothing that affected women in late nineteenth-century America escaped Jane Croly's pen. She wrote about fashions, budgets, diets, the seasons, children. She wrote about duties, manners, cooking, courtship, recreation. But one searches her writing in vain for a consistent viewpoint or an unambiguous philosophic stance. Even on those questions which occupied her centrally for forty years, Jenny June was hopelessly inconsistent. The vast majority of her work concerned itself with a cluster of issues centering around the problem of women's proper "sphere" in society. But in the end she failed to offer her readers any sure and unshakable position even on those issues.

Regular readers of Jenny June, for example, found much in her work (contrary to the example afforded by her own career) that supported the traditional notion that women were happiest when they married, raised families, and remained at home where they belonged. "All women should have homes and children, and should be taught that therein is their life work," she wrote. "A woman is not a woman until she has been baptized in her love and devotion to home and children." "If the wife goes out to earn money . . . ," wrote Mrs. Croly, who consistently earned more than her husband, "the interests of the family must suffer."[12]

[11] Because the memorial book *Memories* was compiled by fellow clubwomen, it is replete with accounts of Mrs. Croly's club work. See particularly Haryot Holt Dey, "Mrs. Croly's Club Life," *Memories*, 82–84; and Miriam Greeley, "Jane Cunningham Croly: An Appreciation," ibid., 186. The best accounts of the founding of Sorosis are an eighteen-page handwritten manuscript, dictated by Mrs. Croly and transcribed by her daughter, Vida Croly Sidney: "Jane Croly," n.d., Susan B. Anthony Collection, New York Public Library, and Blair, *The Clubwoman as Feminist*, ch. ii. See also Ross, *Crusades and Crinolines*, ch. v; Mrs. Croly's still serviceable *The History of the Woman's Club Movement in America* (New York, 1898); and "Charlotte B. Wilbour," in *National Cyclopaedia of American Biography* (New York, 1906), 13: 370. For a nearly contemporary report of the clubs' purposes, see Helen M. Winslow, "Literature via the Woman's Club," *The Critic*, 44 (March 1904): 237–44. The organization's own account is Mary I. Wood, *The History of the General Federation of Women's Clubs for the First Twenty-two Years of Its Organization* (New York, 1912). See also Carl N. Degler, *At Odds: Women and the Family in America from the Revolution to the Present* (New York, 1980), 315–27.

[12] *Jennie Juneiana: Talks on Women's Topics* (Boston, 1869), 31; *For Better or Worse: A Book for Some Men and All Women* (Boston, 1875), 159. For additional examples, see

As unequivocal as these statements seemed, they did not represent the entire range of her feelings about women and the world outside the home. She also espoused the opposite view, warmly supporting the efforts of women to forsake a life of marriage and to strike out bravely on their own. Marriage, she sometimes argued, was not the joy that most girls imagined. Men possessed absolute authority and "from the moment a woman becomes a wife she is in a state of subjection."[13] Sadly, moreover, men were usually despotic seekers after personal pleasure and amoral tyrants, indifferent to the needs, the longings, the agonies of their wives: "Men accept difference of [sexual] function as evidence of inferiority, and practically act upon the proposition, that, not being able to contend for them, women have no rights that men are bound to respect."[14] Given the unhappiness of modern marriage, Mrs. Croly sometimes argued, women had no choice but to turn to professions outside the home. "The silly pride which makes a virtue of helplessness, which considers money given better than money earned, is fast disappearing, and the pace becomes accelerated with every financial success achieved by women on their own account." Indeed, "it is a crime in parents to compel their daughters to look forward to marriage as the only prospect for occupation, position, or livelihood."[15] Herbert's mother seemed sufficiently supportive of the idea of women in business to prepare an entire book, *Thrown on Her Own Resources; or, What Girls Can Do*, designed to be a handbook for women in search of careers.

Demorest's, January 1865, 115; August 1866, 203; June 1873, 230; and March 1880, 128; *Better or Worse*, 19–20, 66–68, 72–74; and *Home-Maker*, May 1892, 162. Also see Schlesinger, "Nineteenth Century Woman's Dilemma," 370–71.

[13] *Demorest's*, November 1867, 337 (reprinted in *Better or Worse*, 136). See also *Demorest's*, January 1868, 15; and *Better or Worse*, 173.

[14] *Better or Worse*, 76. Pouring scorn upon men was one of Mrs. Croly's favorite pastimes and she sometimes grew curiously vicious: "Men are naturally dirty;—they can go to sleep at night with bodies reeking with the exhalations which have accumulated during an active day." *Juneiana*, 117–18; or "Men have nothing to dread with reference to children, no physical risks or suffering, no sacrifice of personal comfort or pleasure. If they 'take the baby,' it is as a plaything to amuse an idle moment, not as a duty to which every other consideration must give way." *Better or Worse*, 106–107. For other, rather random examples of man-baiting, see *Demorest's*, March 1865, 161; April 1865, 187; June 1865, 234; May 1866, 118; July 1866, 176; November 1867, 337 (reprinted in *Better or Worse*, 135); January 1868, 16; February 1873, 60; January 1877, 32; *Better or Worse*, 30, 110, and 125.

[15] *Thrown Upon Her Own Resources; or, What Girls Can Do* (New York, 1891), 24–25; *Demorest's*, July 1866, 176. See also *Demorest's*, March 1865, 162; November 1865, 114; August 1866, 204; November 1866, 287; November 1867, 337; *Better or Worse*, 96, 104–19, 137; and *Thrown on Her Own Resources, passim*.

When Jane Croly was consistent, she was consistently conserva-tive. She was an excellent example of Victorian gentility—that unique, middle-class mixture of complacency and fear, which characterized so much "respectable" opinion in the late nineteenth century. Social reform of a certain sort was permissible of course, and she unhesi-tatingly supported such genteel movements as those to improve ed-ucation, ensure international peace, preserve natural resources, or es-tablish a Central Park where New Yorkers might take their leisure.[16] But Mrs. Croly was ultimately more significant for the "dangerous" and "radical" reforms she opposed. Under no circumstances were the poor to be aided directly by the government or by private citi-zens—to do so would be to undermine habits of independence and self-reliance. The immigrant (immigrant Croly argued) was "an un-lettered, ignorant man, who has seen nothing, who knows nothing, who has read nothing, who has drifted between his potato patch and his cabin until he found himself in the hold of a ship, the most un-clean part of its cargo. . . ."[17] Citizenship was conferred too easily on these newcomers and should be earned. Mrs. Croly opposed the admission of Negro women into Sorosis.[18]

In typical genteel fashion, moreover, Jenny June despised the world of politics. In 1877, when Herbert was eight years old, she repeated her distaste for political life: "Assured position in science, in litera-ture, or in art is infinitely higher than any position in politics, . . . I should like my boy to be distinguished in literature, science, art, or journalism, but if neither of these were possible, I would infinitely rather he were a first-class farmer, or engineer, or printer, or carpen-ter, than one of the large army of legal politicians depending upon street fights and bar-rooms for their constituency and support."[19]

Jenny June's harshest words, however, were reserved for those re-formers who would lead the ladies too far astray. Up to a point, of course, she sympathized with and encouraged (at least sometimes) the new yearnings and aspirations of women. After all, she was her-self the product of the very forces which stirred the "new woman."

[16] On education, see *Demorest's*, February 1865, 137–38; June 1873, 230–31; May 1877, 243; and Morse, ed., *Memories*, 188. On the peace crusade, see *Demorest's*, Au-gust 1876, 409–10; and on conservation and the park system, see *Home-Maker*, March 1897, 533; *New York Times and Noah's Weekly Messenger*, January 20, 1860 (these ci-tations are from Schlesinger, "Nineteenth Century Woman's Dilemma," 374ff).

[17] On the poor, see *Demorest's*, July 1876, 348–49; on immigrants, ibid., June 1877, 306–307.

[18] See her "Letter to Mrs. Dimies T. S. Denison, October 3, 1900," reprinted in Morse, ed., *Memories*, 158–59. See also Blair, *The Clubwoman as Feminist*, 108–11.

[19] *Demorest's*, June 1877, 307.

But when those forces seemed to lead toward any relaxation of sexual relations, Jane Cunningham Croly unleashed the full fury of her pen. She warned young girls against the "impertinent familiarity" of men.[20] She opposed women's suffrage in the most violent and uncompromising terms—pure women, she was sure, would have no desire to associate themselves with the sordid world of politics.[21] And despite her own sporadic denunciations of marriage, she regarded those women who agitated for any easing of the divorce laws as nothing more than "reckless, egotistic, subversive, and insurrectionary . . . social incendiaries, sowing the seeds of dissatisfaction and revolt which are the outgrowth of their own want of truth, honor, and integrity."[22]

Perhaps the secret of Jenny June's immense popularity was the very inconsistency of her views. By arguing both sides of the fundamental questions of the day, she was able to hold a great variety of women readers—partly because she may have succeeded in touching identical ambivalences in some of them, partly because if she seemed to scold today, she would surely praise tomorrow. No doubt, some of the unsteadiness of her opinions may be accounted for by the necessity to please particular audiences and particular editors. But the fluctuations of her views can also be ascribed to a pervasive internal conflict, which she was never quite able to resolve. Herbert Croly's mother was simply a woman caught in a trap. On the one hand, she was a "pioneer"—she had successfully, even spectacularly entered the male world of New York journalism as no woman had done before her. On the other hand, she was emotionally incapable of flouting the conventions. This tension between the radicalism of her life and the gentility of her opinions helps to explain her inconsistencies. She had to defend the emancipation of women to justify her career. But she had to maintain the ideal of Victorian womanhood in order to retain respectability in an America suspicious of the "new woman," and because temperamentally she could never wrench herself away from that ideal completely.

The conflict must have been terribly painful for her, but it was one which many adventurous women in the late nineteenth century were beginning to experience. She attempted to ease the strain by vigorously defending "civilized" morality from those aggressive forces in American culture which seemed to threaten it—materialism, unas-

---

[20] *Juneiana*, 22–24, 28–29, 73–75; *Thrown on Her Own Resources*, 101–102.

[21] *Demorest's*, August 1866, 203; *Better or Worse*, 190–91.

[22] *Better or Worse*, 146–47. See also ibid., 3, 35–37, 111, 154, 172–76, 185–89; and *Demorest's*, March 1865, 161–62 and January 1867, 15.

similable immigrants and Negroes, crass politics, sex reform.[23] She could not pursue her defense of social and sexual purity into the evil realm of political action the way some women could.[24] But she did the next best thing by organizing thousands of like-minded women into genteel and civilized associations. Whether or not this was sufficient to release her from the contradictions and ambiguities of her life is impossible to know. But it should go without saying that the home which Jane Croly would supervise and dominate would be deeply affected.[25]

II

Herbert's father was David Goodman Croly, the editor of the *New York World*. He was a handsome man with clear, deep-set eyes, strong features, and a fantastic moustache that surrounded his mouth like two long braids and hung down to shoulder level.[26] He had been born in Cloghnakilty, County Cork, only forty-one days before Jane Cunningham's birth across the Irish Sea. His mother, Elizabeth, was of Huguenot descent. His father, Patrick, a man of wide reading and literary tastes, brought the family to New York City when David was still a small boy. Financial necessity forced young David to the silversmith trade, but an old friend from those early days recalled that "whatever of leisure was left to him after his long day's labor

[23] See Nathan J. Hale, *Freud and the Americans: The Beginnings of Psychoanalysis in the United States, 1876–1917* (New York, 1971), ch. ii.

[24] David J. Pivar, *The Purity Crusade: Sexual Morality and Social Control, 1868–1900* (Westport, Conn., 1973).

[25] For some interesting, though highly theoretical suggestions, see Peter T. Cominos, "Late-Victorian Sexual Respectability and the Social System," *International Review of Social History*, 8 (1963): 18–48, 216–50; and Stephen Kern, "Explosive Intimacy: Psychodynamics of the Victorian Family," *History of Childhood Quarterly*, 1 (1974): 437–61.

[26] The principal sources for his life are "In Memoriam. David Goodman Croly. Estimates of the Man, His Character and His Life's Work," an eleven-page memorial published as a supplement to *The Real Estate Record and Builders' Guide*, 43 (May 18, 1889); Clinton W. Sweet, "David Goodman Croly," *Record and Guide*, 43 (May 4, 1889): 613–14; *New York Times*, May 1, 1889, an obituary with several errors. The article in the *Dictionary of American Biography*, 4: 560, by Muriel Shaver (who also wrote Mrs. Croly's *DAB* article) contains many errors, omissions, and misinterpretations. See also Charles Forcey, *The Crossroads of Liberalism: Croly, Weyl, Lippmann, and the Progressive Era, 1900–1925* (New York, 1961), 11–18; Sidney Kaplan, "The Miscegenation Issue in the Election of 1864," *Journal of Negro History*, 34 (July 1949): 274–343; and Thaddeus B. Wakeman, "The Positivist Episode," in Morse, ed., *Memories*, 51–76. For a portrait, see "In Memoriam," frontispiece; or, Morse, ed., *Memories*, 60. For a verbal description, see J. D. Bell, "In Memoriam," 4.

was turned to good account in the cultivation of his mind." He joined the Young Men's Debating Society where, from the start, he expressed "the most advanced views on all the political, industrial, and social questions of the day."[27] He learned shorthand, taught it to others, and, with the money saved, enrolled for a year at New York University.[28] He got a job as a reporter for the *Evening Post*, and began learning journalism under two superb tutors, William Bartlett and the venerable William Cullen Bryant.[29] After a friend from the debating society introduced him to Frederick Hudson, Croly was hired by the *Herald*, and it was while working there that he met and married Jane Cunningham.

After a year, the Crolys were persuaded by William Gore King (who had married Mrs. Croly's sister Mary) to take over his faltering *Rockford Democratic Standard*. The young couple moved to Illinois, bought the publication, changed its name to the *Rockford Daily News*, and achieved a temporary rebirth for the paper. Despite their efforts, however, the venture failed—although it was sufficiently popular with the Douglas Democrats in the neighborhood that a group of them offered to help refinance it. "We worked night and day," Mrs. Croly remembered, "but at the end of fifteen months had sunk everything, even the proceeds of our furniture in our work." Partly because of the financial stress, partly because Mrs. Croly wanted a larger field for their endeavors, the Crolys returned to New York City and "went hopefully to work again."[30]

David Croly's new position was in the editorial office of the *New York World*. He became the city editor of that brand-new paper just as the Civil War began; by 1863 he was the managing editor, and he kept that position for a full decade. Croly's dozen years with the *New*

---

[27] Sweet, "David Goodman Croly," 613; R. F. Gaggin, "In Memoriam," 9; and John Mullaly, ibid., 7.

[28] *The General Alumni Catalogue of New York University, 1833–1905* (New York, 1906), 43. See also Sweet, "David Goodman Croly," 613; and Mullaly, "In Memoriam," 7.

[29] Allan Nevins, *The Evening Post: A Century of Journalism* (New York, 1922), 338–63.

[30] Jane Croly to Manton Marble, cited by M. James Bolquerin, "An Investigation of the Contributions of David, Jane, and Herbert Croly . . . ," 27–28. See also, Sweet, "David Goodman Croly," 613; and Jane Croly, "In Memoriam," 3. In later years Mrs. Croly ascribed the return to New York not to a financial failure in Rockford but to Rockford's uncongenial climate. See Helen M. Winslow, "Some Newspaper Women," *Arena*, 17 (December 1896): 128. Probably the likeliest explanation for the paper's failure is the depression of 1857, which ruined many small newspapers throughout the nation.

York World were the most productive of his life, for, in addition to the arduous job of preparing a large and important metropolitan daily, he embarked upon a series of intellectual adventures so apparently unrelated, one to the next, that it is hard to imagine them all springing from the same mind. The first adventure began in late 1863 when David Goodman Croly perpetrated one of the most curious hoaxes in American history.[31]

With some help from another *World* journalist, Croly wrote and published anonymously a pamphlet entitled, *Miscegenation: The Theory of the Blending of the Races, Applied to the American White Man and Negro.* The pamphlet argued that "the miscegenetic or mixed races are much superior mentally, physically, and morally to those pure and unmixed." And "all that is needed to make us the finest race on earth is to engraft upon our stock the negro element which providence has placed by our side on this continent." The Civil War ought to continue, the pamphlet suggested, until all Americans recognized "that it is desirable the white man should marry the black woman and the white woman the black man. . . ."[32] And where—of all places!—did the pamphleteer pretend to see the most encouraging signs of race mixing? "Wherever there is a poor community of Irish in the North," wrote Irishman Croly, "they naturally herd with the poor negroes . . . connubial relations are formed between the black men and white Irish women . . . pleasant to both parties." Such mixing, moreover, "will be of infinite service to the Irish" because they are "a more brutal race and lower in civilization than the negro."[33]

Skillfully baiting this hook with copious praise for leading abolitionists, Croly, always acting anonymously, fished around to see what he could catch. He mailed copies to antislavery leaders, and before long had received replies from several of them. These responses, though evasive and cautious, contained just enough praise of the secret writer's courageous thinking to prove extremely embarrassing to abolitionism, to the Republican party, and to Lincoln himself, who expected the approaching election to be close enough without the charge of race-mixing being leveled at Republicans.[34] The pamphlet pro-

[31] Excellently retold in Sidney Kaplan, "The Miscegenation Issue in the Election of 1864."

[32] *Miscegenation: The Theory of the Blending of the Races Applied to the American White Man and Negro* (New York, 1864), 8, 11, 18–19. The word "miscegenation" was quite consciously coined by Croly and co-author George Wakeman, see p. ii.

[33] Ibid., 30.

[34] Kaplan, "The Miscegenation Issue," 286. The texts of the letters were reprinted in the *New York World*, November 18, 1864.

voked widespread controversy. Angry pamphlets were written in reply, and the debate ultimately reached the House of Representatives. Naturally, Croly's own *New York World* (by this time the leading Democrat organ in the country) assumed a shocked and indignant defense of race purity. Shortly after the election, the *World* smilingly admitted the hoax. Neither author ever publicly admitted writing the pamphlet, but ample evidence proves their complicity.[35]

Undaunted by his failure to defeat the Republicans in 1864, Croly determined to try again in 1868. He prepared a campaign tract, *Seymour and Blair, Their Lives and Services*, a book which the *World* advertised as "not only an invaluable work for the campaign, but . . . an important contribution to the permanent history of the period." Historians have rightly tended to dismiss it as "typical campaign hackwork."[36]

David Croly's next project was the most profitable. In early March, 1868, Croly happened to mention to his best friend, Clinton Sweet, that there was a great need for a journal to serve the city's real estate interests. Millions of dollars worth of property changed hands every month; real estate values rose steadily, and with the constant inflow of immigrants, there seemed no end in sight to the rising prices. Nevertheless, the large numbers of New Yorkers involved in planning, building, and selling residences had no way to keep themselves informed about the many matters which vitally affected their interests. Two weeks later, the first issue of *The Real Estate Record and Builders' Guide* appeared. Within two years, six thousand New Yorkers were subscribing.[37] Sweet and Croly put the paper out jointly from 1869 to 1873, when Croly's other interests forced him temporarily to leave *The Record and Guide*.

The most fantastic of Croly's literary undertakings—a radical periodical entitled *The Modern Thinker*—appeared in 1871. "No journal heretofore published in the United States," he announced, "has made it its special business to give expression to the advanced thought of the time on philosophical, scientific, and religious questions." *The*

[35] The evidence includes a letter from Mrs. Croly dated twelve years after her husband's death: "The little brochure was the joint work of Mr. D. G. Croly, and a very clever young journalist, Mr. George Wakeman." Cited by Kaplan, "The Miscegenation Issue," 285. See also *New York World*, November 18, 1864, and Wakeman's obituary, probably written by David Croly himself, ibid., March 21, 1870.

[36] *New York World*, August 15, 1868; Kaplan, "The Miscegenation Issue," 338; Stewart Mitchell, *Horatio Seymour of New York* (Cambridge, Mass., 1938), 464.

[37] Sweet, "David Goodman Croly," 613; *Record and Guide*, 1 (March 21, 1868): 1; ibid., 7 (February 4, 1871): 61. For a brief history of the journal's first twenty years, see ibid., 41 (March 24, 1888): 354.

Modern Thinker would "employ the best minds of the age as contributors." And Croly mentioned Spencer, Huxley, George Eliot, Ernest Renan, Darwin, and the four leading disciples of Auguste Comte: Littré, Harrison, Bridges and Congreve.[38] Although the contributors proved to be somewhat less spectacular than advertized, they were distinguished, and the new magazine was intelligent, provocative, and filled with radical ideas.

Unfortunately, *The Modern Thinker* never received the attention it deserved, and only two issues ever appeared—the second, in 1873, two full years after the first. A major reason for the inadequate critical attention might have been that those who ventured to comment at all were too easily distracted by the magazine's outlandish appearance. One of David Croly's many pet ideas was that the combination of black print upon white paper injured the human eye. Consequently, *The Modern Thinker* made its appearance in various combinations of colored inks upon variously colored paper. Croly smugly (and accurately) predicted that "the great, idiotic, stupid reading public will jeer and howl at this attempt to save their eyes," but he was confident that he had inaugurated an important reform.[39]

Still another product of Croly's twelve years on the *New York World* was an amazing little book called *The Truth About Love*. A first edition appeared in early 1872, a second, somewhat toned down in its language, later the same year. Both editions were published anonymously. The book was written in Croly's favorite style, an extended Socratic dialogue between a teacher and a group of students, each representing an established position, all putting questions to their instructor.[40] The purpose of the book was revealed in the teacher's first comment: "I propose to discuss fairly and without reserve the relation of the Sexes, the Passion of Love. My object is the service of Humanity—human betterment—the lessening of human misery— the betterment of the race, and the improvement of its environment."[41] Croly went on to castigate Orthodox Priest, to comfort Wanton, and to espouse views on sexual matters which were hardly

[38] David G. Croly, "Egotisms," *Modern Thinker*, No. 1 (1871): 1–7.

[39] Ibid., 2–3; and ibid., No. 2 (1873): 142–45. Croly himself suffered from failing eyesight, which he attributed to the amount of reading he did.

[40] Many of Croly's works, including all of his books except the campaign biography of Seymour, were done in the conversational manner—a reflection, perhaps, of Croly's own skills. His friends reported that while writing came to him with difficulty, he was a brilliant conversationalist.

[41] *The Truth About Love. A Proposed Sexual Morality Based Upon the Doctrine of Evolution, and Recent Discoveries in Medical Science* (New York, 1872), 9.

typical of the prevailing attitudes of the 1870s.[42] One historian who made a short survey of early American sex manuals believed that Croly's had "no peers in nineteenth-century culture. . . . In his determination to speak the truth as he saw it, nobody went beyond Croly."[43]

Meanwhile, however, that same determination was getting him into trouble at the *New York World*. Disagreements with his publisher, Manton Marble, led to bitterness and frustration. Croly and Marble differed in what kind of news the paper should carry. They differed in questions of economic policy, principally the tariff and labor issues. Finally, in the early 1870s, the two quarreled over the *World*'s handling of the Boss Tweed story, the Franco-Prussian War, and the candidacy of Horace Greeley.[44] A few weeks after Greeley's defeat, Croly resigned.[45]

Within a short time he was a leading stockholder and the chief editor of a new journalistic venture, the *Daily Graphic*. The paper began publication on inauguration day, March 4, 1873, and frankly rested its bid for popularity almost entirely upon its illustrations. "We propose to illustrate daily occurrences in such a way that the life of our times shall become photographic, and the illustration of events will be as accurate and pleasing and elegant as any word painting in the text." Despite Croly's usual confidence that "our success is already assured beyond peradventure," the paper never did very well. Croly's friend Sweet asserted that "there probably never was a paper more applauded and commended than the *Daily Graphic* between 1873 and 1878"; nevertheless, he weakly concluded, "the times were against it."[46] Croly resigned in 1878 in another dispute about the extent of his editorial authority.

[42] For example, "If every church in the city of New York was shut up for the next six months, very little harm would result to society. If it were possible to entirely stop all sexual practices in connection with bawdy houses and assignation-houses for that length of time, our city would be the theater of the most frightful outrages the world has ever viewed." Ibid., 90.

[43] Carl Bode, "Columbia's Carnal Bed," *American Quarterly*, 15 (Spring 1963): 57, 59–60.

[44] The most careful examination, day by day, of the *New York World* during the years Croly was its editor is J. M. Bloch, "The Rise of the *New York World* During the Civil War Decade" (Unpublished Ph.D. dissertation: Harvard University, 1941). See also George T. McJimsey, *Genteel Partisan: Manton Marble, 1834–1917* (Ames, Iowa, 1971), ch. viii.

[45] David Croly to Manton Marble, February 5 and 21, and November 24, 1872, Manton Marble mss., Library of Congress. See also Sweet, "David Goodman Croly," 613, and McJimsey, *Genteel Partisan*, 147.

[46] *New York Daily Graphic*, March 4, 1873; Sweet, "David Goodman Croly," 613.

In 1880, he rejoined *The Record and Guide*, after a hiatus of seven years, and there embarked upon what was probably his most significant as well as his most ignored work. Hidden away in the little-read real estate trade journal, Herbert Croly's father offered "Our Prophetic Department," a weekly column in which various imaginary inquirers would put questions about the future to "Sir Oracle." Often the sessions only secured Sir Oracle's predictions about the stock market or the prices for grain in the coming season.[47] In weeks when the market was dull, however, Sir Oracle would speculate about larger problems—the future of labor and business, of religion and American political life, of Negroes and cities and the family.[48] It is in "Our Prophetic Department," between the years 1880 and 1889 (for he wrote his column until the week he died) that David Goodman Croly published the bulk of his mature thought and opinion. It is here that historians will discover the final product of a life of wide reading and intensive original thought.

Given the variety of David Croly's intellectual endeavors and the sheer boldness of his far-flung projects, it is not surprising that when his friends evaluated his career they always came back—with stunning unanimity—to a single trait: the astounding fertility of his mind. "We used to call him the 'Great Suggester' in the *World* office," St. Clair McKelway remembered, ". . . he was the most suggestive man I have ever encountered." One old friend believed that "a leading and peculiarly marked trait of his mind was its fertility of resources. It was singularly rich in suggestions." Wrote another, "He had an

---

See also Croly's later observations on the *Graphic* in *Record and Guide*, 40 (October 22, 1887): 1317. Once again, the most probable explanation for the paper's failure was the bitter depression, which created difficulty for all segments of American business in the 1870s.

[47] Croly was rather an expert on the stock market and an incurable dabbler himself. His daughter-in-law reported that "He always had an account with Stock-brokers. Herbert said in the course of his life a lot of money passed through [David's] hands." Louise Emory Croly to Felix Frankfurter, April 2, [193?], Frankfurter mss. See also *Record and Guide*, 38 (August 7, 1886): 998.

[48] The art of looking into the future fascinated David Croly for many years, and he became impressively accurate in many of his guesses. He predicted with tolerable and often stunning accuracy business cycles and both national and municipal elections. He is generally credited for knowing months in advance about the panic of 1871 and even that Jay Cooke's firm would be the first to falter. He also gave considerable coverage to the social and economic predictions of other "prophets." Some of his columns were collected into his final book, *Glimpses of the Future: Suggestions As to the Drift of Things. To Be Read Now and Judged in the Year 2000* (New York, 1888). In the first few pages of that work he gives his reasons for being attracted to this particular form of social speculation.

extraordinary capacity . . . for suggesting ideas to others without oppressing by his individuality." And another, "He was a storehouse of suggestions." An old *World* reporter, Montgomery Schuyler, thought that "his was the most prolific mind I ever knew. For . . . seven years my association with him was daily, and during all that period he teemed with suggestions. He was never at a loss for assignments to unoccupied reporters or for topics to editorial writers." Even Jenny June (whose view of her husband, interestingly, was mostly rather petulant) admitted that "he had enough original elemental ideas to have supplied a dozen men."[49]

And so the home at 119 Bank Street, into which Herbert Croly was born and in which he was raised, was in some ways an ideal training ground for the intellectual life. It was a home in which reading and thinking and writing were as much parts of the daily routine as were eating and sleeping. It was a home of swirling, stimulating ideas and colorful personalities. It was frequented by fascinating men and women who dealt in unorthodox philosophies and who gathered at the behest of a brilliant conversationalist and an equally brilliant hostess. It was a home in which journalism—the regular and systematic conversion of thought into publication by means of writing—was not so much a trade as it was a way of life. The home of young Herbert Croly, however, was not without its tensions.

III

David Goodman Croly was warm, friendly, leisurely, and full of wit; he liked talking with his friends better than he liked doing almost anything else. His wife was more businesslike. Her brother admitted that "humor and wit can hardly be said to have been marked traits in her mentality. There was something delphic and oracular often in her familiar conversation. Sentimentalism had no place in her nature." Even the clubwomen noticed it: "Drawn to her at the first greeting one was soon convinced of the hidden forcefulness of her nature which could be likened to the resistless, unyielding undercurrent, rather than to the wave which visibly and noisily assails the shore."[50]

Mrs. Croly had no hesitations about discussing her husband's ir-

[49] St. Clair McKelway, "In Memoriam," 6; John Mullaly, ibid., 7; Charles F. Wingate, ibid., 8; Frederick Creighton, ibid., 9; Montgomery Schuyler, ibid., 9–10; and Jane Croly, ibid., 3.

[50] John Cunningham, "A Brother's Memories," Morse, ed., *Memories*, 11; and "Tribute from Izora Chandler," ibid., 192.

ritating traits. She readily acknowledged, of course, that her husband had a fertile mind, even that his originality as a journalist was unexcelled. On the other hand, she complained, "this amazing fertility was in some respects a detriment, for it led him into too many projects, and made him careless whom he enriched, while his dislike of the mechanism of his work made profit for others at his expense." And even if Mr. Croly did happen to possess an original mind, "the time has gone by for ideas. It is not that they are a drug in the market, but that there is no market for them." Although her husband's principal asset had not been particularly marketable in nineteenth-century America, his principal defects were nonetheless annoying. Jenny June was prepared to enumerate those defects with astonishing care. "His faults were those of a nervous temperament, combined with great intellectual force, and a strength of feeling which in some directions and under certain circumstances became prejudice. . . . He cultivated the 'unexpected' almost to a fault." "He was the most utterly destitute of the mechanical or 'doing' faculty of any man I ever saw, and never used his own hands if he could possibly help it." "His pessimistic and unhopeful temperament was doubtless due to inherent and hereditary bodily weakness, and lack of muscular cultivation in his youth, which might have modified inherent tendencies."[51]

The petulance of her remarks reveals the unhappiness of her marriage. "There is no remorse so bitter," Jenny June once wrote, "and none so unavailing, as that of a woman who repents the wickedness of a thoughtless and ill-starred marriage. Through life she is not only tied, but subordinated to a man perhaps greatly her inferior, obliged to submit to his neglect, endure his pretensions, see produced in her children his meanness, his selfishness, his appetites, his passions, and his vices." "How many wives," she wondered, knew the agony of discovering that "instead of a hero . . . they had only married a very ordinary man, with an extraordinary opinion of his own personal qualities."[52] Mrs. Croly's frequent condemnations of marriage were written with such force, with such a profound depth of feeling, moreover, that the reader cannot escape the conclusion that a real and personal regret was being shared.

In fact, Jane Croly's entire career was an attempt to flee from her marriage. She was simply a woman who sought her satisfactions and

[51] Jane Cunningham Croly, in "In Memoriam," 3–4. Mrs. Croly's comments are all the more indicative when one remembers that she wrote them as a widow of less than three weeks.

[52] *Demorest's*, November 1866, 287; and ibid., June 1865, 234.

fulfilled her needs away from home. She was haunted by the fear that marriage subordinated women and that home and children stifled creativity and trapped mothers in a thankless drudgery that suffocated the spirit. Herbert Croly's mother was going to be very careful not to let that happen to her.[53]

In a remarkable article entitled "Modern Bridals," she warned that "girls now enter matrimony blindfolded. They imagine, poor fools, that it is going to give them freedom, state, protection, support, and the *éclat* of established social position." They would soon learn better:

> How quickly the spirit of their illusive dreams would change if they could catch a glimpse of the grinning skeleton which not unfrequently presides over the marriage feast. If they could look into the future, which now seems so bright, and see the solitary woman, the unloved woman, the neglected woman, the woman absorbed by cares, and out of whose life has dropped, little by little, all the beauty and sunshine of which it once seemed so full. . . .
>
> The bridal . . . should be the solemn taking upon oneself the burdens, the pains, the trials, as well as the joys of womanhood. It should be for women, at least, an act of self-renunciation, and a cause for humiliation, rather than self-elation.[54]

Her reservations about marriage included some doubts about having children: "The bearing of a child involves a long period of inconvenience, and more or less of suffering; it involves that mortal agony which is all the human system can endure, and live; it involves a future of unceasing watchfulness and care. Is all this worth nothing? It ought to be the best paid work in the world." And if the "inconvenience" of motherhood were not enough, Herbert's mother had another complaint: in "being compelled to be the mother of the race," women were subjected to all those social, economic, and legal penalties which turned their lives into ordeals of unhappiness.[55]

When Herbert was eight, his mother shared with her readers some

---

[53] An extensive literature has emerged in recent years on the weakening hold of the family on women and the pull of professional work outside the home. Among the most stimulating works are William R. Taylor and Christopher Lasch, "Two Kindred Spirits: Sorority and Family in New England, 1839–1846," *New England Quarterly*, 36 (March 1963): 23–41; Ann D. Wood, " 'The Scribbling Women' and Fanny Fern: Why Women Wrote," 3–24; Nancy F. Cott, *The Bonds of Womanhood: "Woman's Sphere" in New England, 1780–1835* (New Haven, 1977); and Barbara J. Harris, *Beyond Her Sphere: Women and the Professions in American History* (Westport, Conn., 1978), chs. ii–iv.

[54] *Demorest's*, January 1868, 15–16.

[55] *For Better or Worse*, 106; ibid., 77–78.

ideas about raising sons. A long series of articles appeared in *Demorest's* under the title of "Our Boys." Simply stated, the central theme of the articles was that if all children involved inconveniences, boys were especially troublesome and particularly unrewarding. The basic difficulty with boys, she felt, was that they were too much like men, too quick to copy those same traits Jenny found so irritating in their fathers. In the first article of the series she observed that sons "very soon begin to assume toward their mothers an air of patronage, even of authority, inexpressibly galling to her who has suffered for him, who has protected his infancy, who has watched and fostered his growth, who has worked for him, lived for him, and woven into the web of his young life the best and brightest years of her own." Naturally, "under these circumstances it is not surprising that the mother's heart rarely realizes the satisfaction which she hoped for in the birth and possession of a son."[56]

The only way to handle the pretensions of sons was the firm hand of their mothers. Plainly, "boys are usually allowed too much freedom, and are put under too little discipline in this country."[57] And an excellent disciplinary technique for showing boys that they were no better than their sisters was to refuse to recognize any differences: "Boys in the family should be subjected to precisely the same laws as girls." Mothers should "utilize the strength of the boys in household works of various kinds, and exercise their patience in sewing on their own buttons, and even mending their own hose if necessary." The reason for this discipline was simple: "The man would have more sympathy with his wife, if the boy had known just how many steps it takes, and how many movements of arms and body to prepare one meal, to do the work of a single house for a single day."[58] In an article called "The Genius of the Family," Jenny June cautioned against bookish boys. "They grow up selfish and exacting, with the most exalted ideas of their own qualities, desires, and destiny, and a disposition to underrate whatever belongs to the plain and practical in the world around them." Mothers had to resist this particularly subtle form of male domination, she thought; and they had nobody but themselves to blame if "they foolishly indulge and make the whole family yield to the whims and caprices" of such a boy.[59]

Once, in her first article about "Our Boys," Herbert's mother came right out and said it: "Boys, it is said, are especially dear to a moth-

---

[56] *Demorest's*, January 1877, 32.
[57] Ibid., November 1877, 592.
[58] Ibid., July 1877, 336.
[59] *Juneiana*, 68–70.

er's heart, and in a sense they may be so; but I doubt if they are as closely enshrined, or if she feels for them the same anxious solicitude that she does for the girls, whose peculiar difficulties, disadvantages, and helplessness she perfectly understands, and who awaken all her sympathies, and often all her fears."[60]

Personality differences between the parents, even the wife's uneasiness about home and children, might have been smoothed and quieted if the couple had shared a set of intellectual convictions and could have joined in promoting them. Unfortunately, even this realm of friendly cooperation seemed closed to them.

IV

Jenny June wrote almost entirely about a single question—the role of the woman in nineteenth-century America. Yet within the comparatively limited range of this problem she managed to wander aimlessly for forty-five years, neither proclaiming a consistent body of opinion nor writing from any kind of recognizable philosophic position. Meanwhile, her husband, who let his mind and pen range freely over a multitude of topics, brought to much of his work a remarkably unified and persistent approach, a generally consistent set of ideas. Occasionally he changed his mind about some issue, and, as a journalist, he often suppressed his own views in favor of those of the subscribers or the policy of the paper. When Croly was his own man, however, when the responsibility for what he wrote in a book or an article or a column would quite obviously fall upon him as an independent author, then his work revealed a philosophic base and a continuity of thought. Nearly everything Croly wrote on his own was informed by his philosophy of life.

David Croly took that philosophy from the controversial French thinker Auguste Comte, and it was no accident that he consecrated his infant son in Comte's controversial faith. An active and enthusiastic "Positivist," a warm advocate of the "Religion of Humanity," Croly, according to one co-religionist, was "the man who *planted Positivism in America*."[61] When Henry Edgar, who "had the seed from

---

[60] *Demorest's*, January 1877, 31.

[61] Thaddeus B. Wakeman, in Morse, ed., *Memories*, 60. Wakeman, the father of the young *World* reporter who had collaborated with Croly in the *Miscegenation* hoax, was closely associated with Croly in the attempt to spread positivism in America. For proof that the elder Wakeman was too enthusiastic on behalf of his friend, and that positivism had already been well planted and tended in this country, see Richmond Laurin Hawkins, *Auguste Comte and the United States (1816–1853)* (Cambridge, Mass.,

Comte direct," lectured in New York City in 1868, it was David Croly who paid for the hall. When the enthusiasm resulted in the formation of a circle, it was Croly who provided the organizing force and often the Croly home that served as the meeting place. As the movement roused interest, it was Croly who got John Fiske of Harvard to publish his lectures, "Positive Philosophy," in the *World*. And, in 1871, it was David Croly who attempted to popularize and explain Comte's positivism with a handbook (yet another intellectual adventure of his years with the *New York World*), entitled *A Positivist Primer*. As far as Herbert Croly's father was concerned, Auguste Comte was "probably the greatest brain and heart that this planet has ever seen."[62]

It is hard to know how sincerely Jane Croly was committed to the positivism of Auguste Comte. Her "Sunday evenings" at home, the weekly social gatherings for Positivists and others, were compared to Parisian salons so often that it is probable the comparison was made consciously by the participants themselves.[63] She also lent her name to the first number of *The Modern Thinker* by publishing an article on the "Love-Life of Auguste Comte." In her writings, moreover, she frequently discussed the problem of individualism as opposed to social responsibility (an important theme in Comte's writing), and her condemnation of rampant individualism was often made in Comtean terms. Finally, several of the old Positivists insisted that positivism was a family affair with the Crolys.

Nevertheless, there are grounds for suspecting that Jane Croly was far less devoted to the Religion of Humanity than was her husband. She rarely mentioned Comte's name and borrowed only the simplest of his ideas. She evidently felt no compulsion to instruct women in

---

1936), and Hawkins, *Positivism in the United States (1853–1861)*. The date is also set earlier by Frederic Harrison, "Auguste Comte in America," *The Positivist Review*, 9 (June 1901): 121–25. Moreover, Harriet Martineau's translation of Comte's *Cours de philosophie positive*, originally published in London, was republished in New York City (by Calvin Blanchard) under the title, *The Positive Philosophy of Auguste Comte* as early as 1855. Also Henry Edgar (sometimes Edger), whom Croly had hired to lecture in 1868, had already published, a dozen years earlier, *The Positivist Calendar* (New York, 1856).

[62] "C. G. David" [pseud.], *A Positivist Primer: Being A Series of Familiar Conversations on the Religion of Humanity* (New York, 1871), 81.

[63] The comparison to Paris is inevitable with any account of Mrs. Croly as a charming hostess. See for examples "Tribute of T. C. Evans," in Morse, ed., *Memories*, 210–11, or "Tribute from Margaret Ravenhill," in ibid., 208. Her guests included Robert Ingersoll, Louisa May Alcott, Oscar Wilde, E. C. Stedman, and Bayard Taylor.

Comte's positivism, and, in general, did not write as if Auguste Comte had changed her way of looking at things.

Her devotion to the Christianity of her father and brother remained firm—despite the fact that her husband, like any good Positivist, considered Christianity outmoded. She wrote frequently about Christ and God's will for men and men's duties to the Divine. She reminded oppressed wives that "there is One who knows, One who understands, and who can bring out of this pain, a great joy, a never-ending peace." She reassured women whose babies had died that they would be happily united in heaven. In 1869, she comforted her readers with the promise that "when we die, only a cold, inanimate shell will be laid in the narrow grave; and who shall say that the spirit, the real self, will not wake to sights and sounds more charming, and odors more sweet, than our coarse senses are capable of revealing to themselves here?"[64] Her brother John, who naturally detested David Croly's unorthodoxy, emphasized Jenny June's traditionalism. Pointing out that Jenny "never called in question the deeper realities of soul-life," he went on to describe the man she had married as "a radical in religion, and [one who] had but little appreciation of the deeper forces at work in society. . . . 'Jenny June' was a person of very different mental and moral mould."[65]

Perhaps the crucial factor in making Jane Croly less than a complete Positivist, however, was the way in which Comte chose to handle the "female question." The French philosopher left no doubt about the proper place of women in society. The female sex, Comte once wrote to John Stuart Mill, "is constituted in a kind of radically infantile state, which renders it essentially inferior." He ridiculed "the theatrical declamations on the pretended abuse of force on the part of the males" and announced that "the social subordination of women will be necessarily indefinite . . . because it directly reposes upon a natural inferiority which nothing can destroy." A woman is a passive creature, sexually and socially, Comte declared, and her life "should be concentrated in her family, and . . . even there her influence should be that of persuasion rather than of command."[66] Anyone who knew

[64] *Demorest's*, January 1865, 117; ibid., November 1865, 114–15; *Juneiana*, 143. Statements reflecting a consistent devotion to traditional Christianity are scattered throughout her writings. For some random examples, see *Juneiana*, 13; *Demorest's*, December 1865, 138, and June 1866, 145; *Better or Worse*, 87–90; *Thrown on Her Own Resources*, 164–65; and the selections from her letters reprinted in Morse, ed., *Memories*.

[65] John Cunningham, "A Brother's Memories," in Morse, ed., *Memories*, 6–7.

[66] Auguste Comte to John Stuart Mill, July 16 and October 5, 1843, published in "The Subjection of Women by Auguste Comte," *Modern Thinker*, No. 1 (1871): 171;

anything about Jane Cunningham Croly knew that she did not like that kind of talk.

When it came time for her husband to explain this aspect of Comte's thought in his *Positivist Primer*, he staunchly ignored the example provided by his wife and endorsed the Frenchman's teaching to the letter. "Clearly, it is the office of the adult woman to bear and rear the child. This is her peculiar function as a woman. . . . Now, we insist that the female should not be asked to bear and rear the child and to work also." One wonders what thoughts were passing through David Croly's mind when he wrote:

> The notion at present agitating the most advanced of the sex in Europe and America is that women should enter every kind of employment, the same as men, of course taking into account the physical differences of the two sexes. But it is clear that if all women work the same as men, the continuance of the race will become a secondary consideration. The working-woman, using the title in the same sense as the working-man, can not be a good mother.[67]

Mrs. Croly's friends noticed the intellectual tension in the Croly home and they were willing to discuss it. Assuring the ladies that the Crolys' home life was essentially happy, Caroline Morse hastened to add that "between any two minds when both are strong and original there will generally be a divergence; and it has always seemed to me that the origin of Sorosis might be traced by the psychological analyst to some such divergence between Mrs. Croly's lines of intellectual development and those of her equally gifted husband, David G. Croly. The power of initiative was strong in each of these two, and in each it produced excellent though differing results." St. Clair McKelway insisted that the Crolys' marriage was "congenial" despite their "marked dissimilarity of convictions on cardinal subjects."[68]

But many years later, long after both Jenny June and the Great Suggester were dead, even after the death of their son Herbert, Louise Croly, Herbert's widow, dropped even the pretense that Herbert's

---

Auguste Comte, *A General View of Positivism*, trans. by J. H. Bridges (Stanford, 1953 edition), 273. The Crolys were undoubtedly familiar with Comte's letters to Mill since they were published in David's magazine. See also Comte, *System of Positive Polity*, 2: 163.

[67] *A Positivist Primer*, 70–71.

[68] "Tribute from Caroline M. Morse," in Morse, ed., *Memories*, 230–31; "Tribute from St. Clair McKelway," ibid., 214–15.

parents had ever been "congenial." She gathered up some old letters written to Herbert by his father, and sent them to Felix Frankfurter, one of Herbert's closest friends.[69] Frankfurter was considering a biography of his friend, and Louise thought the letters would be helpful. She included some remarks of her own too: Herbert's father, she wrote, "was a great talker, and had many friends."

> He & Mrs. Croly never got on together. Their temperaments were utterly dissimilar. She was very clever, ambitious & a tremendous worker & not in the least domestic. They say each time she had a baby she was in the office in a week. She simply didn't know what it was to be maternal & proably wouldn't have been bothered with children [had she lived] in another period. Mr. Croly on the other hand had no ambition, never was interested in worldly things, was very generous & emotional as you will see [from the enclosed letters] & affectionate. In fact what maternal care there was in the family came through him. Herbert's sister probably had all the duties etc.[70]

Jane and David Croly had five children. Minnie, the eldest sister, married a sailor named Roper and, still youthful, died sometime before 1900. The second child, a boy, died in infancy. The third, Herbert, was followed by two sisters, Vida and Alice.[71] Herbert, therefore, was raised in a house with four women. While the precise nature of the effects on the children cannot be known with certainty, one result of the strained relations between the parents was that it drove

[69] A word of explanation about these letters between HC and his father is necessary. When Herbert went to Harvard in 1886, a long and intimate exchange began. Unfortunately, HC destroyed his own letters, but he saved those his father had written to him. After his own death in 1930, Herbert's widow, Louise Emory Croly, typed extracts from fifty-three of these letters. She deposited one copy of these extracts in Houghton Library, Harvard University, and she gave a second copy to HC's longtime friend Felix Frankfurter. This copy is presently in the Felix Frankfurter mss. at the Library of Congress. HC comments on his correspondence with his father in HC to Louise Emory, June 11, 1891, a copy of a letter made by Louise Emory Croly and deposited in the Houghton Library. These letters will be cited *Extracts* hereafter. It is, of course, impossible to know what Mrs. Croly left out, or how accurately she transcribed her father-in-law's handwriting (she was at best a mediocre typist, and her eyesight was rapidly failing), but except for correction of obvious errors, the quotations from the letters will necessarily appear as she copied them.

[70] Louise Croly to Felix Frankfurter, April 2, 193?, Frankfurter mss., Library of Congress.

[71] John Cunningham, "A Brother's Memories," in Morse, ed., *Memories*, 8–9. Vida married an obscure English playwright named Frederick Sidney, and Alice married a New York lawyer named William F. Mathot.

the two men of the family closer together. Herbert and his father found refuge, companionship, and, soon, intellectual adventure in each other's company.[72]

One of his closest friends recalled that Herbert adored his father and spoke of him often, but had never, as far as he could remember, mentioned his mother.[73] Herbert wrote a long and tender contribution to his father's memorial tribute, but he made none to his mother's. He dedicated his most important book to his father's memory, but never offered a similar dedication to his mother. And when he was in his mid-fifties and sat down to write some of his memories, he lingered long and lovingly over his companionship with his father while mentioning his mother only once and in passing.

When Herbert's widow sent the packet of fifty-year-old letters to Felix Frankfurter, she explained, "we have had them all these years but I had never read them before. When I began to copy them I did it because I thought it might bring out in Herbert some new fresh things which would help you [with the proposed biography], but as I read on I became so deeply interested in Mr. Croly and so moved by the relationship existing between Herbert and him I felt I had opened up something which had value in itself. It may be because I am so deeply involved in these two persons, but there seems to be such a situation in it, such a moving simple story of the relation of two people, I wondered if it could ever be used in any form. I think it would touch people."[74]

Although Louise Croly had caught a glimpse of that relationship when Herbert was seventeen, it had begun much earlier. "While I was still so young that I could hardly walk without being led, he would on Sundays take me by the hand and conduct me along the . . . by-ways of Central Park; and as we walked he would tell me about the kind of world in which we lived and what I ought to do

---

[72] In an interview with Professor Charles Forcey, for example, HC's friend Judge Learned Hand hinted that the shyness, which was one of HC's chief personal traits, stemmed from his home life. In Forcey's recollection of the conversation: "Hand, interestingly enough, brought up spontaneously my theory of C[roly]'s shyness and thwartedness having something to do with the relationship with his mother . . . and that he and others did feel there was some definite tension or unhappiness there." Charles Forcey, "Interview with Judge Learned Hand, April 5, 1956," 4, in Forcey's possession.

[73] Ibid.

[74] Louise Croly to Felix Frankfurter, April 2, 193?, Frankfurter mss. For a superb and provocative psychological case study with many remarkable similarities to the Crolys—as well as some important differences—see Bruce Mazlich, *James and John Stuart Mill: Father and Son in the Nineteenth Century* (New York, 1975).

27

and think about it. . . . I was proud to own a father who would discourse for my benefit copiously and persuasively about so many wonderful aspects of life, and I felt superior to other little boys whose fathers talked to them only about childish affairs."[75]

At first the trips to the park consisted of listening to lectures from his father "that I could so little understand that it was like pouring water on a flat board."[76] To the boy it seemed as though his father was "a running brook of ideas on every subject in which a citizen of the world ought to be interested, and he literally poured a part of this flood into my little mental receptacle without noticing or caring how much of it overflowed." It was a marvelous experience, and until the end of his own life, Herbert could remember "individual Sundays and the glimpses of the visionary landscapes which on particular occasions he unfolded before my wondering eyes."[77] In time, Herbert understood what his father was imparting, and the lectures of his youth were gradually transformed into long and earnest discussions. By the end of his father's life, "I was his constant companion for about three or four years. I used to act as his amanuensis and we used to have long discussions about every aspect of modern literature, economics, and politics."[78]

More than anything else, David Goodman Croly talked about positivism with his son. "From my earliest years," Herbert wrote in the flowery language of his memorial tribute, "it was his endeavor to teach me to understand and believe in the religion of Auguste Comte. One of my first recollections is that of an excursion to the Central Park on one bright Sunday afternoon in the spring, and there, sitting under the trees, he talked to me on the theme which lay always nearest his heart—that of the solidarity of mankind. There never, indeed, was a time throughout my whole youth, when we were alone together, that he did not return to the same text and impress upon me that a selfish life was no life at all, that 'no man liveth for himself, that no man dieth for himself.' "[79]

Arising out of an unpleasant situation at home, growing steadily as the son's mind matured, the companionship of Herbert and David

[75] HC, "Fragment," 5. See also HC to Royal Cortissoz, October 7, 1916, Autograph File, Houghton Library, Harvard University.

[76] HC, in "In Memoriam," 7.

[77] HC, "Fragment," 5. See also HC to Royal Cortissoz, October 7, 1916, Autograph File, Houghton Library, Harvard University.

[78] HC to Royal Cortissoz, October 7, 1916, Autograph File, Houghton Library, Harvard University.

[79] HC, "In Memoriam," 7.

Croly was probably one of the most gratifying experiences in the life of the father. It was easily the most critical influence in the life of the son. The long talks in Central Park constituted a crucial legacy for Herbert Croly—a legacy of concrete ideas and opinions, a consistent and useful approach to social problems, and an encompassing set of ideals and goals for his own life. Half a century later, Herbert Croly summarized in a single sentence what it had meant to him: "If I have felt impelled to occupy my life with the pursuit of ideas," he wrote, "I probably owe the impulse to my father."[80] And everything that David Croly tried to teach his son stemmed from his devotion to Auguste Comte's teachings and his own intense efforts to apply Comte's thought to the American scene.

V

Comte's most important work, undertaken between 1830 and 1842, was the six volume *Cours de philosophie positive*; it attempted to do three things. At the start, Comte proclaimed the law of three stages. All departments of thought, he announced, invariably evolve through three phases: the theological, the metaphysical, and the positive. In the theological stage men spontaneously ascribed causation to gods, and eventually to one God. In the second, or metaphysical stage, phenomena were accounted for not by attribution to gods but by reference to some impersonal abstraction, some non-material power or force. Just as the theological stage culminated in a single God, so did the metaphysical culminate in a single abstract force, Nature. But the real importance of the metaphysical stage was in its transitional character. It lifted men away from theological superstition and raised them to a level from which they might approach the third, the positive, or scientific stage. Then men finally abandon the fruitless search for Absolutes, Essences, and Final Causes, and seek answers on the basis of their own empirical experiences, realizing, at last, that "there can be no real knowledge but that which is based on observed facts." Laws may then be defined and true sciences formed that will avoid metaphysical abstractions and rest on the concrete observations of the relations existing between concrete phenomena.[81]

The second task of Comte's *Cours de philosophie positive* was a clas-

---

[80] HC, "Fragment," 5.

[81] Auguste Comte, *The Positive Philosophy Freely Translated and Condensed by Harriet Martineau* (New York, 1856 edition), 25–38. For a consideration of the strengths and weaknesses of this translation and condensation, upon which David Croly relied, see Hawkins, *Positivism in the United States*, 18–26.

sification of sciences in order of their increasing complexity. Mathematics, at the bottom of his list, was the first developed, the first to arrive at the positive stage, the least complex—it was almost entirely a positive science. Sociology, at the opposite end of the list, however, was only beginning to throw off its theological and metaphysical mistakes. "The general revolution of the human mind is nearly accomplished," Comte believed. "We have only to complete the Positive Philosophy by bringing Social phenomena within its comprehension."[82] And the business of putting the last great science, the science of society, on a positive basis was Comte's third purpose in the *Cours*.

The theological polity, Comte contended, had attained its peak in the "Catholic and feudal system," which dominated Europe in the late Middle Ages. If societies developed by alternating elements of Order and Progress, the theological form emphasized Order and resisted change. Temporal authority was merely a subordinate branch of the spiritual, ruling with divine sanction. This theological stage was destined to be replaced by the metaphysical, and, as in all the other sciences, so in sociology, the second stage had a double task: it had to destroy theological foolishness; and it had to set the stage for positive progress. Naturally, in battering down the fortifications of the old system, the newer one took up weapons most suitable for the siege. Since the old theological party had stressed Order, the battle cry of the metaphysical school became Progress, and Order be hanged. If the old system had cherished stability, the new brandished the sword of revolution. Where the retrograde had seen the temporal connected with and subordinate to the spiritual, the revolutionary metaphysical school demanded a separation of the two with the spiritual in the inferior position. Where the old had talked about "the Will of God," the new cried "human rights" and "the will of the people."

But then, Comte argued, a curious thing happened. The ideas underlying the metaphysical polity (which deserve praise for destroying their theological predecessors) were themselves erected into an absolute dogma. Anyone could see that both the tactics and the ideology of the revolutionary party were designed as destructive tools, not as building blocks for a new society. The ideal of "equality," to take one example, was once necessary to combat feudal distinctions; but now that it was taken as an absolute, it stood in the way of those classifications so necessary for the efficient reorganization of society

[82] Comte, *Positive Philosophy*, 36–37.

along scientific lines. Likewise, the antagonism to the ancient order and the understandable desire to limit its powers, quickly ossified into a terribly dangerous tendency "to represent all government as being the enemy of society." The revolutionary party of Progress now hysterically insisted upon "a perpetual suspicion and vigilance, restricting the activity of government more and more, in order to guard against its encroachments, so as to reduce it at length to mere functions of police, in no way participating in the supreme direction of collective action and social development"[83] In short, the metaphysical stage of political behavior succeeded in routing the theological. In the process, however, the new system turned its weapons of attack into weapons for defending its own abstractions.

For Comte, needless to say, the answer to the prevailing confusion in social speculation was precisely the same instrument that had ended confusion in all the other sciences. The Positive Philosophy was "the only possible agent in the reorganization of modern society."[84] Minds that rebelled against theological fictions and were uneasy about metaphysical abstractions would eagerly submit to a scientific study of society. And the key to such a study was the discovery of a set of unchanging natural laws (based this time not on Nature but on scientific certainty). Such laws would explain social behavior with the same surety that natural laws commanded in the other sciences, for "the conception of invariable natural laws," Comte was confident, ". . . would have the same efficacy here as elsewhere."[85] Moreover, since "true liberty is nothing else than a rational submission to the preponderance of the laws of nature," sociology must uncover those laws so that men might submit to them. The chaos which characterizes our social life will continue, Comte solemnly warned, until we finally realize that "there is no chance of order and agreement but in subjecting social phenomena, like all others, to invariable natural laws, which shall, as a whole, prescribe for each period, with entire certainty, the limits and character of political action."[86] Men were not

[83] Ibid., 408–11.

[84] Ibid., 431–37.

[85] Ibid., 456–57. Comte understood, of course, that "elsewhere" natural laws gave men the ability to know the future: a law of physics not only explains what has happened, it assures us that if the same things are performed in the future, men can predict the results beforehand. Comte did not shrink from the implications of the analogy. Once men had discovered a natural law of social behavior, he affirmed, social theories and social facts "may admit of our foreseeing them." Undoubtedly David Croly's fascination with social prophecy and prediction can be traced to this possibility opened by Comte.

[86] Ibid., 454–55.

powerless to order society rationally, but their efforts had to be subject to and in harmony with the discovered scientific laws. History was littered with the wreckage of men and societies that attempted to reverse the inevitable and invited disaster instead.

For example, Comte argued, it was an incontestable law that human society grew ever more complex. The resulting specialization of men's functions was simultaneously a product of intellectual progress and the chief prerequisite for continued progress. Unfortunately, the steadily developing division of labor not only furthered progress, it threatened it as well. Men grew more isolated in their specializations, private interests became separated from public ones, and the public interest became more remote. Men of the same calling banded together and refused to worry about society as a whole. "Thus it is that the principle by which alone general society could be developed and extended, threatens, in another view, to decompose it into a multitude of unconnected corporations. . . ." But once we understand this fearful potential for disintegration, Comte contended, we may gain an insight into the "social destination of government." Government must function to prevent the dispersion, lest, in their isolation, the parts neglect to think in terms of the whole; it must "intervene in the performance of all the various functions of the social economy, to keep up the idea of the whole, and the feeling of interconnection; and the more energetically, the more individual activity tends to dissolve them. . . . Moreover, this ruling function must become more, instead of less necessary as human development proceeds."[87]

Between the publication of the *Cours* and his second major work, Auguste Comte suffered a shattering emotional crisis. He fell in love with young, charming Clothilde de Vaux; but after a year of passionate letters and clandestine meetings (both were already married and neither believed in divorce), Clothilde contracted tuberculosis and died. The experience produced profound changes in the philosopher's life. His second book, *Système de politique positive*, a four-volume work, was published between 1851 and 1854.[88] It advocated a complete reorganization of society. The agent in the reorganization, however, was not science at all, but a new kind of religion—the Religion of Humanity. From an objective, rationalistic, often brilliant

[87] Ibid., 511–12.
[88] Available as Comte, *System of Positive Polity.* Most of the system can be found in a six-chapter preface published separately as Comte, *A General View of Positivism.*

analyst of scientific and social thought, Comte became the intensely mystical, intensely emotional high priest of a new cult.

Of course Comte could never return to the traditional Christian deity of the theological stage. Instead, he presented a new, tangible, "scientific" deity, Humanity. This new object of worship, the Goddess to whom Herbert Croly was consecrated as an infant, was the only Being deserving of worship, praise, and sacrifice. But except for this substitution, Comte's cult resembled other religions—and especially Catholicism—closely. There were sacraments and prayers, there were regular private devotions of stipulated length, periodic public ceremonies, a "catechism," and a calendar of secular saints. And pervading the Religion of Humanity was an ethic of extreme altruism. Every human act had to be judged by how much it helped as opposed to how much it hindered Humanity; and men and women were obligated to "live as far as possible, for others; and this in public as well as private."[89]

Thus Auguste Comte, by means of a unique and original combination of ideas, succeeded in erecting a system that was inherently unable to strike an alliance with any other system in Europe or America. Virtually every philosophic school with an articulate spokesman joined in the attack on positivism, and if nothing else could unite two sets of widely divergent ideas, they usually shared an implacable hostility toward positivism and its Religion of Humanity. Frederic Harrison complained that "the press and society, platform and pulpit, are continually resounding with criticism, invective, and moral reflection, arrayed against this system."[90]

No one could have been surprised at the hostility of those Comte had labelled "theologians." His assertion that mankind could progress only by throwing off the chains of religious belief and his advocacy of a new religion which dethroned Almighty God were ideas scarcely calculated to win the support of Europe's religious leaders. By the time his views arrived in America, Comte had been branded one of the "boldest atheists of the present century, whose hand is against every man and every man's hand against him. . . ."[91]

Nor could the Positivists have expected encouragement from those Comte called metaphysicians. It was never quite clear whom Comte meant when he used the term, but it was likely that he had in mind

[89] Comte, A General View of Positivism, 444.

[90] Frederic Harrison, "The Positivist Problem," Modern Thinker, No. 1 (1871): 49.

[91] Thomas Hill, Unitarian minister of Waltham, Mass., and destined to become president of Harvard, quoted in Hawkins, Auguste Comte and the United States, 17–18.

two separate schools of thought.[92] German idealism, culminating in the work of Hegel, epitomized for Comte the evils of abstractionism: the Idealists, after all, dealt in Absolutes and Essences and took a foolishly light-hearted view of the outward "reality," which was so important to Comte.[93] The second school of metaphysics Comte attacked centered in his own country. The philosophers of the French Enlightenment typified the dangerous tendencies of the second stage of social thought. They wielded the abstraction of Natural Law in the battle against feudalism, but having won the battle they became an obstacle against any truly constructive approach to a new social order. They were forever attempting wild social experimentation without proper regard for the necessity to submit to scientific laws. Naturally, the descendants of the Enlightenment—nineteenth-century French and English liberals—rejected Comte's allegation that they had turned liberty of conscience, equality, parliamentary deliberation, separation of church and state, limited government into dogmas of their own. To them it must have seemed as if Comte's system, one combining frank élitism and an unobstructed central authority with vast powers extending into the private lives of citizens, had been specifically designed to alienate the liberals.

Marxian socialism, to some extent the intellectual heir of both the Enlightenment and a modified German idealism, also had little in common with positivism. Comte detested and feared revolutions while Marxists encouraged them. Comte envisioned a government balanced between labor and capital with power placed in the hands of the benevolent capitalist (where it was gravitating inevitably anyway, with all the force of a natural law); to Marx the notion was naive and abhorrent. Finally, Comteans argued that wealth in an industrial society flowed into fewer and fewer hands, that this flow was essentially beneficial, and that any attempt to reverse it was doomed to the same failure that awaited every foolish attempt to reverse a natural law.[94]

[92] According to one of Comte's most astute nineteenth-century commentators, Comte "uses the word 'metaphysic' in a narrow and mistaken sense . . . he conceives it, as well as theology, to be bound up with a kind of 'transcendentalism,' which all the great metaphysicians of modern times agree in rejecting." Edward Caird, *The Social Philosophy and Religion of Comte* (New York, 1893), 54.

[93] For the opposition of Hegel and Comte, see Herbert Marcuse, *Reason and Revolution: Hegel and the Rise of Social Theory* (Boston, 1960 edition), 323–60.

[94] For disparaging comments about Comte and Positivism, see Karl Marx to Frederick Engels, July 7, 1866; Marx to E. S. Beesley, June 12, 1871; and Engels to F. Tönnies, January 24, 1895, all in *Karl Marx and Frederick Engels, Selected Correspondence* (Moscow, 1956), 218, 322, and 559–60.

The Positivists never had much hope of attracting those whom the Master had dismissed as theologians and metaphysicians, but they were profoundly disturbed by a revolt from within their own ranks. Two English philosophers of immeasurable influence, whose approach to problems was similar to Comte's and who were often classed by others as his disciples, rose up against positivism and attacked it vigorously.

It would not have been difficult to have mistaken Herbert Spencer for a Positivist. He was, after all, quite as conscious of the importance of science to the study of society as Comte was. Spencer also saw history moving steadily toward a better day, moving from simple to complex, from homogeneous to heterogeneous. Nevertheless, despite some similarities of method and goal, Spencer and the Comtists disagreed bitterly over a number of crucial ideas. Spencer attacked Comte's classification of the sciences and propounded a doctrine of agnosticism, assuring his many readers that religion and science were not in conflict, that whatever science might discover, the true purpose of religion—worship of the Unknowable—was secure.[95] But what really ended the possibilities for intellectual harmony was the conflict over the role of government. Where Comte had called for steadily increasing central authority, Spencer argued that the proper role of government was to refrain from almost any interference whatsoever. In 1864 Spencer formally denied that he was a member of Comte's school. "On all . . . points that are distinctive of his philosophy I differ from him. . . . His ideal of society I hold in detestation. . . . From everything which distinguishes Comtism as a system, I dissent entirely."[96]

John Stuart Mill, the second English philosopher whose thought bore clear similarities to that of Comte, had not agreed with everything in Comte's first major work, but his objections seemed minor—he wished Comte had listed psychology as a separate science, for example, and he disagreed with the Frenchman's disparaging remarks about women. But otherwise, Mill was so full of praise for Comte's achievement that Comte assumed that he had discovered just the man to spread his positivism in England. There followed an earnest correspondence during which Mill's suspicions grew steadily. Mill found Comte to be intransigent, unwilling to accept new sci-

[95] Herbert Spencer, "The Genesis of Science," *British Quarterly Review*, 20 (July 1854): 108–62; Spencer, "Religion; A Retrospect and Prospect," *Nineteenth Century*, 15 (January 1884): 1–12. See also David Duncan, *The Life and Letters of Herbert Spencer* (London, 1908), 254–66.

[96] Duncan, *Life and Letters*, 113.

entific evidence when it contradicted his conclusions, and excessively patronizing. Mill was willing to grant individual men and women far more power in societal improvement than Comte was, and he came to see that in many of its aspects positivism was merely an apology for the existing division of wealth. Comte seemed willing to place his faith in eventual social harmony under "scientific" leadership; Mill continued to believe in the necessity for intellectual and political conflict. Finally, Mill was repulsed by much of the Religion of Humanity (calling it "ineffably ludicrous") and by all of the political arrangements which accompanied it. In 1865, Mill set down his views—both praise and condemnation—in his judicious, devastating, celebrated criticism, *Auguste Comte and Positivism*.[97]

And in the end the Positivists stood alone. Thinkers who might have been sympathetic to Comte's social conservatism were repelled by his heresy; the many scientists and others who might have been attracted by his methodological approach were disgusted by his concrete applications of that approach; those most likely to have accepted a religious skepticism were least likely to tolerate a social conservatism. And so, although the followers of Auguste Comte marched into the second half of the nineteenth century resolutely, they marched alone.

VI

One such isolated marcher was Herbert Croly's father. David Croly accepted with few questions the religious system of Comte. His *Positivist Primer* was dedicated to "the only supreme being man can ever know, the great but imperfect god, HUMANITY, in whose image all other gods were made, and for whose service all other gods exist, and to whom all the children of men owe labor, love and worship." He ended letters to Herbert with the prayer, "May Humanity have you in her lovely keeping."[98] In the *Positivist Primer* he specifically rejected Spencer's doctrine of the Unknowable, and defended Comte's

---

[97] John Stuart Mill to Sir E. Lytton-Bulwer, March 27, 1843, in Hugh S. R. Elliott, ed., *The Letters of John Stuart Mill* (London, 1910), 1: 124. See also Iris Wessel Mueller, *John Stuart Mill and French Thought* (Urbana, Ill., 1956), 92–133; and Walter M. Simon, *European Positivism in the Nineteenth Century: An Essay in Intellectual History* (Ithaca, 1963), 172–201.

[98] David G. Croly to HC, February 8 and May 11, 1887, *Extracts*. See also *Positivist Primer*, 7–10; and "What We Believe: A Dialogue," *Modern Thinker*, No. 1 (1871): 148–50.

complicated rituals as "the noblest and most elaborate of which the human mind can conceive."[99]

Likewise, Herbert's father fully accepted Comte's view of the limited extent of men's powers in altering their environment. Mankind, like everything else on earth, was terribly constricted by unchanging natural laws, and it was the business of men to discover those laws and to set about softening their harshness, modifying—weakly, of course, but at least a bit—their awesomeness. In *The Truth About Love* he drew an instructive analogy:

> If I am in the stream above Niagara, which threatens to carry me over into the roaring gulf, it would be folly for me to turn my boat about and attempt to pull against the current. My strength would be exhausted in a fruitless struggle with the inevitable. Yet it would be equally criminal for me to sit down and fold my hands, and calmly let the cataract wash me away to destruction. The wiser course for me to adopt would be to take advantage of the flowing of the stream; to enlist its forces on my side; to steer my boat to some point on the shore; and employ the momentum of the current to dash me upon safe ground.[100]

Man was not powerless to reform his society, Croly argued, but the reformation must be in accord with those powerful, those virtually irresistible forces that have come roaring out of history and that carry us, like it or not, in certain predictable directions.

Yet it would be an error to see David Croly simply as an unoriginal disciple of Comte, parroting the opinions of his master. In applying Comte to the American scene, in taking the ideas of a philosopher of the 1840s and 1850s and making them relevant to the Gilded Age, David Croly made some prophetic contributions to American social thought.

It required no special gift for prophecy to observe, in post–Civil War America, that the age was one of industrial development. If any phenomenon in American life was clearly a natural law in the way Comte had meant, it was that the economic life of the nation was changing inevitably from an agricultural base to an industrial one. Herbert Croly's father, however, moved a half-step ahead of most of his generation by observing still another natural law within the framework of industrialism. "In noting the progress of modern society," he wrote in 1871, "one remarkable tendency has not escaped

[99] *Positivist Primer*, 14.
[100] *The Truth About Love*, 37–38. See also *Positivist Primer*, 34–35, 55, 90–91.

us. It is the great concentration of wealth into a few hands."[101] A few others had marked the trend as early as Croly; some of them, captivated by Darwinian notions on the one hand, or prevailing doctrines of Christianity on the other, had even judged that the process was more or less inevitable.[102] Nevertheless, at a time when the vast majority of American authorities still placed their faith in the automatic and self-adjusting mechanisms of a laissez-faire economic system, Croly argued that it was precisely this setting which gave the consolidation of wealth its Comtean inevitability.[103] By the time the large trusts began to appear, Croly was convinced that they were merely "a natural evolution from pre-existing industrial conditions, and that to criticise or condemn them was about as sensible as to object to an eclipse or denounce an earthquake. They have come to stay."[104] Consolidation is "the inevitable destiny of modern industrialism," Croly judged, ". . . whether we like it or not."[105]

And then Croly advanced a full step ahead of his generation by deciding to like it. More and more commentators also came to see that wealth was indeed flowing into fewer hands, and a handful of ultra-conservative apologists for the corporations—approaching the problem with opposite assumptions from Croly's and advocating opposite solutions—also wrote in praise of corporate consolidation. But

---

[101] *Positivist Primer*, 57.

[102] For the alliance between Christianity and the accumulation of wealth, see Irvin G. Wyllie, *The Self-Made Man in America: The Myth of Rags to Riches* (New Brunswick, 1954), 55–74; Eric F. Goldman, *Rendezvous with Destiny: A History of Modern Reform* (New York, 1952), 89–90; Ralph H. Gabriel, *The Course of American Democratic Thought* (New York, 1956 edition), 155–58; or William McLoughlin, *The Meaning of Henry Ward Beecher: An Essay on the Shifting Values of Mid-Victorian America, 1840–1870* (New York, 1970), 114–18, 140–48. For the relation between Darwinism and the consolidation of wealth, see Richard Hofstadter, *Social Darwinism in American Thought, 1860–1915* (Philadelphia, 1944), 30–36; Goldman, *Rendezvous with Destiny*, 90–93; Sidney Fine, *Laissez Faire and the General Welfare State: A Study of Conflict in American Thought, 1865–1901* (Ann Arbor, 1956), 99–101; or Robert C. Bannister, *Social Darwinism: Science and Myth in Anglo-American Social Thought* (Philadelphia, 1979), 84–88.

[103] For the universality of laissez-faire economic theory, see Fine, *Laissez Faire and the General Welfare State*, 47–48.

[104] *Record and Guide*, 41 (March 3, 1888): 262. The inevitability of the consolidation of wealth is a constant theme in Croly's writing for the *Record and Guide*. For rather random examples, see 32 (July 28, 1883): 543–44; 32 (October 13, 1883); 779; 33 (April 12, 1884): 371; 37 (March 13, 1886): 312; 38 (July 31, 1886): 970; 38 (October 23, 1886): 1292–93; 39 (May 7, 1887): 621; 40 (November 19, 1887): 1438; 40 (November 26, 1887): 1473; 40 (December 3, 1887): 1502; 41 (January 28, 1888): 103–104; 41 (February 11, 1888): 175–76; 42 (August 25, 1888): 1040; 43 (April 6, 1889): 457. See also *Positivist Primer*, 57.

[105] *Record and Guide*, 37 (June 26, 1886): 827.

while Croly's generation almost universally condemned trusts and monopolies and the huge aggregations of wealth they involved, he moved to a position that was not to have acceptance until well into the twentieth century—and then only by a small but influential group of speculative thinkers led by his own son.

Although Croly acknowledged that the trusts were guilty of abuses, he maintained that "they will succeed, because they ought to succeed."[106] Large corporations organized to eliminate competition unintentionally bestowed genuine benefits upon the community. Monopolies could more accurately gauge the demands of the market and plan production accordingly, avoiding the inevitable piling up of surplus products which resulted when dozens of independent producers each tried to guess how much of their product the public would buy. Distribution of products could be stabilized, avoiding those wild fluctuations of transportation costs that occurred when railroads tried to play one producer off against another. Generally monopolies offered better products, and at an average rate that did not rise and fall violently. Their ability to gauge the market meant the ability to employ labor steadily, and the strength to set prices meant that the hired laborer could generally be offered a fair wage. In short, David Croly concluded, "capital in mass can be more effectively used in the business world than if broken up and used in a competitive way."[107]

Croly realized that "it is the fashion to inveigh against monopolies," and he often predicted that the next few years would see many attempts to break down the trusts and restore competition. In spite of these efforts, however, the fight against the great trust organizations could never be successful. In the first place, the consolidation of wealth progressed with all the steady sureness of any natural law— and attempts to reverse natural laws were roughly analogous to turning the boat around and trying to paddle back from Niagara Falls. In the second place, the monopolies and trusts served the community far better than the old system of individualistic competition could ever hope to do.

The problem of what to do about the abuses of large corporations bothered David Croly for a long time. In the early 1870s he was

---

[106] Ibid., 42 (August 25, 1888): 1040.

[107] Ibid., 40 (November 19, 1887): 1438. For some examples of David Croly praising the consolidation of wealth by means of trusts and corporations which benefit society, see ibid., 31 (April 28, 1883): 165; 33 (June 29, 1884): 695; 37 (June 26, 1886): 827; 38 (October 23, 1886): 1292–93; 38 (November 6, 1886): 1352; 40 (November 26, 1887): 1473; 40 (December 3, 1887): 1502; 41 (December 22, 1888): 1510. See also *Positivist Primer*, 59; and *Glimpses of the Future*, 107–108.

convinced that the problem was a moral one, to be solved by a kind of religious awakening on the part of American capitalists. In this early phase of his thinking, Croly's ideas resembled those of any "gospel of wealth" propagandist. The wealthy man, ennobled by the conception of Humanity, aware that his wealth was social and not personal, would "live for others" as truly as anyone else. He would treat his workers with justice, donate his fortune to museums and libraries, schools and galleries.[108] Before long, however, Croly had changed his mind. The 1870s had convinced him that American capitalists were not particularly sensitive to their moral obligations. William H. Vanderbilt's easy epithet, "the public be damned" (which seemed to David Croly "a social philosophy worthy of a hog"), appeared to sum up the attitude of many of the most powerful men in the country.[109] The watered stock, the bribed legislatures, the illegal maneuverings, the ghastly working conditions, the proliferation of preposterous mansions, the stories of incredible waste and unbelievable indulgence, all were convincing indications that capitalists were not yet living for others in the way Comte would have liked. By the 1880s, Croly was describing Vanderbilt as "this creature of the public bounty, bloated into prosperity and into insolence by the contributions of the public," and insisting that Jay Gould "has done many things which ought to have landed him in States prison."[110]

Despite the immunity of wealthy men to the altruism of the Religion of Humanity, Croly never doubted his basic assumption that the corporations were more beneficial than harmful. But if moral awakening could not control their abuses, he puzzled, what could? More and more, Croly found himself turning to the federal government, and by 1882, he was convinced that "All corporations must be subordinated to the greater corporation which sits in its place of power at Washington."[111] The time had come when government must "exercise functions which would have been considered despotic in times past."[112]

---

[108] For examples of Croly's reliance on "moral suasion" during these years, see "Stewart—Astor—Vanderbilt: Letters Addressed to Three Millionaires on the Social Function of Wealth," *Modern Thinker*, No. 2 (1873): 21; "King Wealth Coming," *Galaxy*, 8 (November 1869): 706–708 (reprinted in *Modern Thinker*, No. 1 [1871]: 45–47); *Positivist Primer*, 98.

[109] *Record and Guide*, 30 (October 14–21, 1882): 16.

[110] Ibid.; and ibid., 41 (March 31, 1888): 390.

[111] Ibid., 30 (October 14–21, 1882): 15.

[112] Ibid., 32 (October 13, 1883): 779. For other pleas for federal intervention, see ibid., 32 (September 1, 1883): 643–44; 32 (September 15, 1883): 685; 32 (September 29, 1883): 732; 37 (January 9, 1886): 31; 37 (March 6, 1886): 281; 38 (September 11,

If the federal government was to regulate the trusts, it was apparent to Croly that the Constitution would have to be amended. In an editorial in *The Record and Guide* for October 7, 1882, he announced the intention of the paper to urge constitutional reform. A National Convention to re-examine the Constitution, Croly argued, would be a most fitting way to observe the centennial celebration of 1887. And the very first demand made by the paper revealed the motivation behind the idea: "The relations of the government to questions growing out of the existence of monopolies is of first importance."[113] For five years, Croly ceaselessly urged a convention, but by 1888 he had given up hope: "Our Constitution is so difficult to change that I do not see any way to reform it. Our fundamental laws are like the decrees of the Medes and Persians—practically unalterable. This is one of the great perils of the country."[114]

The reason why American law was "practically unalterable," and the reason why American political parties were reluctant to advocate any addition of powers to the central government, Croly believed, was an intellectual predisposition against government generally. The fear of government—which Auguste Comte had isolated as a chief characteristic of the metaphysical party, necessary to destroy the old theological society, but quite useless for constructive purposes—was rampant in America. Comte had hated the philosophers of the French Enlightenment; David Croly put the blame on their American counterpart, Thomas Jefferson.

Clearly, Jefferson had developed his famous notion, "That government is best which governs least," as a response to British tyranny; his mistake (typical of the metaphysical stage) was in transforming that principle into an absolute. New forms of wealth, changes in the way wealth was created, social conditions Jeffersonians could never have imagined had combined to build a new kind of society. The working classes desperately needed the protection of the government against the onslaught of corporate greed; yet that very government, paralyzed by eighteenth-century abstractions, was powerless to act. The abuses of the trusts must be controlled, Croly wrote in 1883, "but the only solution of the war against the corporations would be the assumption of control over them by the Federal Government, and this would be utterly antagonistic to the Jeffersonian ideal of

---

1886): 1120–21; 38 (October 9, 1886): 1226–27; 40 (December 31, 1887): 1640; 41 (January 28, 1888): 103–104; 41 (March 3, 1888): 262–63; 41 (March 17, 1883): 330; 41 (May 26, 1888): 669.

[113] Ibid., 30 (October 7–14, 1882): 1–3.

[114] Ibid., 42 (August 11, 1888): 997. See also *Glimpses of the Future*, 18.

government." As long as American political parties were committed to an extreme economic individualism, an ideal of laissez faire, and a consistent policy of hostility and suspicion toward Washington, social progress was unlikely. Indeed, the mere refusal to grant the central government more power was sufficient in itself to fortify the present system—abuses and all. "Now from my point of view," Croly pleaded, "the Jeffersonian theories are as out of place in our politics as would be the Ptolemaic scheme in our modern astronomical discussions. Every government on earth, imperial, kingly, aristocratic and republican, is taking on additional responsibilities."[115]

What America needed was a political party which would espouse economic justice under a federal government of far greater powers. The Republican party was too much under the control of the trusts to be serviceable. The Democratic party, however, carried the possibilities of such a change. The Democrats would soon have to seek a new source of popular support in the working classes; to win that support, they would have to promise to enlist the government on behalf of the oppressed. The new Democratic party, therefore, will have to be "in one essential particular the very antithesis of that inspired and organized by Thomas Jefferson."[116]

These were difficult ideas. They were complicated, sometimes unpopular, easy to misunderstand, misinterpret, and ridicule. David Croly's determination to share them with his only son was an indication of how important they were to him, and the process of instruction on those walks in the park must have required patience and love and an intense belief in the value of what was being explained. And yet, by some miracle, David Croly succeeded in his instruction and succeeded, probably, better than he ever dared to hope: the ideas and opinions of the father, his point of view and even his way of life were destined to survive in the work of his son. A generation later, in a more hospitable America, Herbert would offer his father's Comtean analysis and, this time, the results would be heard respectfully.

[115] *Record and Guide*, 31 (April 21, 1883): 158.

[116] Ibid., 32 (November 3, 1883): 852. David Croly attacked "Jefferson" or "Jeffersonianism" by name in the following places: Ibid., 26 (October 16, 1880): 896; 32 (July 29, 1883): 544; 32 (September 15, 1883): 685; 32 (October 13, 1883): 799; 32 (October 20, 1883): 805; 36 (August 1, 1885): 859; 36 (December 19, 1885): 1390; 37 (January 9, 1886): 31; 37 (March 6, 1886): 281; 38 (September 25, 1886): 1171; 38 (October 2, 1886): 1198; 38 (October 9, 1886): 1126–27; 38 (November 6, 1886): 1353; 38 (December 4, 1886): 1477; 39 (April 9, 1887): 474; 39 (April 16, 1887): 512; 40 (November 19, 1887): 1439; 41 (February 18, 1888): 205; 42 (August 25, 1888): 1040. See also *Glimpses of the Future*, 7–17.

Harvard College versus
David Croly

ALTHOUGH Jenny June and the Great Suggester disagreed about many things, they had little quarrel when it came to the importance of education. Mrs. Croly was too astute an observer of polite society not to realize that education was the gateway to respectability and advancement. David Croly, while undoubtedly agreeing about the social advantages of education, had additional reasons for believing that learning was crucial: "We rely primarily upon education," he asserted in the *Positivist Primer*. "The labor question,—the woman question,—the governmental question,—all must wait for their final solution until the minds of the great mass of the community are scientifically trained. We hold that every individual born into the world should be given the very best education that it is in the power of society to bestow. There must be no exceptions to this rule. Ignorance must be absolutely banished, to secure the highest good of the community."[1] Like thousands of other self-taught, middle-class American parents, therefore, the Crolys were determined that their son would get "the very best education that it is in the power of society to bestow."

J. H. Morse's English, Classical and Mathematical School for Boys on West Thirty-eighth Street was what they had in mind. One of his students described James Herbert Morse as "a Harvard graduate of fine taste and character, with pretensions to being a poet."[2] His school was frankly devoted to a single purpose: "to prepare boys thoroughly for the best colleges and scientific schools. . . . Harvard, Yale, Co-

---

[1] "C. G. David" [pseud.], *A Positivist Primer: Being a Series of Familiar Conversations on the Religion of Humanity* (New York, 1871), 98–99. For David Croly's views on education, see *Real Estate Record and Builders' Guide*, 32 (August 11, 1883): 587; and 33 (January 26, 1884): 109. Jane Croly also advocated "the right of every child, boy or girl, to the best education the country can afford." "Women's Clubs and Their Uses," *Galaxy*, 7 (1869): 902. See also her "What Children Should Read," *Demorest's*, February 1865, 137–38.

[2] Oswald Garrison Villard, *Fighting Years: Memoirs of a Liberal Editor* (New York, 1939), 27–28.

lumbia, etc."[3] The boys got the usual classical training in modern and ancient languages, a smattering of physics and mathematics, and some work in composition and penmanship. Oswald Garrison Villard, son of one of the wealthiest men in America and one of Herbert Croly's schoolmates, rode his pony up Fifth Avenue to Morse's school. "Its curriculum was conventionally barren," Villard remembered. The families who sent their boys to Morse "represented the steadiest kind of solid bourgeois citizens of the Republic—conservative, of course, and generally Republican in politics." Compared with the German schools Villard later attended, Morse's operation seemed "small and relatively easy-going and superficial."[4]

In 1884, Herbert Croly, now fifteen years old, continued his preparation by enrolling for classes at the City College of New York. He took the standard freshman courses: French and German, mathematics, history, natural history, drawing, and English. In June he ranked fifty-fifth in a class of 130. His strengths and weaknesses were clear enough. He finished a poor sixtieth in mathematics, sixty-third in natural history, and sixty-seventh in drawing; on the other hand, he was thirty-fifth in his class both in modern languages and in history and fourteenth in English.[5] If David Croly still harbored any serious hopes for turning his son into a physical scientist, one of the heroes of the Positivist society, the year at City College should have been sufficiently illuminating and disappointing. Herbert was too much like his father to deal with science in any but a theoretical way—Herbert was interested in social science, in history, in communication.

Then, in the third week of September, 1886, when he was four months shy of his eighteenth birthday, he packed his bags, left home for the very first time, and traveled up to Cambridge, Massachusetts. He began his much-interrupted, fourteen-year career as a Harvard undergraduate on Thursday morning, September 30. For some reason he had not passed the usual entrance examination and was ad-

---

[3] *J. H. Morse's English, Classical and Mathematical School for Boys: Announcements for 1882* (New York, 1882), 5–6. Villard indicated in his *Dictionary of American Biography* article that HC attended more than one grammar school. His name appeared on the class lists for the Morse school for 1880–1881 (copy found in the Villard mss., Houghton Library, Harvard University), and for 1881–1882 (in *Announcements*). How long before or after he attended this particular school is unknown; the other schools he attended are also unknown.

[4] Villard, *Fighting Years*, 27–28, 72.

[5] *Thirty-sixth Annual Register of the College of the City of New York, 1884–85.* For HC's record, see *Merit Role of the College of the City of New York. First and Second Academic Terms, September, 1884 to June, 1885*, 12.

mitted as one of ninety-six "special students." Not technically a candidate for the Bachelor of Arts degree, therefore, but in every other way a student at Harvard College, he moved into his room at 25 Holyoke Street (an address made notorious by the antics of young William Randolph Hearst, who had been expelled the year before) and settled down to his studies.

David Croly, now suffering from nephritis and diabetes, and alternating his residence between New York City and a resort in Lakeside, New Jersey, watched his son's education with the closest possible attention. His letters were filled with fatherly concern and advice, and on October 4, in Herbert's first week at school, he set down some basic rules of good conduct:[6]

Dear Bert—We were glad to get your letter this A.M. I do hope you will give a good account of yourself at college. You have a splendid chance to improve yourself and to get a good start in life. Do try to form regular habits. Be methodical. Keep the following in mind.

1. —Form the best acquaintances: it is as easy to know the cream of the college as the dregs.
2. —Avoid all billiard playing. This I must insist upon.
3. —Impress the professors you are studious and desirous of improving yourself; let them know that you do not belong to any fast set. Write plainly, punctuate your sentences, take pains to be accurate. Avoid slovenliness in thought, writing, or expression. . . . Give me a schedule of your daily studies.[7]

Half of David Croly's letters to his son were filled with just such commonplace counsel: "Be very careful that you do not get into pool playing or into playing cards for even the smallest stakes. You will regret it bitterly if you do not heed this warning." "Train yourself to tell stories well, and have a store of apt anecdotes. . . . But be careful not to get tangled up with young women of any kind. You are of an age when there is every possibility of your being impressed and thinking some ordinary young person is an angel." "Try and become a speaker as well as a writer. Then read–read–read. Be careful, be correct, be ready." "Aim high, don't waste your time, take exercise and try to be an all-round man."[8]

[6] See chapter 1, note 69.
[7] David G. Croly to HC, October 4, 1886, *Extracts*.
[8] David G. Croly to HC, October 10, 1886, November 28, 1886, and January 6, 1887, *Extracts*.

These admonitions, which might have come from any socially ambitious father whose son had left home for the first time, were not, however, all that David Croly wrote to Herbert. It did not take the father long to discover that a Harvard education involved some terrible dangers.

I

Herbert Croly arrived at Harvard at a most auspicious moment. The school was celebrating its 250th birthday that fall. The President of the United States had come to sanctify the event, and the air was filled with self-congratulation and confidence. Most of the boys who came to study at Cambridge agreed that Harvard was a wonderful place. The excitement of new ideas, the bold questioning of old values proved to be a widening, exhilarating experience for nearly all of the students of the 1880s and 1890s who later commented on their years there.

If one arrived from the chilly, decorous, dignified, orthodox New England aristocracy, one inevitably discovered in Harvard an openness which accorded "radical" notions their fair hearing, a freedom where one could feel in daily life the broadening and heady sense of limitless intellectual adventure. Robert Morss Lovett's ancestors had been in Boston since the 1630s. He had been raised on "the New England maxims," and was sent to the Monroe Street School because the nearer Quincy Street School had too many Irish. Bob Lovett found a new world at Harvard: "The setting sun of the classics cast a mellow glow from the horizon, like Christianity in an age of science," he recalled. He remembered the contagious "intellectual excitement" of the new elective system, whose "immediate effect was stimulating and broadening."[9]

The same feeling of liberation was experienced by Norman and Hutchins Hapgood. The brothers had come to Harvard from Alton, Illinois, a town Hutchins characterized as "sadly bare and unfortunate, dry and uninspiring." Hutchins Hapgood grew lyrical when he remembered what Harvard had done for him. "I found freedom of the spirit all about me. . . . I found free instead of imprisoned souls. I had come from a town where most people seemed to me painful or benumbed slaves, where the intensity of life revealed itself only in ugly passion, inarticulate. I came into serene elevation, into a feeling of relatively general freedom. . . . I unfolded as a flower unfolds

[9] Robert Morss Lovett, *All Our Years* (New York, 1948), 33–34. For Lovett's New England upbringing, see 3–30.

when the physical conditions are right."[10] His brother Norman echoed the view: "If there could be a place intellectually more attractive than Harvard University toward the end of the Nineteenth Century, my imagination does not give it form."[11]

There was much to substantiate this view of Harvard. At the center of the College was its flinty, forthright, solitary, energetic president, Charles William Eliot. "He stood as straight as Bunker Hill Monument and was obviously as unshakable on his foundations," wrote Croly's contemporary Oswald Villard. "One looked at him and felt our institutions were justified when they produced one such as he."[12] Eliot had been president since 1869, and from the start he relentlessly pushed forward his plans for Harvard, supervising the difficult transition from college to university. Under Eliot's leadership Harvard was modernized, and his years of educational reform constituted a turning point in the history of American higher learning. As John Jay Chapman, another of Croly's contemporaries, remarked, he was "the nonpareil schoolmaster to his age."[13]

Two especially important reforms, achieved just before young Croly's entrance, reinforced the view that Harvard was, perhaps, a little too radical for its own good. In the academic year 1883–84, the elective system was extended to the freshman year. So successful had Eliot been in limiting the number of required courses, that when Croly's class entered, students had to enroll for freshman English and either German or French, sophomore and junior themes or forensics, and two half-year courses in physics and chemistry. Otherwise, students followed their own inclinations in what Robert Morss Lovett called "the intellectual cloud-cuckoo land under the elective system."[14] The second important reform, abolition of compulsory attendance at daily religious exercises, went into effect only a few months

[10] Hutchins Hapgood, *A Victorian in the Modern World* (New York, 1939), 49, 66–67.

[11] Norman Hapgood, *The Changing Years* (New York, 1930), 46.

[12] Villard, *Fighting Years*, 84–85.

[13] John Jay Chapman, *Memories and Milestones* (New York, 1915), 165. For other personal reminiscences of Eliot from HC's generation of students, see Villard, *Fighting Years*, 84–85; Lovett, *All Our Years*, 47–48; Norman Hapgood, *Changing Years*, 48–49; Chapman, *Memories and Milestones*, 165–90; Mark A. DeWolfe Howe, *Classic Shades: Five Leaders of Learning and Their Colleges* (Boston, 1928), 163–99; Rollo W. Brown, *Harvard Yard in the Golden Age* (New York, 1948), 23–40. See also Hugh Hawkins, *Between Harvard and America: The Educational Leadership of Charles W. Eliot* (New York, 1972). Still valuable is Henry James, *Charles W. Eliot: President of Harvard University, 1869–1909*, 2 vols. (Boston, 1930).

[14] Lovett, *All Our Years*, 32. See also Samuel Eliot Morison, *The Development of Harvard University Since the Inauguration of President Eliot, 1869–1929* (Cambridge, Mass., 1930), xli–xlv.

before the opening of Croly's first year. Naturally such an open invitation to wickedness called down the wrath of many New Englanders. Even before the final decision had been made, physicist John Trowbridge reported back from his travels that Harvard was regarded as "a hotbed of atheism & of dissipation."[15]

In the end, however, Harvard's reputation did not rest on Eliot's reforms, but on that remarkable band of dedicated, gifted, gentle, and challenging scholars who comprised the faculty. Eliot had been able to strengthen each of Harvard's departments by astute and fortunate appointments in the 1870s and 1880s, and there could be no doubt that Harvard had the most distinguished faculty of any college in America. Looking back on his teachers a half century later, Villard wrote, "If I aver that we have not their equals today, I must not be accused of looking at the past through the rosy spectacles with which the old always seek to regard the days of their youth. They were the flowering of an age. Their disappearance marked the end of an era."[16] And particularly noteworthy were developments in two departments destined to be important to Herbert Croly.

At the urging of Francis J. Child, described by Chapman as "an old fashioned, caustic, witty little fellow," Harvard established English as a legitimate field of study in the 1870s. Child brought his student, George Lyman Kittredge ("an iron man who would be seen stalking about Cambridge with a vicious looking small bag filled with burglar's tools and footnotes on Othello"), who began his three decades of illustrious teaching in 1888.[17] President Eliot persuaded Adams S. Hill, to leave the *Chicago Tribune* in 1872, for the difficult task of teaching undergraduates how to express themselves clearly. In 1883, LeBaron R. Briggs, best known as Harvard's first college dean, came over from the Greek department to teach sophomore rhetoric with Hill. Perhaps most important of all, Barrett Wendell began teaching in 1880—composition at first and later American and comparative literature. Soon other gifted teachers were recruited: Lewis E. Gates came in the mid-1880s, George P. Baker in 1888, the leg-

[15] Cited in Hawkins, *Between Harvard and America*, 123. For the abolition of compulsory chapel attendance, see ibid., ch. iv; and Morison, *Development of Harvard*, li-lviii.

[16] Villard, *Fighting Years*, 80. For a departmental breakdown of this distinguished faculty, see Morison, *The Development of Harvard University*. See also Henry James, *Charles W. Eliot*, 1: 250–59. In 1886, Harvard employed 61 professors and 118 teachers below professorial rank. *Harvard University Catalogue, 1886–87* (Cambridge, Mass., 1886), 153.

[17] Both comments are cited by Melvin H. Bernstein, *John Jay Chapman* (New York, 1964), 54.

endary Charles Townsend Copeland in 1892. "Our system of English training at Harvard is by no means ideal," wrote Barrett Wendell in 1888, "but it is . . . the most thoughtfully developed in America, and I believe anywhere."[18]

Unquestionably, though, both those who looked askance at Harvard unorthodoxy and those who recalled with pleasure Harvard "freedom of spirit," were most often thinking about the remarkable Department of Philosophy. For three decades after 1850, philosophy at Harvard had been preparing for the eventual flowering of the 1880s and 1890s. Gradually loosening its connection with theology, no longer the exclusive province of the university president, shifting hesitantly from recitation to the lecture method, changing from an exclusive adherence to the Scottish common-sense school to include some attention to the exciting German metaphysicians, the study of philosophy at Harvard was vigorous and mature when Herbert Croly arrived as a freshman.[19]

Next to the venerated Francis Bowen, the senior member of the department was forty-five-year-old George Herbert Palmer, who had come as Bowen's assistant in 1872. The fifteen thousand students who passed through Palmer's classroom found it difficult to classify him. He was never a system-builder like his more brilliant colleagues, and his writings were confined largely to criticism. In the lecture room, it was precisely his ability to adopt completely the point of view of any philosopher that made his famous Philosophy 4 so memorable. He referred to himself as a "moderate idealist," and although the designation may have been logically untenable, it described his views with reasonable accuracy. He abhorred philosophic materialism; he agreed to the principle of the organic interconnectedness of all things; and he held that individuals were insignificant, effective only in relation to all the other individuals who composed society. But when idealism confined human freedom, when it clouded moral distinctions, when it devolved into a kind of monism of its

[18] Barrett Wendell to Edward F. Lowell, January 7, 1888, in Mark A. DeWolfe Howe, ed., *Barrett Wendell and His Letters* (Boston, 1924), 75. The single most useful examination of the English department is in Morison, *Development of Harvard University*, 65–105. See also Rollo Brown, *Dean Briggs* (New York, 1926); Blake Nevius, *Robert Herrick: The Development of a Novelist* (Berkeley, 1962), 35–39; Villard, *Fighting Years*, 89–91; Lovett, *All Our Years*, 32–33, 45–46.

[19] Benjamin Rand, "Philosophical Instruction in Harvard University from 1636 to 1906," *Harvard Graduates' Magazine*, 37 (1928–29), 29–47, 188–200, 296–311; Bruce Kuklick, *The Rise of American Philosophy: Cambridge, Massachusetts, 1860–1930* (New Haven, 1977), ch. vii.

own, Palmer refused either to follow along or to iron out the intellectual difficulties of the argument.

Small, frail, with bushy eyebrows and a full moustache, the picture of dignity and integrity, invested with a kind of romantic mystery in 1886, as rumors spread about his courtship of Alice Freeman, president of Wellesley, George Herbert Palmer made his profoundest impact by introducing young men to the breadth of philosophic thought.[20] It never mattered that his own thought lacked creativity. His impact was always his teaching. It was Palmer, above all, who attracted to Harvard some of the most brilliant philosophers in America.

One of them was William James. After abandoning a career in art and trying to teach physiology and psychology in Harvard's Department of Natural Science for eight years, James joined the Department of Philosophy in 1880. Although he was not, in 1886, the world-famous philosopher he was later to become, the forty-four-year-old James was a popular teacher and a maturing original thinker. Throughout the 1880s he devoted himself principally to psychological studies; nevertheless it was possible to detect in James's thought the leading ideas of his important work of the 1890s. He had already rejected abstract rationalism in favor of a thoroughgoing empirical approach to knowledge—truth was not that which harmonized with some clever intellectual system or some insistent law of logic; truth must constantly submit itself for substantiation or refutation to the concrete environment and the observed data of experience. He had already made tentative approaches to that pluralism which was to command so much of his attention in the last years of his life—reality was not part of a harmonious and unitary Whole; reality was remarkably diverse, multiple, interpenetrating, and even contradictory. Other characteristic Jamesian ideas—respect for religious emotion and mysticism, a commitment to human freedom, democracy, the power of the individual will, and the pragmatic test of truth—could also be easily seen in his writings and lectures of the 1880s.[21]

[20] The leading source for Palmer's life is his *The Autobiography of a Philosopher* (Boston, 1930). See also Charles M. Bakewell, "The Philosophy of George Herbert Palmer," in *George Herbert Palmer, 1842–1933: Memorial Addresses* (Cambridge, Mass., 1935), 3–43; William E. Hocking, "Personal Traits of George Herbert Palmer," ibid., 47–65; Kuklick, *Rise of American Philosophy*, ch. vii; Morison, *Development of Harvard University*, 20–21; Brown, *Harvard Yard*, 48–49, 67–74; and Rand, "Philosophical Instruction," 298–99. The winning of Alice Freeman is charmingly reconstructed in Palmer, *An Academic Courtship: The Letters of Alice Freeman and George Herbert Palmer, 1886–1887* (Cambridge, Mass., 1940).

[21] For James's early philosophical leanings, see Ralph Barton Perry, *The Thought and Character of William James* (Boston, 1935), 1: 449–808, and Kuklick, *Rise of American Philosophy*, ch. ix.

Although James was never a spellbinding lecturer, those who took his courses recalled the experience with pleasure and gratitude. Despite his lack of organization, his hesitancy, the habit of working slowly to new conclusions in front of the class, James's openness, his wit, his humanity, his flashing insights and love of dialogue on important questions all shone through. It mattered little whether he was teaching, walking across the Yard, entertaining students in his home. To Norman Hapgood, he was "the best of all the good teachers I have known." "Where he walked, nothing could touch him," wrote another former student, ". . . it was impossible not to be morally elevated by the smallest contact with William James."[22]

At James's urging, twenty-seven-year-old Josiah Royce came to Harvard in 1882. Initially Royce held several beliefs in common with James. He was a voluntarist, for example, and, like James, saw the will actively engaged in the fashioning of thought.[23] Both men were empiricists, and both ridiculed romanticism in philosophy. The two were also united by a philosophic tolerance and a mutual respect, which permitted each to criticize without hesitation—in the classroom, in articles and books, in private and spirited talk as they walked together through the streets of Cambridge—the most cherished beliefs of the other. Their similarities in doctrine and their personal friendship would need all the strength possible to encompass their ever-growing differences.

From the start Royce found himself in that train of philosophic idealism which was formulated by Kant and modified and elaborated by Fichte, Schelling, and Hegel.[24] So much was Royce identified with his belief in a transcendent, all-embracing, all-knowing Unity that even the undergraduates joked about "Royce's old Absolute."[25] His

[22] Norman Hapgood, *Changing Years*, 60; and Chapman, *Memories and Milestones*, 20. For reminiscences of James as a teacher, see Perry, *William James*, 1: 441–46; Norman Hapgood, *Changing Years*, 60–73; Brown, *Harvard Yard*, 74–84; Walter Lippmann, "An Open Mind: William James," *Everybody's Magazine*, 23 (December, 1910): 800–801; Horace M. Kallen, "Remembering William James," in *In Commemoration of William James, 1842–1942* (New York, 1942), 11–23; Dickinson S. Miller, "William James, Man and Philosopher," in *William James: The Man and the Thinker* (Madison, Wis., 1942), 29–52; or Josiah Royce, *William James and Other Essays on the Philosophy of Life* (New York, 1912), 3–34.

[23] John Dewey, "Voluntarism in the Roycean Philosophy," *The Philosophic Review*, 25 (1916): 245–54, reprinted in *Papers in Honor of Josiah Royce on His Sixtieth Birthday* (New York, 1916), 17–26; and James Harry Cotton, *Royce on the Human Self* (Cambridge, Mass., 1954), 73–106.

[24] Vincent Buranelli, *Josiah Royce* (New York, 1964), 48–76; Gabriel Marcel, *Royce's Metaphysics* (Chicago, 1956).

[25] Norman Hapgood, *Changing Years*, 58.

tendency to see the Whole, to universalize the data, to notice the harmony, to exalt the community, to argue for the underlying unity of the Absolute, and James's fascination with the discrete parts, his proclivity for particularization, his exaltation of the individual, his impassioned defense of the plural universe—these provided the meat of their twenty-eight-year dialogue. Yet throughout the long debate each man retained his poise, his tolerance and good humor, and an unwavering respect for his opponent.[26]

Josiah Royce was an intense teacher. Even his humor had seriousness in it. By all accounts he was an encyclopedic storehouse of information. He loved to talk and to listen; and, as Royce paused thoughtfully to consider some student's question, one was automatically made to feel that even a poorly stated question was an important thing. Chapman recalled his accessibility (his seminars were open to everyone): "You could join in the discussion and challenge the champion if you had the brains. . . . He had fixed hours when anyone could resort to him and draw inspiration from him."[27]

In 1886, with Palmer, James, and Royce, the philosophy department at Harvard was, easily, the most distinguished in the United States. In 1889 it added to its roster Royce's stormy and brilliant pupil, George Santayana. And in 1892, James brought in Hugo Münsterberg to handle the psychological-philosophical studies in the department. "What the students saw in the five, felt in them, was a vitality from which there was no escape."[28] As an introduction to the world of abstract thought, what Palmer called "this philosophical menagerie"[29] must have made a profound impression on the young men who came to Cambridge. But in that respect, philosophy was merely symbolic of what so many remembered about the place as a whole: the earnest discussion of even the most securely enshrined

[26] For the relationship between Royce and James, see Ralph Barton Perry, "Two American Philosophers," in *In the Spirit of William James* (Bloomington, 1958 edition), 1–43; and Perry, *William James*, 1: 778–824. See also James's captivating letter to Royce in Henry James, ed., *The Letters of William James* (Boston, 1920), 2: 136; and Royce's warm tribute in *William James and Other Essays*. The general topic is well handled in Kuklick, *Rise of American Philosophy*, chs. viii, and xiv-xvi.

[27] John Jay Chapman, "Portrait of Royce," *Outlook*, 122 (July 2, 1919): 372, 377. For other personal reminiscences of Royce as a teacher, see Richard C. Cabot, "Josiah Royce as a Teacher," *Philosophical Review*, 25 (1916): 466–72, reprinted in *Papers in Honor of Josiah Royce*, 68; Morison, *Development of Harvard University* (the reminiscence of Palmer), 9–15; Norman Hapgood, *Changing Years*, 58; W.E.B. DuBois, "A Negro Student at Harvard at the End of the Nineteenth Century," *Massachusetts Review*, 1 (Spring 1960): 439–58.

[28] Brown, *Harvard Yard*, 50.

[29] Quoted in Bliss Perry, *And Gladly Teach: Reminiscences* (Boston, 1935), 223.

values; the strenuous intellectual combat of energetic minds and gentle, tolerant spirits; the thrill of a plunge into the enlivening and liberating atmosphere of Harvard College.

II

But there is danger in overstating the case. Not everyone found the intellectual and social atmosphere widening, liberating, and free— because not everyone who came to Harvard in the 1880s arrived fresh from the New England aristocracy or the intellectual wastes of Alton, Illinois. Henry Adams, who had too restless a mind to dwell contentedly in his social position, had been a student in the 1850s and a teacher in the 1870s. Both experiences he thought were wasted and debilitating. His final verdict: "In spite of President Eliot's reforms . . . the system remained costly, clumsy and futile."[30] Adams's complaint—that Harvard was essentially an eighteenth-century institution in a world roaring madly into the twentieth—was echoed by a group of students and faculty of the 1880s. To them, Harvard was socially conservative, politically naïve, and intellectually stultifying.

Young W.E.B. DuBois, who arrived in 1888 and became the first Negro Ph.D. in Harvard's history, remembered, "I was in Harvard but not of it and realized all the irony of 'Fair Harvard.' I sang it because I liked the music."[31] Socially ostracized, DuBois associated the university with exclusive clubs, sheltered lives, endless talk about one's Puritan ancestors. Oswald Garrison Villard, who inherited his radicalism from his famous abolitionist grandfather, summed up his classmates: "As a whole I cannot say, as I should dearly like to, that '93 has been a class to which the university might refer with special pride. But at least we have upheld the Harvard tradition of contributing greatly to the steadfast bourgeoisie and the satisfactory maintenance of the *status quo*."[32]

A glance at Herbert Croly's class of 1890 substantiates the complaints of social inbreeding and conservatism. The class came complete with its Wheelright, Wentworth, and Washburn; its Cotton, Endicott, Mather, and Brooks; its Babbitt, its Cabot, its Abbot. More students were from Massachusetts than from all the other states combined; and Episcopalians, Unitarians, and Congregationalists outnumbered all the other denominations combined—indeed, in the class of 284, no other formal sect could claim more than seven adherents.

[30] Henry Adams, *The Education of Henry Adams* (New York, 1931 edition), 304.

[31] W.E.B. DuBois, *Dusk of Dawn: An Essay Toward an Autobiography of a Race Concept* (New York, 1940), 37.

[32] Villard, *Fighting Years*, 87.

There were, of course, more Republicans than there were members of all other parties combined.[33]

While some were uneasy in Harvard's social climate, there were also objections to her political apathy. Henry Adams complained that neither Auguste Comte nor Karl Marx had been mentioned in the Harvard of his day.[34] DuBois, writing about the 1880s and 1890s, made a similar observation: "Karl Marx was hardly mentioned and Henry George given but tolerant notice. The anarchists of Spain, the Nihilists of Russia, the British miners—all these were viewed not as part of the political development and the tremendous economic organization but as sporadic evil."[35] Villard, who was fascinated by politics, found few students who shared his tastes, and "practically nobody in the class was interested in world events."[36] The phrase "Harvard indifference," much in the air, meant many things. Quite clearly, however, the phrase implied a kind of complacent self-satisfaction coupled with a disdain for politics. When Villard had to choose between teaching at Harvard or becoming a journalist, his wealthy father urged Harvard. But Villard told his father that "at Harvard one was too safe, too sheltered, too at ease. 'It is,' I assured him, 'like sitting in a club window and watching the world go by on the pavement outside.' "[37]

Thus, though Harvard was denounced by some in the community as radical and a few parents hesitated about sending sons into so contaminating an environment, the reputation was probably undeserved. In at least two critical areas, Harvard was unwaveringly orthodox. In economic thought no one questioned the broad principles of Adam Smith's laissez-faire free-trade system. A small, noninterfering central government, the gradual reduction of all trade barriers, and the freest possible play of individuals engaged in competitive struggle—these tenets were as securely enshrined at Harvard in 1886 as they were anywhere else in the United States; Charles F. Dunbar and Frank W. Taussig carefully explained the catechism to generations of young men.

In addition to this devotion to classical economics, Harvard was also firmly committed to a belief in the essential truth and beneficence of Christianity. The abolition of compulsory attendance at chapel, in the summer of 1886, was not an anti-Christian act. The reform

[33] *Harvard College Class of 1890, Report 1* (Cambridge, Mass., 1891), 5–14.
[34] Henry Adams, *The Education of Henry Adams*, 60.
[35] DuBois, *Dusk of Dawn*, 39–40.
[36] Villard, *Fighting Years*, 88.
[37] Ibid., 105.

was initiated, after all, by Francis Greenwood Peabody, Plummer Professor of Christian Morals, and it received full support from Phillips Brooks, the famous Episcopal preacher of Boston and one of the university preachers. President Eliot was not the infidel he was sometimes accused of being; he was, in fact, a pillar of the Unitarian church, attending chapel frequently, and always ready to admit that his faith was an important fact of his life.[38]

That the great majority of the faculty were practicing and devout Christians could hardly be questioned. Even Harvard's philosophic triumvirate of 1886—men, it was widely assumed, who challenged everything—even they were all theists and all at least partial to Christianity. "In Religion all Philosophy culminates," Palmer summed up his consistent belief, "or rather, from it all Philosophy flows." Palmer could not accept the literal interpretation of the Bible, and he questioned doctrines like the Virgin Birth, but his devotion to Christian ideas and Christian forms was beyond doubt.[39]

William James's religious views are well known. His biographer argued that half his philosophy was religious: "He was solicited on the one side by religion and on the other side by science. He felt the appeal of both religion and science, and his central intellectual compulsion was the necessity of providing for both."[40] James too could be seen at Harvard chapel regularly, but he could never properly be labelled as a member of a particular Christian sect, though emotionally he was clearly a Protestant and understood himself to be one. He was committed to a theistic conception of the universe, for it was only the theistic scheme, he felt, which could answer the moral, emotional, and volitional demands of human nature. James's God was a personal Helper to Whom men's souls aspire. And since James believed that everything experienced was real, he found ample proof for the existence of God in the collective religious history of mankind and in the compelling and transforming mystical experiences of individual men and women. Those accustomed to identifying rigid empiricism with heresy were destined to be surprised by William James.[41]

[38] Hawkins, *Between Harvard and America*, ch. iv; and James, *Charles W. Eliot*, 1: 297–302.

[39] Palmer's religious views are explained at great length in *The Autobiography of a Philosopher*, 73–113.

[40] Ralph Barton Perry, "William James," in *Dictionary of American Biography*, 9: 594. The analysis in Theodore Flournoy, *The Philosophy of William James* (New York, 1917), 134, is almost identical: "James' special philosophic preoccupation seems to have been to reconcile the demands of the moral and religious life with those of science. . . ."

[41] For James's religious views, see Julius Seelye Bixler, *Religion in the Philosophy of*

For Josiah Royce the problem of religion loomed quite as large as it did for James. In the preface of his first philosophic work, *The Religious Aspect of Philosophy*, Royce carefully explained that "religious problems have been chosen for the present study because they first drove the author to philosophy, and because, they, of all human interests, deserve our best efforts and our utmost loyalty."[42] Although Royce had serious questions about Christianity and, like James, joined no particular sect, in the end, he argued that "both by reason of its past history and by reason of its present and persistent relation to the religious needs of men, Christianity stands before us as the most effective expression of religious longing which the human race, travailing in pain until now, has, in its corporate capacity, as yet, been able to bring before its vision. . . ."[43]

The difficulty, then, of talking about Harvard is clear. If a young man approached the experience from the New England establishment, if he came from a religiously orthodox home, if he arrived fresh from some chilly intellectual wasteland, then naturally Harvard was a liberating adventure.

But what if the young man came straight from an intellectually alive home in New York City? What if, instead of tracing his ancestry to seventeenth-century Boston, his parents were immigrants? And even more to the point, what if he were raised to believe that laissez-faire economic theory was the pernicious vestige of the second stage of human progress, and, worse yet, that Christianity was the pernicious vestige of the first?

III

Freshman Croly's program was typical. In French 2 he read the classics from Voltaire to Balzac under the guidance of Ferdinand Bocher, who, according to Norman Hapgood, "was said to be lazy, and who

---

William James (Boston, 1926); Flournoy, *The Philosophy of William James*, 134–65; Richard P. Brennan, *The Ethics of William James* (New York, 1961), 44–67; Perry, *William James*, 2: 352–59.

[42] Josiah Royce, *The Religious Aspect of Philosophy* (New York, 1958 edition), ix.

[43] Josiah Royce, *The Problem of Christianity* (New York, 1913), 6–13. For Royce's religious views, see George Dykhuizen, *The Conception of God in the Philosophy of Josiah Royce: A Critical Exposition of Its Epistemological and Metaphysical Development* (Chicago, 1936); Mary Whiton Calkins, "The Foundation in Royce's Philosophy for Christian Theism," *Papers in Honor of Josiah Royce*, 54–68; William Adams Brown, "The Problem of Christianity," ibid., 77–86; Cotton, *Royce on the Human Self*, 266–94; and John E. Smith, *Royce's Social Infinite: The Community of Interpretation* (New York, 1950), 109–25.

appeared to me to be lazy, but whose humor, taste, and pleasant malice were the Gallic mind accurately embodied at its best."[44] Croly continued his study of French into the second semester with the reading course, French 8, also under Bocher. He dutifully entered LeBaron Briggs's English A and B, Rhetoric and Composition, for Eliot's elective system had not removed those requirements. Three times a week he listened to Silas Macvane repeating the textbooks in Henry Adams's old course, History 2, "Constitutional Government in England and America."[45] Nothing terribly challenging and nothing terribly difficult. Croly made "B"s in English and French and got an "A" from Macvane in history.[46]

Three additional courses taken in his first year were a good deal more traumatic: Croly registered for Philosophy 1, "The History of Philosophy," with Palmer; Philosophy 2, "Logic and Psychology," with James; and Political Economy 4, "The Economic History of Europe and the United States since 1763," with the old laissez-faire proponent, Charles Francis Dunbar. Herbert's work in these three courses commanded not merely his own effort but the anxious interest of his father as well. A dramatic struggle ensued between Herbert's teachers and his father, who, despite his illness, battled desperately to keep Herbert from falling prey to the wiles of Palmer, James, and Dunbar. All his hopes, after all, rested on the willingness of the son to carry on his teachings, and with so much in the balance it was no wonder that David Croly fought as hard as he did.

For two weeks everything went smoothly; it was sufficient that Herbert was engaged in philosophic thought: "I am delighted with the kind of works you are reading," his father wrote. "Had I free choice and no living to make, my life would have been spent in just such studies as you are practising. I fear you are too young to take much interest in philosophical works but I will be pleased if I am mistaken."[47] By the end of October, however, some of Herbert's thirty- and forty-page letters home had begun to raise questions. David Croly countered with frankness, tolerance, and a reading list of his own that would have surprised George Palmer:

> My dear Boy — You said something about the divergence between my ideas and those of the philosophers you are reading

[44] Norman Hapgood, *Changing Years*, 55.

[45] Lovett, *All Our Years*, 32.

[46] *Harvard University Rank Lists, 1886–1905* (Cambridge, Mass., published by the university annually).

[47] David G. Croly to HC, October 16, 1886, *Extracts*.

at college. Let me beg of you to form your own judgment on all the higher themes—religion included—without any reference to what I have said. All I ask is that you keep your mind open and unpredisposed. . . . Be careful and do not allow first impressions to influence your maturer judgment. . . . I wish during your college year that you would read:

(1) Miss Martineau's translation of Comte's "Positive Philosophy."
(2) Mill's Estimate of Comte's Life and Works.
(3) [J. H.] Bridges' Reply to Mill.
(4) All of Frederic Harrison's writing that you can find.
(5) All of Herbert Spencer's works that are not technical.
(6) John Fiske's works.
(7) The works of the English Positivists, such as Congreve, Bridges, and Beesley.

By noticing the dates I think you will find that Spencer appropriates a great deal from Comte and that he tries to shirk the obligation. It would be well to read the latter's "General View of Positivism" further along.

My dear son, I shall die happy if I know that you are an earnest student of philosophic themes. Do cultivate all the religious emotions, reverence, awe and aspiration, if for no better reason than as a means of self-culture. Educate, train every side of your mental and emotional nature. Read poetry and learn the secret of tears and ecstacy. Go to Catholic and Episcopal churches and surrender yourself to the inspiration of soul-inspiring religious music.

Ever your affectionate,
Father[48]

By November 6, David Croly was growing concerned about what was going on in Palmer's classroom. "On one point let me put you on your guard. Do not become bewitched by brilliant or showy paradoxes. . . . There was something in your long letter recently about the 'becoming' which had a flavour of Hegel. Beware of metaphysics, my son. We live in a real world and should not be fooled by words or phrases." And, before closing his letter, a slash at Professor Dunbar too: "Ricardo, the Manchester school, Bastiat, and the rest have discredited political economy with practical people. Do not be

[48] David G. Croly to HC, October 31, 1886. This letter was separated from the others in 1889, when Herbert submitted it for publication in his father's memorial collection in *The Real Estate Record and Builders' Guide*, May 18, 1889, supplement, 3.

cajoled by definitions and phrases however apparently self-evident."[49]

Three weeks later the father was making frank pleas for Comte's scientific approach. "What you say about Modern Philosophy repeating the ancient is all true enough. . . . Man made no progress by simply interrogating consciousness. He went from realism to Idealism, then to Materialism and Scepticism. . . . But when man's intellect was brought to bear upon the phenomena of the objective world, then Science was born and the basis laid for the great inventions of our Modern Era. Hence the superior fruitfulness of the objective as compared with the subjective method."[50] More and more, David Croly invested his hopes in Herbert's eventual study of the "modern" philosophers. "Do not take stock in all Fiske and Spencer say about Comte," he wrote regarding his son's outside reading. "Suspend your judgment until you have read more. When you study Comte (he died in 1857) you will find that he anticipated nearly all that is valuable in the thinkers who have followed and reviled him."[51] "Is it worth while to thoroughly understand Descartes, Spinoza, or any of the metaphysical philosophers? The ones to be constantly studied, to my mind, are Kant, Hume, Berkeley, J. S. Mill, Comte, and H. Spencer, but life is too short to master the unfruitful thinkers such as Hegel and the lesser lights."[52]

By the end of Herbert's first year at Harvard, David Croly felt that he had weathered the storm. He discouraged his son from spending the summer vacation studying theology ("The pros and cons of theism might be unprofitable because there is no solution to that problem. . . .") and turned him instead to poetry (". . . an improvement of your ear, taste and style would help in your future progress.")[53] As the first year drew to its close, David Croly breathed easier. "Happily you see Palmer and James's shortcomings in Philosophy. . . ."[54] Unfortunately, the father had counted the victory prematurely. The son had not yet encountered the philosopher whose intellectual impact would dwarf both James and Palmer. Herbert Croly was not to meet, and David Croly was not to battle, the compelling and persuasive and brilliant Josiah Royce until the next academic year.

Meanwhile the struggle raged along another front. There were grave

[49] David G. Croly to HC, November 6, 1886, *Extracts*.
[50] David G. Croly to HC, November 25, 1886, *Extracts*.
[51] David G. Croly to HC, January 16, 1887, *Extracts*.
[52] David G. Croly to HC, March 20, 1887, *Extracts*. See also the letter of May 1, 1887.
[53] David G. Croly to HC, March 4, 1887, *Extracts*.
[54] David G. Croly to HC, May 18, 1887, *Extracts*.

problems in the world, and David Croly had his doubts about Harvard's approach to them. He sent Herbert the latest articles of Henry George; he congratulated his son for sympathizing with the striking cab drivers: "These people sacrifice themselves for us and we ill-treat them because they become coarse and ignorant in serving us." And always the Comtean admonition: "Remember . . . the highest morality is altruistic. 'Live for others' is the Motto always to be kept in mind. A purely selfish life is necessarily a base one."[55] Particularly worrisome was Harvard's conservative approach to economic problems. "Do not commit yourself against state socialism," cautioned the father. "There is a good deal to be said for government ownership of natural monopolies, such as telegraph, railroad, etc. Try not to be biased until both sides are presented. The tendency all over the civilized world is for the great corporation of the nation to do what has so far been relegated to the irresponsible private corporations. . . . The labour movement all over the world is of vast significance."[56]

Naturally, the prospect of studying political, economic, and social questions with men such as Dunbar, Taussig, Peabody, and J. Laurence Laughlin filled Herbert's father with uneasiness. "I almost dread your going through a course of Political Economy at Harvard," he wrote. "The theories which prevail there are, I apprehend, a quarter of a century behind the age." Although Herbert had seen some of the weaknesses of Palmer and James, David Croly could not help wondering whether his son would "be able to look at practical, and political questions with more modern eyes than the Harvard Professors who secured their present position a decade back by advocating views which to my mind are antiquated."[57]

Finally, as the first year of college came to its close, Herbert and his father exchanged some letters on the question of a career. The extent to which Auguste Comte dominated even this dialogue is obvious from the prophetic letter David Croly sent his son on March 10, 1887:

Dear Bert — I was very much pleased with the letter you last sent me. It seems that your aims are high and that you intend to devote your life to worthwhile uses. Keep constantly in mind

[55] David G. Croly to HC, January 16, 1887, February 9, 1887, and April 17, 1887, *Extracts.*

[56] David G. Croly to HC, May 11, 1887, *Extracts.*

[57] David G. Croly to HC, May 18, 1887, *Extracts.*

the highest moral law which is "Live for others." . . . It seems
to me our two main objects in life should be

1 —Improve man himself by heredity and education
2 —To improve man's environment by trying to create conditions to make his life as useful and pleasant as possible. Hence
after you have got through with the older and Middle Age
Philosophies I hope you will turn your attention to the Science of Sciences the sum and end of Philosophy—Sociology.
. . . So far the foundation of this noblest of Sciences has not
been laid. Why not make it the work of your life? The field
is virgin, almost, and a well-equipped University student
such as you ought to be at the end of two years, might reap
an honorable fame by trying to think out some of the mighty
problems connected with man's future on this planet. . . .
Society is an organism controlled by laws of development
which when discovered can be modified by man himself.
Here is a career for you, my son, a noble one. By following
it you can take your place in the front rank of modern thinkers and devote your life to the holiest uses.[58]

Having fortified him by a summer of serious discussion, David
Croly released his son to the dangers of Cambridge for a second year
of intellectual combat. Herbert enrolled for English C, Forensics,
which David Croly hoped would instill confidence in the boy. In
addition, Herbert registered for History 16, "Comparative Religion," under Charles C. Everett. Hutchins Hapgood remembered
Everett as "one of the most charming professors it has ever been my
lot to meet. Under his genial touch knowledge became one of the
highest pleasures." Hapgood spoke of his simplicity and unselfish-
ness, but what really made the profoundest impression was the teacher's religious devotion. "The great appeal that this old scholar had
for me was undoubtedly due to his religious nature, which expressed
itself without theology, and so broadly that it included science and
every kind of criticism. . . . It sprang from a constant recognition of
God in all things."[59] The importance of Everett for Herbert Croly—
in the crucial year when he discovered Christianity—is impossible to
estimate.

Herbert also enrolled in English 12, the course in composition made
famous by the already legendary Barrett Wendell. Nearly everyone

[58] David G. Croly to HC, March 10, 1887, *Extracts*.

[59] Hutchins Hapgood, *Victorian in the Modern World*, 73–74. For another student
whom Everett nearly attracted into the ministry, see Lovett, *All Our Years*, 44.

who sat in Wendell's classroom had something to say about him. His high-pitched voice, the pointed beard, the twirling watch chain, his eccentricities and his outrageous opinions all combined to make him a "character," the professor every undergraduate went around imitating. Despite the fact that he required daily themes, Wendell's course was an extremely popular elective, the enrollment frequently passing two hundred.[60] In politics, Wendell was "an ultra Back Bay conservative" who thought that Henry Cabot Lodge was the greatest man in public life, and his literary tastes were equally fastidious.[61] He demanded high moral tone (condemning, for example, deMaupassant for writing about things "no decent man out of France would for a moment think worthy of his pains," and Walt Whitman for being "too eccentric"). Most important, he was a stickler for "good use." No word or phrase was permitted unless it was "Reputable, National, and Present"; there was no excuse for vulgar, eccentric, slangy, local, obsolete, technical phraseology. Herbert Croly's personal style, which so many have rightly found plodding, academic, and colorless, may have owed some of its pedantic tone to the teaching of Barrett Wendell.[62]

Once again, however, the centers of action and conflict, the sources of questioning and intellectual struggle were political economy and philosophy. Herbert Croly heard lectures from J. Laurence Laughlin in the first semester and Frank W. Taussig in the second semester of Political Economy 1. The course was typical Manchester School laissez-faire theory; the text was John Stuart Mill and some chapters from the work of Harvard's own Charles Dunbar.

Bravely, despite considerable pain and collapsing health, David Goodman Croly once again attempted to counter the influence of an economic theory he thought was outmoded. "What I dread," he wrote early in Herbert's second year, "is that your political economy course will give you a bias towards believing that what is, is right. You ought to read Comte on Political Economy in his Positive Philosophy. You should also read up Bridges, Marx and the Socialist writers, not that they are right but that they are the most recent studies

[60] The leading source for his life is Howe, ed., *Barrett Wendell*. Personal reminiscences of this colorful teacher abound, but see Rollo Brown, *Dean Briggs*, 60–61; William R. Castle, Jr., "Barrett Wendell—Teacher," in *Essays in Memory of Barrett Wendell by His Assistants* (Cambridge, Mass., 1926), 1–10; and Daniel Sargent, "Professor Wendell and the Philosophers," in ibid., 11–20.

[61] Villard, *Fighting Years*, 91.

[62] I am relying on the intelligent analysis of Wendell's possible influence on one of HC's classmates, in Blake Nevius, *Robert Herrick*, 35–39.

on the wealth and Labour problems."[63] The fundamental assumption of Harvard's political economy courses was that if men were granted complete freedom to compete with one another, the struggle would be fierce, but (just as Darwin had shown in biology) would lead to steady improvement. David Croly warned his son about being too sure:

> Be careful how you accept Laughlin's Political Economy. The bitter struggle for life which we find in Nature and which is so remorseless in its operation, also prevails in human society with equally terrible results; but to properly serve man, the brutal and blind forces of Nature must be manipulated. Competition in the world about us gives us the shark, the tiger, and the poisonous snake as well as the more innocent animal kingdom suitable to its environment; but man almost recreates the vegetable world, develops wheat out of a useless weed, gives us by cultivation the fruit and sunflower, tames the wolf or fox into the dog and practically creates the horse, sheep, cow and hog. My quarrel with Political Economy is its limitation. I beg of you to read what Comte says of it in Miss Martineau's Translation of his philosophy.[64]

Unfortunately, the anxious father had to fight off Laughlin and Taussig with his left hand; his right, as usual was directing blows at the Department of Philosophy. Herbert enrolled for Palmer's Philosophy 4, "English Ethics," and Philosophy 13, "Monism and the Theory of Evolution in Their Relation to the Philosophy of Nature," under Josiah Royce. The approach of both men was in direct opposition to that of David Croly. Both were committed to theistic conceptions of the universe; both were philosophic Idealists—if not formal Hegelians, then closer to Hegel than to any other major philosopher. In short, as David Croly saw it, both suffered from outworn vestiges of the two primitive stages of human development. Naturally, these teachers dealt with philosophers who shared their beliefs in a Supreme Being and a harmonious world whose concrete phenomena were merely the poor shadows of a transcendent and intangible Truth. And, just as naturally, David Croly kept wondering when Herbert would get done with the unimportant thinkers and get down to business.

When Herbert was required to write essays on Shaftesbury and

---

[63] David G. Croly to HC, October 22, 1887, *Extracts*.
[64] David G. Croly to HC, November 24, 1887, *Extracts*.

Butler, for example, his father erupted. "Why spend so much time on such a third rate philosopher as Shaftesbury? . . . Bishop Butler and his antiquated theological arguments are surely out of date." When Herbert tried to defend his course of study, his father got even angrier: ". . . here you are advocating the study of theology which is without a glimmering of modern scientific truth. . . . Life is too short to study exhaustively the works of the Butlers, Baxters, and the other expounders of creeds outworn." Three weeks later: "I am just a little dubious as to the wisdom of spending so much effort to set forth ethical theories of these 17th century moralists. I wish your studies were more in the direction of modern scientific thought." Again Herbert tried to explain, and again his father grew impatient. "Of course you have to accept the task assigned to you. I realize the History of the course of philosophic thought is indispensable to a student, but I do not quite see the utility of spending so much time and effort upon antiquated systems. Surely it would not pay to try and master Hutton or Werner on Geology or to reproduce the antiquated chemistry of fifty years ago." Finally, after what must have been a spirited reply by his son, David Croly backed off: "We will not discuss that Butler matter any farther. Our positions really do not differ, but it is the misery of all controversy to find differences rather than agreements. I agree that all the links of a chain should be considered, what I feared was the minor links would take up more of your time than the larger and more important departments of Philosophy. So no more on that head."[65]

By the end of Herbert's second year at Harvard, David Croly was frustrated and angry. In its political, economic, and philosophical instruction, the school was hopelessly conservative and perniciously old-fashioned. Whether it was Royce or Laughlin, James or Dunbar, Palmer or Everett or Taussig, Harvard College was obviously staffed by men without insight or imagination, men who had apparently given up the search for truth. And whenever David Croly was frustrated and angry he went to the public. No sooner had Herbert returned in June 1888, and delivered in person his account of what had transpired at Harvard, than his father addressed himself to what must have been the most baffled audience in the whole history of American journalism. All over the city of New York, real estate dealers, brokers, contractors, carpenters, plumbers, and architects picked up their copies of *The Real Estate Record and Builders' Guide*, where with what feelings of horror we can only guess, they learned:

[65] David G. Croly to HC, December 8, 1887, December 14, 1887, January 9, 1888, January 16, 1888, and January 21, 1888, *Extracts*.

What is known as advanced scientific thought has very little show in any of our colleges, even in Harvard. The Professional chairs represent the creeds of the past, not the living and advanced thought of the present. It may not be generally known but at Harvard the philosophy taught the pupils is Hegelianism, which has been discredited in the country of its birth for the past fifty years. The political economy taught in the same institution is that of the Manchester school, which is thirty years behind the age.[66]

We may assume that this announcement of Harvard's delinquency unleashed a wave of consternation among the real estate dealers of New York City. Unfortunately, the various ways they chose to channel their fury have not been preserved in the public record.

IV

Throughout that crucial second year of college, Josiah Royce was Herbert Croly's favorite teacher. "I am glad to learn from one of your previous letters," the as yet unsuspecting David Croly wrote at the beginning of the school year, "you feel attracted towards one of your professors. It puts a good influence into a young man's life when he is profoundly impressed with the culture and intellect of some teacher with whom he is associated." When Harvard announced a leave of absence for Royce and his replacement by Francis E. Abbot, David Croly consoled his son, "I am sorry you have lost Prof. Royce. The danger is that with Abbot, your antagonism will be aroused and you will not do him justice."[67] By the year's end it was clear that Royce had engaged the son's mind and challenged the father's ideas as had no other teacher. It was also clear that the impact of this brilliant and sophisticated thinker was primarily religious.

Herbert himself saw the change in his thinking almost wholly in religious terms. When it came time for him to contribute to his father's "Memorial," it was precisely this conflict between Harvard and his father that he chose to discuss. Writing with what he later called "a detestable flavour of priggishness which I did not in the least feel," Herbert tried to explain what had happened to him at Harvard College.[68]

[66] *Record and Guide*, 41 (June 23, 1888): 800.
[67] David G. Croly to HC, October 20, 1887, and February 16, 1888, *Extracts*.
[68] HC to Louise Emory, June 1, 1891, a copy made by Louise Emory Croly and deposited in Houghton Library, Harvard University.

First, the son remembered fondly the childhood talks in Central Park, the discussions of Comte and the Religion of Humanity, the beauty of a life of altruism. But, Herbert reported, his father's teachings were "as largely negative as positive." He never understood Christianity, and when it came to Jesus, "his attitude was one, I judge, of sympathetic scepticism." True, he had admitted that there had to be something in a faith which had inspired so many; on the other hand, "it was incomplete . . . very often the followers of Christ gave more to the doctrine than they received from it." Above all, he had argued that "it was the teaching of Auguste Comte that supplied what was lacking in the teaching of Jesus Christ." "Under such instruction," Herbert wrote, "it was not strange that in time I dropped insensibly into his mode of thinking, or, more correctly, into his mode of believing." Then came Harvard and Professor Royce:

> While I was at college I was surrounded by other influences, and while retaining everything that was positive and constructive in his teaching, I dropped the negative cloth in which it was shrouded. My change in opinion was a bitter disappointment to him, as several letters which he wrote at the time testify. But intense as was his disappointment, it never took the form of a reproach. This is very remarkable when we consider what an essential part of his character his beliefs constituted. Here was an end, for which he had striven through many years, failing at the very time when it should have become most fruitful. And his disappointment must have been all the more severe because he exaggerated the differences that existed between us. It was his opinion that his negative opinions were necessarily connected with those which were positive. . . . His opinions, crystallized by opposition which they met on every side, were so very much the truth to him that he wished his son to perceive them clearly and cherish them as devoutly as he did. That wish became impossible of fulfillment. Part of his life work had failed.[69]

What plainly emerges from this incredibly pompous exposition of twenty-year-old Herbert was the fact that the disagreement between him and his father was neither social nor political, but religious. Harvard, and particularly Josiah Royce, had soured Herbert Croly on the Religion of Humanity.[70]

[69] HC, "In Memoriam," *Record and Guide*, May 18, 1889, supplement, 7.

[70] HC was not the only student on whom Royce had a religious influence. Rollo Brown reported: "A third of a century later a man of the most practical concerns said: 'Not all the clergymen and theologians of a lifetime ever gave to me any such feeling of the reality of God as I once got from old Josiah in one lecture.' " *Harvard Yard*, 57.

Considering the unfriendly state of the intellectual climate at Harvard, then, David Croly had not come off badly in the struggle for the mind of his son. He had sent Herbert to college with three important beliefs. First, he had imparted a Positivist metaphysics (although Comte would have detested the thought of a Positivist "metaphysics"); second, he had indoctrinated his son in the Religion of Humanity; and third, he had given Herbert a Comtean analysis of political, economic, and social problems.

The metaphysical opinions of the young Croly are difficult to know. No doubt they were modified by Roycean idealism at least enough to comfortably encompass a theistic view of the world—at the end of his life Herbert described his philosophical view, after Royce, as being "a qualified but warm adherence to Hegelianism," which he very soon abandoned.[71] At the same time, Royce's respect for empirical evidence, like James's respect for it, harmonized entirely with David Croly's positivism. The second belief of the father, perhaps his most doubtful and vulnerable, the Religion of Humanity, was plainly defeated at Harvard. There would always be undertones of it in Herbert's work, but the kind of fervent devotion to its ritual and its precepts, which David Croly wanted to instill in his son, became impossible after 1888. Finally, there is no evidence that Harvard's conservative economic and political approach made any impression at all on Herbert. In this third area, the area of social analysis, David Croly's teachings remained firm, and Herbert Croly left Harvard in 1888 as he had entered it in 1886, steadfastly committed to his father's diagnosis of American society. It was, of course, precisely in this field of social and political analysis that Herbert Croly made his reputation as an intellectual and his contribution to American life and thought.

Viewed in another way, of course, the age had passed by both Herbert's father and Herbert's college with a fine impartiality. What David Croly regarded as "advanced" and "modern" turned out to be neither. By the late 1880s, positivism, which might have been a promising intellectual stance in the 1860s and 1870s, had ceased to be attractive to the avant-garde. The most creative and original young thinkers were finding it sterile and irrelevant. Indeed, the chief unifying characteristic of the intellectuals of the 1890s was what H. Stuart Hughes has called "the revolt against positivism." According to Hughes, "Their insistence on the radical insufficiency of merely 'naturalistic' explanations of human conduct was the crux of their po-

---

[71] "Fragment," 13–14.

lemic with the generation of their fathers."[72] Herbert Croly had come to Harvard at the dawn of a new philosophic era.

Everywhere what was "advanced" constituted a rejection of the purely scientific approach. The importance accorded to the subjective and the intuitional, the new respect for the uncivilized and the primitive, the new concern with the mental and emotional "set" of the social observer himself, all created a fresh climate of opinion.[73] Novel and challenging questions were soon to be raised by men such as Nietzsche, Freud, Bergson, and Weber, but they would be questions Auguste Comte had not considered. It was Comte's irrelevance that must have shocked Herbert Croly most. Probably his father had prepared him for a debate; if Harvard had only dared to launch a frontal attack on Comte, David Croly would undoubtedly have relished the engagement. The trouble was the absence of an engagement. James, Palmer, Laughlin never crossed swords with Comte, and Josiah Royce dismissed "probably the greatest brain and heart that this planet has ever seen" with a single sentence in *The Religious Aspect of Philosophy*.

But the "creative" answers to the purely scientific approach, the "newest" movements of sociological, philosophical, and psychological thought, were as foreign to Harvard as was positivism. Outside of William James, who kept abreast of the latest developments in European psychology and philosophy and who was shortly to enter the dialogue as a respected and influential contributor, Harvard had little contact with the rising generation of Western thought. David Croly's criticism of Harvard was entirely justified; the Hegelianism and Manchesterism that Herbert encountered there was pre-Comtean and, in some measure, outdated.

Where Herbert's father went astray, however, was in his belief that if Harvard had suddenly become "modern," Auguste Comte would suddenly come into his own. Positivism certainly had contributions to make—its consistent and devoted empiricism was a useful antidote to Romanticism and the philosophy of Hegel; in addition, Comte's notions of "progress" squared nicely with the other philosophies of progress of the nineteenth century. But these Comtean ideas were easily absorbed and assimilated without the other, more dubious and

[72] H. Stuart Hughes, *Consciousness and Society: The Reorientation of European Social Thought, 1890–1930* (New York, 1958), 30–31; chs. i and ii.

[73] George Mosse, *The Culture of Western Europe: The Nineteenth and Twentieth Centuries, An Introduction* (New York, 1961), 213–30. "This change of public spirit after 1870 tended toward a recapturing of the irrational—a revolt against positivism. . . . Many people accepted the positivist definition of the universe, to be sure, but the dominant modes of thought tended to become increasingly antipositivistic" (214).

bizarre, tenets of Comte's philosophy. Everyone, more or less, believed in progress, especially after Darwin and Spencer. And everyone—James, Freud, Weber, even the Idealist Royce—was an empiricist. Comte had become irrelevant.

V

One day, when Herbert was a boy of fourteen, according to an old family story, he was having lunch with his mother. "Herbert you are very silent," said his mother. "I have nothing of importance to communicate," he replied.[74] The parents sent him off to Harvard hoping that the experience would correct the reticence and shyness, that college would somehow open him socially, render him more outgoing and articulate. His father's letters expressed continual concern about it. "I hope you will take advantage of your elocution lessons and will debate as often as you have a chance." "How about your debating and elocutionary exercise? I hope you will have a chance to talk and recite." "Do not be discouraged at your failure to speak on your legs. . . . You are young, only 18 and have made wonderful progress in a very short time." "Facility of expression will come to you when your mind is full and your feelings are keenly interested." "The matter of your conversation is very good, but you should improve your manner." "You know I have been somewhat disappointed at your not learning to talk on your legs. I had wanted you to be able to express yourself in public. I never could quite understand your reluctance to follow my advice in this matter."[75]

Unfortunately, while Harvard had thrown many of Herbert Croly's ideas into confusion, it did nothing to overcome his natural reserve. When he left Cambridge in June 1888, at the age of nineteen, his personality was indelibly stamped. Despite his father's urging, Croly remained painfully shy and hopelessly unsocial for the rest of his life. His inability to communicate with new acquaintances, moreover, depressed him; and the depression sometimes spilled over into self-doubt and despair. "Among your shortcomings," his father wrote, "I think lack of self-confidence is one. . . . A little assurance and push is very necessary to those who want to make their way in the world."

[74] Jane Croly told the story to her daughter-in-law, and Louise passed it to George Soule, who vouched for the wording. Author's interview with Soule, October 7, 1963.

[75] David G. Croly to HC, October 28, 1886; November 28, 1886; January 25, 1887; February 16, 1887; October 19, 1887; January 21, 1888, all in *Extracts*. See also, the letters of October 10, 1886, and December 8, 1887, *Extracts*.

"You are disposed to be gloomy and to undervalue yourself. . . . You have a bright future ahead of you, but you must cultivate self-confidence and look on the bright side of life." "Cultivate cheerfulness above all things. I think you inherit from me a disposition to be apprehensive."[76] Over the Christmas holiday in 1887, Herbert dutifully had come to New Jersey, where his father was recuperating. He returned to school haunted by the feeling that he had made a fool of himself. "You seem to be in a morbid strain of mind just now," his father tried to console him. "No one thought ill of you at Lakewood. On the contrary you were regarded as a modest well behaved young gentleman. You made a very good impression. Do not indulge in feelings of morbid self-deprecation."[77]

He had been bookish before he came to Harvard. His studies and compositions, in addition to the extra reading he undertook at the instigation of his father, left little time for social life. Moreover, his lack of connections to the established Harvard families closed off many aspects of the college's club life and certain homes in Boston. He joined no clubs; he was a member of no clique; he published nothing in the exciting new *Monthly*. Studiousness, lack of social connection, shyness and self-doubt, then, combined to make Croly what the students called "a grind." He read books, thought through problems, and made good grades (earning all "B"s in his second year), but he probably did very little else.

There were many gifted and interesting young men at Harvard during Croly's first two years, some of whom were destined to become friends and associates. Among them were the Hapgoods and Oswald Villard, with whom Croly would unite in many progressive crusades. There was George Rublee, soon to be a neighbor, and Bob Lovett, who was to help Croly edit *The New Republic*. There was Robert Herrick, the novelist, William Vaughn Moody, the poet, Charles Platt, the architect. Croly was casually friendly with a few, but of those who wrote about Cambridge and their golden memories there, none remembered Herbert Croly at Harvard College. No classmate was as close, no professor as important to him as his father was. And even though they were miles apart, their relationship was very nearly an obsession: "We were very good correspondents one to another," Herbert recalled with stunning understatement. "I used to send him packets of thirty or forty pages every other day, which

[76] David G. Croly to HC, February 13, 1888; November 5, 1887; and February 8, 1887, *Extracts*.

[77] David G. Croly to HC, January 9, 1888, *Extracts*.

he used to answer with marvelous regularity and unfailing kindness. . . ."[78] There is something quite pathetic, something almost frightening in the picture of young Herbert writing a hundred pages of letters to his father each week. That he felt compelled to do so may be taken as a measure of both his dependence and his loneliness.

Perhaps the best indication of his isolation was the unwitting testimony of two men who were to one day be among his closest friends. Philip Littell thought he first met Herbert Croly in 1905.[79] Learned Hand was not quite sure, but he believed he first met Croly in 1908 or 1909.[80] Both men were thinking of their introductions to Croly in the relaxed atmosphere of his summer retreat in Cornish, New Hampshire. But not only were both of them at Harvard with Croly, they both took courses with him and sat in the very same classrooms. Lovett, who wrote of Croly at Harvard, "I think he was lonely," attributed that loneliness to Croly's intellectual concerns.[81] But it is probable that Croly was lonely because, at nineteen, he was already terribly uncomfortable with strangers, slow to make friends, tortured by feelings of social inadequacy.

In his after-dinner speech, "The True Harvard," William James attempted to justify such loneliness. He might have been talking about Herbert Croly, who had come to Cambridge flushed red hot with his father's radical ideas, who had some of them cooled-off, who spent two years reading and thinking, puzzling and alone. "The true Harvard," said James, "is the invisible Harvard in the souls of her more truth-seeking and independent and often very solitary sons. . . . The University most worthy of rational admiration is that one in which your lonely thinker can feel himself least lonely, most positively furthered, and most richly fed. . . . [A]s a nursery for independent and lonely thinkers I do believe that Harvard still is in the van. Here they find the climate so propitious that they can be happy in their very solitude."[82]

[78] HC to Louise Emory, June 11, 1891, a copy made by Louise Emory Croly and deposited in the Houghton Library, Harvard University.

[79] Philip Littell, "As a Friend," *NR* 43 (July 16, 1930): 243.

[80] Learned Hand in an interview with Charles Forcey, April 5, 1956.

[81] Lovett, "Herbert Croly's Contribution to American Life," *NR*, 43 (July 16, 1930): 245.

[82] William James, "The True Harvard," in *Memories and Studies* (New York, 1911), 354–55.

THREE

The Blank Years
1888–1909

HISTORIANS have never been able to discover much about Herbert Croly's life in the period before the publication of his major work, *The Promise of American Life*, in 1909. He was not yet well known as a writer or a thinker, and few letters written to him or by him during these years have survived. Indeed, a dozen years after his death, his old friend Oswald Garrison Villard, who agreed to write the account of Croly's life for *The Dictionary of American Biography*, ended by complaining to his editor, "I am astonished how little source material there is. . . ." And a quarter century later, historian Christopher Lasch echoed that observation: "One reason why Herbert Croly remains a somewhat mysterious figure in American political thought," Lasch wrote, "is that the first forty years of his life are largely a blank."[1] Nevertheless, it is possible to piece together, in at least a fragmentary fashion, Herbert Croly's principal activities and central intellectual concerns during the obscure period, prior to 1909.

I

Croly returned home from Harvard in June 1888, and immediately began serving as his father's private secretary, inseparable companion, and intellectual sparring partner. The two were constantly together for nearly a year, until David Croly's death on April 29, 1889. Herbert may have worked for *The Real Estate Record and Builders' Guide* even before his father's death, but from the spring of 1889, when he inherited a part interest in the paper,[2] until the summer of 1891 he both edited and wrote for *The Record and Guide*.[3] So similar,

---

[1] Villard to Harris E. Starr, March 30, 1942, Villard Mss., Houghton Library, Harvard University; and Christopher Lasch, "Herbert Croly's America," *New York Review of Books*, 4 (July 1, 1965): 18.

[2] David Croly's Last Will and Testament, Liber 415, 314ff, New York Surrogate Court, New York City.

[3] Villard, "Herbert Croly," *Dictionary of American Biography*, supplement 1, 209–10; George Soule, "Herbert Croly," *Encyclopedia of the Social Sciences*, 4: 603; and R.M.L.

moreover, were these articles and editorials to those written by his father, that if one had not been certain of his death, one might easily have believed that David was still at work.

In one of his earliest editorials, printed only six weeks after his father's death, Croly addressed the question, "What has sociology to say about the trusts?" The application of scientific principles to social questions was valid, he argued, because "societies develop not in a haphazard way according to individual caprice, but in accordance with certain laws. Wherever there is development it is along well-defined lines."[4] Nobody familiar with the views of the father could have been terribly surprised to observe the son invoking science and referring to social laws. Neither could the regular subscribers have been astonished to find young Herbert drawing the familiar conclusions about the trusts.

To begin with, he argued, trusts and monopolies were distinctive features of the economic development of the age; they were here to stay, and it was time that this was more clearly recognized. The trusts were not the reprehensible creatures of evil men nor the unnatural offspring of evil laws like the tariff. They were simply the predictable outgrowth of the American way of doing business. In addition, their potentiality for efficient production and low prices promised many material benefits for the community.[5] "Of course," Croly added, "the 'trust' or combination, is not without danger to Society. . . ."[6]

That danger had to be met by resolute and unprecedented action by government. Other nations had made enormous strides toward solving this problem and America must follow their examples. Unfortunately, Croly continued, the United States was prevented from doing what needed to be done by an ideological obstacle: the unyielding belief in laissez-faire theory and Jeffersonian government. In a letter to the editor (which might very well have been Croly's own fictitious creation), a "Correspondent" wrote, "I am an old subscriber . . . and an older Jeffersonian, a believer in the good doctrine

[Robert Morss Lovett], "Herbert Croly," *Harvard Class of 1890, Fiftieth Anniversary (Report IX), 1930–1940* (Norwood, Mass., 1940): 112–14. These three short biographical articles are more helpful than many because each was written by one of HC's friends. Some uncited statements in this chapter derive from one of these articles.

[4] *Record and Guide*, 43 (June 15, 1889): 834.

[5] For some of HC's most typical comments about the trusts in the *Record and Guide*, see 43 (June 15, 1889): 834; 44 (August 24, 1889): 1153; 44 (August 31, 1889): 1181; 44 (September 7, 1889): 1232; 45 (April 19, 1890): 557–58; 45 (May 17, 1890): 731–32; 46 (October 25, 1890): 538.

[6] *Record and Guide*, 43 (June 15, 1889): 834.

under which this nation has increased so marvelously in numbers and wealth—that the people that are governed least are governed best: that the activity of the 'State,' outside of very narrow limits, is evil; and that the individual is much better qualified and much more able to manage his own affairs and look after his own interests than a lot of politicians." Provided with this straw man, twenty-year-old Herbert Croly got on with the congenial task of knocking him down. "It is worth pointing out to our Jeffersonian friend that the long reign of Individualism in this country . . . has been preparing the way and is still preparing the way for Socialism. . . . The Jeffersonian idea might continue to be the safest guide if this country continued as it was under Jefferson. But in many respects we are as far away from Jefferson as from Sesostris."[7]

If the consolidation of industry was natural and inevitable, so also was the consolidation of other elements of American life. The new farmers' organizations proved that even the most individualistic Americans were suddenly willing to join forces to get what they wanted. The rumblings of organized labor also illustrated the inevitability of combination.[8] Croly gave sympathetic attention to all kinds of voluntary associations—industrial mergers, farmer alliances, workingmen's unions—because all of them indicated that consolidation was one of the "laws" presently controlling American economic development.

Even though the bitter struggle between capital and labor was destined to continue for a while, Croly believed that it could not go on much longer. The warfare was detrimental to both parties, and as soon as both realized that fact, extreme demands would be dropped and a compromise reached. "The shape that this compromise will take no one can say. It is very certain to be something that both sides would declare an impossibility today."[9] In a striking editorial of 1890, Croly compared the consolidation movement in the economy to the Protestant Reformation and the rise of democracy, calling consolidation the third great force of recent history:

> The world has witnessed in modern times a religious and a political revolution, and there can be little doubt that the rapid

[7] Ibid., 43 (June 1, 1889): 762–63. Sesostris was the legendary lawgiver and king of ancient Egypt. For HC's comments on European advances in the social control of industrial problems, see 44 (July 13, 1889): 975–76; 44 (July 27, 1889): 1045; 46 (October 11, 1890): 459–60.

[8] For HC's editorials on labor and farmer associations, see ibid., 46 (August 30, 1890): 272; 46 (September 6, 1890): 297–98; 46 (October 4, 1890): 423; 46 (December 27, 1890): 866–67.

[9] Ibid., 44 (September 6, 1890): 297–98.

organizing of capital and labor these days are a part of an industrial revolution. That the outcome of it will be exactly what either Capital or Labor expects is scarcely probable. Some middle way between the clash of interests will no doubt be found to the advantage of all concerned. In the meantime there will be strikes and boycotts, injustices committed on both sides and much wrong-headedness, after the manner of men.[10]

Although Croly, at this stage in his career, did not suggest an exact blueprint of this new "middle way" between consolidated capital and consolidated labor, the authority of the central government would certainly be employed as a regulating and moderating agent. "As has been pointed out repeatedly in this paper, . . ." modern industrial methods are "working a deep and enduring change in the application of the principle of federation and home rule which lies at the basis of our government. . . . The history of our National government has been a history of the assumption of new functions."[11] To make his point even clearer, Croly sprinkled *The Record and Guide* with reviews of the latest works of such economists as Simon Patten, E.R.A. Seligman, and Richard T. Ely, who had begun to attack the inadequacies of a strictly limited central government.

One can only regret that Herbert Croly did not retain his position at *The Record and Guide* throughout the 1890s. His unfolding political and social philosophy might be traced with infinitely greater certainty had he continued his weekly editorial observations of the swirling events of that stormy decade. As it was, circumstances took him in other directions.

The F. W. Dodge Corporation, which specialized in business services and published *The Record and Guide*, had shown an interest in architecture for some time. The paper had been attempting to attract architects as well as contractors and dealers, and it probably surprised no one when on June 15, 1891, *The Record and Guide* announced the creation of a new sister periodical, *The Architectural Record*.[12] "The purpose of the new publication," its promoters promised, "will be to keep the architects and the general public of the United States and Canada in touch with the progress of architecture, building, and decoration at home and abroad. . . ." The magazine would seek out the

[10] Ibid., 46 (August 30, 1890): 272.

[11] Ibid., 45 (February 15, 1890): 220–21. See also 43 (June 22, 1889): 869.

[12] There is a confidential history of the Dodge Corporation, which I was not permitted to consult: Thomas S. Holden and Frederic H. Glad, Jr., "The House that Dodge Built: Story of a Service Organization," written in 1954 and unpublished. See also "Clinton W. Sweet," *National Cyclopaedia of American Biography*, 20: 353.

leading architectural writers of the day, and readers would find "numerous illustrations of a high order." The tone of *The Architectural Record* was to be popular, not strictly technical, "but by 'popular,' adherence to low artistic standards must not be understood."[13]

Either by his own request or because of the demands of the office situation, Herbert Croly was transferred from *The Record and Guide* to the staff of the new magazine. The first piece of writing to bear his by-line, an undistinguished and slightly pretentious article about "Art and Life" ("Therefore, I say, friend Smith, bring art into your life, that you may have a high and temperate soul."), appeared in the first issue. Undoubtedly, Croly wrote some of the chatty editorials, signing himself sometimes "Primus" and sometimes "Secundus." He probably also did some of the book reviews as well as other editing and compiling chores. But his first term of duty with *The Architectural Record* lasted for only a year; other ambitions, problems, and influences were meanwhile making themselves felt.

One new influence was named Louise Emory. The daughter of a well-established Baltimore family, she had been educated in private schools before coming North. Herbert met her while she was a student at what was then called "Harvard Annex" and was soon to become Radcliffe. While not a particularly attractive young lady—smallish, with kinky hair, blue eyes, and an unusually rosy complexion—Herbert found her charming, lively, and outgoing. They were engaged in the spring of 1891 and married a year later, on May 30, 1892. Herbert was twenty-three and his bride was twenty-six.

Louise was, in many ways, the ideal wife for Herbert Croly. After nearly four decades together, one friend of the couple would refer to their marriage as "the perfect relationship at the center of his life."[14] She brought to that relationship many of the things her husband lacked. She was gregarious and friendly. She enjoyed meeting important people and the duties of hostess were congenial to her. She liked to cook and to garden and to keep house, and she seemed generally content to remain quietly in the background. At the same time, Louise Croly was highly intelligent and articulate. She read widely, enjoyed music and the drama, and won the respect and admiration of Herbert's friends. Throughout his life he read aloud to her the piece he was working at, seeking her comments and criticisms before submitting the composition to a larger audience. For her part, Louise was sympathetic to her husband's ideas and goals and proud of his

---

[13] *Record and Guide*, 47 (June 13, 1891). See also 47 (June 27, 1891): 1215; and Harry W. Desmond, "By Way of Introduction," *Architectural Record*, 1 (July–September, 1891): 3–6.

[14] Dorothy Straight Elmhirst, "Herbert Croly," *NR*, 63 (July 16, 1930): 243.

achievements. They were a close and affectionate couple, genuinely fond of one another. They never had a child.[15]

II

The Crolys decided that Herbert should quit the plodding world of obscure trade magazines and continue his education, majoring in philosophy with an eye to writing and teaching. After the wedding, therefore, the couple moved to Cambridge and Herbert enrolled in Harvard for the academic year 1892–1893.

One of his courses was the well-known and exclusive English 5, under Adams S. Hill. Limited to twenty-five advanced students, the course consisted of the preparation of themes, which were read before the class and freely criticized. A frail, almost cadaverous little man of poor health, Hill brought his journalist's training in clarity and conciseness to bear upon undergraduate writing. "Never was there a more biting tongue," wrote Oswald Villard, who took the course along with Croly. "After a theme was read aloud by the author he would often allow two or three minutes to elapse while the class shiveringly anticipated the coming verbal execution of the criminal who had just performed."[16] Herbert's ponderous style must surely have resulted in periodic executions.

Croly also enrolled in Economics 3 with his former English instructor, Edward Cummings. His course, "The Development of the Modern State and Its Social Functions," unquestionably interested Croly. Cummings was particularly engrossed, at the time, with problems of labor organization, arbitration of labor disputes, and recent experimentation in voluntary cooperation both in Europe and the United States. One could hardly imagine topics more attractive to Croly.[17] As usual, however, the most challenging and disturbing courses were those of the Department of Philosophy.

In Philosophy 8, "Aesthetics," a new, romantic personality entered

[15] See also Louise Croly's obituary, *New York Times*, October 1, 1945, 19. Interview with Miss Frances Arnold of Cornish, N.H., October 15, 1963, and with George Soule, October 7, 1963.

[16] Villard, *Fighting Years: Memoirs of a Liberal Editor* (New York, 1939), 89–90. See also Robert Morss Lovett, *All Our Years* (New York, 1948), 32–33; and Rollo W. Brown, *Dean Briggs* (New York, 1926), 50–52.

[17] The article on Cummings in the *DAB* (4: 594–95) is inadequate. The best guide to his economic views and interests are the ten articles he published for Harvard's *Quarterly Journal of Economics*, 1–13. See particularly "The English Trade Unions," 3 (July 1889): 403–35; "Industrial Arbitration in the United States," 9 (July 1895): 353–71; "Co-operative Stores in the United States," 11 (April 1895): 226–71; and the reprinted speech, "Charity and Progress," 12 (October 1897): 27–41.

Herbert Croly's intellectual life. George Santayana devoted the course to studying the psychology of "taste" and the history of aesthetic theories. Brilliant, pensive, intense yet somehow detached from so much of American life, Santayana was always a controversial figure at Harvard. His lectures in Philosophy 8 were preliminary to his *Sense of Beauty* (1896), an ambitious effort to reconcile the newest findings in the psychology of perception with his personal philosophic idealism.[18] In addition to Santayana's course, Croly also enrolled in Josiah Royce's Philosophy 3, "Cosmology," which was Royce's attempt to fit the theory of evolution into the Idealist framework.

In late January 1893, before taking his semester examinations, Herbert Croly suffered a nervous breakdown. He withdrew from Harvard on February 2, ten days before the second semester began.[19] It is impossible to be sure what caused the collapse. New domestic responsibilities, the absence of steady income, the apparent lack of direction in his life, his slow progress at Harvard (he was still classified as a "Special Student," and not yet a candidate for any degree), increasing difficulty with his health—all might have contributed. He never talked about it later. Alvin Johnson, who was to work with Croly on *The New Republic*, reported that "Croly was utterly reticent as to his own spiritual career. In the seven years of our intimate association I cannot recall a single conversation revealing any part of Croly's early life." But, Johnson went on to add, "his oldest friends could tell of a profound spiritual crisis he went through in revolt against Auguste Comte, the god of his father."[20] Whether or not Croly's friends were talking about his collapse in 1893, and whether or not they were correct in ascribing it to strictly intellectual causes can never be known. Certainly it was likely that Santayana, Royce, and even Cummings were either totally indifferent to positivism or overtly hostile to it. Perhaps the continuing battle between Harvard and the now dead David Croly contributed to Herbert's illness, but there is simply not enough evidence to make a final determination.

[18] For Santayana's aesthetic theory at this time, see *The Sense of Beauty* (in *The Works of George Santayana* [New York, 1936], vol. I); "A Brief History of My Opinions," in Irwin Edman, ed., *The Philosophy of Santayana* (New York, 1942), 1–21; Irving Singer, *Santayana's Aesthetics: A Critical Introduction* (Cambridge, Mass., 1957); and George W. Howgate, *George Santayana* (Philadelphia, 1938), 92–102. For contemporary views of Santayana at Harvard, see Hutchins Hapgood, *Victorian in the Modern World* (New York, 1939), 76–77; and Norman Hapgood, *The Changing Years* (New York, 1930), 53.

[19] *Harvard University Catalogue, 1892–93*, 9.

[20] Alvin S. Johnson, *Pioneer's Progress, An Autobiography* (New York, 1952), 241.

Croly's collapse was responsible for introducing him to Cornish, New Hampshire, a place where he was always able to find comfort, refreshment, and friendship. Augustus St. Gaudens, the most important sculptor in America, had settled in Cornish in the 1880s. By the early 1890s, he had attracted a sizable colony of artists and architects, among them George Brush, Thomas Dewing, and Henry Walker. In 1892, Walker brought his intimate friend and Herbert Croly's classmate Charles A. Platt, the architect. And in the summer of 1893, the Crolys went to Cornish with Louise's best friend at college, Ellen Biddle Shipman, and her husband Louis, a young playwright. The Shipmans were the Crolys' closest friends, and the two couples shared a big, square, white, century-old farmhouse, surrounded by stately elms and overlooking picturesque Mt. Ascutney. That summer was sufficient to captivate both the Crolys and the Shipmans. After sharing the Johnson farmhouse for one more summer, both couples decided to build summer houses nearby.[21]

The Croly house and garden were designed by Charles Platt. Small, comfortable, airy, hidden from view by hillocks and pine trees, it was built in Platt's favorite Italian style on a fifty-five-acre site. It combined Platt's usual restraint and modesty ("He never made a flamboyant design in his life," commented one architectural writer) with the financial necessities of his client. Croly had no income, after all, so the house had to be financed by his mother; it was therefore designed in such a way as to be easily enlarged over the years.[22] The Crolys spent most of their summers in Cornish from the 1890s until Herbert's death in 1930.

Meanwhile, the community of intellectuals in Cornish was growing rapidly. New York City was only eight or nine hours away by train, and writers and artists who wanted to retain contact with the city found the scenery, companionship, and convenience of Cornish attractive. Among the regular visitors and summertime residents were Emma Lazarus, Maxfield Parrish, Kenyon Cox, Henry Fuller, and Percy MacKaye. Winston Churchill, the novelist, came in 1898; Cro-

[21] William H. Child, *History of the Town of Cornish, New Hampshire, with Genealogical Record* (Concord, 1910), 1: 220–32; Hugh Mason Wade, *A Brief History of Cornish, 1763–1974* (Hanover, N.H., 1976), 43–94.

[22] I am indebted to Mr. and Mrs. Burnham Carter, who purchased the Croly house in 1946 and who took me over the grounds, showed me the house, and talked about its history. For Charles Platt, see Royal Cortissoz, ed., *Monograph of the Work of Charles A. Platt* (New York, 1913), introduction; and HC, "The Work of Charles A. Platt," *Architectural Record* 15 (March 1904): 181–244. There are many examinations of individual Platt houses in the *Architectural Record* during the period 1900–1910. For pictures of the Crolys' house and garden, see HC's article, 193, 194, and 195.

ly's classmate, Norman Hapgood, arrived in 1902; Hapgood attracted another classmate, the inveterate public official, George Rublee, in 1907; and Rublee, in turn, brought still another classmate, his best friend, Phil Littell, in 1908.[23] A young lawyer named Learned Hand settled nearby.[24]

The relaxed and informal life of Cornish worked its gentle influence on Croly—not only during the summer of 1893, but for the rest of his life as well. There, as no place else, he was able to break free of the crippling shyness and the anguished seriousness that so often hampered his personal relations. There, for some reason, he seemed able to open himself to sociability and friendship. It is not surprising, therefore, that both Littell and Hand mistakenly believed they had first met him there. Nor is it surprising that the most intimate and trusted companions of his life, Littell and Hand, Rublee, Hapgood, Platt, Felix Frankfurter, were associated with Cornish.[25] In that atmosphere, Herbert Croly talked freely and intensely, played poker and bridge with gusto, even proved capable of tennis, although one long-time resident recalled that "he played with great solemnity!"[26] Again and again, the time spent at Cornish braced and strengthened Croly for the duties ahead.

Having recuperated from his breakdown during the summer of 1893, the Crolys spent the next two years traveling and relaxing in Cambridge, Cornish, and Europe. They probably lived on funds supplied either by Herbert's mother or by Louise's parents; the countries they visited and the people they met remain unknown. But, finally, having regained his health, Herbert Croly, now twenty-six years old, returned for his final engagement with Harvard College. That he returned with the intention of preparing himself to teach philosophy is clear from the courses he chose. Beginning right where he had left off when he dropped out two years before, he enrolled in Royce's lectures on the theory of evolution. Before these last years

[23] For Littell's view of the colony, see his "A Look at Cornish," *Independent*, 74 (June 5, 1913): 1297–98.

[24] Child, *History of Cornish*, 1: 224–31; George Rublee, "Oral History," Columbia University Oral History Project, 46–48; Interview with Miss Frances Arnold, October 15, 1963; Learned Hand, "Oral History," Columbia University Oral History Project, 46–47. For descriptions of the community at Cornish, see Blake Nevius, *Robert Herrick: The Development of a Novelist* (Berkeley, 1962), 159–60; or, Edith Bolling Wilson, *My Memoir* (Indianapolis, 1938), 69–74.

[25] For the information regarding Frankfurter's introduction to HC by Learned Hand at Cornish, I am indebted to Mr. Justice Frankfurter himself, who, though ill, relayed the story through his secretary in response to my question.

[26] Interview with Miss Frances Arnold, October 15, 1963.

of college ended, Croly studied with each of Harvard's philosophic giants, exploring all the branches of philosophy in two courses with Royce and one each with James, Palmer, and Santayana. Moreover, he bravely confronted that tender area where Harvard had disagreed most notably with his father—he took "The Philosophy of Religion" and "The Content of the Christian Faith" under saintly, pious Charles C. Everett. And, as if he were determined to leave no stone unturned, he took three courses from the history department in the history of Christianity and of Christian thought.

His other work during these last four years was mostly supplementary to the work in advanced philosophy: two courses in German, and one each in Semitic and Greek; a smattering of economics with Cummings and William Cunningham, a visiting professor from Cambridge. Croly also studied literary criticism with Lewis Edward Gates, who possessed, according to Robert Lovett, "the qualities of a first-rate critic of literature—scholarship, sensibility, a sure sense of values, and a brilliant style."[27]

Finally, Herbert Croly took a course in fine arts with Charles Eliot Norton, one of the genuinely colorful teachers of his day. The work of Norton's life, wrote John Jay Chapman, "consisted in making the unlettered, rough youth of America understand that there were such things as architecture, painting, and sculpture. Norton could do this on a grand scale, to two hundred men at once; he did it as a giant crane-shovel digs the Panama Canal. He did it with great strokes of natural power, often with tears in his eyes, sometimes with sarcasm, sometimes dogmatically, but always successfully."[28] He was merciless in his indictment of America: "Nowhere in the civilized world are the practical concerns of life more prosaic; nowhere is the poetic spirit less evident, and the love of beauty less diffused."[29] This seemed particularly sad because, in Norton's view, a nation's ultimate place in the history of civilization depended upon its ideal of beauty. To many of the undergraduates who took his course, however, Norton was as much renowned for his caustic commentary on contemporary politics as for his pronouncements on the arts.[30]

---

[27] Lovett, *All Our Years*, 45–46.

[28] John Jay Chapman, *Memories and Milestones* (New York, 1915), 139–40.

[29] Charles Eliot Norton, "The Educational Value of the History of the Fine Arts," *Educational Review*, 9 (April 1895): 343–48 (quoted in Mark A. DeWolfe Howe, ed., *The Letters of Charles Eliot Norton with Biographical Comment by His Daughter* [Boston, 1913], 2: 8–9).

[30] For Norton as a teacher, see Howe, ed., *Letters of Charles Eliot Norton*, 2: 7–9; Barrett Wendell, "Charles Eliot Norton," *Atlantic Monthly*, 103 (January 1909): 82–88;

Herbert Croly marched through this array of philosophy, language, and art in remarkably good style. In 1897 he became a "regular" student and was listed as a sophomore. The *Catalogue* of 1898–1899 mentioned him as a student of "marked excellence of the second rank." His grades were good, consisting of more "A"s than "B"s, and he finished his last year at Harvard with "A"s from Emerton in history, John White in Greek, and William James, George Herbert Palmer, and George Santayana in Philosophy.[31] After the impressive performance of 1898–1899, however, Herbert Croly left Harvard—fourteen years after first entering and still not the recipient of his bachelor's degree—and he never returned. Ostensibly he went to Paris to continue his study of philosophy. With whom he studied, whether he studied at all is not known. What is known, however, is that sometime in the year 1899–1900, he changed his plans. He gave up forever any idea of teaching philosophy and embarked instead upon a career in journalism and free-lance writing.

The best clue to the factors that impelled his decision was contained in two letters he wrote thirteen years later to Felix Frankfurter. In the summer of 1913, Frankfurter was offered an appointment by the Harvard Law School ("If I had received a letter from an Indian princess asking me to marry her, I wouldn't have been more surprised," Frankfurter later remarked). Having serious doubts about teaching, he rushed out pleas for advice to those men he most trusted, Oliver Wendell Holmes, Louis D. Brandeis, Henry L. Stimson, Theodore Roosevelt, and Croly. After summarizing the advantages of a teaching job, Croly advised Frankfurter to turn it down:

Taking a professorship is like getting married. After doing so you have got to be good, and good along certain particular lines. In its way it is almost like becoming a Bishop. Whether you like it or not you are one of the Pillars of Society. Your freedom of movement is hampered, and what is worse, you are almost committed to thinking along certain lines. Most of your time would be given to teaching and in that case it is only a really blithe spirit that can escape the fate of being a pedagogue. The vocation of pedagogy is a noble one, but in this country at least it has rarely proved a help to liberal thinking. Of course there are many

Chapman, "Charles Eliot Norton," in *Memories and Milestones*, 129–45; Lovett, *All Our Years*, 37–38; Villard, *Fighting Years*, 82–83; Norman Hapgood, *Changing Years*, 56–57.

[31] *Harvard University Catalogue, 1897–98; 1898–99;* and *Harvard University Rank Lists, 1886–1905.*

exceptions, and conditions are better than they used to be. Still I feel sure that with any but unusual minds the necessity of teaching tends to make one a routine thinker. . . . I am afraid that after the first few years of it you would find the confinement irksome.

Croly also had a few things to say about Cambridge, Massachusetts. Frankfurter would find it, Croly thought, "a poor place in which to live. A college town society is one of the most limited social medium [sic] in the world. The proximity of Boston would help, but Boston itself lacks vitality. In so far as you need to keep in touch with the real pulse of American life, in so far as you get your real insight from social experience, New York & Chicago are the only places in which to live." Continuing his argument in a second letter two weeks later, Croly spoke about his own decision, a dozen years earlier, against teaching:

> My own instincts were against [your] accepting, partly because of my own personal experience. I lived in Cambridge for six years as a graduate student with the intention of becoming an instructor in philosophy. I abandoned the plan, partly because I found the atmosphere of the place illiberal and petty. All college towns seem that way, but, of course, I would not have changed my plans in case I still had felt a strong desire to teach philosophy. While I retained my interest in philosophy itself, the work of a teacher made no appeal. One trouble with teaching is not that it is uninteresting but too interesting. I used to know many graduate students at Harvard years ago, who were full of ideas for books on various phases of philosophy, but who in every case have become so absorbed in teaching, that they have produced nothing. If one wants to do some solid thinking, it is not necessary to retire to a college town for the purpose. You will find it just as difficult in Cambridge to get time for your own personal work as you would in New York. I never knew a professor there, who did not consider himself burdened with administrative duties.[32]

Despite the decidedly disingenuous claim that he had been "a graduate student" all those years, Croly was undoubtedly sharing with

[32] HC to Felix Frankfurter, June 29, 1913, and July 14, 1913, Frankfurter mss., Library of Congress. See also Harlan B. Phillips, ed., *Felix Frankfurter Reminisces* (New York, 1960), 77–86. For an elaboration of HC's view that New York was the best place for an intellectual, see HC, "New York as the American Metropolis," *Architectural Record*, 13 (March 1903): 193–206.

Frankfurter an honest explanation of his decision. At the end of his life, however, Croly revealed still another reason for abandoning academic philosophy. He had been confused by the disagreements among his teachers. He soon found Royce's Hegelianism unsatisfying, but discovered that James and Santayana "pulled me in different ways." He felt himself "the victim of an incoherent eclecticism" and blamed "a lack of dialectical ability which prevented me from thinking out satisfactory reasons for choosing among conflicting doctrines."[33] Whether that combination of doubts about teaching and doubts about his philosophic dexterity were the entire explanation, or whether, to take an obvious possibility, Croly expected an offer from Harvard (like the one Royce's other student, George Santayana once received) and that offer never materialized, cannot be known.

In any case, the Crolys returned from Europe not to Cambridge but to West Twenty-third Street, New York City. And in 1900, Herbert Croly returned to that establishment where, apparently, he was always welcome. He went up to see Clinton Sweet, his father's old friend at the F. W. Dodge Corporation. And from 1900 to 1906, he worked as an editor for *The Architectural Record*.

III

Obviously he was better equipped for work on an architectural journal than he had been ten years earlier. Besides being more settled and mature, Croly had undergone experiences that could hardly have helped but shape and sharpen his tastes. He had travelled in Europe and America; his wanderings probably took him to the Chicago World's Fair, and he certainly witnessed both the Universal Exposition in Paris during the summer of 1900 and the Pan-American Exposition in Buffalo a year later—all three being important from an architectural point of view.[34] In addition to his travels, of course, he had studied fine arts and aesthetics with Norton and Santayana, both men of decided opinions and the most thoughtful approach to beauty. Finally, he had built his own residence, learning first-hand about site, setting, interior decoration, the way a professional confronts the technical problems that are part of every building; and since Croly's architect was also a neighbor and a personal friend, it is likely that the experience was particularly educational.

[33] HC, "Fragment," 14–15.

[34] For a strong indication that HC saw the giant Paris exposition, and for proof of his attendance at Buffalo, see HC, "The Pan-American Exposition," *Architectural Record*, 11 (October 1901): 590–614. I infer from several comments in this and other articles that HC might have seen the Chicago exposition in 1893.

Croly made good use of his new competence at *The Architectural Record*. Over his own name or over the initials "H.D.C." Croly wrote twenty-nine articles in the seven-year period; in addition, he did seventeen articles under the pseudonym "A. C. David."[35] Besides the two sets of signed articles, Croly's style and philosophy identify dozens of unsigned articles, editorials, and book reviews. He also prepared two architectural books: *Stately Homes in America from Colonial Times to the Present*, written with another *Architectural Record* editor, Harry W. Desmond, appeared in 1903, and *Houses for Town or Country*, a collection of articles that had been previously published in the journal, appeared in 1907.[36]

He gained noticeably in competence and technical skill as the years passed. His first articles were admittedly written from the layman's perspective; some of them even contained apologies: "It is on the supposition that one who is neither artist nor learned in the arts may yet have something to say on art matters that is of possible value to layman [*sic*] like himself, that the present writer ventures a few remarks concerning the effect of art on life."[37] Before leaving *The Architectural Record*, however, Croly handled even technical architectural problems with confidence. Moreover, within the framework of his criteria, Herbert Croly was extremely tolerant. Anxious for con-

[35] There can be no doubt that A. C. David was really Herbert David Croly. In the first place, the pseudonym was reminiscent of C. G. David, a pen name often used by HC's father, David Goodman Croly. But even if this clue were not decisive, the briefest comparison of the subjects, ideas, and language (down to dozens of favorite expressions, phrases, and stylistic characteristics) of A. C. David's articles with those signed by HC erases any doubt. Key phrases such as "New York as America's metropolis" and "the nationalization of American art" appear under both names. In addition, both write about the same things, and when one changes, the other soon follows. When HC, to take only one example, took a trip to California, A. C. David began writing articles on California architecture. Moreover, aside from work in the *Architectural Record*, A. C. David was a totally anonymous figure. If this were not sufficient, on one occasion (but I believe only on one) the journal slipped and listed in the table of contents an article by HC that was signed by A. C. David (see the issue of March 1908). One more bit of proof exists: in his memorial tribute Charles Platt wrote, "It was of a badly designed theater that I remember his writing, 'It belongs to the numerous group of the American architectural hybrid.' That remark was characteristic of Herbert Croly in its forthright expression of disapproval" (*NR*, 63 [July 16, 1930], 257). But the remark appeared in an article signed by Arthur David, "An Intimate Auditorium: The Interior of the New Stuyvesant Theatre in New York," *Architectural Record*, 23 (March 1908): 226.

[36] *Stately Homes in America from Colonial Times to the Present Day* (New York, 1903); William Herbert (pseud.), *Houses for Town or Country* (New York, 1907).

[37] HC, "Art and Life," *Architectural Record*, 1 (October–December 1891): 221. For a similar admission of ignorance, see "American Artists and Their Public," ibid., 10 (February 1901): 258.

structive experimentation, willing to trust the professional as far as he possibly could, respectful of the artist's individuality—Croly was almost always willing to give the benefit of the doubt. He did not particularly like Richardson's Romanesque revival, to take one example, but was willing to judge each building within the architect's own objectives—this was a good Romanesque attempt, that was a bad one. He discussed architecture "generously and understandingly," thought Charles Platt.[38]

Despite his sizable output and his growing competency, Croly never became the adherent of any recognizable school of architecture. He believed, almost instinctively, that some buildings were "good" and that some were "bad." After that initial judgment had been made, the examination was conducted largely through the skillful and persistent use of a number of favorite adjectives. Good buildings, Croly kept saying, were "positive," "virile," "tasteful," "modest," and "honest"; they invariably revealed "quality of feeling," and "sincerity." Bad buildings were "stiff," "ineffective," "crude," "pretentious," or "too severe." What made for pretention or modesty or virility were matters he never systematically revealed. His criticism and his praise were, at bottom, subjective and even whimsical. This is not to argue that Croly had no preferences, for he did both criticize and praise; nor is it to minimize the extent to which the problem of definition is an abiding problem of aesthetics.[39] It is merely to observe that Croly's judgments were rendered in adjectives he never fully explained.

When he consciously tried to define his criteria he was unsuccessful. A building was either "festive" or "cluttered," he would sometimes insist, because of a mysterious quality called "integrity." In addition to having integrity, the good building had to be "appropriate to its site," "make the best use of its materials," and "retain a Wholeness and Unity of design."[40] Again and again, consequently, his criticism of architecture fell back upon a single, nebulous concept. Again and again, Croly deprecated buildings because they lacked what he called "propriety" or praised them because they manifested "propriety" in their design and decoration. With only a handful of exceptions, therefore, every architectural article written by Herbert Croly

---

[38] Charles A. Platt, "H. C. and Architecture," *NR*, 63 (July 16, 1930): 257; reprinted in *Architectural Record*, 68 (August 1930): 138.

[39] See for example the discussion by HC's teacher, George Santayana, "Preference is Ultimately Irrational," in *The Sense of Beauty*, 18–21.

[40] *Houses for Town or Country*, 86; "Art and Life," 219–27.

contained the word *propriety*, and, in some measure, final judgment rested on that single word.

At the time, opinion in America was sharply divided over what constituted proper architectural performance. The struggle between those who favored selective derivation from European models and those who urged the development of native art raged furiously during the years that Croly edited *The Architectural Record*. "We are at that dramatic moment in our national life wherein we tremble evenly between decay and evolution," wrote the hardly impartial Louis Sullivan, "and our architecture . . . reflects this equipoise."[41] Croly was caught up in this conflict and his criticism reflected the tension between the two often contradictory ideals. After all, Croly had imbibed at Harvard the keen, often devastating criticisms of American culture that were the specialities of Charles Eliot Norton and George Santayana. Their erudite condemnation of American gaudiness and showy materialism, and their emotional rhapsodies over European standards of art undoubtedly helped to inform Croly's own tastes. Yet, at the same time, Croly found himself yearning for and sympathetic toward an indigenous American architecture, and this preference stemmed from social as well as purely aesthetic considerations.

Although he rarely strayed from his central, architectural purpose, it is possible to detect social and economic commentary, particularly in the articles written before he had achieved a mastery over technical detail. These political observations in *The Architectural Record* ranged from an occasional nod of approval for the vigorous leadership of President Roosevelt to regular praise for innovations in the municipal and state control of private interests.[42] Initiatives undertaken by progressive city governments in city planning were welcomed by *The*

[41] Quoted in Henry Steele Commager, *The American Mind: An Interpretation of American Thought and Character Since the 1880s* (New Haven, 1950), 397. For general discussions of the intellectual climate of American architectural debate during these years, see ibid., 391–405; Wayne Andrews, *Architecture, Ambition and Americans: A Social History of American Architecture* (New York, 1964 edition), 152–238; John Burchard and Albert Bush-Brown, *The Architecture of America: A Social and Cultural History* (Boston, 1961), 193–296; or William H. Jordy and Ralph Coe, Introduction to *American Architecture and Other Writings* by Montgomery Schuyler (Cambridge, Mass., 1961), 1–89. For a discussion of the general "nationalization" of American culture during this period, see H. Wayne Morgan, *Unity and Culture: The United States 1877–1900* (Harmondsworth, England, 1971), 75–109.

[42] "New York as the American Metropolis," 205. See also three unsigned editorials probably written by HC: "A Captain of Culture," *Architectural Record*, 12 (June 1902): 238–40; "Democracy and Fine Art," ibid., 14 (September 1903): 225–32; and "A Successful Meeting," ibid., 17 (April 1905): 343.

Architectural Record; the construction of park areas, the social control of skyscrapers, which shut out light and air from the city streets, the demands of conservationists—all were given a favorable hearing under Croly's editorship.[43]

Aside from these chance notices and passing comments, however, Croly's social observations were notable for their development in three particular areas. He became fascinated by the American millionaire as a social type; he began to tinker with the idea of a "nationalization" of American artistic life; and he worried over the role of the artist in modern American society. In each of these three fields, moreover, his thought was torn by an ambivalence. And it is a measure of the strength of his mind and the maturity of his judgment that he was willing to live with that ambivalance.

It was inevitable that the commentator on recent American architecture, the author of two books on American residences, should sooner or later confront the problem of the millionaire. Aside from a few adventuresome municipal projects, the new and exciting architecture in America was the result of the vast accumulations of money and power in the hands of individual men. The millionaire, Croly argued, was an unprecedented phenomenon. He was still, in 1900, usually a self-made man, deeply engaged in the struggle, exulting in and fascinated by the excitement of the game. He was daring, audacious, and, unlike the European aristocrat, he was the recipient of unexpected new money. In addition, unlike even the wealthiest European bourgeoisie, he had nothing to fear from an entrenched class of social superiors. He was free to exercise his personal inclinations and tastes, unmindful of appearing pretentious and ridiculous. The principal difference between the millionaire and the monied European, however, involved the exercise of power. The American businessman had obtained tremendous economic power, but it had no institutional outlet. In any other civilized nation the possessor of such strength would occupy some official place in society, but the American millionaire was in the uncomfortable position of being an unofficial celebrity—his private life was watched eagerly by his countrymen, his personal decisions affected thousands of smaller men, but

---

[43] See two unsigned editorials: "Do Skyscrapers Pay?" ibid., 12 (May 1902): 109–11; and "The Improvement of Washington," ibid., 12 (September 1902): 456–58. Also HC, "What is Civic Art?" ibid., 16 (July 1904): 47–52; HC, "The Promised City of San Francisco," ibid., 19 (June 1906): 425–36; and HC, "Civic Improvements," ibid., 21 (May 1907): 347–52.

he had no official standing, no official duties, and no formal restraints upon his activity.[44]

And how was the millionaire performing? On the whole, Croly thought, it was still too early to tell. The charitable work millionaires did was certainly impressive. They probably had few political ambitions for themselves, and were committed to the prosperity of the Republic and the preservation of democratic forms. Their houses were beginning to be built with a dignity and a conservatism that revealed a healthy desire to gain the respect of other Americans ("Indeed the 'palatial' period of American democratic architecture is already on the wane. The newer houses, while they still proclaim loudly their owners' opulence, indicate the influence of better ideas of propriety, architectural and social").[45] At the same time, Croly never deluded himself about the millionaire's motives. Too often the wealthy businessman acted without the slightest consideration of his larger, public responsibility. Government officials had certainly been bribed; illegal maneuvers had certainly been employed; natural resources had certainly been squandered—and all without a thought for the social context in which the millionaire operated. Croly was confident that some kind of social control would be necessary. The nature of that control, its stringency, and the precise moment of its application, however, could not be decided until it became clearer how the millionaire would behave. Croly was willing to suspend judgment for the present.

A second question with which Croly wrestled in these years, a question as much aesthetic as social, involved the eventual "nationalization" of American architecture. Croly observed that with the passing of the Georgian period by the second quarter of the nineteenth century, the way had been opened for architectural experimentation. Although American architecture in 1900 was still heterogeneous, it was far less chaotic than it had been. Types were emerging. And while some of these types could be criticized, Croly felt that they "have all some measure of propriety."[46] The rise of dominant local architecture, he had always insisted, constituted progress in American art. The question that bothered him was how society ought

---

[44] HC, "Rich Men and Their Houses," ibid., 12 (May 1902): 27–32; *Stately Homes in America*, 15, 16–26, 31, 293–317, and 343–44; *Houses for Town or Country*, 76.

[45] *Houses for Town or Country*, 77. See also *Stately Homes in America*, 12, 222–27; HC, "The Contemporary New York Residence," *Architectural Record*, 12 (December 1901): 704–22; "The Finest Store in the World," ibid., 17 (January 1905); and "New York as the American Metropolis," 201.

[46] *Houses for Town or Country*, 4.

to set about achieving this nationalization. What was the responsibility of the architect, the citizen who decided to erect a new building, the architectural critic, the municipal commission planning a new city hall? To what extent, in other words, should men and women of taste copy European forms and to what extent should they consciously strive for an original American kind of architecture?

Again Croly was caught between alternatives. He believed that "a spontaneous and instinctive art is not one which has dispensed with traditions; it is rather one which cordially accepts the traditions it possesses and is thoroughly satisfied with them."[47] The pioneers came to America for social and economic freedom, Croly argued, and they created an original society, but their "power of being original was thereby exhausted." In nonpractical matters, particularly in aesthetics, American instincts turned to Europe for ideas; and "unless the persistence and . . . legitimacy of this instinct be granted, the history of this country in ideas and aesthetic forms cannot be at all understood."[48] But borrowing was only a temporary expedient. Americans had to experiment, adapt, and search for "appropriate" local and national art. Once traditional forms had been mastered, then Americans might "demand that these forms be modified, with a special view to giving them a higher degree of individual, local and national propriety."[49] Croly had cautious praise for the new midwestern architects who departed from the tradition—particularly Louis Sullivan and "a very able architect, who issued from Mr. Sullivan's office, Mr. Frank Wright."[50]

The reason for both his wide tolerance and the hesitation and sub-

[47] *Stately Homes in America*, 128. See also ibid., 47–48; *Houses for Town or Country*, 37–38, 225–26, and 229; "The New World and the New Art," *Architectural Record*, 12 (June 1902): 149–51; "The St. Regis—The Best Type of Metropolitan Hotel," ibid., 15 (June 1904): 553–600; and "A Modern Instance of Colonial Architecture, the House of Mr. B. W. Arnold at Albany, New York," ibid., 17 (April 1905): 305–17.

[48] "What is Civic Art," 49; *Houses for Town or Country*, 77; "The Architectural Work of Charles A. Platt," 181; and *Stately Homes in America*, 36.

[49] "The Architectural Work of Charles A. Platt," 181. In 1902, HC wrote: "What the United States needs is a nationalization of their intellectual life comparable to the nationalizing, now under way, of their industry and politics; and in the fullness of time American culture will be invigorated and informed by the same enterprising and co-operative spirit which has distinguished its industrial successes." ("New World and the New Art," 153.) See also *Houses for Town or Country*, 225; "A New Use of Old Forms," *Architectural Record*, 17 (April 1905): 271–93; "The Architecture of Ideas," ibid., 15 (April 1904): 361–84; and "What Is Indigenous Architecture?" ibid., 21 (June 1907): 434–42.

[50] "Architecture of Ideas," 363. See also "Houses by Myron Hunt and Elmer Grey," *Architectural Record*, 20 (October 1906): 281–95.

jectivity of his strictly aesthetic criticism becomes clearer when one understands that Croly saw America in a transition period architecturally as well as politically. Auguste Comte and David Goodman Croly had argued, after all, that a society functioned best politically when it had one radical and one conservative party; Herbert Croly felt that society functioned best aesthetically when it had one conserving and one innovating school. "In a country, such as the United States, which is in the process of making and naturalizing its local architectural traditions and forms," Croly summed up his difficulty and offered his solution, "it is a good thing both that some of the leading practitioners should intentionally cleave to the standard authoritative historic styles, and that others should propose, also intentionally, to depart from strict allegiance to the time-honored tradition, and to substitute types of design that have a manifest local propriety."[51]

Finally, Croly faced a third dilemma fraught with social implications: the conflict in America between the demands of intellectual and artistic integrity and technical skill on one hand and the prevailing shoddiness of popular taste on the other. "That the plastic arts in a modern democratic community can ever be both genuinely popular and thoroughly self-respecting is at least a very dubious question," he complained.[52] The requirements of a business civilization—its premium on efficiency, standardization, and stunning effect—worked at cross-purposes with the requirements of great art. "And so American artists . . . adapt themselves to business conditions and compromise the integrity of their work or they are forced aside and continue to work conscientiously along their own lines, and are 'good but lonely.' "[53]

Croly refused to dismiss this problem by resorting to simple clichés about artistic integrity. Popular standards, he argued, had a right to make themselves felt, and this was particularly true in architecture. The rich businessman who built a palatial house had the right to expect that house to meet his needs (including his need for showy advertisement) and suit his tastes (including tastes that could only be deemed wretched). An architect could not, and should not, impose his better judgment on a determined client if the client was unwilling. Popular taste in a democracy must be elevated if society is to produce great representative art; but it was impossible to elevate taste by de-

[51] "Architecture of Ideas," 363. See also "What Is Indigenous Architecture?" and "American Architecture," *Architectural Record*, 23 (February 1908): 111–22.

[52] "American Artists and Their Public," 260.

[53] "The New World and the New Art," 151.

cree. The public had to be led gradually to appreciate beauty, and, in the beginning, the education must take place amidst familiar surroundings, even if those surroundings happen to be shoddy at first.[54] But what did this do to the artist? Obviously it tended to make him a prostitute—debased, careless, the very antithesis of a creative spirit. It was hard to see how artistic standards could be raised if the artist forced himself to produce compromising and popular work.

Herbert Croly fought valiantly with this question, returning to it many times during these years. Undoubtedly, *Unleavened Bread*, a novel by Robert Grant about an architect caught in exactly this trap, stimulated his thinking. Reading into the novel more than it contained, Croly sought to clarify the issues raised by Grant and to arrive at a solution.[55] The problem, he concluded, resulted from the traditional American distrust of the "expert," a distrust inherited from the Jacksonian exaltation of the versatile, unskilled, practical yeoman. Americans always looked with suspicion upon men of special training and special sensitivity, seeing in their specialness a threat to the democratic homogeneity of the community. The artist was just such a specially trained individual, so it was not surprising that "wherever the genuine artist comes into contact with the public he is placed on the defensive."[56]

Croly's solution to this problem—like his solutions to the nationalization of American art and the problem of the American millionaire—was unclear. Usually he tried to find a way out: perhaps the artistic élite might educate the public to an appreciation of beauty; or, perhaps, the children of millionaires, growing up in elegant surroundings and accustomed to better standards of beauty, might someday cause more tasteful, dignified, and appropriate residences and statues and paintings to be created. Perhaps. But in the meantime, Croly was forced to conclude, "the modern artist is surrounded

[54] *Stately Homes in America*, 525–32; *Houses for Town or Country*, 37–38, 77, and 230; and "New York as the American Metropolis," 198.

[55] Robert Grant, *Unleavened Bread* (New York, 1900). The novel centers on the ambitions of a social-climbing American woman, Selma White. Only about a third of her story touches her marriage to the struggling architect, Wilbur Littleton. For HC's early warm references to this book, see "New York as the American Metropolis," 200; and "The Architect in Recent Fiction," *Architectural Record*, 17 (February 1905): 137–39. For the novel's composition and reception, see Robert Grant, *Fourscore: An Autobiography* (Boston, 1934), 219–32.

[56] "American Artists and Their Public," 257. See also *Stately Homes in America*, 101–102, 107–108, and 212–18; "Democracy and Fine Art," 231; and "The Architect in Recent Fiction," 140.

by conflicting and distracting voices."[57] And when he was pressed, and unwilling to take refuge in a pious hope for the future, he usually ended by nodding to the rights of public standards, but enshrining above them the rights of the creative artist. In the last analysis, Croly usually argued, it would be better for all concerned if the artist remained true to his inspiration and reconciled himself to being good but lonely.[58]

In addition to his work at *The Architectural Record* between 1900 and 1906, Croly also managed to find time for some free-lance writing. He wrote five short articles for other periodicals. Two of them were strictly technical and merely extensions of his architectural work.[59] The other three, however, were written for *The Lamp* and revealed a wider field of interest. In "Some Really Historical Novels," Croly reviewed recent attempts at historical fiction by Winston Churchill, Edith Wharton, Gertrude Atherton, and Maurice Hewlett. In a splendid and perceptive article, "Henry James and His Countrymen," Croly tried to evaluate James's expatriation in terms of what his art had gained and what it had lost by the writer's removal from the contemporary American scene. And in "An American Farmer," Croly wrote a straightforward short review of a new edition of the letters of Crèvecoeur.[60] Although the three literary articles were interesting and intelligent (particularly the piece on Henry James), they were more important for what they said about Croly than for what they said about their subjects. His thoughts were beginning to wander away from purely architectural themes. At the same time that his technical writing was growing more competent, his mind was asking other questions and exploring larger areas.

[57] "American Artists and Their Public," 261. See also *Stately Homes in America*, 279–80; "The Pan-American Exposition"; "The New World and the New Art," 151; "Rich Men and Their Houses," 32; and "Democracy and Fine Art," 232.

[58] "If we are obliged to make a choice, we should say that it were far better for a painter to paint entirely for his brother painters, to paint even from a frank delight in his own technical mastery and cleverness, than to compromise the native virtue of his art. . . ." ("American Artists and Their Public," 258–59.) See also "Criticism that Counts," *Architectural Record*, 10 (April 1901): 398–405; "A Captain of Culture"; "Committee Meeting Sculpture"; and "Painting and Illustration," *Architectural Record*, 19 (January 1906): 70–71.

[59] "The New York Rapid Transit Railway," *Review of Reviews*, 30 (September 1904): 305–11; and "A California Country House," *Sunset Magazine*, 18 (November 1906): 50–65.

[60] "Some Really Historical Novels," *Lamp*, 26 (July 1903): 509–13; "Henry James and His Countrymen," ibid., 28 (February 1904): 47–54; and "An American Farmer," ibid., 28 (July 1904): 477–78.

IV

In the summer of 1905, Herbert Croly made another momentous decision about his life. No one with his background and with his lively interest in politics could have failed to notice the quickening of political activity during the first decade of the new century. Stimulated by the growing awareness of economic injustices and political corruption, focused to some degree by the frenetic leadership of President Theodore Roosevelt, the nation was rapidly moving toward a concerted effort at social reform. It seemed obvious to Croly, however, that the infant movement lacked direction and purpose. To be effective, progressive instincts needed to be guided by rigorous thought. Americans would have to consider many questions as they set about addressing their institutions, but the fundamental questions concerned the extent to which the nation would be content with repairing the existing system and the extent to which it would be willing to embark on a basic reconstruction of American life. By 1905, Croly had come to believe that he had some ideas that might be helpful in achieving a better understanding of the problem, and he decided to have a try at providing guidance and direction to his countrymen.

Interrupting his life as he had done in 1893 and again in 1900, he loosened his connection with *The Architectural Record*. He remained an associate editor of the journal until 1913, contributing occasional articles until 1928. But his chief occupation for four hours every morning (and never more than four hours for the sake of the work) became a book of political commentary designed to offer a thoughtful critique of progressive reform and to point a more fruitful direction for its impulses. He wrote a first, hurried draft in 1905, rewrote it in 1906 and 1907, and then rewrote it again in 1908 and the early months of 1909.[61]

Given his fascination with ideas, and particularly with political ideas, and given his propensity for concentrated, private thought, the surprising thing is not that he quit an architectural trade magazine in order to write *The Promise of American Life* but that he could have restrained himself for so long. The book was not, after all, the product of four hours a day for three or four years; it was the product of twenty-five years of reading and thinking and talking by a pensive, reserved, highly intelligent man. It stood as the culmination of everything that had happened to him intellectually, and it was his greatest masterpiece.

[61] Philip Littell, "As a Friend," *NR*, 63 (July 16, 1930): 243; HC, "Fragment," 20.

Whether or not the book was, as so many have claimed, a turning point in the progressive movement, it was certainly a turning point in the life of Herbert Croly. The argument of his book almost instantaneously established its author as the leading political philosopher in the United States.

FOUR

The Promise of American Life

In 1910 the Kansas editor William Allen White opened his new book, significantly entitled *The Old Order Changeth*, with a comparison between Tocqueville's America and his own: "The two—politically, economically, and socially—are almost utterly dissimilar," he wrote. "Something has intervened." Four years later, twenty-five-year-old Walter Lippmann observed that "those who are young today are born into a world in which the foundations of the older order survive only as habits or by default."[1] White and Lippmann had seen something that historians two generations later would resolutely try to analyze and document. They would invent terminology like "the revolt against formalism," "the watershed of the nineties," "the search for order," or "the end of American innocence" in order to explain the gulf that separated nineteenth from twentieth-century America. They would only echo the wonderment of the men and women who had lived through the time.

White and Lippmann were not the only contemporaries to notice a discrepancy between the nineteenth and twentieth centuries—countless observers whose lives had spanned the transition stared in amazement at "modern" America. As early as 1893, Frederick Jackson Turner announced the closing of "the first period of American history." By 1906 the mystified Henry Adams was passing among his friends a manuscript autobiography purporting to show that nothing he had received from a brilliant eighteenth-century inheritance or a brilliant nineteenth-century education was worth a thing in the modern world. William James and John Dewey demanded a new kind of philosophy to meet the needs of a new kind of social order. Patten, Veblen, and Ely made the same demand for economics, and Holmes and Brandeis for law. Norris and Dreiser answered the call for a new kind of literature. "The jocund youth of our people now passes away never to return," observed Captain Alfred Thayer Mahan as he sur-

---

[1] William Allen White, *The Old Order Changeth: A View of American Democracy* (New York, 1910), 3; Walter Lippmann, *Drift and Mastery: An Attempt to Diagnose the Current Unrest* (New York, 1914), xvii–xviii.

veyed the United States at the close of the Spanish-American War. "The cares and anxieties of manhood's years henceforth are ours."[2]

Herbert Croly saw the changes too. He fully accepted the notion of a transformed America, fundamentally different, requiring fresh assumptions and techniques, and *The Promise of American Life* was his attempt to offer an explanation and present a plan.[3] He devoted a large part of the book to the argument that the change stemmed from the fact that individual interests and the national welfare had somehow fallen out of harmony. In a happier nineteenth century, the American could usually pursue his own economic interest and simultaneously benefit his country. A set of changed circumstances, however, now made this less and less possible. In short, "the plain fact is that the individual in freely and energetically pursuing his own private purposes has not been the inevitable public benefactor assumed by the traditional American interpretation of democracy."[4] The end of the harmony between economic individualism and national stability, he argued, gave rise to many of the perplexities, confusions, and dangers of the twentieth century.

I

Although Croly was inconsistent and vague in his periodization throughout *The Promise of American Life*, it nevertheless emerges with tolerable clarity that he considered the "pioneer period" to stretch from the establishment of American independence to the end of the Civil War. The first and formative epoch in American history, therefore, encompassed the formation of a new government, the growth of political parties, the rise of democracy, the settlement of the West, and the confrontation of the crisis of human slavery. But in addition to the drama and importance of these developments, this classic age was crucial for three additional legacies.

First, the years between the Revolution and the Civil War were significant because they bequeathed to future generations a tension in

[2] Quoted in W. D. Puleston, *Mahan: The Life and Work of Captain Alfred Thayer Mahan, U.S.N.* (New Haven, 1939), 201.

[3] HC, *The Promise of American Life* (New York, 1909). The book was reprinted in 1910, 1911, 1912, and 1914. There were five reprints in the 1960s. One from Archon Books, 1963; one introduced by Charles Forcey (Dutton, 1963); one introduced by Cushing Strout (Capricorn, 1964); one introduced by Arthur M. Schlesinger, Jr. (Harvard, 1965); and one introduced by John W. Ward (Bobbs-Merrill, 1965). All editions employ the same pagination.

[4] *PAL*, 106.

political philosophy, a conflict between two organizing principles for American government. Although the roots of the controversy stretched back to the Revolution itself, the two schools of thought were summed up, and, in the end, symbolized by the towering figures of Thomas Jefferson and Alexander Hamilton. Although Croly acknowledged that both men could be criticized for possessing an incomplete vision, he began his analysis with a frank confession: "I shall not disguise the fact that, on the whole, my preferences are on the side of Hamilton rather than of Jefferson."[5]

Alexander Hamilton's great vision was of "a vigorous, positive, constructive national policy. . . . a policy that implied a faith in the powers of an efficient government to advance the national interest." Hamilton clearly and correctly saw the new nation's need for a government that would not merely maintain the new Constitution, but would firmly and imaginatively "promote the national interest and . . . consolidate the national organization." Hamilton's view implied "an active interference" in all aspects of the country's political, social, and economic life, a steady "regulation and guidance in the national direction." It implied, moreover, the ascendancy of men who could "discriminate between those ideas and tendencies which promoted the national welfare, and those ideas and tendencies whereby it was imperiled."[6] Nevertheless, Hamilton's views were open to a most serious objection. Unfortunately, the great proponent of American nationalism feared democracy, and he believed, "far more than he had any right to believe," that the new government had to be based upon the wealthy and well-educated classes. "Instead of seeking to base the perpetuation of the Union upon the interested motives of a minority of well-to-do citizens he would have been far wiser to have frankly intrusted its welfare to the good-will of the whole people."[7] The tragic result of Hamilton's narrowness was one of the genuine dangers to the Republic. The plain people came—with a measure of justice—to identify nationalism with an aristocracy; they turned away from the praiseworthy principle of national integrity because they could see, lurking behind it, preferential treatment for the wealthy and a haughty distrust of everyone else.

Before long Hamilton found himself battling "one of the most implacable and unscrupulous oppositions which ever abused a faithful public servant." Thomas Jefferson's influence was "baleful," and

5 Ibid., 29.
6 Ibid., 38–40.
7 Ibid., 40–41.

his tactics were "unfair," but in one way he was perfectly correct. "Jefferson was filled with a sincere, indiscriminate, and unlimited faith in the American people." Hamilton's opponent was "wholly right in believing that his country was nothing, if not a democracy." The trouble with Jefferson, however, was that his vision was also incomplete. He talked about democracy, but his democracy was "meager, narrow, and self-contradictory." He mistakenly saw only a "collection of individuals, fundamentally alike in their abilities and deserts." To Jefferson, "democracy was tantamount to extreme individualism."[8] The role of government was to destroy special privilege and to leave people alone. The best government was local and limited. The greatest threat to American society was centralized power. Thus Jefferson emerged as the symbol of that distrust of an active and vigorous central government which was to work so much evil in American life.

The lines drawn in the 1790s were unfortunately persistent, and the debate between Hamilton's inadequate concept of nationalism and Jefferson's inadequate concept of democracy continued to the Civil War. For seventy-five years and more, then, the American discussion of government suffered from what Croly called "this double perversion."[9] Even worse, the clear winner was Thomas Jefferson. "During the next fifty years," Croly unhappily reported, "the American democracy accepted almost literally this Jeffersonian tradition." "The triumph of Jefferson and the defeat of Hamilton" meant the victory of unfettered individualism, the ascendancy of a suspicious and irrational antinationalism.[10] Jefferson's most spectacular successor, Andrew Jackson, continued true to the faith by destroying a perfectly useful financial institution and uprooting an efficient and honest office-holding class—and all in the name of "democracy." The Whigs, who inherited the philosophy of Hamilton, quickly proved themselves ineffective in opposition and so greedy for office that they willingly ignored any principle that seemed to stand in the way. The inability of either party to face up to the slavery crisis merely proved that both were operating under distorted conceptions. The only responsible political figure who seemed able to combine properly the right elements of democracy and nationalism was Abraham Lincoln. He, at least, understood that any viable democratic theory precluded one man owning another man; and yet he also fully realized that the

[8] Ibid., 42–43.
[9] Ibid., 29.
[10] Ibid., 48–49.

Union was more than a lifeless legal framework designed simply to bind the states together.[11]

If the first legacy of the pioneer period was this tension in political philosophy, a tension generally resolved in favor of the Jeffersonian view, the second bequest to modern America was a particular sort of individual. The Western Democrat of ante-bellum America emerged as an ideal type, a symbol for the nation. The pioneer—with all his strengths and all his weaknesses—succeeded in making his personality, his character, his achievements and failings stand for those of all Americans.

In many ways, modern society was better because of him. It was the pioneer who cleared the trackless forests, supplied the agricultural bounty, built the cities and the railroads and the governments of most of the nation. In the process he developed certain admirable traits—flexibility, alertness, energy, practicality—which have become useful national characteristics. Perhaps most important of all, the pioneer, with his natural informality and his "freedom of intercourse," lifted and advanced the democratic ideal. True democracy must be based upon that "easy and effortless sense of companionship" the pioneer so naturally exemplified. On the other hand, Croly insisted, we must never blind ourselves to the less desirable half of the story. This typical American was almost exclusively interested in wringing personal wealth out of the land. His preoccupation with getting rich obscured every other consideration, and he pursued his own interest "energetically and unscrupulously." Since the development of the country was in general harmony with the pioneers' economic individualism, and since the most pressing national need coincided with their selfishness, each one could feel that his labor enriched both the nation and himself. But this "licensed selfishness" was a potentially worrisome element in the pioneer's legacy to America, and it was not the only one.

Conditions in the wilderness rewarded versatile men. "In such a society a man who persisted in one job, and who applied the most rigorous and exacting standards to his work, was out of place and was really inefficient." Moreover, the specialist's work was an implied criticism of the crude work of his neighbors; he interfered with the "rough good-fellowship" of his society. It was not surprising, therefore, that Americans came to view "with distrust and aversion the man with a special vocation and high standards of achievement."

[11] HC's analysis of American history from the presidency of Jefferson to the end of the Civil War can be found in ibid., 52–99.

The expert, the man of knowledge, the skilled craftsman threatened the homogeneity of the community. Public opinion was "taught to approve of the average man as the representative type of the American democracy." The unfortunate result of this worship of the average was an abiding suspicion of moral and intellectual excellence.

Thus modern Americans had to be cautious and balanced in their evaluation of this second bequest of the pioneer period. The faults as well as the virtues of the frontiersman had to be remembered. Croly offered a warning to those of his contemporaries who might be prone to overidealize:

> If we study the Western Democrats as a body of men who, on the whole, responded admirably to the conditions and opportunities of their time, but who were also very much victimized and impoverished by the limited nature of these conditions and opportunities—if we study the Western Democrat from that point of view we shall find him to be the most significant economic and social type in American history. On the other hand, if we regard him in the way that he and his subsequent prototypes wish to be regarded, as the example of all that is permanently excellent and formative in American democracy, he will be, not only entirely misunderstood, but transformed from an edifying into a mischievous type.[12]

The third legacy of the formative period of American history was the definition in the popular mind of what Croly called "the Promise of American life." Americans, he argued, had always seen their country in terms of its promising future. Belief in a national destiny offering the prospect of a better life to come was so firmly embedded in the consciousness of America that it was probably the leading idea in the national tradition. "From the beginning Americans have been anticipating and projecting a better future. From the beginning the Land of Democracy has been figured as the Land of Promise."[13] What were the elements of this national Promise? What was it that Americans had always anticipated for themselves and for their children?

In the first place, the Promise was economic. "America has been peopled by Europeans primarily because they expected in that country to make more money more easily." Whatever else the future might hold, Americans would consider themselves cheated if material prosperity was not part of the bundle. "With all their professions

---

[12] HC's discussion of the pioneer democrat can be found in ibid., 62–63.
[13] Ibid., 3.

of Christianity their national idea remains thoroughly worldly. . . . The Promise, which bulks so large in their patriotic outlook, is a promise of comfort and prosperity for an ever increasing majority of good Americans."[14] But the ideal of the Promise was not exhausted by purely economic hopes. A second element, "absolutely associated in the American mind" with growing prosperity, was the growth of personal freedom through a system of free political institutions. Indeed, the two elements were inseparably merged: "Our democratic institutions became in a sense the guarantee that prosperity would continue to be abundant and accessible. In case the majority of good Americans were not prosperous, there would be grave reasons for suspecting that our institutions were not doing their duty."[15]

But even this difficult dream ("a pervasive economic prosperity guaranteed by free institutions") failed to satisfy the American's hopes for the future. Somehow human nature itself would be transformed. "The implication was, and still is, that by virtue of the more comfortable and less trammeled lives which Americans were enabled to lead, they would constitute a better society and would become in general a worthier set of men." Give men prosperity and make them free, the vast majority of Americans felt, and they will respond to the chance. Part of the Promise, then, was "moral and social."

"Within certain limits," Croly readily admitted, "this system has made good." Americans were, in fact, richer than Europeans. Americans were, in fact, freer than Europeans. And, on the whole, Americans "made their freedom and prosperity contribute to a higher level of individual and social excellence." This was not to say that Americans were innately or genetically or racially superior; it was merely that more of them were leading "alert, active, and useful lives." "In a word, they are more alive, and they must be credited with the moral and social benefit attaching to a larger amount of vitality."[16]

The pioneer period of American history—to Herbert Croly's way of looking at things—had, therefore, been particularly fruitful. A nation had been established and set firmly on its way; a continent had been civilized. In addition, the period between the Revolution and the Civil War had engendered a particular political philosophy, a unique sort of individual, and a special dream for the future—a dream of wealth, liberty, and individual excellence. Best of all, for most of the nineteenth century the three bequests meshed. The combination of

[14] Ibid., 8–10.
[15] Ibid., 11.
[16] Ibid., 12–13.

Jeffersonian government, frontier individualism, and hope in the unfolding future seemed to work smoothly together.

At the very outset of his examination of American historical development in the pioneer period, Croly warned his readers that his exposition was likely to be unorthodox. His view of the past, he acknowledged, was "extremely controversial," and his judgments would differ radically from those of most American historians.[17] Despite the fact that many of his interpretations were comfortably within the tradition (his long eulogy of Abraham Lincoln, for example), the warning was accurate. Croly's discussion of American history was strikingly original and sometimes surprisingly prophetic.

His remarks on the Constitution of 1787, for example, must be seen as anticipating the revolutionary work of Charles A. Beard. Croly's contention that "the Federalists, representing as they did chiefly the people of wealth and education, demanded a government adequate to protect existing propertied rights," and his insistence that the Constitution "did succeed in giving some effect to their distrust of the democratic principle," were certainly not standard interpretations in 1909.[18] While it was true that Beard had many precursors, it was also true that Croly's view of the Constitutional Convention, propounded as it was in an age of unabashed Constitution worship, was historiographically much ahead of its time.[19]

Croly's discussion of the Hamilton-Jefferson debate, often counted as one of his most original contributions, was scarcely as radical. Although by 1909 Thomas Jefferson was securely enshrined above Alexander Hamilton in the national memory, and although he was the publicly acknowledged model for such leading political figures as William Jennings Bryan, Louis D. Brandeis, and Woodrow Wilson, there nevertheless existed a vital school of pro-Hamiltonian historiography. English scholars such as James Bryce and Frederick Scott Oliver had warm praise for Hamilton. Americans as diverse as novelist Gertrude Atherton, historian Henry Adams, and politicians Theodore Roosevelt and Henry Cabot Lodge were all busily engaged in resurrecting Hamilton at the expense of Jefferson. And the fact that Croly's father, a quarter century before, had both delineated the controversy and urged the claims of Hamilton, sufficiently proves

[17] Ibid., 27.

[18] Ibid., 32–33.

[19] See Richard Hofstadter, "Beard and the Constitution: The History of an Idea," *American Quarterly*, 2 (Fall 1950): 195–213; or Lee Benson, *Turner and Beard: American Historical Writing Reconsidered* (New York, 1965 edition), 96–103.

that Herbert Croly's analysis was not ground-breaking historical scholarship but merely an addition to a long-established dialogue.[20]

The remarks in *The Promise of American Life* about the pioneer democrat and his relevance to modern American problems, however, placed Croly in the forefront of the study of American history. The teachings of Frederick Jackson Turner were widely accepted by 1909, and dozens of historians and social critics had elevated the frontiersman into the symbol of all that was unique and valuable in American life. In the two decades after 1909, a small group of liberal historians and other intellectuals began to challenge not only Turner's conclusions but the dangerous implications they believed Americans were drawing from the exaltation of the frontier type. Many of their criticisms, however, merely echoed the earlier objections Croly had made: the pioneer, for all his inventive daring and democratic spirit was often dwarfed and stultified by his surroundings, ruthless in his pursuit of wealth, consistently indifferent to the welfare of the community as a whole, and an insufficient ideal for modern America.[21]

Aside from his suggestive departures from the main currents of American historical interpretation, Croly's discussion of American history was remarkable and provocative for its relative indifference to the strictly political, diplomatic, and military concerns upon which so many historians of the day had focused. Far more than most, he was willing to write about the impact of social and intellectual factors. Partly, of course, his attention to these broader areas of historic interest was the result of the direction of his argument. But partly, too, Croly's concern with ideas in history sprang from his view of the historical process. "The material for this critical estimate [of American history]," he wrote, "must be sought, not so much in the events of our national career, as in the ideas which have influenced its course. . . . Consequently we must go behind these facts and scrutinize, with more caution than is usually considered necessary, the adequacy and consistency of the underlying ideas."[22]

Literate Americans, then, who read the standard historical works

[20] See Merrill D. Peterson, *The Jeffersonian Image in the American Mind* (New York, 1960), 280–346.

[21] For the history of the acceptance and later criticism of the Turner thesis, see Ray A. Billington, *The American Frontier Thesis: Attack and Defense* (Washington, D.C., 1971). For the social critique of the implications of the frontier myth made by intellectuals and radicals after HC, see the superb analysis in Warren Susman, "The Useless Past: American Intellectuals and the Frontier Thesis: 1910–1930," *Bucknell Review*, 11 (March 1963): 1–20.

[22] *PAL*, 28.

of the time—Burgess, Rhodes, McMaster, Schouler, Channing, the American Nation Series—might very well have been surprised by *The Promise of American Life*. Not only were many of Croly's conclusions controversial, but his whole methodology was hardly the kind to which most readers were accustomed.[23] But Herbert Croly neither belabored nor elaborated his historical insights. He wrote about history never as an end in itself but merely in order to advance the central argument of his book.

II

Few Americans of 1865 realized—Croly pressed that argument forward—that a new set of circumstances was about to intervene. The Civil War had interrupted the characteristic American activity—an activity "which from the public point of view, was described as the economic development of the country, and which from an individual standpoint meant the making of money." Naturally, the war over, the country plunged back to work. "A lively, even a frenzied, outburst of industrial, commercial, and speculative activity followed hard upon the restoration of peace," and this outburst and its results constituted "the most important fact in American life during the forty years" since 1865. Not many suspected, as they rushed into the last half of the nineteenth century, that events would force the first two elements of the pre–Civil War inheritance (exaltation of both Jeffersonian government and the pioneer democrat) to give way to the third, the continuing pursuit of the Promise of American life. If the Promise was to be achieved at all in the twentieth century, a new kind of government and a new kind of citizen would be required.

According to Herbert Croly, the most significant change brought about by the explosion of economic enterprise was an increased and persistent demand for "specialists," those "well-paid and well-trained men, who could do one or two things remarkably well, and who did not pretend to much of anything else." Thus specialization, which had been distrusted and scorned by the pre–Civil War pioneer dem-

---

[23] See Michael Kraus, *The Writing of American History* (Norman, 1953), 177–241; John Higham, "The Rise of American Intellectual History," *American Historical Review*, 56 (April 1951): 453–71; Robert A. Skotheim, *American Intellectual Histories and Historians* (Princeton, 1966), 66–172; Charles Crowe, "The Emergence of Progressive History," *Journal of the History of Ideas*, 28 (January–March 1966): 109–24; Cushing Strout, *The Pragmatic Revolt in American History: Carl Becker and Charles Beard* (New Haven, 1958); Richard Hofstadter, *The Progressive Historians: Turner, Beard, Parrington* (New York, 1968); and Lee Benson, *Turner and Beard.*

ocrat, became an increasing necessity after 1865.[24] It pervaded all areas of national life until "Americans are divided from one another much more than they were during the Middle Period by differences of interest, of intellectual outlook, of moral and technical standards, and of manner of life." The rough good-fellowship of a homogeneous population had given way, under the pressure of new economic forces, to specialized organization in all practical matters.[25] And if the particularization was a universal problem, in certain "primary American activities" some especially perplexing problems were being raised.

The most perplexing expert to appear after the Civil War was "the business specialist." In Europe, where opportunities and resources were less spectacular, businessmen might prosper by employing sound, conservative methods. In the United States, however, the businessman found both unlimited scope and "more severe, more unscrupulous, and more dangerous competition." The choice he faced was "between aggressive daring business operations, and financial insignificance or ruin." Even the successful businessman was denied the luxury of relaxation, realizing that in this "war to the knife" he had to be constantly on the lookout for competitors who might suddenly drive him to the wall.[26] Naturally, business specialists sought ways to escape the savage warfare and to consolidate their precarious ascendancy. The results of these rational desires were those questionable, competition-stifling measures that had so visibly upset the muckrakers. Rebates, mergers, interlocking directorates, trusts—all were the perfectly understandable attempts of the largest industrialists to limit the dangers of the battle by crushing their potential rivals at birth.

These attempts at eliminating competition were often successful. In the first place, economic opportunities were simply not what they had been forty years before, and the firmly established corporation was now more difficult to assail. In addition, the weakness of the central government, the inability of Washington to assert and defend a "public interest" in the economic warfare, the inability to police questionable activities, even the inability to enforce existing regulations, gave powerful corporations a free hand with which to destroy their enemies. But the most important factor in the triumph of the large corporations was that they performed a genuine, perhaps even an indispensable, public service. Precisely because they had the new-

[24] PAL, 101–104.

[25] Ibid., 138. On this general point, see Robert H. Wiebe, *The Search for Order, 1877–1920* (New York, 1967).

[26] PAL, 106–107.

est machinery, the most efficient plants and expensive terminals, the best experts, the influential government connections, precisely because of their advantages they could reduce waste and produce low-priced goods of uniform quality with unprecedented efficiency. In short, the business specialist, with his new organization, "has created an economic mechanism which is capable of being wonderfully and indefinitely serviceable to the American people."[27]

Why then did the new businessman constitute so grave a threat to American democracy? One reason was that the system amounted to economic privileges for the few; and these few wrung personal profits from the nation far in excess of the economic services they were performing. More important, however, this new power occupied an equivocal position under the law. The new corporations evaded, broke, or adversely influenced the regulations under which they were supposed to operate. Their tremendous power resulted in "the corruption of American public life and in the serious deterioration of our system of local government." Despite the benefits it brought, business specialization also involved an overwhelming difficulty: "The rich men and the big corporations have become too wealthy and powerful for their official standing in American life."[28]

The modern businessman was only one example of the transformation of American society through specialization. The professional politician was another, and in some ways he was a counterpart of the new businessman: "Business efficiency under the conditions prevailing in our political and economic fabric demanded the 'Captain of Industry.' Political efficiency under our system of local government demanded the 'Boss.' " Given America's inherent, Jeffersonian suspicion of governmental authority, some informal way of getting the public business accomplished was a necessity. Somebody had to keep the local and state machinery staffed and oiled, somebody had to negotiate with the corporations for franchises and legislation. And, like the business specialist, the professional politician should not be condemned and dismissed. He too performed indispensable services and provided specialized leadership. For, although he was primarily interested in his personal income, the boss—or in complex urban or state politics, the boss's lieutenant—could only maintain his power by aiding his constituency. He got jobs, provided picnics, interceded with the police, and, above all, understood the problems of his followers in the best democratic tradition.

[27] Ibid., 115.
[28] Ibid., 116–17.

On the other hand, the boss could only sustain himself by petty graft and corruption. Since the system was built entirely on the satisfaction of merely individual, class, or neighborhood needs, moreover, "the local representative system was poisoned at its source." Even more dangerous was the fact that, like his business counterpart, the boss and the machine politicians who supported him were the sources of immense political power free from political responsibility. They usually held no office, but they jealously directed the affairs of the city or the district or the state. In short, they too had erected a power base quite outside the official power structure.[29]

A final example of specialized organization of immeasurable importance, rising to unprecedented heights of power year after year, yet operating independent of adequate public control, was the labor union. In many ways, Croly pointed out, unions formed exact counterpoises to the giant corporations. Both demanded the traditional forms of competition for the other while rejecting those forms for themselves; both firmly opposed federal intervention unless it was intervention on their own behalf; and both had achieved power by taking advantage of weak state governments. But the challenge of the labor union was more complex than the challenge of the corporation. The union was composed of men dangerously dissatisfied with the present ordering of American society; they were committed to significant, sometimes even to radical change. Indeed, "inasmuch as their power is likely to increase . . . the American people are confronted with the prospect of persistent, unscrupulous, and increasing agitation on behalf of an economic and political reorganization in favor of one class of citizens."[30]

The transformation of American society since the Civil War, then, had resulted in a specialization and a disintegration hitherto unimaginable. "The vast incoherent mass of the American people is falling into definite social groups, which restrict and define the mental outlook and social experience of their members. The all-round man of the innocent Middle Period has become the exception."[31] But Croly was always quick and careful to point out that specialization was not to be considered an evil. On the contrary, "the specialized organization of American industry, politics and labor" indicated greater efficiency, greater bounty, and "a promise of individual moral and intellectual emancipation." Nevertheless, it would be absurd to deny

[29] Ibid., 118–22.
[30] Ibid., 130.
[31] Ibid., 138.

that perplexing problems accompanied the change, problems that might even threaten the stability and coherence of the nation itself. And upon the ability of the American people to hold firm to the new gains while finding solutions to the new problems rested the fulfillment of the Promise of American life. But what was to be done?

III

Croly began his discussion of alternatives with a spirited, almost an eloquent analysis of what must *not* be done; and the bitterest phrases in *The Promise of American Life* were reserved for those men and women, operating out of ignorance or dishonesty, who insisted that nothing needed to be done at all. The experience of the pioneer period had lulled many into the belief that "they were able, in a sense, to slide down hill into the valley of fulfillment." With the abundant resources and opportunities of the nineteenth century there had been some reason for believing that the Promise could be captured "merely by virtue of maintaining intact a set of political institutions and by the vigorous individual pursuit of private ends."[32] But in modern America troublesome obstacles had intruded on the landscape, and obstacles are particularly dangerous when one is sliding downhill. In fact, Croly warned, "to conceive of the better American future as a consummation which will take care of itself . . . is admirably designed to deprive American life of any promise at all."[33]

Fortunately, more and more Americans were coming to realize that the new conditions required some sustained response. Movements of criticism and protest had grown steadily "until at the present time average well-intentioned Americans are likely to be reformers of one kind or another, while the more intelligent and disinterested of them are pretty sure to vote a 'reform' ticket."[34] Calling oneself a reformer, however, was only the first step away from the heresy of complacency; and for Croly, at least, two modern reformist types were worse than useless—they were positively harmful.

Those who would attempt to "restore" America to some previous age were so terribly ineffectual because their analysis of the sickness was so terribly naïve. The trouble with American society, they innocently maintained, was simply that corrupt and ruthless men had selfishly exploited economic and political opportunities. These so-

[32] Ibid., 17–21.
[33] Ibid., 5.
[34] Ibid., 141–42.

109

called reformers, therefore, called for "no more than moral and political purification"; they were satisfied to "cleanse, oil, and patch a
piece of economic and political machinery, which in all essentials is
adequate to its purpose." Their diagnosis was too simple: millionaires
had too much money; corrupt politicians had too much power. Their
solution, therefore, was too simple: "Reform must restore to the
people the opportunities and power of which they have been deprived."[35] Of course it could never work.

The millionaire and the boss, being inevitable results of traditional
ideals and present needs, could not be dismissed as mere abuses within
a workable system; they were the result of that system. Americans,
supposing that no conflict could possibly exist between self-interest
and patriotism, had given enormous freedom to individuals and sharply
restricted the power of the central government. "Under such a system unusually energetic and unscrupulous men were bound to seize
a kind and an amount of power which was not entirely wholesome.
They had a license to do so; and if they failed to take advantage
thereof, their failure would have been an indication, not of disinter-
estedness or moral impeccability, but of sheer weakness and inefficiency." How confused and foolish, therefore, were those who "consider reform as equivalent merely to the restoration of the American
democracy to a former condition of purity and excellence." The former condition had been purchased at a great sacrifice of individuality,
intellect, and excellence. It could never be reinstated, even if we wanted
it—the abuses were inevitable, given the society, and would soon
reappear even if they could be temporarily eradicated. "Reform exclusively as a moral protest and awakening," Herbert Croly solemnly
announced, "is condemned to sterility."[36]

The second type of reformers doomed to remain ineffectual were
those who espoused antinational sentiments. These critics refused to
admit that the trouble in American life was nationwide. Like the pre–
Civil War Democrats, they insisted that purely local authority was
capable of dealing with abuses that, like the problem of slavery, tran-
scended localities. Because of their blindness and fear, they denied to
the central government those powers absolutely necessary for effective action. If these well-intentioned men and women had only scru-
tinized their philosophies, they would have discovered that they were
modern captives of Thomas Jefferson. And if Jefferson himself had
exerted a "baleful" influence, what could possibly be said in defense

[35] Ibid., 145.
[36] Ibid., 149–50.

of those who stubbornly clung to his philosophy in the face of the changed situation of the twentieth century?

These two erroneous theories of reform, Croly observed, seemed to have captured the liberal wing of the Democratic party, and seemed to cluster about the person of William Jennings Bryan.[37] No one could question Bryan's integrity, courage, or patriotism, but he was simply "a Democrat of both Jeffersonian and Jacksonian tendencies, who has been born a few generations too late." His backing away from the daring proposal to nationalize the railroads was just one example of how both Bryan and the Democrats were bound hand and foot by the Jeffersonian tradition. If there was to be any reform at all—freed from the dangers of complacency, restoration through morality, and antinationalism—that is, if there was to be any "constructive" reform at all, Americans could expect it not from the impotent party of Jefferson and Bryan but from the national party of Lincoln and Theodore Roosevelt.

Luckily for the United States, an increasing number of citizens were waking to the need for constructive governmental reform. Not only did they reject the absurdity of remaining hopefully inactive, they were also beginning to sense the uselessness of Jeffersonianism. They saw that all attempts at moral purification, aimed at some restoration of the pioneer period, ended in failure. They saw that local authority was insufficient for problems that were national in dimension. These constructive reformers were led by ex-President Roosevelt, and Croly devoted eight, praise-filled pages to this leader "whose work has tended to give reform the dignity of a constructive mission." "During the course of his public career, his original integrity of character has been intensified by the stress of his labors, his achievements, his experiences, and his exhortations. . . . He may be figured as a Thor wielding with power and effect a sledge-hammer in the cause of national righteousness."[38]

And what had Theodore Roosevelt done to merit such praise? "He was the first political leader of the American people to identify the national principle with an ideal of reform." He revived the Hamiltonian conception of government from its nineteenth-century slumber. Like Hamilton, he envisioned a strong central government embarked upon an active program of national betterment. But, Croly was quick to add, "Theodore Roosevelt is Hamiltonian with a difference." The old secretary of the treasury had desired to use the

---

[37] HC's discussion of Bryan can be found in ibid., 154–60.
[38] Ibid., 174; HC's discussion of Roosevelt can be found at 167–75.

111

power of the state to thwart the rising tide of democracy. The modern ex-president, explained Croly in a phrase destined to become
important, symbolized a "new Federalism or rather new Nationalism
[which] is not in any way inimical to democracy." Indeed, "the whole
tendency of his programme is to give a democratic meaning and
purpose to the Hamiltonian tradition and method."[39]

The chief characteristic of a democracy, Croly argued, was not
easy to pinpoint. Democracy, for example, must not be confused
with its basic machinery—representative assemblies might act in an-
tidemocratic ways and the French were perfectly capable of using
universal suffrage to choose an emperor. Thus the customary tools
of the democratic process cannot constitute democracy in themselves.
Popular sovereignty was the start of a true democracy, not the end.[40]
Nor did democracy mean a government devoted to enforcing
"equality." That Jeffersonian slogan was outworn, sterile, and inefficient. It was so ambiguous that both radicals and businessmen could
appeal to it in the very same battle. Moreover, the government that
tried to enforce equality was trying the impossible. If it decreed, for
example, that equal rights demanded that corporations be unencum-
bered by special regulations, it was, in fact, discriminating on behalf
of corporations; but if it decreed that equality required control of
corporations, then it was discriminating against one class in society
and on behalf of others.[41]

What then was "democratic" government? It was simply government whose goal was "bestowing a share of the responsibility and
the benefits, derived from political and economic association, upon
the whole community."[42] The democratic ideal implied popular sovereignty, of course. But it also implied a machinery actively, persistently, candidly employed on behalf of social and economic amelioration. The central authority had to make decisions, and it had to
discriminate (for even the decision to do nothing was discrimination
in favor of the *status quo*); but this interference was only justifiable if
it constructively enhanced the democratic purpose of social and economic betterment.

America, then, required a conscious union "between democracy
and nationality." Theodore Roosevelt had made some encouraging
first steps, but they were only first steps. Democracy, at the present
moment in American history, needed a wholesale abandonment of

[39] Ibid., 168–69.
[40] Ibid., 179.
[41] For HC's attack on the equal rights philosophy, see ibid., 179–85.
[42] Ibid., 194.

Jeffersonian superstition and some fundamentally new ideas, if not some fundamentally new institutional forms. Croly began laying out his concrete program for the achievement of the Promise.

Most obviously, state and municipal governments, those persistent sources of confusion and corruption, had to undergo extensive alteration. Local authority certainly had its role in a federal system—it had to preserve order, administer justice, undertake certain economic functions, collect taxes for local purposes, and provide for the education of the community. States and municipalities, therefore, had to possess powers necessary to fulfill those functions. But they had to be content with a restricted area of operation. A state constitution ought not to be a copy of the federal, burdening its efficiency with complicated checks and balances—the powers of the governor in state government, for example, should be vastly strengthened; nor should state constitutions assume complete authority in all aspects of the social, political, and economic life of the citizenry. Local governments were notoriously corrupt, not only because they were run by evil men but because they were institutionally and administratively designed to perform tasks they should never have been expected to perform. Their power must be restricted to meet their legitimate functions.[43]

Conversely, more power must be granted to the central government. Each proposal to strengthen the federal government must be treated on its merits and not simply dismissed as an unqualified evil. If the addition of a particular power enabled the central authority to discharge its responsibilities thoroughly, efficiently, and in harmony with the democratic purpose, then that power ought to be speedily engrafted. Properly strengthened and faithfully representing the public interest, the federal government could supervise the quest for the Promise of American life.

The central power, for example, must be made ultimately responsible for the corporation problem. The states were simply unable to cope with the complexities of interstate commerce, and they had to give up the foolish and corrupting attempt. The national government must recognize the corporations and, instead of breaking them to pieces, allow them to grow freely in efficiency and strength; but it must always stand ready to prevent abuses and to insure that the corporations remained useful social servants, not dangerous economic tyrants. Under certain circumstances, when the activities of a corporation ran directly counter to the interests of the country and

[43] For HC's discussion of state and municipal reconstruction, see ibid., 315–50.

after extensive experimentation had failed to adjust the difficulties, public ownership might prove necessary.[44]

In addition, the invigorated and democratically oriented central government had to assert candidly and energetically its responsibility for a more equitable division of wealth. Differences in income were inevitable and, within limits, stimulating and healthy, but the creation of extremes of wealth and poverty were unjust, discouraging, and possibly dangerous to the stability of the society. There was a clear public interest in avoiding such polarization, and the federal government could meet its obligation by progressive taxation, particularly by boldly moving to tax corporate profits and inherited wealth.[45]

The national government also had to embark upon an energetic and imaginative foreign policy. Isolation and noninterference could no longer constitute the automatic American response to every international question. Americans needed to understand that they now possessed legitimate and far-flung interests in the world, and that those interests would increasingly involve them in world politics. The nation had better be prepared to employ the tools of power in defense of peace and security—Washington's Farewell Address and the Monroe Doctrine had ceased to be totally adequate guides to the problems of war and peace, commerce and colonization.[46]

Finally, the new nationalism had to confront the problem of organized labor. The formula of the Sherman Antitrust Act, which was being used to condemn both trusts and unions, was clearly untenable. In the case of the unions, the proper course was "substantial discrimination by the state in their favor." The central government had to recognize unions as honestly as it recognized corporations. "The labor unions deserve to be favored, because they are the most effective machinery which has as yet been forged for the economic and social amelioration of the laboring class." They advanced the national interest by helping to accomplish the necessary redistribution of wealth and by serving as an effective check on the power of the corporations. Just as the government had to surrender a policy of favoritism for small independent businessmen who could not compete with corporations, so was the "industrial derelict," the laborer who refused to join a union, to be similarly surrendered.[47]

[44] HC's program for the corporations can be found in ibid., 351–85.

[45] HC's discussion of the distribution of wealth is in ibid., 369–85.

[46] HC's analysis of the future of American foreign policy can be found in ibid., 289–314.

[47] For HC's views on the government and labor, see ibid., 385–98.

The key then to Herbert Croly's political reorganization was a central government strong enough to achieve the Promise. The new central authority would not merely assert American interests abroad but bind up and unite struggling factions at home. Committed to bigness and efficiency, the federal government would persistently intervene in the interests of the whole community, deftly wielding its power on behalf of democracy.

IV

The final chapter of *The Promise of American Life* was to be the source of countless misunderstandings and distortions, caused in part by the fact that it seemed to be devoted to considerations that seemed, at first, far removed from the concerns of the rest of the book. The title of that chapter, "Conclusions—The Individual and the National Purpose," moreover, seduced many superficial readers into an expectation of discovering therein the author's general and summarizing conclusions. When perused that way, the chapter unfortunately imparts to the whole book a mysticism, an élitism, and a general tone that, while certainly a part of the entire work, is not nearly so important as some have maintained. To be properly understood, the final chapter has to be read with a clear understanding of Croly's overarching argument, an argument developed carefully throughout the work.

Croly was troubled by the breakdown of the inheritance of the pioneer period. Then, the Promise could be approached by means of an individual (typified by the Western Democrat), whose private selfishness coincided, in general, with the patriotic task of building a nation. Then, a Jeffersonian government, which allowed individual freedom the greatest possible play, may have been appropriate and, to some extent, justifiable. But conditions had changed; and the new conditions, Croly believed, demanded a new philosophy of government and a new kind of individual citizen. Throughout much of *The Promise of American Life* Croly outlined the ways in which that new government had to move closer to a democratic Hamiltonianism. In the last chapter, however, he turned his attention to the second problem and tried to propose an alternative to the traditional Western Democrat.

"Americans have always associated individual freedom with the unlimited popular enjoyment of all available economic opportunities." Unfortunately, however, that assumption was tragically wrong. In fact, "it would be far more true to say that the popular enjoyment

115

of practically unrestricted economic opportunities is precisely the condition which makes for bondage." Indeed, "It is the economic individualism of our existing national system which inflicts the most serious damage on American individuality."[48] Where was the individuality in the common, headlong, unscrupulous struggle for money? Some of the participants might exhibit more energy than others, some more daring, some more immorality; but if viewed from the proper distance, they were all alike.

Genuine individualism implied a wholehearted and single-minded devotion to some unselfish social purpose. Since projects of economic and social amelioration were (by definition) democratic projects, the citizen who would be a true individual must necessarily be a democrat. And since the new democracy was so intimately tied to a new national strength and integrity, the citizen who would be a democratic individualist must necessarily be also a nationalist who directed his efforts, however indirectly, to the attainment of the Promise of American life. In short, "just in so far as a people is sincerely seeking the fulfillment of its national Promise, individuals of all kinds will find their most edifying individual opportunities in serving their country." And, best of all, while working to help America, "they will be increasing the scope and power of their own individual action."[49] Croly's demand, then, was that men stop their relentless devotion to the ideal of making money and somehow transfer that energy to the pursuit of less selfish but more fruitful goals, goals that had to be national in scope and democratic in practice. The demand implied a certain faith in human nature, but a faith in human nature, Croly hastened to point out, was the fundamental assumption of any democracy.

Naturally, the average citizen would be unable, at first, to convert his loyalty to money into a loyalty to the democratic nation. Some Americans—the educated, the intelligent, the idealistic—saw the need already. What could they do? It was the responsibility of each to fulfill his own purpose—which in most cases meant devoting himself to excellence in his own occupation. It would be a difficult undertaking for this special American—his country traditionally laughed at excellence and was suspicious of any craftsman, professional, artist, or intellectual who dared to pursue it. These courageous few, nevertheless, were the natural leaders of the American people. They had to strike the balance between the demands of the populace and the

[48] Ibid., 409.
[49] Ibid., 406.

demands of their personal consciences. Later, as more and more saw the value and the necessity of this course, the task would become easier.

The final goal for America—a goal so far into the future that it was idle to predict its attainment—was a society based on "the religion of human brotherhood." Men must come to know "the loving-kindness which individuals feel toward their fellowmen and particularly toward their fellow countrymen; and it is through such feelings that the network of mutual loyalties and responsibilities woven in a democratic nation become radiant and expansive." Such a sublime future was the real Promise of America. For the present, the evangelist had to content himself with the first steps, which could be accomplished by conscious dedication. He could only hope for a few converts at first, but slowly he could, perhaps, lead substantial numbers of his fellow citizens to see the necessity for political and personal rebirth. The gifted evangelist and his first, far-seeing and idealistic converts would have a difficult time. They would surely need to combine, Croly agreed with George Santayana, the attributes of hero and saint. But if the common citizen is ever enabled to rise to an imitation of that kind of élite leadership, Croly concluded, it "will depend upon the ability of his exceptional fellow-countrymen to offer him acceptable examples of heroism and saintliness."[50]

V

Although *The Promise of American Life* has generally been recognized as a major classic of the progressive era, commentators have disagreed sharply about the ideas and influences that combined to fashion it.[51] Unfortunately, Croly's single published attempt to offer an ex-

[50] Ibid., 453–54.

[51] The two most authoritative readings of *PAL* illustrate the diversity of interpretation. Both David Noble and Charles Forcey agree that HC experienced a profound "revolt" against his father's positivism while a student at Harvard. Noble, who has probed HC's writings several times (see "Herbert Croly and American Progressive Thought," *Western Political Quarterly*, 7 [December 1954]: 537–53; and *The Paradox of Progressive Thought* [Minneapolis, 1958], 34–77), concluded that it was the philosophy of Hegel that imparted the decisive influence to HC's book: "It is clear that Croly, a serious student of philosophy, when faced with the problem of creating a theory of social reform that would replace the ideas sanctioned by Herbert Spencer, was unable to escape from principles very similar to the other important philosophic tradition of the late nineteenth century, Hegelian idealism." Noble seemed to base this conclusion entirely upon HC's discussion of the nation-state. To account for elements in HC's book that seem decidedly un-Hegelian, Noble condemned him for "arguments which

planation of his own fails to shed much light on the book's intellectual origins. In June 1910, Croly wrote a short article for *World's Work* entitled "My Aim in *The Promise of American Life.*" In five brief paragraphs, fewer than four hundred words, Croly suggested that "the idea which lies at the basis of 'The Promise of American Life' first occurred to me about ten years ago, during a reading of Judge Robert Grant's novel, 'Unleavened Bread.' "[52] Croly acknowledged no other spur to his thinking and no other source for his ideas.

His explanation, we may assume, was a sincere one. He had previously praised Grant, and the conflict between the creative individual and American society, which Grant had developed in *Unleavened Bread*, was a theme that did, in fact, appear in Croly's book, particularly in the final chapter. Grant's novel might very well have triggered Croly's imagination and set into motion the writing that would eventually become *The Promise of American Life*. And yet, after reading his father's work before 1889 and his own writing before 1900, one cannot help but feel that Herbert Croly incorrectly assessed the importance of Grant's novel and the questions it raised.[53] At most, *Unleavened Bread* may have served as a trigger, releasing whole sets of ideas, opinions, prejudices, and hopes, which had been stored in

---

were inescapably tortuous and somewhat contradictory." A very different reading is found in Forcey's *The Crossroads of Liberalism: Croly, Weyl, Lippmann and the Progressive Era* (New York, 1961) and again in his introduction to the Dutton edition of *PAL*, xiii–xiv. Professor Forcey, whose work was based on the most meticulous research and stands at the beginning of any serious study of HC's life and thought, argued that "Croly took the pragmatism of William James as his creed." Whether HC learned his pragmatism directly from James or not, Forcey contended, is uncertain. But the pragmatic philosophy "was so much in the air" during the years that HC wrote that he might have been influenced by it indirectly. See *Crossroads of Liberalism*, 20–21. Other historians have also accepted the view that HC rejected Comtism while at college. "Positivism as an ideological commitment quickly evaporated upon exposure to Harvard Yard," according to Arthur M. Schlesinger, Jr., in his introduction to the 1965 edition of *PAL*. Eric F. Goldman contended that "David Croly . . . was shocked to receive a letter [from his son] which said, with a minimum of circumlocution, that Auguste Comte was a pompous fool." *Rendezvous with Destiny: A History of Modern American Reform* (New York, 1952), 191. My own opinion, which should be clear in these pages, is that these writers seriously underestimated the importance of the Positivist legacy from HC's father and either overestimated or misunderstood the nature of the "revolt" which HC experienced at Harvard.

[52] HC, "My Aim in *The Promise of American Life*: Why I Wrote My Latest Book," *World's Work*, 20 (June 1910): 13086.

[53] For the view that Grant's novel was more important than I believe it is for understanding the origin and essential meaning of *PAL*, see Forcey, *Crossroads of Liberalism*, 22–23; and introduction to the Dutton edition of *PAL*, xiv–xv.

Croly's mind for many years and which had come to him from some curiously diverse places.

Most clearly, the origins of *The Promise of American Life* are to be found in the social, political, and economic thought of Auguste Comte as that thought was applied to American conditions by David Goodman Croly. The briefest glance at the book's central ideas indicates the magnitude of Herbert Croly's intellectual debt to his father. The famous distinction between Thomas Jefferson and Alexander Hamilton—for which the book was best known in the popular mind—was taken nearly word by word from David Croly.[54] Similarly, Auguste Comte had predicted that a government's social destiny consisted of actively uniting the disparate parts of society as specialization and compartmentalization proceeded and as men became engrossed in their private affairs. Herbert Croly's discussion of the corporation and its "captain," the labor union and its leader, the political machine and its "boss" was conducted as an exploration into post–Civil War specialization and the need for the expert in the new America. It is scarcely surprising, therefore, that he also argued in behalf of a vitalized central government whose function would be the active pursuit of the welfare of the entire society, the conscientious defense of the whole community from the special, narrow, blind, and irresponsible actions of its parts.

Thus Croly's most popular concepts, the Hamilton-Jefferson distinction and the plea for a powerful central government, were borrowed from his father's positivism. But they were only the first in a long line of borrowed concepts. The compulsion to examine the transformation of institutions historically provides another example. For Comte the historical approach was a necessity—how could one discern a sociological law except by studying the drift of events over time? Herbert Croly's unusually long historical essay on the development of American life—always with an eye toward what one might expect as the main trends moved majestically into the future—was merely an exercise in Comtism, the attempt to apply the positive approach to a particular sociological problem.

Like Comte and like his father, moreover, Croly emerged from this historical search for long-range trends finding the consolidation of society inevitable. Like Comte and like his father, Croly recognized the modern industrial corporation as the necessary, irreversible culmination of everything that had come before. Like Comte and like his father, Croly argued that such concentration carried with it im-

---

[54] See the discussion above, pp. 41–42.

mense possibilities for human betterment. Despite the vain efforts of deluded reformers (Comte would have called them "metaphysicians," the Crolys called them "Jeffersonians"), industrial consolidation was a present fact of social existence; trusts could not be "busted," and even if they could be, they should not be.[55] To Auguste Comte, the deplorable confusion in human affairs was, at its base, an intellectual confusion. Social theorists were failing to be effective, he had argued, because only a few had discovered the Positivist approach to problems; the others were still stumbling stupidly along with the heavy and useless baggage of metaphysical beliefs. If the proper methodology could prevail, Comte insisted, progress would follow quickly. Herbert Croly thought so too. For Croly as for Comte, the real difficulty was the intellectual approach to social problems. What was immediately required was a reorientation of thinking, a recognition that some ideas were outmoded, useless, and fast becoming harmful. If right ideas were widespread, Croly echoed Auguste Comte, if America's heroes and saints could skillfully sow and cultivate more modern seedlings upon American soil, fruitful growths would spring into existence and progress would quickly follow.[56]

Herbert Croly, therefore, not only borrowed from his father's positivism the best known and most influential concepts of *The Promise of American Life*, but he borrowed as well Comte's historical approach to social problems and Comte's consistent commitment to the primacy of intellectual reorientation to social change. But even then the borrowing did not end. Virtually dozens of the smaller ideas and personal prejudices of the father appeared in the work of the son. Their writing about the conflict between the individual and the community was similar, and for both men, "individualism" emerged as the sum of all evil. The call for "altruism" and human brotherhood, which was the message of the last chapter of *The Promise of American Life*, was merely an echo of the social philosophy of the Religion of Humanity as explained in David Croly's *Positivist Primer*. The two men wrote in precisely the same terms about a score of things: both were critical of lawyers, both tolerant of big-city bosses;[57] both understood the psychology of the millionaire's pursuit of wealth in the same way; both favored an active, imperialist foreign policy and

[55] See the discussion above, pp. 37–39.

[56] This helps account for HC's heavy emphasis on the role of ideas in American history. See *PAL*, 28.

[57] For these themes in David Croly's writing, see *Glimpses of the Future: Suggestions as to the Drift of Things* (New York, 1888), 24–26, 41–42; *Record and Guide*, 38 (August 28, 1886): 1025; 40 (November 1887): 1379; 42 (August 11, 1888): 963.

advocated the creation of a big navy;[58] both predicted an increase in executive power and a diminution of the power of the legislature.[59]

Another "similarity" was so uncanny that one hesitates to mention it. On April 26, 1884, David Goodman Croly suggested that young Theodore Roosevelt be given the Republican nomination for the presidency at the approaching Republican convention.[60] That this was the first time Roosevelt's name had been mentioned in connection with the presidency seems obvious. It was, after all, two full years before the aspiring young politician finished a poor third in the New York mayoralty; it was, astonishingly, nine full years before the twenty-six-year-old Roosevelt would be constitutionally eligible for the office! Clearly, the preference for Theodore Roosevelt by Herbert's father, at a time when Herbert was still at Morse's grammar school, was coincidental and unimportant. Whether the Herbert Croly of 1909 even remembered his father's early enthusiasm for Roosevelt is highly doubtful, and the notion that the praise for Roosevelt in *The Promise of American Life* was "influenced" by David Croly's earlier praise is far-fetched. Still, seen in another way, there is an indication here of how closely the mind of the son resembled the mind of the father. The similarity was not only one of intellectual constructions, but of emotional predispositions and responses as well—they responded to the same qualities of leadership. That the possessor of the qualities of "heroism" happened to be the same individual (a quarter-century later) was meaningless and entirely coincidental; that their criteria for "heroism" were so obviously identical, however, cannot be dismissed as trivial.

In all the pages of *The Promise of American Life* Herbert Croly disagreed with his father only once. Although they both contended that

[58] For David Croly's views, see *Record and Guide*, 32 (August 18, 1883): 604; 32 (October 13, 1883): 780; 32 (October 20, 1883): 808; 33 (April 12, 1884): 371; 42 (September 15, 1888): 1132; 42 (October 20, 1888): 1312.

[59] For David Croly's views of the relations between the executive and the legislative, see *Glimpses of the Future*, 24–25; *Record and Guide*, 32 (November 10, 1883): 877; 38 (November 27, 1886): 1452.

[60] *Record and Guide*, 33 (April 26, 1884): 431. The editorial paragraph reads, in its entirety: "Theodore Roosevelt heads the New York delegation to the Chicago convention. How would he do to head the ticket nominated at Chicago? His record is a splendid one for a dark horse. The Democrats of this State piled up a tremendous majority for an ex-mayor of Buffalo for Governor whose name had scarcely been mentioned before the convention met. Theodore Roosevelt might be equally available as a presidential candidate although he has never been more than a State Assemblyman." For other instances of David Croly's praise for Theodore Roosevelt, see *ibid.*, 38 (September 11, 1886): 1113; and 38 (December 4, 1886): 1477–78.

society functioned best with one party holding fast to existing arrangements and the other pushing for constructive change, they disagreed about which party was which in America. David Croly, who had tried to sink Lincoln with the miscegenation hoax of 1864 and who wrote the campaign biography of Democrat Horatio Seymour in 1868, believed that the Democratic party was the party of progress. The Republicans, he had argued, were too deeply indebted to the great corporations; the Democrats, gaining support from labor and the farmers, cleansing themselves of their Jeffersonian-Jacksonian philosophy, were the best hope. Herbert Croly was convinced that the years since his father's death had proved the opposite. Theodore Roosevelt had rescued the Republicans from their bondage to big business; and meanwhile William Jennings Bryan was busy leading the Democrats into such a pervasive and debilitating Jeffersonianism that no one could tell for sure how many years would have to pass before a hero or a saint could conscientiously vote Democratic. This disagreement aside—and it was, of course, not really a disagreement, for Herbert and his father were judging political parties on the basis of identical criteria—David Croly could have subscribed wholeheartedly to everything in *The Promise of American Life*. It was not accidental—indeed, it was simple justice—that the book bore the dedication, "to the memory of David Goodman Croly."

So ingrained and fundamental was Herbert's debt to his father, moreover, that he had to be forceably aroused to actually "remember" how many of those ideas he had always taken for granted stemmed from his father's thought. In 1916, Royal Cortissoz, an art critic and friend of the Croly family, sent Herbert a copy of an old interview David Croly had once given to a newspaperman.[61] "It was extraordinarily good of you to take the trouble of having this interview typewritten and transmitted to me," Croly replied. "It brought back my father's whole method of thought more vividly than anything which has happened in a great many years. He was a man of enormous fertility of mind. He could, I think, originate more ideas in less time than any man I ever met. . . . I found it extremely suggestive 45 years after it was given." And after reminiscing about the long rambling talks in Central Park, Croly confessed in closing, "I was very much amused when it suddenly occurred to me after I had written 'The Promise of American Life,' how many of its leading trains of thought I could trace back to those discussions and which

---

[61] Probably the interview in Charles F. Wingate, ed., *Views and Interviews on Journalism* (New York, 1875).

were directly prompted by things he had said. I am telling you this so that you can understand what keen pleasure I received from the opportunity you let me have of hearing him talk once again."[62] Similarly, at the end of his life, when he sat down to write some autobiographical reflections, Herbert acknowledged that "many a time . . . I have waked up in the midst of giving expression to what seemed to be an idea of my own, to a sudden recollection that I was only obeying the orders of some early suggestions of my father's."[63] There was no mention at all, in his autobiographical fragment, of Robert Grant's novel. At moments, then, when he examined the origins of his thought most carefully and searchingly, Herbert Croly could see below the transitory influence of Grant's *Unleavened Bread* and recognize the true source of his opinions.

When the boys at the office of the *New York World* began calling David Croly "the Great Suggester," they created a nickname better than they could ever have imagined. David Croly was not merely adept at offering interesting approaches to green *World* reporters; he "suggested" a coherent, viable, influential social philosophy to a nation confronted by overwhelming industrial problems. And when David Goodman Croly invested in his son those endless hours of talk, he invested more wisely than he could ever have dreamed.

VI

If *The Promise of American Life* had turned out to be only David Croly's positivism brought up to date, it would still have been an impressive work. That Herbert Croly's book was something more, however, that it was as original and exciting as so many critics have believed, is because Croly did more than just parrot his father's positivism. He embellished, augmented, illustrated, and tempered that philosophy with ideas gathered from many sources. Dozens of allusions to non-Comtean sources crowded *The Promise of American Life*. They ranged from a reference to Gilbert and Sullivan's *Pinafore* to a play on words from *Macbeth*; from Crèvecoeur to H. G. Wells; from Tocqueville to Henry George. There were, however, three major intellectual influences, that supplemented the Positivist core of *The Promise of American Life*.

In the first place, Croly's attention to cultural problems—embod-

[62] HC to Royal Cortissoz, October 7, 1916, Autograph File, Houghton Library, Harvard University.
[63] HC, "Fragment," 5–6.

ied for him in the terrible conflict between the harried individual and the crass materialism of American life—is an element of the book that has no very precise echo in the thought of Comte or his father. Herbert Croly's eye was always focused beyond particular social and political reforms, to the kind of men and women a reformed society might produce. "American individual achievement in politics and science and the arts will remain partially impoverished as long as our fellow-countrymen neglect or refuse systematically to regulate the distribution of wealth in the national interest,"[64] he wrote. This belief that individual excellence went hand in hand with social reform, the persistent hope that educated and creative American idealists could transform a pursuit of money into a less selfish and more social pursuit, the faith that these regenerated men and women would courageously pursue excellence in a society that traditionally suspected excellence, the conviction that such men and women were America's natural élite—all these tenets were basic to *The Promise of American Life*.

In fact it was precisely this set of beliefs that imparted to Croly's nationalism a tone and a purpose, which distinguished him from many of the other nationalist writers of the time. He shared with many of them an organic view of the American nation and rejected the merely legalistic formulation, which had characterized patriotic formulations before the Civil War. In addition, he probably supported the programs of many contemporary nationalists; his advocacy of a large navy and his frank imperialism, for example, were in harmony with the main currents of nationalist thought. But Croly's emphasis was always on nationalism as a vehicle for individual improvement and the elevation of American intellectual development: "It is, then, essential to recognize," Croly summarized his view, "that the individual American will never obtain a sufficiently complete chance of self-expression, until the American nation has earnestly undertaken and measurably achieved the realization of its collective purpose. . . . Any success in the achievement of the national purpose will contribute positively to the liberation of the individual . . . by enveloping him in an invigorating rather than an enervating moral and intellectual atmosphere."[65]

This cultural concern and the subordinate ideas that sprang from

[64] *PAL*, 409. See also, 399, 409–21, 427–41.

[65] Ibid., 409. For the state of nationalist thinking, see Merle Curti, *The Roots of American Loyalty* (New York, 1946), 173–222; Hans Kohn, *American Nationalism: an Interpretative Essay* (New York, 1957); or Boyd C. Shafer, *Nationalism: Myth and Reality* (New York, 1955), 153–241.

it—a desire for excellence in a nation that prided itself on an easy homogeneity, a fear that the blind pursuit of wealth might crush true individuality, and a profound and hopeful faith in America's real leadership—comprised the first non-Comtean addition to the Comtean core of Croly's book. Undoubtedly the source of this train of thought was Croly's aesthetic training: Norton and Santayana, work on *The Architectural Record*, and Robert Grant's *Unleavened Bread*. It was certainly significant that Croly chose American architects to illustrate how an enlightened and creative minority could raise the level of appreciation among their countrymen.[66]

A second contribution to the core of *The Promise of American Life* becomes apparent when one compares the son's writing about "the nation" with the writing of the father. Both men agreed that the nation would exert an ever-more pervasive influence upon the private lives of its citizens and both agreed that this increased influence would serve the purposes of coordination, elevation, and direction. Both men thought that the whole process of centralization would be beneficial to an America plagued by excessive individualism. Yet one cannot escape the observation that Herbert Croly invested more in his discussion of the nation than did his father. He added an element of emotional commitment. Men had to redirect their spiritual loyalties; they had to stop their exclusive dedication to private pursuits and transfer their love to the national community. Too many radical and enthusiastic democrats, Croly complained, mistakenly saw in the nation the great threat to democracy, but this Jeffersonian vestige was "a disastrous error." "It is not too much to say that no permanent good can, under existing conditions, come to the individual and society except through the preservation and the development of the existing system of nationalized states."[67] Nationalism had to be accepted as "loyally and unreservedly" as democracy.

Read on one level, this commitment to the union between democracy and nationalism was merely a working out of Herbert Croly's most popular idea, the necessity of combining Jeffersonianism and Hamiltonianism. What Herbert Croly added to the purely intellectual construct was the element of "loyalty." His entire discussion of the coming devotion to American nationalism centered on the problem of where loyalty was owed and where it was not. "Loyalty to the existing system of nationalized states does not necessarily mean loyalty to an existing government merely because it exists." Loyalty, he

[66] *PAL*, 444–45.
[67] Ibid., 211.

elaborated, "does not necessarily mean the uncritical and unprotesting acceptance of the national limitations and abuses." Instead, "the loyalty which a citizen owes to a government is dependent upon the extent to which the government is representative of national traditions and is organized in the interest of valid purposes."[68] There is no reason to suspect that David Goodman Croly would have disapproved of his son's much repeated addition of the element of "loyalty" to the nation; the only certainty is that he himself never spoke of this kind of passionate gift of loyalty to America.

But there was one thinker who spoke about a commitment of faith to society, and he spoke about it as "loyalty to the community." In a history of his native California, Josiah Royce set up the dichotomy: there were the selfish and irresponsible pioneers on one side and the higher demands of the civilized community on the other. In the final paragraph of that book, Royce drew his moral: "It is the State, the Social Order, that is divine. We are all but dust, save as this social order gives us life. When we think it our instrument, our plaything, and make our private fortunes the one object, then this social order rapidly becomes vile to us; we call it sordid, degraded, corrupt, unspiritual, and ask how we may escape from it forever. But if we turn again and serve the social order, and not merely ourselves, we soon find that what we are serving is simply our own highest spiritual destiny in bodily form."[69] Royce's history of California urged a spiritual dedication to society, and he attacked the problems involved in achieving this dedication again and again. The titles of his works are significant: in books such as *The World and the Individual, The Philosophy of Loyalty,* and *The Hope of the Great Community,* and in articles such as "The Idea of the Universal Community," "Loyalty and Insight," and "Some American Problems in Their Relation to Loyalty," Royce returned repeatedly to the problem of the individual and society.[70] No one at the dinner honoring Professor Royce at the end of his life should have been surprised at the way he extemporaneously summarized his social philosophy. "When I review this whole process," he said, "I strongly feel that my deepest motives and prob-

[68] Ibid.

[69] Josiah Royce, *California from the Conquest in 1846 to the Second Vigilance Committee in San Francisco: A Study of American Character* (Boston, 1886), 501.

[70] My interpretation of Royce relies heavily on R. Jackson Wilson's discussion, *In Quest of Community: Social Philosophy in the United States, 1860–1920* (New York, 1968), 144–70. But see also John E. Smith, *Royce's Social Infinite, The Community of Interpretation* (New York, 1950).

lems have centered about the Idea of Community, although this idea has only come gradually to my clear consciousness."[71]

Croly's acceptance of Royce's particular formulation of the dichotomy between selfish individuals and a community interest, and the fact that Croly borrowed Royce's particular solution—the emotional commitment of loyalty to the community—were purely fortuitous. Croly followed Royce because of his devotion to a favorite teacher. If Royce had never lived, however, or if Croly had never met him or read his work, *The Promise of American Life* would have been different, but only slightly different. Clearly, the conflict between individualism and community interest was explicit in the writing of Comte and an important element in the thought of David Croly. And if the problem was part of Croly's intellectual inheritance, there were many intellectuals besides Josiah Royce searching for a possible solution. An entire generation of American thinkers between 1880 and 1920 wrestled with the task of taming the traditional American individualist so that he might function satisfactorily in an industrial society. Men as diverse as Charles S. Peirce, Richard T. Ely, G. Stanley Hall, Lester Frank Ward, Edward Bellamy, and E. A. Ross involved themselves in defining the limits of individualism and the new areas for the exercise of community responsibility. Croly's formulation happened to make use of Royce's concept of loyalty; but the whole question was being so widely discussed that fully half a dozen alternative formulations might have served Croly's purpose as easily.[72]

The third additional source of Herbert Croly's *The Promise of American Life* cannot be defined as easily as the other two. It lacks the compact unity of a body of related ideas, like the first, nor can it be associated with a single philosopher, like the second. Nevertheless, Croly's thinking was stimulated and *The Promise of American Life* was forceably influenced by that curious combination of ideals, prejudices, plans, and hopes known as the progressive movement. Dozens of historians have examined the first decade of the twentieth century and virtually all of them have agreed that something unusual was afoot. They are scarcely in harmony when it comes to assessing the movement's origins or its underlying ideology or the ultimate significance of its concrete achievements; but they universally acknowledge that the period was a time of special enthusiasm, of a

---

[71] "Words of Professor Royce in the Walton Hotel at Philadelphia, December 29, 1915," in *Papers in Honor of Josiah Royce on His Sixtieth Birthday* (New York, 1916), 282.

[72] Wilson, *In Quest of Community, passim.*

special and searching concern with the evils of American society, and of a special willingness on the part of thousands of average Americans to involve themselves in programs of social reform. In the end, the progressive movement may be seen as the disorganized but urgently felt impulse to accommodate the strains within American society caused by the economic and social dislocations of the late nineteenth century. And progressivism made itself felt in *The Promise of American Life* in several ways.

To begin with, the agitation of the progressive movement, including the sensational disclosures of the muckrakers, imparted to Croly's book a sense of gravity, which was apparent on every page. Back in 1890, young Croly had written an interesting editorial for *The Record and Guide* entitled, "Our 'Problems.' " In it, he surveyed the American scene and assured his readers that there was nothing to worry about. "There are, in truth, to-day, in this country no problems of a vital nature that so press upon our civilization with so much of persistency and urgency that consideration and action become imperatively necessary." Twenty-one-year-old Croly was confident that "there are yet no difficulties that have come so close to our very existence as a people that it is thereby restricted or confined."[73] Surveying the scene at the other end of two decades of strife, agitation, exposure, and sensationalism, Herbert Croly was far more nervous.

By 1909, he thought that "grave national abuses cast a deep shadow across the traditional American patriotic vision."[74] For all their beneficial economic services, the giant corporations were now the symbols of privilege and dangerous irresponsibility; for all their indispensable political services, the political bosses had shown their capacity for corruption, which threatened to eclipse democracy in the United States. Also troubling was the shadow cast by elements of organized labor. Despite his open sympathy with the labor movement, and despite his recognition of the need to further labor's legitimate demands, Croly felt obliged to warn his readers that "the militant unionists are beginning to talk and believe as if they were at war with the existing social and political order." Indeed, the discontent of labor "affords to a substantially revolutionary purpose a large and increasing popular following."[75] The Promise of America was in obvious danger, Croly was convinced by 1909, and unless Americans acted decisively and immediately, American life would cease to have

[73] *Record and Guide*, 45 (February 22, 1890): 255–56.
[74] *PAL*, 20.
[75] Ibid., 128, 130. See also, 100–40.

any Promise at all. By 1909 he had the distinct suspicion that "the traditional American system is breaking down," and that "the serious nature of contemporary American political and economic symptoms at least pointedly suggests the existence of some radical disease."[76] Twenty years of muckraking, the political appeals of social reformers, and the heightened concern that characterized the progressive movement had not been wasted on Herbert Croly.

The spirit of progressivism influenced *The Promise of American Life* in other ways, too. The wave of social reform and political interest had deposited in the public consciousness a series of commonly used catch phrases, commonly debated questions, and commonly discussed personalities. These "live issues" found a prominent place in Croly's book. In undertaking to write a useful and timely critique of American politics, Croly probably felt obliged to mention, at least in passing, the burning questions of the hour. Consequently the book was crowded with the most common expressions in the contemporary reform lexicon: "the money power," "the Square Deal," "home rule to the cities," "graduated inheritance tax," "the relations between labor and capital," "naval strength in the Pacific." These and dozens of additional slogans indicated how deeply Croly was absorbed by the current literature of social debate and how that literature was reflected in *The Promise of American Life*.

Croly also felt compelled to deal with the most controversial issues and men of the day and to offer opinions on virtually all of them. The book contains, therefore, discussions of everything progressives were talking about. Croly's view of civil service reform, the Australian ballot, imperial expansion into the Philippines, the care of the insane and the criminal, the closed shop, reciprocity with Canada—all found room in the book.[77] His view of the Sherman Antitrust Act, the Interstate Commerce Commission, the Pure Food and Drug Act, and plans for the initiative, referendum, and recall were all presented in detail. William Randolph Hearst, William Jennings Bryan, Henry George, Theodore Roosevelt were discussed favorably or unfavorably.[78] Obviously, many of these comments on issues, laws, and men were necessary to Croly's central purpose. Some, however, such as a four-page examination of the reform career of New York's dynamic but ephemeral District Attorney, William Travers Jerome, were forced.[79] Necessary or not, Croly's continual references to the

[76] Ibid., 25.
[77] Ibid., 334–37, 341–42, 308–309, 345, 127–31, 304–306.
[78] Ibid., 274, 359, 351–57, 191, 320, 327–28, 332–33, 142–44, 156–59, 168–75.
[79] Ibid., 160–63.

vocabulary of reform and the political debates and personalities of the hour revealed the extent to which the progressive movement made itself felt in *The Promise of American Life*.

But the most important impact which progressivism had on Croly's work was neither the sense of urgency it imparted nor the particular catalogue of issues Croly felt compelled to discuss. More important than either were the criticisms this wave of reform sentiment called forth. Progressivism caused Croly to examine the nature and course of contemporary activity, and, as often as not, he found himself in violent disagreement with what he saw happening in the name of reform. At a time when reformers, in Eric F. Goldman's phrase, "swept each other over ideological difficulties in a tide of emotion," Herbert Croly managed to maintain an ideological independence and a posture of skepticism.[80]

His condemnation, for example, of those reformers who contented themselves with striving to infuse a new sense of morality into American politics indicated Croly's unwillingness to equate good intentions with constructive work. His denunciation of antinationalist reformers such as Bryan revealed his refusal to equate any reform program with useful planning. For Croly, mere activity—even when accompanied by incorruptible integrity and high idealism—was never sufficient; he forthrightly proclaimed the dangers that many reformers represented. They misunderstood corporations; they misunderstood the challenge of labor; they misunderstood the sources of political corruption; they misunderstood the choices that faced the United States. They never even suspected their intellectual bondage to Thomas Jefferson.

The absolute condemnation of the trusts by some progressives, therefore, was merely a product of the movement's ignorance,[81] and civil service reform was merely the misguided and doomed attempt to "restore" by the infusion of moral revival.[82] Measures to make the federal judiciary elective, or to diminish the authority of the president by allowing him only a suspensive veto, were simply vestiges of the democratic faith of the Middle Period.[83] From Croly's viewpoint, anti-imperialists were men who had no adequate concept of a national interest or a national destiny;[84] those who would have increased the powers of state or municipal governments had no ade-

---

[80] Goldman, *Rendezvous with Destiny*, 192.
[81] *PAL*, 143, 158, 351–57.
[82] Ibid., 334–37.
[83] Ibid., 119–20, 159.
[84] Ibid., 259–63.

quate understanding of the beneficial trends in the opposite direction;[85] those who campaigned for a forced equality in economic pursuits could not see that the real need was for constructive discrimination in behalf of a public interest;[86] those who filled the air with cries for the initiative, referendum, and recall were just old Jeffersonians who yearned to blame selected individuals for the fundamental weaknesses of the institutional structure of our government.[87] All such "reformers"—whatever their reputations in progressive circles—Croly dismissed as the unthinking spokesmen of a deluded and empty-headed enthusiasm.

The progressive movement, therefore, stood as the third non-Comtean influence upon *The Promise of American Life*. It provided the moment; it persuaded the author that basic American institutions and hopes were in crisis. Progressivism, in addition, spun off a series of shibboleths, issues, and personalities, which Croly had firmly fixed in mind as he wrote. Finally, progressivism changed *The Promise of American Life* by driving its author into a critical review of the recent efforts toward reform.

But the progressive movement—like Croly's cultural concern and the Roycean idea of community—must be kept in perspective. They augmented the core of the book, they enriched it and widened its concerns; they convince one that Herbert Croly was more than a copyist, that he could skillfully and smoothly combine distinct trains of thought into a coherent whole. Nevertheless, *The Promise of American Life* was essentially the application of the thought of Auguste Comte to the industrial society of the United States. The debt to Comte and to his American disciple, David Goodman Croly, was so fundamental and preponderant that the other influences on Herbert Croly's masterpiece were distinctly subordinate to it.

[85] Ibid., 317–29, 143, 348–50.
[86] Ibid., 182–83, 185–206.
[87] Ibid., 320, 327–28, 332–33.

FIVE

"Taking on the Form of
the Sun God"

The Promise of American Life was an instantaneous success. The book appeared in early November 1909, and the apprehensive author sent copies to some of his friends. Their replies were reassuring. Arthur Colton, the librarian of the New York University Club, thought it was "the solidest piece of consecutive thinking on the subject that I have met with in some if not many years. . . . I would venture to prophesy that the book will make its mark."[1] Another friend wrote Croly, "You've done a big thing in that book and I haven't the least doubt but that it will come to be recognized, one of these days, as a landmark in the progress of our national development."[2] One of Croly's closest companions, Judge Learned Hand, confessed to being "lost in a maze of admiration at your excellent work. . . . I mean you to believe quite literally what I say when I tell you that I consider it a most remarkable work of reasoning and certainly it is the result of the best reflection which any man of my acquaintance and any where near my age has given forth, with perhaps the exception of Santayana." "Your reference to the book overwhelmed me," Croly wrote back. "Is it really as good as that?"[3]

Within six months Croly had ample evidence that the book was good. *The Promise of American Life* was being widely noticed and reviewed. "This is an eminently notable book," began the review in *The Nation.* "It is one of the best examples in recent years of a long-sustained flight in the region of realistic philosophical politics." *The World Today* thought Croly "a man of keen insight and clear vision," his book, "a contribution of marked value." The enthusiastic reviewer at *The Bookman* regarded it as "the most remarkable book on this subject that has appeared since Bryce's *American Commonwealth.*" *The Review of Reviews* went one step further and, in a joint review,

[1] Arthur Willis Colton to HC, November 15 [1909], Autograph File, Houghton Library, Harvard University.

[2] J. W. Howard to HC, January 5, 1910, Autograph File, Houghton Library, Harvard University.

[3] Learned Hand to HC, December 3, 1909; HC to Learned Hand, December 5, 1909, both in the Hand mss., Law School Library, Harvard University.

confused the two as "Herbert Bryce" and "James Croly"! Theodore Roosevelt's magazine, *The Outlook*, not surprisingly, was the most impressed of all. *The Promise of American Life*, it solemnly announced, "will beyond doubt be recognized by students of the great philosophical currents of American history and political development as an unusual and remarkable work. Its character and scope cannot adequately be indicated by a brief note." And from across the Atlantic, London's *Saturday Review* acknowledged, "this is a very clever and candid book, which we advise all who think about politics to read."[4]

The book was also noticed in several scholarly journals; and although a few reviewers had reservations about some of Croly's conclusions, they generally agreed, in the words of one of them, that Croly had written a "singularly original and thoughtful work."[5] In addition, *The Promise of American Life* was the subject of several longer review articles. Particularly significant was the piece in *The Outlook* of April 16, 1910. In a perceptive and prophetic article entitled "At the Parting of the Ways," the anonymous author examined Croly's book side by side with a recent address delivered by Woodrow Wilson. "The one represents the new Jeffersonianism, the other the new Hamiltonianism," he stated. And after summarizing the views of each, the article suggested that "the American Nation is at the parting of the ways. These two leaders, each of whom sees with greater clearness and speaks with greater courage than the newspaper editor or the practical politician usually possesses, lead in opposite directions. . . . A great debate between these two principles of national action

[4] "The Future of Democracy," *Nation*, 90 (March 3, 1910): 209–11; *World Today*, 18 (June 1910): 670; *Bookman*, 31 (June 1910): 343; *Review of Reviews*, 41 (January 1910): 127; *Outlook*, 93 (December 4, 1909): 788–89; *Saturday Review* (London), 109 (April 2, 1910): 433–34. For other reviews of *The Promise of American Life*, see *New York World*, November 13, 1909; *St. Louis Globe-Democrat*, November 13, 1909; *Providence Journal*, November 21, 1909; *Philadelphia North American*, December 11, 1909; *Milwaukee Sentinal*, December 12, 1909; *Boston Transcript*, December 22, 1909; *Chicago Record-Herald*, December 27, 1909; *Louisville Journal*, December 11, 1909; *Los Angeles Herald*, December 12, 1909; *Hartford Post*, December 29, 1909; *The Churchman*, January 15, 1910; *London Daily Chronicle*, January 18, 1910; *Collier's Weekly*, January 1, 1910; *Cincinnati Enquirer*, January 16, 1910; *London Daily Mail*, January 22, 1910; *Education*, January 19, 1910; *San Francisco Chronicle*, January 15, 1910; *Ladies Home Journal*, February, 1910; *New York Examiner*, February 17, 1910; *Newark News*, March 26, 1910; *Philadelphia Telegraph*, March 7, 1910; *Chicago Post*, February 18, 1910; *New Orleans Picayune*, February 6, 1910; *Pittsburgh Dispatch*, March 13, 1910; *Columbus State Journal*, March 20, 1910; *Manchester Guardian*, March 29, 1910; *North American Review*, March 1910.

[5] Henry Jones Ford in *American Political Science Review*, 4 (November 1910): 614–16. See also *Annals of the American Academy of Political and Social Science*, 35 (January 1910): 191; and Royal Meeker in *Political Science Quarterly*, 25 (December 1910): 688–99.

would be a great education not only for America but for all peoples with democratic institutions or democratic proclivities."[6]

All this was doubtless heady and gratifying for Croly. He had been an obscure editor of an architectural journal; he was suddenly a recognized political authority whose opinions were being contrasted with those of a man being prominently mentioned for public office and whose controversy with the Princeton alumni was capturing the attention of the nation. But Croly maintained from the beginning that his book had been written to change minds, to influence powerful men, ultimately to divert the course of national policy into more fruitful channels. "Naturally I hope that it is really good not merely because I have my own share of spirit," he explained to Learned Hand, "but because it needs to win friends. It is essentially a reconnoitering expedition into territory evidently not very well occupied in this country; and I cannot expect to hold my ground unless I obtain support. . . . I have always hoped that it would win some converts because they & I should feel encouraged to seek other applications and to fortify the position already assumed."[7]

The fact that only 7,500 copies had been sold at the time of Croly's death, twenty years later, seems to indicate that, numerically at least, the converted probably failed to affect American political life very noticeably.[8] There was, nevertheless, some indication that a few young men destined to be important (the very kind of élite whom Croly had hoped to reach) were impressed by *The Promise of American Life*. Henry L. Stimson, for example, read the book and was soon quoting Croly in speeches (the two men became friendly).[9] Ray Stannard Baker told his father that Croly's book was "the very best thing of its kind I have seen."[10] By the start of 1911, Learned Hand playfully reported to the author, "I have no doubt that in a few years, myths will be established about you. Perhaps you will take on the form of the Sun-God. That is the common retroactive metamorphosis of heroes. . . .

[6] "At the Parting of the Ways," *Outlook*, 94 (April 16, 1910): 830–31. For other longer review articles, see *Political Science Quarterly*, 25 (December 1910): 688–99; "The Future of Democracy," *Nation*, 90 (March 3, 1910): 209–11; and Spectator, "The American People," *Living Age*, 264 (March 26, 1910): 817–19.

[7] HC to Learned Hand, December 5, 1909, Hand mss.

[8] The estimate of 7,500 is from Felix Frankfurter, "Herbert Croly and American Political Opinion," *NR*, 63 (July 16, 1930): 247.

[9] Henry L. Stimson and McGeorge Bundy, *On Active Service in Peace and War* (New York, 1947), 58–59. See also HC to Stimson, ?, 1911; Stimson to HC, April 8, 1911; HC to Stimson, September 20, 1913; HC to Stimson, October 18, 1913; and HC to Stimson, March 27, 1914, Stimson mss., Yale University.

[10] Ray Stannard Baker to Joseph S. Baker, December 12, 1910, Ray Stannard Baker mss., Library of Congress.

You are quite the rage. Stimson is reported to have read the book over three times. I doubt not he could recite parts of it by heart. . . . The local insurgents are a forlorn hope and just at present I think are in some danger of canonizing you."[11]

Many participants in the age of reform who looked back on the exciting days of their youth were very sure that Herbert Croly's book had something to do with the climate of opinion. Robert Morss Lovett thought that it "lifted the study of political science in American colleges to a higher plane."[12] John Chamberlain remembered it as "a book whose influence spread in a wide circular ripple. . . ."[13] "To omit Croly's 'Promise' from any list of half a dozen books on American politics since 1900 would be grotesque," insisted Frankfurter in 1930. "It became a reservoir for all political writing after its publication. . . . The 'Promise' may fairly be called seminal for American political thinking."[14] Walter Lippmann summed up the view of many of the progressive activists: "I should say that 'The Promise of American Life' was the political classic which announced the end of the Age of Innocence with its romantic faith in American destiny and inaugurated the process of self-examination. That is, of course, the opinion of a very grateful friend; yet I believe it will be justified when our history is sufficiently distant and neutral to be interpreted."[15]

Whether or not the progressive era is, even now, sufficiently distant to be definitively interpreted is debatable. But those historians who have made the attempt tend to agree with Lippmann. They see Croly's contribution in less powerful terms, but the leading historians of the period nearly all acknowledge Croly's influence. Richard Hofstadter, George E. Mowry, William E. Leuchtenburg, Daniel Aaron, Samuel P. Hays, Arthur M. Schlesinger, Jr., Henry F. May, Russel B. Nye, Arthur S. Link, Eric F. Goldman, and Christopher Lasch disagree about the nature and extent of Croly's impact, they even disagree about whether his influence was pernicious or beneficial, but they all assume that *The Promise of American Life* made its presence felt in the debate.[16]

---

[11] Learned Hand to HC, February 6, 1911, Hand mss.

[12] Robert Morss Lovett, "Herbert Croly's Contribution to American Life," *NR*, 63 (July 16, 1930): 245.

[13] John Chamberlain, *Farewell to Reform: The Rise, Life and Decay of the Progressive Mind in America* (Chicago, 1965 edition): 223. For Chamberlain's changing views of the book, see "Croly and the American Future," *NR*, 101 (November 8, 1939): 33–35.

[14] Frankfurter, "Croly and Opinion," 247, 249. See also Harlan Phillips, ed., *Felix Frankfurter Reminisces* (New York, 1960), 88, 165.

[15] Walter Lippmann, "Notes for a Biography," *NR*, 63 (July 16, 1930): 250.

[16] Richard Hofstadter, *Age of Reform* (New York, 1960 edition), 246–47; George E.

Whether or not the book was of shaking importance, however, was less crucial than the fact that a great many people *thought* the book was of shaking importance—a terribly influential piece of work. And that impression derived almost entirely from the book's close association with a single individual.

I

Croly's most important reader was the flamboyant ex-President Theodore Roosevelt. Having broken decisively with the conservative wing of his party, and entrusting the burdens of his office to his friend William Howard Taft, the still energetic Colonel left the White House on March 4, 1909. Three weeks later he was off to Africa to have a try at killing lions. Eleven months passed and Roosevelt emerged from the jungle with his 296 trophies. After a head-spinning tour of European capitals, he landed in America on June 18, 1910. Then, sometime in the late spring or early summer of 1910, Roosevelt read *The Promise of American Life*.

In April he had been urged to read the book by two curiously dissimilar men. "I am recalling to you an acquaintance, long since past," began the author's own ambassador, Learned Hand, "to send to you a book of my friend, Herbert Croly, 'The Promise of American Life.' "

I hope that you will find it as comprehensive and progressive a statement of American political ideas and ideals as I have found. I think that Croly has succeeded in stating more adequately than

Mowry, *The Era of Theodore Roosevelt and the Birth of Modern America, 1900–1912* (New York, 1962), 55–57; and Mowry, *Theodore Roosevelt and the Progressive Movement* (New York, 1950 edition), 146; William E. Leuchtenburg, ed., introduction to *The New Nationalism* (Englewood Cliffs, N.J., 1961), 11–17; Daniel Aaron, *Men of Good Hope: A Story of American Progressives* (New York, 1961 edition), 250–51; Samuel P. Hays, *The Response to Industrialism, 1885–1914* (Chicago, 1957), 88; Arthur M. Schlesinger, Jr., introduction to *The Promise of American Life* (Cambridge, Mass., 1965 edition); and Schlesinger, "Croly and 'The Promise of American Life,' " *NR*, 152 (May 8, 1965): 17–22; Henry F. May, *The End of American Innocence: A Study of the First Years of Our Own Time, 1912–1917* (New York, 1959), 304, 317–18; Russel B. Nye, *Midwestern Progressive Politics: A Historical Study of Its Origins and Development, 1870–1950* (East Lansing, 1951), 274–78; Arthur S. Link, *Woodrow Wilson and the Progressive Era, 1910–1917* (New York, 1963 edition), 18–19; and Link, *American Epoch: A History of the United States Since the 1890s* (New York, 1963 edition), 79–80; Eric F. Goldman, *Rendezvous with Destiny: A History of Modern American Reform* (New York, 1952), 188–207; Christopher Lasch, "Herbert Croly's America," *New York Review of Books*, 4 (July 1, 1965): 18.

anyone else,—certainly of those writers whom I know—the bases and prospective growth of the set of political ideas which can fairly be described as Neo-Hamiltonian, and whose promise is due more to you, as I believe, than to anyone else. I do not suppose that you will agree with it all, but I should be much disappointed if you failed to be interested in much the greater part of it, if you could find a chance to read it.[17]

Three weeks of anxious waiting and Roosevelt acknowledged the gift: "I look forward with real pleasure to reading it." From Cornish, a delighted Croly rejoiced, "You certainly hit the game. Now let's see whether he drops."[18]

Meanwhile a friend much closer to the ex-president than Hand was also urging Roosevelt to read *The Promise of American Life*. "I have just finished a book . . . by Herbert Croly, of whom I have never heard before," wrote Henry Cabot Lodge. "There are plenty of things in the book with which you will disagree as I do but you will not say of any of them that the writer has not thought hard about it." Roosevelt, from Paris, assured Lodge, "I have at once ordered Herbert Croly's 'The Promise of American Life' from the Macmillans of London."[19] (Either Hand's gift, sent separate from his letter, had not yet arrived, or the Colonel simply forgot that Judge Hand had sent him the present over a week before Lodge's letter.)[20]

The "game" which Hand and Lodge had aimed at finally "dropped" on the last day of July 1910. Croly's joy must have been delirious as he read the most important letter he was ever to receive:

My dear Mr. Croly:

I do not know when I have read a book which I felt profitted me as much as your book on American life. There are a few points on which I do not entirely agree with you, yet even as to

[17] Learned Hand to Theodore Roosevelt, April 8, 1910, Hand mss.

[18] Theodore Roosevelt to Learned Hand, April 30, 1910, and HC to Hand, May 6, 1910, Hand mss.

[19] For Lodge's letter to Roosevelt, see Charles Forcey, *The Crossroads of Liberalism: Croly, Weyl, Lippmann, and the Progressive Era, 1900–1925* (New York, 1961), 124; for TR's reply, see either *Selections from the Correspondence of Theodore Roosevelt and Henry Cabot Lodge* (New York, 1925), 2: 378, or, Elting E. Morison, ed., *The Letters of Theodore Roosevelt* (Cambridge, Mass., 1954), 7: 76. Lodge's letter was written on April 19, 1910, and TR's reply was dated April 27, 1910.

[20] We may dismiss as fanciful Matthew Josephson's view that "in the trunks that went to Africa there had been placed by chance a copy of Herbert Croly's *The Promise of American Life*. . . ." Josephson, *The President Makers: The Culture of Politics and Leadership in an Age of Enlightenment, 1896–1919* (New York, 1940), 369.

these my disagreement is on minor matters; indeed chiefly on questions of emphasis.

All I wish is that I were better able to get my advice to my fellow countrymen in practical shape according to the principles you set forth.

I shall use your ideas freely in speeches I intend to make. I know you won't object to my doing so, because, my dear sir, I can see that your purpose is to do your share in any way for the betterment of our national life; that what you care for is to see this betterment secured.

Can't you come in to see me at the Outlook office? I want very much to have a chance to talk to you.

Sincerely,
Theodore Roosevelt[21]

Croly was ecstatic. "Whatever gratification I may feel as an author in receiving such a letter," he told Hand, "is entirely swallowed by my sentiment of personal loyalty to the man in his position who could lend me so firm & cordial a hand."[22] After the letter from Roosevelt, it was at least an open question who was the hunter and who was the fallen game. It may not be an exaggeration to assert that the ex-president had returned to the United States with 297 trophies!

On the other hand, the Colonel had really read the book. He was undoubtedly not above flattering authors whose work he had merely skimmed; but Eric F. Goldman's suggestion that "it is doubtful whether Roosevelt read many of Croly's 454 pages, which include a good deal of labyrinthine analysis and even more tedious writing," is without foundation.[23] Actually Roosevelt read Croly's book rather carefully, and an obscure but convincing substantiation does in fact exist.

Sometime in the late summer of 1910, Ray Stannard Baker had run into Roosevelt at the big conservation conference in St. Paul. Although relations between the two men had been cooler since the Colonel's "muckrake" speech back in 1906, the ex-president invited the reporter to pay a call. On October 5, Baker dutifully caught the 9:00 A.M. train to Oyster Bay and by 10:30 he was at Sagamore Hill. The next day he wrote in his diary: "I was shown into T.R.'s library,

---

[21] No original of this letter survives. This version was copied by HC and sent to Learned Hand: "What you say about T.R. & The Promise of American Life is confirmed by the following letter received yesterday, which I transcribe." HC to Hand, August 1, 1910, Hand mss.

[22] Ibid.

[23] Goldman, *Rendezvous with Destiny*, 189.

being informed that T.R. was out on horseback and would return very soon. I had opportunity to look over his books somewhat. The familiar books of the library are about evenly divided between hunting books & books on American history and American affairs. Almost no fiction (except a few of Kipling's) and no poetry to speak of. Of new books, I found Herbert Croly's 'Promise of American Life' with many passages heavily scored & pages on the fly-leaf with references. I understand T.R. has been confirmed in his position on the 'New Nationalism' by this book."[24]

The question of Croly's influence on Roosevelt is a difficult one. Certainly the notion—once widely held—that Croly suddenly converted a relatively conservative Roosevelt into the strident liberalism of the 1912 campaign is a vast overestimation of the book's effect. Nearly all the distinctive ideas in *The Promise of American Life* had found some expression in Roosevelt's letters, speeches, and messages to Congress (particularly in the last two years of his administration) long before the publication of Croly's book. Roosevelt was a vocal Hamiltonian and often publicly critical of the influence of Thomas Jefferson. The ex-president's vigorous nationalism needed no prod from Herbert Croly. Even Croly's solution to the trust problem— the point at which the strongest case for Croly's influence can be made—echoed Roosevelt's hesitant and experimental attempts to control big business while he was president.[25] On the other hand, those historians who argued that it was really Roosevelt who influenced Herbert Croly might have gone too far.[26] Too zealous, per-

[24] See Baker, Diary, Container 121, Notebook "K," 151–53, Ray Stannard Baker mss.

[25] For the convincing argument that Roosevelt held many of Croly's ideas before the publication of *The Promise of American Life*, see Forcey, *Crossroads of Liberalism*, 127–30; Leuchtenburg, ed., *New Nationalism*, 11–17; E. E. Morison, ed., *Letters of Theodore Roosevelt*, 7: 76–77n; Schlesinger, Jr., introduction to *PAL*, xxiii–xxiv; William Henry Harbaugh, *Power and Responsibility: The Life and Times of Theodore Roosevelt* (New York, 1961), 337–48. HC himself recognized that TR's Hamiltonianism was evident prior to 1909. In May 1910, he wrote Hand, "Of course it is absolutely true that he is the original and supreme Hamiltonian revivalist. I have just been reading his book on Gouverneur Morris, written about 1887; and have been amused to find how closely I merely followed after many of his judgments of the Federalist epoch."

[26] Professor Forcey writes: "When the measure of Croly's influence on Roosevelt is taken, moreover, the profound impact of Roosevelt's own career on the philosopher has to be counted. The relation of the two men was one of interaction, with Roosevelt's impress much the stronger. Croly was quite consciously trying to formulate and carry further tendencies which had been manifest in Roosevelt's Presidency." (*Crossroads of Liberalism*, 130.) Similarly, Professor Leuchtenburg, in his superb introduction to *The New Nationalism*, argues (12) that HC's book "is less important for the impact Croly had on Roosevelt than as evidence of the impact Roosevelt had on Croly."

haps, in their correction of an admitted historical myth, these writers' contentions do not adequately consider the roots of Croly's thought in the pre-Rooseveltian teaching of Comte and the author's father.

Part of the difficulty in this particular historical quibble has been the attachment, on both sides, to a rather narrow conception of what really constitutes "influence." Suppose a traveler, journeying eastward on a carefully planned, publicly announced mission, suddenly encountered a stranger who urged him to travel west instead. If the traveler listened to the stranger and decisively reversed his course, then surely one could strongly argue that the stranger had influenced the traveler. It is difficult to believe, however, that such a dramatic and sudden reversal is required before one may fairly ascribe influence. Such startling conversion experiences are rare in the history of men, rarer still in the biographies of public figures with established reputations, successful careers, and trademarked ways of thinking. It is abundantly clear that Theodore Roosevelt had no such experience as he put down his copy of *The Promise of American Life*.

But suppose the traveler encountered a stranger who intelligently, persuasively, and sympathetically urged him to continue in the direction he was heading. If the traveler proceeded more confidently, if he proceeded better aware of the complexities and dangers of the road ahead, if he had been given a compelling vision of the ultimate destination, if he quickened his pace—then surely one can suggest that the stranger had influenced the traveler. The obvious problem is that influence such as this, however real, is perceived intuitively; it is hard to document and a potential source of endless controversy.

This kind of unspectacular, quiet, confirming influence is, of course, much more common. Perhaps when a public man has committed himself to a set of basic beliefs this is the only kind of appeal that can be effective at all. Carl Becker was not far wrong when he asserted, referring to an entirely different historical setting, that "generally speaking, men are influenced by books which clarify their own thought, which express their own notions well, or which suggest to them ideas which their minds are already predisposed to accept."[27] Even if there were not direct evidence that Croly helped to draft Roosevelt's famous speech at Osawatomie, Kansas—delivered only thirty days after he told Croly he would be using his ideas in future speeches— one cannot read that important address without feeling that Roosevelt had been strongly confirmed in his views by reading Croly's

[27] Carl Becker, *The Declaration of Independence: A Study in the History of Political Ideas* (New York, 1958 edition), 28.

book.[28] "Combinations in industry are the result of an imperative economic law which cannot be repealed by political legislation," Roosevelt proclaimed his New Nationalism: ". . . the way out lies, not in attempting to prevent such combinations, but in completely controlling them in the interest of the public welfare."

In any case, the important phenomenon, once again, was not the extent to which Croly influenced Theodore Roosevelt, it was that Herbert Croly's generation harbored no doubts about the relationship between *The Promise of American Life* and Roosevelt's new radicalism. *The American Magazine*, in November 1912, merely asserted what everybody already knew. In capital letters the caption under Croly's picture read: "THE MAN FROM WHOM COL. ROOSEVELT GOT HIS 'NEW NATIONALISM.' "[29] The *Cleveland Leader* insisted: "Herbert Croly, quite as much as Theodore Roosevelt, is the author and the prophet of the 'New Nationalism.' . . . He is everywhere credited by the well informed with the right to speak as one having authority on the great changes even now in progress."[30] *The Independent* called him simply, "the author of the New Nationalism."[31] "My dear friend, you are becoming an authority," reported Learned Hand. "I find that by actual mention of my intimacy with you, I acquire a distinct political significance."[32]

Naturally, being an authority carried with it new honors and new opportunities.

II

To begin with, Harvard College was now happy to claim the illustrious author as one of her own. Although he had never completed the requirements for his degree, the authorities seemed willing to accept *The Promise of American Life* as sufficient evidence of erudition; at Hand's urging, Croly was awarded his bachelor's degree in 1910, "as of the class of 1890." "I shall be your older college brother," he informed Hand ('93).[33] The graduate's first response was to round up

[28] For evidence that HC helped draft the speech, see Walter Lippmann, "Oral History," Columbia University Oral History Project, 6–7. Gifford Pinchot also worked on the speech—see his *Breaking New Ground* (New York, 1947), 385–86; and Amos R. E. Pinchot, *History of the Progressive Party, 1912–1916* (New York, 1958 edition), 112–15.

[29] *American Magazine*, 84 (November 1912): 23.

[30] *Cleveland Leader*, March 17, 1911.

[31] *Independent*, 74 (June 5, 1913): 1297.

[32] Learned Hand to HC, February 6, 1911, Hand mss.

[33] HC to Learned Hand, June 30, 1910, Hand mss.

letters of recommendation for the University Club of New York City.

Meanwhile, Croly's literary reputation was enhanced by his new stature, and he set busily to work writing articles. In May 1910, he shared with the readers of *World's Work* some thoughts about the newly announced Rockefeller Foundation. The short article ended with a plea that the Foundation consider establishing a national school of political science. Located in Washington, the institution might help to prepare able public officials for government service. Repeating his contention in *The Promise of American Life*, Croly argued that "the prosperous future of a democratic nation depends upon the foundation and diffusion of sound, progressive ideas and authentic information in relation to living political problems."[34] Once again Croly was insisting that intellectual orientation must precede constructive social change.

Those who happened to pick up *The North American Review* that month found Croly speculating about the latest political developments in a full-length article, "Democratic Factions and Insurgent Republicans." The piece was an intelligent attempt to bring *The Promise of American Life* up to date, to encompass within the book's assumptions the exciting and dramatic political events of 1909 and 1910. Given the fact that Americans confronted a new set of problems which required a national solution, how well, Croly asked, were the two political parties prepared to respond?

The Democrats, he thought, were hopelessly ripped by the conflict between the old theories of Jefferson and Jackson and the severe demands of the new situation. Half of them emphasized the need for destroying economic privilege; half of them shrank from the centralizing tendencies such an effort would require. It was not surprising that they were divided into warring factions. Croly gave them "a respectable chance" of electing the next president, but he was convinced that power would only bring to the surface that factionalism which, even when out of power, they were so hard-pressed to quiet. The Republicans, meanwhile, faced their own problem. By tradition, of course, they were the national party, the party that had saved the Union from dissolution. But the nationalism of the Republican party after the Civil War had consisted almost entirely of distributing the nation's land, timber, and minerals, in the faith that the speedy in-

[34] HC, "A Great School of Political Science," *World's Work*, 20 (May 1910): 12, 887–88.

crease in individual wealth meant a speedy increase in the wealth of the nation.

With the diminishing opportunities of the late nineteenth century, Croly continued, some Republicans sensed the end of this splendid harmony between selfishness and national health. Beginning with a concern for conservation or a desire to lower the tariff, these Republicans now voiced ever more serious complaints and demanded more radical changes. They were still national in their outlook, Croly insisted, but they had changed their minds about what constituted the best national policy. The struggle in the Republican party between Insurgents and the Old Guard could be explained in precisely these terms. The conservatives wanted to retain the program that had served party and nation so admirably for so long; the progressives, disturbed by new economic conditions, correctly understood that "the national interest is demanding the modification of every important element in the economic system for which the party has in the past been responsible."[35]

It was a genuine division and it was causing "one of the most difficult and dangerous crises" in the history of the Republican party. Typically, Croly resorted to a pious belief in better ideas: "One can only fall back upon the hope that in the end the crying need for thorough-going economic reform will create the great increase in economic and political intelligence and in disinterested patriotism needed for its satisfaction." Although Croly's "Democratic Factions and Insurgent Republicans" was essentially a gloss on previous work, he did state two propositions in this article with more certainty than ever before. First, he asserted much more strongly than in *The Promise of American Life* that American resources and opportunities were now almost gone: "The Government could no longer encourage the development of the natural resources of the country, because there were, comparatively speaking, no more natural resources to develop." A second argument, put forward with new boldness, was that the Congress of the United States might, in fact, be incapable of solving American problems. Constituted as it was, a gathering of "district and state delegates in a national Legislature," Congress had thus far passed constructive bills only by a combination of log-rolling and party discipline. Worse, national legislation had been passed in the erroneous belief "that national interest [was] . . . a composite

[35] HC, "Democratic Factions and Insurgent Republicans," *North American Review*, 191 (May 1910): 626–35. The quotation is at 634.

version of individual and local interests."[36] New measures, badly needed, might require that some states and districts suffer temporary losses; and it remained to be seen whether the American Congress was equal to the new challenge.

In December 1911, Croly delivered a paper at the meeting of the American Political Science Association in Buffalo. His topic was "State Political Reorganization," and his remarks followed closely the position he took in the eleventh chapter of *The Promise of American Life*. Condemning the "progressive fascination" with such direct programs as referendum, the initiative, and recall, Croly once again urged the integrity of state government. State legislatures must neither be hampered by unworkable institutions nor drowned in a sea of popular distrust; instead the states confining themselves carefully to their proper activities, must be granted full power to perform their special functions. Croly personally favored a system whereby the governor possessed a legislative initiative, the legislature vetoing or amending his suggestions, and the referendum to the people as a last resort when the two disagreed.[37]

Finally, in a series of ten articles written for the *Cleveland Leader*, Croly tried once again to popularize and make current the central teachings of *The Promise of American Life*. The object of the series, Croly confided to Hand, was to correct some of the misunderstandings surrounding the issues, "to rescue the features of the New Nationalism from the disfigurement that infant received at the hands of T.R. & his critics."[38] Although the bulk of the articles was a simple repetition of the book, Croly wrestled hard with a new dilemma— one which would plague him, more or less, until the end of his life.

On the one hand, the Insurgents—those liberal-minded midwestern Republicans who admired Robert M. La Follette and were challenging the stuffy leadership of Taft and the Old Guard—were the most promising political development in years. Their Republicanism had oriented them nationally, and their reformism was an encouraging sign that intelligent young Americans were starting to realize the necessity for constructive national planning. "If the contentions of the preceding articles are true," Croly began his seventh installment, "the progressive wing of the Republican party are the best existing representatives of both the historic mission of Republicanism

---

[36] Ibid., 632–35.

[37] HC, "State Political Reorganization," *American Political Science Review*, 6 (February 1912): supplement, 122–35.

[38] HC to Learned Hand, February 3, 1911, Hand mss.

and the traditional purpose of the American Democracy."[39] Aside from his open devotion to the personal leadership of Roosevelt, Herbert Croly had never before publicly revealed his partisan preferences so frankly.

Nevertheless, despite their hopeful enthusiasm and their progressive intentions, the Insurgents were not a group which Croly could whole-heartedly support. The last installment in the *Leader* series was devoted entirely to criticizing them. It was painfully clear that they had failed to master one of the most important lessons of *The Promise of American Life*. They still did not see that the central government must "discriminate" in favor of those enterprises which strengthened the nation. Instead, the Insurgents kept chattering about "equality," kept hoping that an infusion of "more democracy" into the system would fix everything. Their sermons about restoring morality, their stubborn faith in recall, referendum, and the initiative, their unwillingness to acknowledge the need for specialization, efficiency, and bigness, their backward insistence that government be kept weak and under vigilant surveillance—all these sins marked them as Jeffersonians. Croly surveyed their program with irritation: "It fills the writer with dismay and chagrin. . . . I would very much like to accept their political leadership, but their platform is so appallingly inadequate as the statement of an effective program of political reform and is based upon such a partial and false analysis of the causes of our political and economic abuses that its permanent acceptance as the regular reform political platform will most assuredly result in disaster for the cause of reform."[40]

The *Leader* series revealed one of Croly's abiding difficulties. To what extent were hopeful and promising political movements to be supported; to what extent were their faults to be exposed and criticized? The problem, of course, is an obvious one and every intellectual whose work and thought touches political life is faced with it. Pointing out mercilessly the weaknesses of a movement can only arm its opponents and impede its immediate prospects. Ignoring those weaknesses in the name of a pragmatic effectiveness, or in a belief that, even with the shortcomings, it is the best movement available at the moment, is a clear violation of intellectual integrity. Croly refused to be swept up in the Republican Insurgency regardless of its potential serviceability. He agreed to write the series for the *Leader*,

[39] *Cleveland Leader*, April 3, 1911, 1.
[40] Ibid., April 10, 1911, 1, 3.

he told Hand, because "it would relieve my mind very much to have another whack both at the stand-patters & the Insurgents."[41]

III

While the articles for the *Cleveland Leader* testified to Croly's firm devotion to principle and his high sense of intellectual integrity, these very qualities were called into question by another literary exercise written the same year. Throughout 1911, Croly was at work on *Marcus Alonzo Hanna: His Life and Work*. Ostensibly a biography, Croly dutifully traced Mark Hanna's career: his ancestry, his youth in Ohio, his developing business interests and expanding fortune, his growing interest in Ohio politics. Three-quarters of the book was devoted to recounting Hanna's friendship with William McKinley, his maneuverings on his friend's behalf, his role in the conventions and campaigns of 1896 and 1900, and his own personal influence in the United States Senate from 1897 until his death in 1904. Croly's biography of Hanna appeared in early 1912, and it unquestionably constituted the most compromising intellectual act of Croly's career.

The book's integrity is suspect because of the conditions under which it was written. Croly, who had no steady income, was paid to undertake the biography by the Hanna family, acting through Daniel R. Hanna, the senator's son, and the family was given the power of censorship before publication. From his vacation in California, in February 1911, Croly wrote to Hand: "I wish we could join you & Frances in England this summer, but after I get home, I must remain in Cornish until I get Uncle Mark well-planted in his printed grave. I have not accomplished much since I have been here—so little in fact that I have been obliged to write to Dan [Hanna] and call off my pay checks."[42] When the book was completed, Croly personally took the manuscript out to Ohio. "I am loafing away ten days here," he wrote Hand from Ravenna, "in the effort to get the Biography straightened out with the family. Dan Hanna is all right. . . . Mrs. Hanna had some qualms but she was easily talked down. There remains a brother Leonard who will be harder to line up, but if there is trouble I'll have Dan behind me."[43]

Given these conditions, the book's point of view is scarcely surprising. Even if Croly had somehow managed to win most of the

---

[41] HC to Learned Hand, February 3, 1911, Hand mss.
[42] HC to Learned Hand, February 24, 1911, Hand mss.
[43] HC to Learned Hand [late October], 1911, Hand mss.

disputed points with the family, his realization that the book would be shown to them before publication must have affected his writing. The reviewer for *The Political Science Quarterly* politely suggested that "Mr. Croly may have erred somewhat on the side of sympathy."[44] Arthur C. Cole, who wrote on Hanna for *The Dictionary of American Biography*, echoed that judgment, calling the work "a somewhat over-sympathetic account."[45] Professor Forcey frankly called it "in many ways an apologia."[46] A Negro politician and friend of Hanna thought that the book would be "pleasing to his family, pleasing to his friends. . . . The author has presented a new Hanna, wholly unlike the Mr. Hanna that we personally knew."[47] The distinguished historian James Ford Rhodes disagreed. Choosing Croly to be Hanna's biographer, Rhodes thought, was an "exceptionally happy" choice; and although "some of Hanna's friends, on hearing of the selection, may have shuddered at the thought of an author with socialist proclivities undertaking the biography of a strong individualist," nevertheless Croly "presented the real Mark Hanna with remarkable perspicacity and skill."[48] But then, James Ford Rhodes happened to be Mark Hanna's business associate and brother-in-law. No wonder Dan Hanna wrote to Roosevelt, early in 1912, to tell him now pleased he was with his father's biography.[49]

The principal source for the book was a set of statements by Hanna's friends and associates that had been collected by James B. Morrow, himself a close associate of Hanna. Croly added to these statements by interviewing others who had been connected with Hanna. Particularly significant was Croly's interview with Roosevelt, who invited him for a long stay at Oyster Bay for the purpose.[50] Since

[44] *Political Science Quarterly*, 28 (March 1913): 168–69.

[45] *Dictionary of American Biography*, 8: 225–28.

[46] Forcey, *Crossroads of Liberalism*, 143.

[47] John A. Garraty, ed., "The Correspondence of George A. Myers and James Ford Rhodes, 1910–1923," *Ohio Historical Quarterly*, 64 (1955): 26. Myers continued: HC "smoothed over the rough characteristics, and by the eloquence of his masterly pen through the lavish use of the 'Queen's English' presented his subject to his readers in such a manner that gives no offense to anyone. We knew Mr. Hanna to be a rough brusque character with an indomitable will of his own that respected the rights of no one who stood in the way of his successful accomplishment of the object he had set out to accomplish."

[48] James Ford Rhodes, *The McKinley and Roosevelt Administrations, 1897–1909* (New York, 1927), 8–9.

[49] See TR to Daniel Rhodes Hanna, February 29, 1912, in E. E. Morison, ed., *Letters of Theodore Roosevelt*, 7: 513.

[50] HC, *Marcus Alonzo Hanna: His Life and Work* (New York, 1912), v–vi; Forcey, *Crossroads of Liberalism*, 143. For TR's contribution, see *Hanna*, 311–14.

the papers were either mysteriously lost or destroyed after the completion of the biography, historians can never know how fairly Croly used his bulk of contemporary opinion, nor can they consider those materials Croly decided not to employ.[51]

In several ways, Croly's *Marcus Alonzo Hanna* was a praiseworthy and useful work. The details of Hanna's life were carefully and completely set forth; Croly's book is still the best place to discover precisely what Hanna's activities were. In addition, the biography brought together dozens of letters and many personal reminiscences of considerable historic interest. Most important, Croly's portrait of Mark Hanna served as a worthwhile and necessary counterbalance to the crude popular view. He convincingly showed that Hanna was not a corrupt, rapacious, power-mad political manipulator. Croly's examination of Hanna's private business affairs, his enlightened policy toward organized labor, and his part in the deliberations of the Senate provided a corrective to the often unfair portrayals of Hanna in the popular press. The Hanna who emerged from Herbert Croly's biography was a long way from the bloated, cynical, unscrupulous "Dollar Mark"; he was, instead, a highly skilled organizer and tactician, scrupulously honest about party funds, and, in some economic policies, far ahead of his time.

Much of Croly's presentation, moreover, was not at all a violation of his principles. Sympathy for the "boss," that political specialist required to carry on the public business, had been an important part of *The Promise of American Life*. Hanna's recognition of the permanency of the trusts and his contention that they were useful institutions, his emphasis on consolidation and efficiency, his willingness to use the federal government as an instrument of economic policy (as in his advocacy of ship-building subsidies to revive that lagging industry), his nationalism, his support for an Isthmian canal—all probably elicited sympathetic reactions from Croly.

If the integrity of the biography was questionable, it was questionable for two reasons. In the first place, Croly's assignment of motivation revealed a dubious double standard. He always explained Hanna's actions as indicating highest idealism, unwavering patriot-

---

[51] Croly offered this account to William Allen White many years later: ". . . the Hanna papers are now destroyed. After the work was done, I had them packed in a box and sent to the late Dan Hanna, accompanied by a letter. Apparently they reached Ravenna, Ohio, during one of his many non-lucid intervals. At all events, I never heard from him about them and the box containing the papers disappeared. Subsequently, when we tried to trace the papers we could not." HC to White, May 24, 1927, William Allen White mss., Library of Congress.

ism, and the firmest sense of right and wrong. Croly seldom suggested that Hanna operated for reasons of personal power, private gain, or the establishment of his own ambition and reputation.[52] On the other hand, he rarely ascribed the same kinds of motivation to Hanna's opponents. Those newspapers or political leaders who opposed Hanna—Joseph B. Foraker, his inveterate enemy in Ohio Republican politics, for example—were often accused of petty jealousy, revenge, shortsightedness, and base personal ambition.

Another indication that Croly's book was less than completely honest was what he decided *not* to write. The most thoughtful and redeeming part of the book was the last chapter. Having carried the story of Hanna's life to its end, Croly devoted the "Conclusion" to some personal observations on Mark Hanna's meaning for America. In those last few pages he attempted to fit Hanna's story into the historical framework of *The Promise of American Life*. He accomplished this with skill and insight. Hanna, argued Croly, was the symbol and the culmination of the pioneer period of American history. "In truth, Mr. Hanna did embody the most vital social and economic tradition in American history—the tradition, that is, of the pioneer. He was an incarnation of the spirit and methods of the men who seized and cleared the public domain, developed its natural resources, started and organized an industrial and commercial system and determined most of our political and social habits and forms. All the salient characteristics of the pioneer are writ clear and large in Mr. Hanna's disposition and achievements."[53] Hanna's flexibility, his easy good-fellowship, his combination of a business with a political career, his determined pursuit of personal wealth—all marked the man as a model of the pioneer mentality. Above all, Croly emphasized, Mark Hanna could see no possible contradiction between the private race for wealth and the best interests of the United States. He "honestly identified and confused individual and social interests, and he was honestly concerned as much for the one as for the other." In short, "Mark Hanna's public career coincided with the culmination of an epoch, and he himself was unquestionably the hero of this culminating moment of a century of American development."[54]

[52] In private, however, HC admitted that Hanna fought for one corrupt official "partly because of loyalty to Rathbone but more because Rathbone was *his* appointee and and [*sic*] *he* had engaged in a fight on R's behalf. It became a matter of personal pride to do everything he could to save R. He did not want to be beaten and he loved any decisive expression of his personal power." HC to Learned Hand, May 21 [1911?], Hand mss.

[53] *Hanna*, 465–66.

[54] Ibid., 477, 473.

But then, mysteriously, Croly stopped the analysis. After brilliantly placing Hanna in the historical context that served as the basis for Croly's overarching political thought, he declined to finish the argument. If Croly believed that the pioneer spirit was the natural and fruitful product of nineteenth-century conditions, he also believed that pioneer individualism had ceased being beneficial in the twentieth century; that, in fact, it had become a pernicious and retrograde obstacle to national regeneration. One finds in *Marcus Alonzo Hanna* no such forthright conclusion. Instead of drawing the obvious moral—that Hanna's type in business and politics had served well but had outlived its usefulness—Croly simply praised the type, acknowledged recent strains in the pioneer system and the emergence of a national debate, and ended the book. Friends of Croly, who knew what the author believed, could hardly escape the conclusion that the writer of *The Promise of American Life* was pulling his punches.

The same man who had advised aspiring architects that it was better to be unsuccessful than to violate artistic integrity, and who had warned his readers not to subscribe wholeheartedly to the insurgent movement lest their integrity be submerged by their enthusiasm—that same man, it seems, was guilty of just such a violation of intellectual honesty. There is no evidence that Croly ever compromised his beliefs so seriously again; more important, there is abundant evidence that he sometimes refused to compromise his beliefs despite the severest and most seductive pressure to do so. Nevertheless, the fact remains that Herbert Croly, for whatever reasons, signed his name in 1912 to a book that was one-sided and colored, that defended a man who would have "stood pat," in Hanna's own proud phrase, against many of the most promising reforms of the progressive movement, and that praised a set of social and economic attitudes the author himself believed to be harmful to modern society.

IV

Inevitably, as his writings unmistakably show, Croly was being drawn into the whirlpool of American politics. While he had always watched political developments closely, his public association with Theodore Roosevelt and the kinds of books and articles he was being called upon to write demanded more attentive observation than ever. But fame and literary responsibilities aside, the years between 1910 and 1914 were alive with gripping political drama. Herbert Croly was not the only young American who was drawn into the whirlpool.

Hundreds of intelligent and articulate men and women were finding themselves fascinated and pulled by the swirl of reform politics.

Walter Lippmann wrote in 1914 that the young man "faces an enormously complicated world, full of stirring and confusion and ferment. He hears of movements and agitations, criticisms and reforms, knows people who are devoted to 'causes,' feels angry or hopeful at different times, goes to meetings, reads radical books, and accumulates a sense of uneasiness and pending change." The arch-conservative humanist, Paul Elmer More, also saw the obsession with politics by 1914. He was sick of the "cry of the demagogue," tired of "the excess of emotional humanitarianism," which agitated society at the expense of more important things. "Let us, in the name of God, put some bounds to the flood of talk about the wages of the bricklayer and the trainman. . . ." To the tiresome slogan of American reform: "The cure for democracy is more democracy," More angrily grumbled, "It is a lie, and we know it is a lie."[55] Lippmann and More made their observations from opposite ends of the political spectrum; it would have been astonishing to find them agreeing about any kind of concrete program. Yet they were both convinced that the nation was preoccupied by causes and campaigns, reforms and elections.

And if Americans were obsessed with politics in the years after 1910, it was no wonder. How often in American history did a major political party disintegrate before your very eyes? The spirit of reform, which had been growing since the turn of the century, had resulted in the election of progressives to Congress in unprecedented numbers. President Taft simply failed to keep up with the progressive wing of his party. On the one hand, their demands, growing out of an increased strength and an increased public pressure, seemed to be carrying the country farther and faster than Taft was willing to go. On the other hand, the progressives were dismayed and angered by the posture of Taft and the conservatives in the party in such colorful public fights as those over tariff, the re-election of Speaker Joseph G. Cannon, and the Pinchot-Ballinger conservation controversy. By the end of 1910, the two wings of the Republican party seemed less and less able to cooperate within the same political institution.

Like everyone else, Herbert Croly watched developments. Before

[55] Lippmann, *Drift and Mastery: An Attempt to Diagnose the Current Unrest* (New York, 1914), 17; Paul Elmer More, "Natural Aristocracy," *Unpopular Review*, 1 (April–June, 1914): 272–97, reprinted in More, *Democracy and Justice* (Boston, 1915), 3–38.

the midterm elections of 1910, elections which exposed unmistakably the division in the Republican party, Croly reported to Hand, "All the reformers think that Taft has nailed down his own coffin by vetoing the Woolen Bill. . . . I don't suppose that he is sure Republicans can be saved by any tactics they adopt—and I don't much regret it. We are going to have some troubled years. Let the Democrats carry the load. They are as much at sea as the Republicans about every subject of national legislation. . . ."[56] Six weeks later he repeated, "It is all going to be an awful mess for the next few years, but inasmuch as the Republicans have split, the Democrats . . . are entitled to their innings. Let us see what they can do. It is wholly improbable that they will be able to pull together towards any good purpose but they may do better than we think. . . . Uncle Mark [Hanna] was a wise old boy. He said in 1902 that if the Republican party tried to revise the tariff, it would immediately be torn to pieces."[57]

Roosevelt, meanwhile, was openly in conflict with the party's conservatives and with his former friend, the president. From the outset of the Republican division, Croly (like thousands of other Americans) approached the unfolding drama asking a single question: How would the trouble within the party affect the prospects of Theodore Roosevelt? Although the ex-president had not caused the split (it would have happened, thought Croly, "even if Roosevelt had never returned from Africa"), it was conceivable that he might benefit from it. "Undoubtedly he may come back," Croly ventured, "but he will have a weary road to travel, and it seems to call for qualities of patience and forbearance which he does not possess. . . . It would have been a wonderful opportunity for T. R. if he were returned now with his prestige undiminished, and if he had the quality which I always credited him with possessing, of being able to unite right-minded and disinterested people on programs of national reform."[58] Three weeks later: "The more I watch the effect of T.R. on different classes of men, the more it looks to me as if his peculiar influence was really trembling in the balance. He has to go about things differently and if I get a chance I shall tell him so. *Me Big Injun.*"[59]

While Roosevelt's personal influence was "trembling in the balance," his most promising pocket of support in the party seemed determined to make fools of themselves. As far as Croly was concerned the midwestern Insurgents' stand on the reciprocity treaty with

[56] HC to Learned Hand, September 2, 1910, Hand mss.
[57] HC to Learned Hand, October 20, 1910, Hand mss.
[58] Ibid.
[59] HC to Learned Hand, November 4, 1910, Hand mss.

Canada was dreadful. After clamoring for tariff reform, they had disgraced themselves by refusing to accept a reduction that affected the agricultural products of their own region. Croly thought Taft's tariff message was "magnificent." "He has landed one right on the neck of the Insurgents—as I suppose he intended to do. It shows what kind of tariff reformers they are when the interests of their own locality are affected. They have [been] making me sick." And if their stand on reciprocity was bad, their incessant agitation for more direct democracy was worse. "Nothing but more elections—as if the machinery of elections had not already broken down from overwork." The Insurgents—Herbert Croly solemnly pronounced his ultimate condemnation—the Insurgents represented "simply a new ebullition of the old Jeffersonian spirit." Learned Hand commiserated: "They have about as much sense of what you are after," he consoled the author of *The Promise of American Life*, ". . . as they have of Neo-Cartesianism. . . . Some of them must be disgusting whelps."[60]

Throughout 1911 the political situation boiled. The split in the Republican party widened even further, and Hand and Croly continued to wonder whether or not anything good would come to Theodore Roosevelt. "Every month reassures me of the Colonel's position," Hand wrote. "No one, I think, in the country, has anything like the real breadth of vision that he has; no one the foresight, granting his violence, and his lying, his personal untrustworthiness, he is today the best patriot we have. It seems to me incredible that in the situation which the next ten years will bring us, he should not again come to the front. I believe he will, provided he lives and does not go crazy. It is a pity that the precious liquor is all in one chalice."[61] As 1911 flowed into 1912 and attention focused on the presidential election, the overwhelming question became whether or not the violent, lying, untrustworthy "chalice" would have a try at the nomination.

Croly's relation to the Colonel continued to be loyal and warm. There were at least occasional meetings between the two, and at one of them, Roosevelt apparently admitted to more than a casual interest in the approaching election. On January 9, one of Hand's informants hinted that "Roosevelt had said that he would run but was not a candidate and did not want it." Croly was more than willing to join in the national guessing game. One of *his* sources, confided that "T.R.

---

[60] HC to Learned Hand, February 3, 1911; and Hand to HC, February 6, 1911, both in the Hand mss.

[61] Learned Hand to HC, February 6, 1911, Hand mss.

had consented" and was actively working for the nomination. "Of course he may have exaggerated," Croly cautioned. "T.R. may be seeing local leaders merely in order to size up his situation, but with the intention of quitting in case it does not look good enough. Or he may as usual be deceiving himself. That he will run appears inevitable to me—unless some very stout resistance develops. I don't like it but if he does run, a good strong argument can be made on his behalf." Ten days later Hand agreed: "It looks to me as though the Colonel certainly was the Man of Destiny now. It is quite strange that the President seems incapable of developing any strength."[62]

Roosevelt ended the game on February 22, 1912, by announcing that he was, indeed, a candidate for the presidency of the United States. "I am glad that it has become an open fight," Croly wrote Roosevelt, "and I am glad of the opportunity of wearing a Roosevelt button."[63] Prior to the Republican convention both Hand and Croly were requested to submit planks for the party platform. Hand wrote a few, but Croly declined on the grounds that the planks already written contained "about as much sound doctrine as the 'progressive' following would stand."[64]

The wild scenes at the Republican convention in June no doubt amazed Croly as much as they amazed everyone else. Everybody knew that the progressives supported the Colonel while the conservatives were anxious to renominate Taft. But the bitter fight over contested convention seats and the bolt of Roosevelt and his followers were probably more than even the most optimistic Democrat could have dreamed. American politics had exploded, and when the air cleared there were three major candidates—the Republican Taft, the Democrat Wilson, and the Bull-Mooser, Theodore Roosevelt. There was no question about where Herbert Croly's loyalties were to be found. By mid-July he was convinced that his vision of a national democracy might become a reality:

> There would have been more justification in voting for Wilson— in case Roosevelt had been the regular Republican nominee. But a third party even under the existing somewhat dubious conditions certainly contains more promise for future good government than any recent movement in American politics. You will

[62] Learned Hand to HC, January 9, 1912; HC to Hand, January 12, 1912; Hand to HC, January 24, 1912, all in the Hand mss.

[63] HC to Theodore Roosevelt, February 28, 1912, Theodore Roosevelt mss., Library of Congress.

[64] HC to Learned Hand, June 17, 1912, Hand mss.

find it driven by the logic of its own work and situation toward nationalism. George [Rublee] said that at one of the Chicago conferences the idea of calling it the "National" party without any "Progressive" was strongly supported. Its membership contains for the most part the most forceful ingredients in American political opinion. It contains the men who want to do something and who are willing to use the agency of the government for the realization of their program. A Democracy chiefly of Southerners will be full of scruples and you will find the Democrats gradually pushed into a dogmatic states' rights position—which in the course of time will enable the new party to obtain recruits from the Democracy.[65]

During the campaign the relation between Croly and Roosevelt grew closer than ever. Croly, Hand, and George Rublee worked enthusiastically on the new platform in late July.[66] In one conversation in the same week, Roosevelt intimated that if ever a biography were to be written, he wanted Croly to undertake the task. "Ever since last Tuesday I have been preoccupied by the subject of our conversation," an enthusiastic Croly wrote the candidate. "The confidence in me implied by your suggestion has touched me very deeply, and no matter what comes of it, the sense of loyalty to you already established by your past kindness has been intensified." Evidently, however, Croly had read more into the conversation than Roosevelt had intended. "I am both pleased and surprised at your letter," the Colonel replied. "I had not supposed you would pay any attention to the half-jesting remark I made, but if ever there should be a biography of me there is no one whom I should so like to have write it as you, because I think you understand, as no other literary man does, the kind of things I am striving for in politics. . . . When this campaign is over I hope to have the chance really to visit with you."[67]

Croly made two concrete contributions to the campaign. First, he assigned himself the task of answering Louis D. Brandeis and Wilson on the question of the trusts. Wilson had discovered the issue halfway through the campaign, and under Brandeis's instruction, moved to a powerful and persuasive position. The Democratic party, Wilson repeated again and again in September and October, favored a resto-

[65] HC to Learned Hand, July 13, 1912, Hand mss.

[66] Learned Hand to Felix Frankfurter, July 25, 1912, Frankfurter mss., Library of Congress.

[67] HC to Theodore Roosevelt, July 26, 1912, Roosevelt mss.; Theodore Roosevelt to HC, July 30, 1912, in E. E. Morison, ed., *Letters of Theodore Roosevelt*, 7: 582.

ration of free competition; the new party of Theodore Roosevelt, he charged, was willing to countenance monopoly on the one hand and gigantic government on the other. Wilson and Brandeis availed themselves of a long, honorable tradition of defending the "little man," and they could employ an emotionally powerful rhetoric of equal rights and equality of opportunity. More important, Wilson's campaign was maneuvering Roosevelt into the uncomfortable posture of being the defender of big business, a posture not calculated to win votes.[68]

In the middle of September, Learned Hand informed Frankfurter from Cornish, "I am up here for two or three weeks visiting Croly. . . . We are each independently trying to say something about the trust plank to meet Brandeis's effort to throw us into the camp of the monopolists. Without in the least meaning to question their good faith, I thoroly believe they are falsifying the actual issue, which is a thoroly good one and upon which we are in our proper position and they in theirs." Frankfurter wrote back, "It is good news that you and Croly are working on the trust phase of the campaign. Brandeis, in my opinion, has given, with his wonted power, a very unfair slant to the Progressive position on that issue."[69]

The line which Croly's refutation of Brandeis took had been hammered out in detail long before the 1912 campaign. By the time of the publication of *The Promise of American Life*, Croly's views on the trusts were solidly formulated, and he was not particularly tolerant of heresy. As late as December 1911, for example, Hand had broached the topic. "I suppose that you have read Brandeis's speech to the Senate Committee," he wrote Croly. "That presents very forcibly a

[68] The best statement of the Democratic position on the trust question is Brandeis's confidential memorandum to Wilson, September 30, 1912, published in Melvin I. Urofsky and David W. Levy, eds., *The Letters of Louis D. Brandeis* (Albany, 1971–1978), 2: 686–94. See also Alpheus T. Mason, *Brandeis: A Free Man's Life* (New York, 1956 edition), ch. xxiv; Melvin I. Urofsky, "Wilson, Brandeis and the Trust Issue, 1912–1914," *Mid-America*, 49 (January, 1967): 3–28; William Diamond, *The Economic Thought of Woodrow Wilson* (Baltimore, 1943); or Arthur S. Link et al., *The Papers of Woodrow Wilson* (Princeton, 1978), vol. 25.

[69] Learned Hand to Felix Frankfurter, September 12, 1912; Frankfurter to Hand, September 23, 1912, both in the Frankfurter mss. Brandeis had unleashed a furious attack in a series of articles and interviews. See "Trusts, Efficiency, and the New Party," *Collier's Weekly*, 49 (September 14, 1912): 14–15, or "Trusts, the Export Trade and the New Party," ibid., 50 (September 21, 1912): 10–11. Both were reprinted in *Business—A Profession* (Boston, 1914). It is worth pointing out that Frankfurter, who would be instrumental in bringing HC and Brandeis together after the 1912 campaign, was not yet the inseparable companion and daily correspondent of Brandeis that he later became. At this point, Frankfurter was more closely attached to HC than to Brandeis, but this would soon change.

point of view which is growing in importance in my judgment."
After explaining why he personally found Brandeis's system of pro-
hibitive regulation attractive, he hastened to apologize, lest Croly
suspect his orthodoxy: "Do not on this account think me any the
less of a sound Hamiltonian. I am such in so far as I think that the
community should recognize its responsibility; I am not such in so
far as recognition of that responsibility necessarily involves the assumption of the function by the community itself. As a practical
prima facie rule of presumption I am for the slogan, 'the less regulation the better.' "[70] Unsatisfied by Hand's brand of Hamiltonianism, Croly clarified the doctrine:

> I cannot agree with you about Brandeis. In declaring that large
> scale production has no economic advantages he has the consen-
> sus of expert opinion against him. It has proved its value in
> certain industries, and it has consequently earned its right to fair
> treatment. What Brandeis proposes to do is to prejudge the issue
> of the conflict between large scale & small scale production and
> to discriminate against the former. That is not a wise course &
> it may not be a possible course. But whether possible or not, it
> will demand just as much regulation & interference by the Gov-
> ernment as would a policy of recognizing the economic desira-
> bility of large industrial units. If there is economy in large scale
> production, you can stop business men from taking advantage
> of it only by drastic supervision. . . . In either event some kind
> of administrative influence appears to be necessary. The proper
> course is to let large scale & small scale production fight it out.
> The question is not yet settled how far and in what industries
> each is more efficient, and it should not be pre-judged.[71]

The quarrel between Brandeis and Croly—acted out on the stage
of national politics by Woodrow Wilson and Theodore Roosevelt—
proceeded at two levels. Most simply, they disagreed about what
kind of business was most efficient.[72] Croly was unfair in deciding
that Brandeis had "prejudged" the question, for the Boston lawyer

[70] Learned Hand to HC, December 15, 1911, Hand mss. Hand was referring to
Brandeis's testimony before the Senate Committee on Interstate Commerce, 62nd
Congress, 2nd Session, *Hearings on Control of Corporations, Persons, and Firms Engaged
in Interstate Commerce*, 1 (Pt. 16), 1146–1291 (December 14–16, 1911).

[71] HC to Learned Hand, December 19, 1911, Hand mss.

[72] For the extent to which "efficiency" became a catch phrase of the progressive era,
to which all public advocates had to appeal, see Samuel Haber, *Efficiency and Uplift.
Scientific Management and the Progressive Era, 1890–1920* (Chicago, 1964). Haber gives
special attention to the views of both Brandeis (whom he correctly acknowledges to
be a leading popularizer of the efficiency movement) and HC.

could have shown that his conclusion was based on the meticulous study of several large industries—notably railroading, shoe manufacture, insurance, steel and banking. There could be no doubt that Brandeis's efforts in learning the day-to-day operations of big business surpassed Croly's. On the other hand, Croly concluded that the drive toward consolidation (a drive Brandeis explained as a desire to control the market and fix prices) was impressive proof that efficiencies were to be gained by large-scale economic operations; businessmen, he believed, pursued efficiency with the same passion as they pursued other means for lowering their operating costs, and the fact that they were so willing to move to bigness, showed where efficient management could be found.

At bottom, however, the dispute between Brandeis and Croly was a quarrel over values. Brandeis's program was designed to preserve economic democracy, that free-swinging competition between relative equals, which, Brandeis thought, had contributed so much to American prosperity and vitality. Croly, on the other hand, was convinced, not only that the Brandeis scheme was naïve, nostalgic, and perhaps (in view of the Comtean natural law which seemed to be operating) impossible, but that it exalted a kind of competitive individualism, which was both dangerous to the nation and degrading to those caught up in an ethic of struggle and greed. The real threat to American society, Croly argued, was not efficient, large-scale production, but precisely that sort of ruthless, demeaning, unscrupulous economic warfare that Wilson and Brandeis were trying so hard to re-establish.

Neither Hand, Frankfurter, nor Croly, however, felt any personal enmity toward Brandeis. Long before 1912, the Boston reformer had clearly demonstrated his commitment to progressive legislation; Brandeis shared a great many of Croly's goals and, perhaps most important, saw many of the same dangers that Croly saw. The speed with which Croly and Brandeis forgot the doctrinal differences of 1912[73]—the sincerity with which Croly entered the fight for Bran-

---

[73] As early as December 13, 1913, HC wrote to Hand: "I have seen a good deal of Brandeis during the last few weeks, and have acquired an enormous respect for his ability. He is above all a realist with a comprehensive and thorough understanding of certain concrete questions. But so far as I can make out his mind lacks breadth and power of generalizations. He instinctively does not attach much importance to general ideas or to anything but the needs of the immediate situation. He would make a wonderful administrator and it is an enormous pity that he is not in the cabinet." HC to Hand, December 13, 1913, Hand mss.

deis's elevation to the Supreme Court,[74] and the good will with which Croly urged that Brandeis lead the peace delegation to Paris in 1919—reveals that the breach of 1912 was transient, good-natured, and perhaps exaggerated in the fury of the campaign.

Herbert Croly's second contribution to the campaign was an article in *The American Magazine*. It was called "A Test of Faith in Democracy," and it appeared a few days before the election. The piece was straight campaign progaganda—a last-minute plea that voters cast their ballots for the Bull Moose party: "The very existence of the party is an evidence of faith. Its endurance will constitute a still severer test of faith. Those who lack the faith, let them remain outside; but if a man has seen the light and shared the faith, the National Progressive Party has a right to claim him as its own."[75]

Sufficient numbers of American voters lacked the faith and remained outside, and Woodrow Wilson emerged as the new president. A combination of Wilson's progressivism, stealing votes which the Colonel had counted on getting, and Roosevelt's lack of any "grassroot" political machinery had proved too much to be surmounted in only three months of campaigning. Three weeks after the election Croly dropped a two-line note to Hand: "I am getting down to work again & don't propose to be interrupted until Christmas—unless the country really needs me—which it won't."[76] When Roosevelt offered Croly a position in the Progressive party, Croly politely declined on the grounds of intellectual independence. Roosevelt said he understood: "I am a little ashamed of myself not to have thought of the very considerations you present in your letter. I believe you are right. I believe that your writings will have more weight if you are not an officer of the Progressive Party. Understand me, I think that when the next Presidential campaign comes around, we may very possibly want you on some committee, to show your identification with the movement. . . ."[77]

In January 1913, Croly and his wife moved to Washington, D.C.

---

[74] On the day of the announcement of Brandeis's nomination, HC wrote: "Dear Mr. Brandeis: I have not been so pleased in a great many years over anything connected with the public welfare of the whole country as I have with your appointment to the Supreme Court." So warm was the *NR*'s support of the nomination, throughout the long and bitter confirmation hearing, that Brandeis quipped to HC, "I feel almost as if you and your associates must carry the responsibility." See Urofsky and Levy, eds., *The Letters of Louis D. Brandeis*, 4: 45.

[75] HC, "A Test of Faith in Democracy," *American Magazine*, 75 (November 1912): 21–23.

[76] HC to Learned Hand, November 29, 1912, Hand mss.

[77] Theodore Roosevelt to HC, January 7, 1913, Roosevelt mss.

("Bill Taft's house is over about 200 yards away," he informed Hand); and he settled down to the combined tasks of writing and political observation. He thought Wilson's inaugural address was "fascinating rather than convincing"; but he was heartened by the new president's cabinet choices, particularly Franklin K. Lane in Interior. He was disappointed, as were many progressives in both parties, by the failure to make Brandeis the new attorney general, and he was sure that William Jennings Bryan would be a disaster as secretary of state. "The outlook seems worse than ever to me," he half-jokingly wrote to Hand. "I have a hunch that 1913 is to be a year of riot & bloodshed & sudden death. The Almighty is going to have a little laugh on W. J. B[ryan]. The Mexican business gets worse every day. There is trouble brewing in China and the Lord only knows what will happen in Europe. The only consolation (and it is a damn poor one) it will make us nationalists more necessary."[78]

V

If the years between 1909 and 1914 were exciting for the whole country, they were particularly thrilling for Herbert Croly. He was at the height of his power—alert, alive, and in good health. His work was widely respected. His services were eagerly solicited: to write articles or deliver papers, to prepare planks for the platform of an old party, to serve as an officer for a new one. Alternating between Washington, New York, and Cornish, Croly was always meeting important new people. In addition to his Cornish friends, Platt, Rublee, Littell, Hapgood, and Hand, Herbert Croly came to know a number of Washington luminaries—Henry L. Stimson, Elihu Root, Louis Brandeis, Albert J. Beveridge, William Kent, Felix Frankfurter, the young English diplomat Lord Eustace Percy, and other socially prominent, politically important, artistically interesting men and women.

It was a good time for liberals. Things were humming. What did it matter, ultimately, if your special brand of tariff reform or your special kind of corporation control suffered a temporary setback at the polls? Weren't more Americans interested in progressive reform than ever before? Wasn't it merely a matter of waiting until the sweep of events proved the necessity for your vision of responsible government? Wasn't it just a question of educating Americans to the need, and didn't the fact that four out of every five voters in 1912 cast their

---

[78] HC to Learned Hand, January 28 and February 20, 1913, Hand mss.

ballots for some candidate more sympathetic to social reform than William Howard Taft show that the time was coming soon?

William Allen White probably had it right. In December 1913, he reported the political situation in Kansas to the Colonel. Things looked pretty bad for the Bull Moose party, White wrote; the election of 1914 seemed doubtful. "But it is so much a part of my mind, that I should not be entirely candid with you if I did not tell you how matters look to me. It is really a fine time to be alive; with so much to be done; with such a portentous panorama unfolding in the nation's politics, and with so much strength to work and faith to fire the engine—I am exceedingly happy."[79] White could have been writing for all of them—including Herbert Croly. The years between 1909 and 1914 were vibrant and joyful and exhilarating for them. And they would never be quite so happy about America again.

[79] William Allen White to Theodore Roosevelt, December 8, 1913, White mss.

SIX

Progressive Democracy

AMONG THE honors that came to Herbert Croly as a result of his new importance was an invitation to present the prestigious Godkin lectures at Harvard. Written and delivered in late 1913 and early 1914, the lectures were published as *Progressive Democracy* in October 1914. The book, second only to *The Promise of American Life* in revealing the social and political ideas of its author, was written in a tone of sober conviction and filled with warnings. But it is easy to see in it, despite its tone, the confident optimism so characteristic of the progressive movement.

The central argument of *Progressive Democracy* is straightforward enough. The American people, Croly believed, had entered upon a new age. And while it would have been naïve to name 1912 as the year of abrupt transition, nevertheless, "we have apparently been witnessing during the past year or two the end of one epoch and the beginning of another." The new epoch was marked by progressive ideas, and Croly did not hesitate to call progressivism "the dominant formative influence in American political life."[1] Gradually, since the 1880s, Americans had come to see the need for thorough reform, had come to recognize that they were confronted "not by disconnected abuses, but by a perverted system," had come to understand that halfway measures produced only halfway remedies.[2]

Unfortunately, this awakened and promising spirit had fallen into the hands of Woodrow Wilson. The new president was undoubtedly sincere, Croly insisted, and his version of progressivism had to be recognized as "a high and serious doctrine, which is the outcome of real elevation of purpose and feeling, and which up to date has had on the whole a beneficial effect on public opinion." But Woodrow Wilson was simply no Theodore Roosevelt. Whereas Roosevelt (upon whom Croly lavished the usual praise) fully understood the need for comprehensive reorganization and drastic reform, Wilson lacked the vision: "His version of progressivism, notwithstanding its immediately forward impulse, is scrupulously careful not to be too progres-

---

[1] HC, *Progressive Democracy* (New York, 1914), 1.
[2] Ibid., 10–11.

sive. . . ." It is "either too vague and equivocal to inspire sufficient energy of conviction, or else it is progressivism with its eyes fastened more on the past than on the future."[3]

But vagueness and equivocation would no longer serve. Before long the "acid of progressivism" would disintegrate American political institutions and traditions and force the nation to reconsider what was meant by old classifications like "liberal" and "conservative." "The American democracy is becoming aroused to take a searching look at its own meaning and responsibilities," Croly suggested, and already "a momentous discussion has been started."[4] *Progressive Democracy* was Herbert Croly's attempt to shape the contours of that critical discussion; and it was clear that he saw the debate centering on three crucial areas of American life: the political, the economic, the moral.

I

As befitted a writer of his reputation, Croly devoted most attention to the political crisis in America. That crisis arose, Croly argued, out of one of the deepest and oldest conflicts in American political thought, and in order to give the proper perspective, he embarked upon a historical examination, which eventually occupied more than a quarter of the entire book.

According to Croly's reading of American history, the American experiment in government was launched, in the late eighteenth century, in a divided spirit. On the one hand, the Revolutionary generation made an assertion of popular sovereignty, insisting that the people themselves were "the only source of righteous political authority in the emancipated nation." On the other hand, the same people restricted their own power by means of a "self-denying ordinance."[5] The whole state and federal constitutional system—with its deep suspicion of any authority, its crippling division of powers and restrictive bills of rights—comprised an abdication of popular power at the very moment the American people were asserting their right to exercise it. The exercise of democratic will was "divided, weakened, confined and deprived of integrity and effective responsibility in order that a preëstablished and authoritative Law might be exalted, confirmed and placed beyond the reach of danger."[6] Even

[3] Ibid., 15–18.
[4] Ibid., 26–27.
[5] Ibid., 30–34.
[6] Ibid., 41.

worse, the people were soon persuaded that the constitutional "Word" was eternal wisdom and that to challenge it was heresy. Croly denounced "the kingdom of the Constitution," "the kingdom of the Law," "the monarchy of the Word." But the fact remained that "the American people have been suffering without knowing it from the division of purpose between their democracy and their law."[7] The nation—for a variety of economic and political motives—had consented to the stultification of popular authority. And while there might have been reason to consent to it once, the twentieth century demanded that the people regain their freedom of action.

Throughout *Progressive Democracy* Croly evaluated various political changes—sometimes at length, sometimes briefly. He predicted the weakening of the party system.[8] He summarized the strengths and weaknesses of such "direct democracy" mechanisms as referendum, the initiative and recall; and while he seemed much more favorably disposed to them than he had ever been before, he warned against placing too much reliance on them.[9] He detailed, at considerable length, a possible modernization of state government.[10] He advocated increased authority for federal administrators and new roles for federal commissions.[11] But Croly's specific recommendations were not nearly as important as the general principle: "The character of a nation, like the character of an individual, is wrought not by submissive obedience to the Law, but by the active assertion of the needs and purposes of its own life."[12] Specific reforms, particular versions of the "correct" political arrangement quite aside, progressive democracy could not succeed unless it could free itself from the restricting fetters of Law and rely upon the confident exercise of its own authority.

This crucial question—nothing less than whether the democracy would bravely grasp its destiny or whether it would remain intimidated by an eighteenth-century formulation of political righteousness—outweighed all concrete proposals for changing the system. In addition, that single question served as the best way to distinguish modern conservatives from modern progressives. Conservatives believed that constitutional restraints on the popular will were still required and that without them men would run riot. Progressives be-

[7] Ibid., 158.

[8] Ibid., 343–44.

[9] Ibid., chs. xii and xiii.

[10] Ibid., ch. xiv. Croly borrowed his "visions of a new state" from the plan formulated by the People's Power League of Oregon.

[11] Ibid., ch. xvii.

[12] Ibid., 167.

lieved that while restraints might have been useful in the infancy of the democracy, the time had come to enter into manhood's inheritance—indeed, without the courage to brush aside obstacles and enact the democratic will, America could never overcome the new difficulties.[13]

A large number of those new difficulties, of course, were economic ones; and Croly gave considerable attention to this second crucial area of the American debate. His discussion of economic matters, moreover, bore two distinct similarities to his discussion of political problems. First, he argued that present economic difficulties were incomprehensible apart from their historical background; and second, he once again insisted that particular economic reforms were scarcely as important as the assertion of a general principle.

Throughout the nineteenth century American business and American agriculture, the two chief economic pursuits of the republic, were uneasy allies. The tensions between them were obvious. But both thought that a desirable system was one that left everybody alone to accumulate private property. Under the Jacksonians this goal could be achieved merely by keeping the central government weak and allowing individuals, aided by whatever assistance state and local authorities could provide, to struggle and grasp and, in the process, upbuild the nation.[14] After the Civil War the Republican party united farmers and businessmen into an effective alliance simply by deciding to help both groups exploit American resources. Under the post–Civil War Republicans, therefore, "the economic system of the country was conceived as a vast cooperative productive enterprise, in which the social or the public economic interest was promoted by energetic and promiscuous stimulation of productive agencies in private hands."[15]

This system worked satisfactorily as long as there were enough resources to exploit. By the end of the century, however, the system was disrupted by scarcity, ending the happy harmony between individual greed and social progress.[16] Moreover, the Republican party's success had depended upon "a comprehensive system of special privilege, in the benefits of which all American citizens were supposed to share" (in contrast to the old Jacksonian Democrats, who were foes of any special privileges whatsoever). Scarcity caused not only a rupture between greed and progress, it also caused a rupture in the Republicans' grand alliance. Soon farmers were bitterly com-

---

[13] Ibid., 158–68.
[14] Ibid., 57.
[15] Ibid., 87.
[16] Ibid., 96–97.

plaining that their share of the national spoils was inadequate. The "insurgency" within the Republican party represented the efforts of midwestern politicians to express the discontent of this class and to urge that special privileges be awarded to no person or class. It did not escape Croly's notice that the Insurgents, by rigidly opposing any award of special privileges, constituted merely "a revival of the older Democratic program."[17]

As was the case with his political observations, Croly also punctuated his economic discussion with particular proposals for reform. Wage-earners, a class unrecognized in the early nineteenth century, had become so numerous that specific programs had to be constructed which recognized their needs—insurance against unemployment, sickness, old age, unwholesome conditions of labor, less than adequate wages.[18] Croly discussed unionization and concluded that present unions, while obviously necessary under current conditions, constituted "an inferior kind of emancipation by means of an inferior kind of associated action"[19]—he had higher purposes in mind for labor organizations. He also made a stirring plea for the application of science to industrial productivity; scientific management, despite the unreasoning opposition of many labor leaders, "is coming to be the great critical and regenerative influence in business organization."[20]

But as before, Croly was far more concerned to recommend a general principle than he was to endorse specific reform schemes. That principle was simply that American society must begin to make conscious choices about its economic policies. Talk about abolishing "privileges," Croly thought, was foolish—in a society of scarcity private property itself was a "privilege," and private property will continue to exist for a long time. The old Democrats, "who are firm believers in private property, and yet who insist upon the rules of special privileges for none, are the victims of a flagrant self-contradiction." The old Republicans, who favored special privileges for all, had a more promising program, but they were caught in the "baleful illusion" that privileges could be distributed equally. The new Insurgents merely wanted to take privileges away from the class that now enjoyed them for the benefit of another, more numerous class of farmers and small businessmen who felt beleaguered by giants; but their program of corrective legislation must "not be allowed to impose itself on public opinion as a comprehensive national policy."

[17] Ibid., 107.
[18] Ibid., ch. xviii.
[19] Ibid., 386.
[20] Ibid., 399.

The true progressive, Croly proclaimed, will recognize the inevitability of privilege, but will attempt to make its operation socially useful.[21] Once the nation realized that privilege was here to stay and that the only choice was whether to make decisions about its distribution or to trust innocently in some automatic means of distribution, the way would be cleared for a genuinely progressive economic policy. Such a policy, whatever special reforms were advocated and adopted, would measure its choices against the good of the whole nation. Back when private greed and social progress were in harmony, no such courageous discrimination was required of us; but the time for submitting to the capricious workings of the free marketplace and having everything come out all right, that time has gone forever.

Thus Herbert Croly's economic recommendations were closely related to his political ones. Indeed, the rapid changes in the economic realm, more than any other factor, necessitated changes in the political: "Precisely because the industrial revolution has imparted such an enormously increased momentum and efficiency to the exercise of existing individual and class rights, a corresponding efficiency and momentum must be imparted to the instruments of social policy,— to the active law-making and law-administering functions of society." A better distribution of privilege was the goal; a stronger, more resolute, more efficient central government was to be the tool. "A national economic policy of comprehensive but carefully disciplined privilege demands a strong government as its instrument."[22] And the direction of change, in both the political and economic aspects of American life, was to be the same; away from passive submission to natural law (whether propounded by the Founding Fathers or by Adam Smith) and toward flexibility, experimentation, and the application of real authority in the name of the national interest.

II

For most of the reformers of Croly's generation, stating the case for substantial political and economic changes—as if those changes were proper and sufficient ends in themselves—would have been enough, a satisfactory discharge of the social duties of the reformer. For Croly, however, the argument would never be complete until convincing reasons could be offered for wanting reforms in the first place. To

[21] Ibid., 109–13.
[22] Ibid., 123–24.

what ultimate end, he always asked, was all this furious reform being directed. Croly wrestled bravely with that question and devoted considerable space to it in *Progressive Democracy*. But those other reformers who took the trouble to read all the way through the book must have found the answer imprecise, even a shade mystical.

For Croly, "the common purpose which must determine the activities of a democracy is the enhancement of human life." Indeed, all the political and economic mechanisms in the world were merely tools. The trick was to "convert the necessary mechanism of society into the veritable instruments of its needs; and by the use of these instruments, not merely to accomplish, perhaps, certain useful results, but add to the energy and the wealth of its own life."[23] And the key to the enhancement of American life, the key to adding energy and vitality to the nation was massive, loyal, devoted faith in an ideal of social justice. As Croly surveyed the American scene, he was optimistic about the growth of such an ideal: "The ideal of individual justice is being supplemented by the ideal of social justice," he wrote. Once, social welfare was thought to be secure merely by leaving everyone alone; but "now the tendency is to conceive the social welfare, . . . as an end which must be consciously willed by society and efficiently realized. Society, that is, has become a moral ideal. . . ."[24]

The crucial task, therefore, was to nurture the ideal of social justice, to encourage its continued growth and development, its spread to wider and wider segments of the population. Efforts in that direction Croly called "social education," or "enlightenment." The test of any social mechanism was the extent to which it contributed to this enlightenment.[25] Croly's entire discussion of labor organization, for example, concentrated on its possible service as an educational instrument. Croly envisioned a "new unionism," which would transcend narrow class demands and would "fight and plan for the creation of a new system, based upon the dignity, the responsibility and the moral value of human work." Thus the central task for progressive unionism "consists in the deliberate education of the wage-earners for the position, which they must eventually assume, of being

---

[23] Ibid., 120, 183.

[24] Ibid., 148–49.

[25] Thus, for HC, the federal Constitution was once appropriate because it was "at once authoritative, national and educational. It instructed the American people during their collective childhood" (145–46). Similarly, HC favored state reorganization because it would "promote political education. . . . It must have the chance to be efficient, but only for the purpose of being educational" (283).

responsible . . . for the proper organization and execution of the productive work of society." He offered a plan whereby unions could assist "the process of industrial education" and thereby fulfill their prime responsibility.[26]

Croly suggested some attributes that would stimulate social education and result in the growth of the ideal of social justice. These attributes were self-reinforcing and the determined cultivation of any one of them would inevitably result in the strengthening of them all. One of the chief of these attributes was "faith" in the ability of the people to control their own destiny. "A democracy becomes courageous, progressive and ascendant just in so far as it dares to have faith. . . . Faith in things unseen and unknown is as indispensable to a progessive democracy as it is to an individual Christian. In the absence of such a faith, a democracy must lean, as the American democracy has leaned in the past, upon some specific formulation of a supposedly or temporarily righteous Law; but just in proportion as it has attained faith it can dispense with any such support."[27]

Another quality indispensable to the growth of the social ideal Croly called "will." The monarchy of the law was pernicious precisely because it tried "to bend the living human will to its dictates and demands." But any people that permitted its will—its power to make conscious choices—to be confined, was falling short of its potential vitality. "When the living human will, individual or collective, asserts its own necessary superiority to such dictation, it is always accused of a more or less impious defiance of salutary traditions and experience; but none the less the living human will, if it is to continue to live, must continue to assert itself." Moreover, "the attainment of justice in concrete cases implies the exercise of the will to interpret the law in the interest of justice. . . . It is the will which chooses, insists and dares."[28]

For Croly, the will implied "action"—another requirement for achieving the regenerating and enhancing social ideal—and the willingness to take action implied courage, risk, daring. "A prudential democracy," Croly warned, "would be a democracy without power, without character and without ascendancy." All past experience should testify to the enormity of the risks and the slim chance for consistent success; nevertheless, "changes must be made. Risks must be incurred."[29] In his advice to the "newer unions," for example, Croly

[26] Ibid., 287–90.
[27] Ibid., 168–69.
[28] Ibid., 167–68.
[29] Ibid., 171–73.

promulgated the doctrine of action: "The process of industrial education, like the process of political education, does not, however,
consist primarily in going to school. It consists primarily in active
effort on behalf of an increasing measure of self-government; and the
only form which such effort can take is that of fighting for its attainment."[30]

Croly was too rigorous an intellectual, of course, to permit this
array of social virtues to assume a strident anti-intellectual dimension.
Although advocating "faith" and "will" and "action" had frequently,
in the history of thought, been coupled with suspicion of intellect,
Croly was extremely careful, at virtually every point, to assure his
readers that he harbored no such suspicion. Accurate social knowledge, administrative expertise, political and social scientists of the
highest order would be absolutely required for the realization of any
important social ideal. It was carefully gathered facts that would prevent faith and will and action from becoming blind and dangerous.
Croly emphasized that caution continually, but especially in his advocacy of more responsibility for federal administrative commissions
(staffed by intellectuals) and in his insistence upon the application of
scientific techniques to business practice.

In any case, this far from exact amalgam of social virtues, Croly
thought, would produce a life-enhancing commitment to social justice. It would be wrong to believe that these attributes—faith, will,
action, daring—were very distinct in Herbert Croly's mind. In fact
they were interconnected and interchanged in ways that can only be
called obscure, blurred, mysterious. Croly certainly thought that they
were closely related and that a strong faith would lead to a more
determined will, that vigorous action would lead to ever-increasing
faith, that the exercise of will would strengthen faith and enlighten
and direct action.

In the light of his analysis of the three critical areas of American
life—the political, the economic, and the moral—Croly's introductory condemnation of Wilsonian progressivism took on a special force.
In each of the three realms, Wilson was a bitter disappointment. "Not
a word that President Wilson uttered during or since the campaign
indicated any tendency on his part to substitute for an automatic
competitive economic regime one in which a conscious social purpose, equipped with an adequate technical method, was to play a
decisive part. The 'New Freedom' looks in general like a revival of
Jeffersonian individualism. It proposes to contribute to human amel-

---

[30] Ibid., 390.

ioration chiefly by the negative policy of doing away with discrimination, by expressly disparaging expert contribution to the business of government, by opposing the extension of national responsibility, and by intrusting the future of democracy to the results of cooperation between an individualistic legal system and a fundamentally competitive economic system."[31]

Croly began *Progressive Democracy* with a denunciation of the Wilsonian vision. He ended the book with a four-page vision of his own. It was as close as he had ever come to a euphoric utopian dream. For the rule of live-and-let-live, he suggested, a resolute democracy would substitute the rule of live-and-help-live. From rampant individualism, the society could move to cooperation, mutual assistance, even to brotherly love. "Thus the progressive democratic faith, like the faith of St. Paul, finds its consummation in a love which is partly expressed in sympathetic feeling, but which is at bottom a spiritual expression of the mystical unity of human nature." The day may come when citizens can forget the economic aspect of life, when they can concentrate instead on "an ardent and intelligent cultivation of the essential art of living." Such a society would place a high emphasis upon recreation and playfulness, upon literature and drama; indeed, "it might make every woman into something of a novelist and every man into something of a playwright." This sort of society "would be bathed in eager, good-humored and tireless criticism, and the bath would purify as well as cleanse."[32]

III

Other men, more mindful of propriety than Theodore Roosevelt, might have politely declined to publish a review of a book so loaded with praise for the reviewer. But observing the niceties was never one of the Colonel's chief characteristics, and notwithstanding the fact that he was the book's main political beneficiary and his arch-enemy, President Wilson, its main villain, he plunged ahead. A month after publication, Roosevelt reviewed *Progressive Democracy* together with young Walter Lippmann's new book, *Drift and Mastery*, for *The Outlook*. He was ecstatic: "There are books of which it is impossible to make an epitome, and which therefore it is impossible to review save in the way of calling attention to their excellence," he began. "No man who wishes seriously to study our present social, indus-

[31] Ibid., 16–17.
[32] Ibid., 427–30.

trial, and political life with the view of guiding his thought and action so as to work for National betterment in the future can afford not to read these books through and through and to ponder and digest them."[33]

Other commentators seemed better able to restrain themselves. While the reviews of *Progressive Democracy* were generally quite favorable, they were not nearly so enthusiastic as those written for *The Promise of American Life* five years earlier. Some even found fault. An exceptionally intelligent review in the *New York Times*, published the same week as Roosevelt's effusion, charged that Croly's treatment was "often extremely abstract" and his style "needlessly dry." Henry Jones Ford made a similar complaint in *The American Political Science Review*: "He inspires more than he instructs. There is a lack of concreteness in his proposals; he sets forth ideals, but when it comes to the matter of finding ways and means of realizing them the discussion barely escapes sinking into verbalism and futility." When making fine distinctions, wrote the reviewer for *The Independent*, "he is not seldom hard to follow and occasionally not worth following." Harshest of all was the review in *The Nation*: "But carefully wrought as is the book, it strikes one as essentially a piece of 'closet-philosophy,' built up *a priori*, within four walls, detached and abstract in character rather than actual, concrete, and inductive. It smells of the student-lamp rather than of the streets."[34]

But criticisms like these were always embedded in a context of praise. Most of the reviews were, like Roosevelt's, exceedingly superficial, as if the reviewers had wearied of wrestling with Croly's complex ideas and contented themselves with summarizing two or three of the most obvious arguments in the book.[35] Most of them stayed clear of the mysticism, and concentrated on calling attention to Croly's attack on the Constitution or his introductory comments

[33] Theodore Roosevelt, "Two Noteworthy Books on Democracy," *Outlook*, 108 (November 18, 1914): 648–51.

[34] *New York Times Book Review*, November 22, 1914; *American Political Science Review*, 9 (1915): 409–10; *Independent*, 80 (December 28, 1914): 504; and *Nation*, 100 (April 29, 1915): 469–70.

[35] For some typical reviews of *Progressive Democracy*, see *Cincinnati Enquirer*, November 21, 1914; *Buffalo Express*, November 22, 1914; *Ohio State Journal* (Columbus), November 22, 1914; *New York World*, November 28, 1914; *Brooklyn Daily Eagle*, November 28, 1914; *Detroit Free Press*, December 12, 1914; *Syracuse Post Standard*, December 12, 1914; *Boston Globe*, December 19, 1914; *St. Louis Post Dispatch*, January 5, 1915; *Social Science Bulletin*, January 15, 1915; *Providence Sun Journal*, January 17, 1915; *Des Moines Capital*, March 3, 1915; *Detroit Times*, March 9, 1915; and *Vogue*, April 1, 1915.

on the political history of the preceding ten years. (It was a curious fact that reviews of Croly's first book suffered because many critics read only the last chapter, "Conclusions," while reviews of this book suffered because many read only the first.) In general, that sort of review routinely praised Croly's keen analysis or his spirit of optimism or his thoughtful and objective discussions.

At least three essays on *Progressive Democracy*, however, presented balanced and judicious estimates of the book, their authors exhibiting genuine understanding of Croly's central arguments. J. Salwyn Schapiro, still at the beginning of his distinguished career as a European historian, wrote a perceptive review for *The Political Science Quarterly*. Croly's book, according to Schapiro, was "characterized by fairness, poise, keenness of observation and sympathy with progressive ideas." But Schapiro also took Croly to task for ignoring President Wilson's concrete legislative program—especially the new Federal Trade Commission—as an instance of the very sort of economic nationalism Croly advocated. "Mr. Croly forgets that American statesmen have developed an extraordinary capacity for keeping their philosophy and their practice in two idea-tight compartments."[36] The review in the *New York Times*, while complaining about Croly's abstract writing, offered readers the most acute summary of the book's principal ideas, the subtle ones as well as those that were obvious.[37] It was the review in *The Nation*, however, that best combined balanced judgment, accurate summary, and critical distance. The author of that review was the only one who directly confronted Croly's insistence on the element of "faith" in democracy: "Mr. Croly's structure is nicely compact, entirely logical, . . . All you have to do is to embrace the faith vigorously and the rest is easy. If you can once assume and believe the fundamental dogma that the popular will is inherently good, that it makes necessarily for 'social righteousness,' and that the way to develop it and free it for action is to throw responsibility upon it and challenge it to do its best, then the 'holy city' of 'progressive democracy' is clearly in sight for you. . . . Let him take it who can." The reviewer could not accept it in the end and concluded that the book's "kinship is with the visions of Utopia, that intoxicated men's minds a hundred or more years ago."[38]

Comments from Croly's friends and acquaintances, as one might expect, were generally supportive. Even they, however, harbored

---

[36] *Political Science Quarterly*, 30 (1915): 171–73.

[37] *New York Times Book Review*, November 22, 1914.

[38] *Nation*, 100 (April 29, 1915): 469–70.

reservations. Willard Straight, who was deeply involved with Croly in starting a new journal, thought the book "a corker" and "a marvel." "It's a bigger book than the 'Promise,' more mature and more constructive," he wrote. But he also ventured to suggest that "people won't get it as they did the other. The Promise was specific. You mentioned names. Your vocabulary was familiar. In this work you go to fundamentals and talk the philosophy of it all."[39] Croly also received a long letter from Justice Oliver Wendell Holmes. Naturally, the man who had done so much to advocate flexibility in the law read with "keen pleasure" Croly's attack on the monarchy of the "Word." Holmes also enjoyed the discussions of particular experiments in progressive legislation, and made the usual acknowledgment of the author's candor and thoughtfulness. But the bulk of Holmes's letter was criticism and some of it went to the very heart of Croly's philosophy: "You seem to me to over-emphasize the importance of the particular Club we call nation or State. I am quite ready to agree . . . that personality only realizes itself fully in the group, but I should have thought that now and in the past and I confess that I should have hoped also in the future that the largest part of Man's personality is, has been and will be realized through and in other groups than the State."[40]

Passing time has also failed to enhance the reputation of *Progressive Democracy*. Many of the old reformers remembered the importance of *The Promise of American Life* in helping to create the reform spirit of the age; none of them would ever assign the same importance to *Progressive Democracy*. The friends who memorialized Croly at his death chose to mention the book only in passing, and historians of the progressive era have never discovered in *Progressive Democracy*, as they have in *The Promise of American Life*, a seminal and constructive influence upon the time for which it was written. In short, the book was destined to a cooler reception and a less enduring esteem than the classic work upon which Herbert Croly's reputation as the political philosopher of American liberalism principally rested.

IV

As far as the author himself was concerned, *Progressive Democracy* was a natural outgrowth of *The Promise of American Life*. A few weeks

[39] Willard Straight to HC, March 1 and March 5, 1915, Willard Straight mss., Cornell University.

[40] Oliver Wendell Holmes to HC, November 22, 1914, Autograph File, Houghton Library, Harvard University. Holmes also objected to Croly's view (*PD*, 396) that rent was "appropriation."

after its publication he wrote to Roosevelt: "I hope you will like my book. It carries the argument somewhat further than it was carried in the Promise of American Life, but it remains in my mind only as a supplement thereto. I wish that the two books had been combined into one."[41] In fact, there is considerable justice in Croly's view—the two books had a great many similarities.

Most obviously, they were organized identically. Each opened with a long historical analysis, designed to place recent events in a fresh and useful perspective. Each contained a middle section, which put forward Croly's concrete suggestions for the reorganization of American political and economic life. And both books closed with appeals to higher faiths, better ideals, more thoroughly socialized motives than those that had traditionally moved the American people.

In addition, the opening historical essays are very alike. As might have been expected, numerous historical judgments remained unchanged in *Progressive Democracy*—all the former contentions about the pioneer democrats, the Whigs, the growth of the American economy were repeated. The periodization Croly employed also remained unchanged. In both books, moreover, Croly showed himself to be a sensitive and creative student of the American past. He employed the findings of the best of the contemporary historians and ventured several prophetic interpretations. Both essays, finally, were constructed around the device of discovering a momentous tension running down through American history. In *The Promise of American Life* Croly elaborated the enduring conflict between the political philosophy of Hamilton and that of Jefferson. In *Progressive Democracy* he turned to the enmity between the principle of democratic freedom and the principle of constitutional restraints. In neither essay did Croly disguise his preference, and in both he insisted that for progressivism to win out some resolution of the fundamental conflict in American thought would be required.

Just as there were similarities in his historical approach, there were also similarities in his concrete program. Both works advocated the centralization of functions, rationalized state governments, increased administrative authority, and political "discrimination" in the name of the national interest. Both urged sympathy for labor, steps which would limit the power of lawyers to shape the nation's policies, the use of intellectual, scientific and technical experts, greater efficiency in political and economic undertakings, and a greater role for edu-

[41] HC to Theodore Roosevelt, November 5, 1914, Theodore Roosevelt mss., Library of Congress.

cation. In both books, the great obstacle to achieving a better society was persistent and rampant individualism; in both, the great hope rested in collective national action and a recognition of the spiritual unity of all mankind.

But if the two books were similar in many respects, there were important differences as well. *Progressive Democracy*, for example, offered no advice about foreign policy comparable to the lengthy discussion in *The Promise of American Life*; nor did Croly indulge himself in elaborate comparisons between American and European conditions as he had done in the earlier book. In addition, *Progressive Democracy* was more enthusiastic about the mechanisms of direct democracy; it also assigned a more crucial role to organized labor and a less crucial one to a sensitive élite of heroes and saints. There was less deference to the political boss and to heads of corporations than before, and more respect was given to the potential of the everyday citizen. In these and in other ways, *Progressive Democracy* was not merely a rephrasing of *The Promise of American Life*—it was a distinct book and it revealed the continued growth of its author.

The direction and the source of these modifications and changes, moreover, are not difficult to detect. The influence of American pragmatism upon the writing of *Progressive Democracy* was apparent on nearly every page, and it was that influence which imparted to the book its differences in tone and program.[42] Croly quoted John Dewey (without mentioning his name)[43] and borrowed heavily from both William James and Dewey's one-time colleague and collaborator, Albion W. Small, the leading University of Chicago sociologist.[44] Croly did not, in fact, hesitate to use the word itself; democ-

---

[42] On the influence of pragmatism on *PD*, see Charles Forcey, *The Crossroads of Liberalism: Croly, Weyl, Lippmann and the Progressive Era, 1900–1925* (New York, 1961), 155–60; and David Noble, *The Paradox of Progressive Thought* (Minneapolis, 1958), 66–77. For Professor Forcey, who thought that HC's earlier book was shaped by Jamesian pragmatism, the new book "still clung" to that philosophy. For Professor Noble, however, who thought that *PAL* revealed the influence of Hegel, *PD* marked an important turning point in HC's life: HC was transformed "as he came into contact with the writings of American social psychologists, sociologists and philosophers. . . . Sometime in the years between 1909 . . . and 1914 . . . Croly became acquainted with these technical aspects of the American intellectual environment. These ideas formed a leaven which altered his political philosophy so completely that *Progressive Democracy* escaped the limitations of Hegelian authoritarianism." Noble calls this change "the Americanization of Herbert Croly." While differing with both Noble and Forcey in their interpretations of *PAL*, I am in entire accord with their view of the impact of pragmatism on this book.

[43] *PD*, 423.

[44] Croly borrowed the distinction between "the rule of live-and-let-live" and "the

racy in its truest sense, he wrote, "is necessarily . . . allied to pragmatism."[45] But even if he had avoided the word, there could be no doubt about the extent of Croly's debt to the philosophy.

Few ideas, for example, were so deeply ingrained in the writings of the pragmatists as the belief that the great danger to progress in human affairs was adherence to outworn creeds. Old formulations that pretended to eternal Truth were the enemies; they blinded men to the unique problems of an ever-changing environment, and they excused men from the hard thought required to meet new situations. The pragmatists attempted a "revolt against formalism" in many fields, but in each the thrust was the same: in order to survive, thoughtful men must place their trust in their own intelligence not in absolute and unchanging laws.[46] Dewey attributed the new skepticism about inherited truths to Charles Darwin: "In laying hands upon the sacred ark of absolute permanency, in treating the forms that had been regarded as types of fixity and perfection as originating and passing away, the 'Origin of Species' introduced a mode of thinking that in the end was bound to transform the logic of knowledge, and hence the treatment of morals, politics, and religion."[47]

It was no accident that Herbert Croly's discussion of the Constitution was undertaken in exactly these terms. If progressive democracy was to have a chance, Croly argued, Americans must free themselves from the pernicious notion that "the sacred words must be deposited in the ark of the covenant, there to remain inviolate as long as the commonwealth shall endure." In the United States, unfortunately, the fundamental law had received "a peculiarly sacred and exalted character," and what might once have been a useful, living social mechanism had been "transformed into a Higher Law."[48] The movement of American life since the eighteenth century, however, had made the "monarchy of the Word" an obstacle to the resolute confrontation of industrial problems. And "the future of democratic

---

rule of live-and-help-live" (*PD*, 426) from Albion W. Small, *Between Eras From Capitalism to Democracy* (Kansas City, Mo., 1913). On Small, see Vernon K. Dibble, *The Legacy of Albion Small* (Chicago, 1975). There is nothing adequate on the relationship between Small and the pragmatists, but see Darnell Rucker, *The Chicago Pragmatists* (Minneapolis, 1969).

[45] *PD*, 178.

[46] Morton G. White, *Social Thought in America: The Revolt Against Formalism* (New York, 1949).

[47] John Dewey, *The Influence of Darwin on Philosophy and Other Essays in Contemporary Thought* (New York, 1910), 1–2. See also Philip P. Wiener, *Evolution and the Founders of Pragmatism* (Cambridge, Mass., 1949).

[48] *PD*, 35–37.

progressivism depends upon . . . the emancipation of the democracy from continued allegiance to any specific formulation of the Law, and its increasing ability to act upon its collective purposes."[49] Allegiance to the constitutional system did more than stultify action, it also crippled creative intelligence: reliance on an eighteenth-century authority "not only enfeebled the power of collective action . . . but it also enfeebled its power of thought. The American democracy could not think candidly, sincerely and vigorously, because its thinking, like its action, was circumscribed by the supposed authority of a system of rules."[50]

A related characteristic of pragmatic social thought was the faith in experimentation, flexibility, and the fearless manipulation of alternatives in the service of human amelioration. Ideas, in John Dewey's terminology, were instruments; they were designed to accomplish purposes and destined to be discarded if their consequences were not beneficial.[51] This naturally imparted to any new proposal a tentative, impermanent, experimental quality. The pragmatists, busy rebelling against antiquated creeds, were determined to avoid erecting an orthodoxy of their own.

Those critics who were disappointed at Croly's reluctance to provide concrete "solutions" to American problems failed to appreciate his philosophic reluctance to establish a set of orthodox conclusions. At the outset he warned that "the value of the book, so far as it has any, will consist not so much in the attainment of definite conclusions as in the spirit which characterizes the attempt to reach them."[52] He held to that purpose throughout the book and justified it in plainly pragmatic vocabulary: "The establishment of the progressive democratic faith as the primary creative agency of social improvement necessarily gives to any specific formulations of social law a merely temporary and instrumental value. They have their use for a while and under certain conditions. They constitute the tools which the social will must use in order to accomplish certain specific results or to reach a useful temporary understanding of certain social processes."[53] In the past, Americans harbored an illusion of permanent

[49] Ibid., 154.

[50] Ibid., 328–29.

[51] William James, *Pragmatism: A New Name for Some Old Ways of Thinking* (New York, 1907), 212–13. For Dewey's "instrumentalism," see H. S. Thayer, *Meaning and Action: A Critical History of Pragmatism* (Indianapolis, 1968), 169–74; and George Dykhuizen, *The Life and Mind of John Dewey* (Carbondale, Ill., 1973), 129–33.

[52] *PD*, 25.

[53] Ibid., 177–78.

stability, bequeathed to them by "a presumably permanent body of constitutional law," but "in the future there will probably be substituted for this permanent body of law a social program which will not make any corresponding pretentions to finality."[54]

Just as Croly borrowed from the pragmatists their suspicion of inherited absolutes and their experimental and instrumental approach to problems, he borrowed other concepts as well. It was not hard to detect in Croly's appeals to faith and to will the influence of his old teacher William James.[55] Similarly, Croly adopted the pragmatists' insistence on the interrelatedness of thought and action. To Croly, as to the pragmatists, thought and action could never be separated— thought was the civilized human response to problematic situations (such as the ones America faced in modern times); but thoughts were plans of action, and it was action that tested the value of thoughts, and all thoughts had to be referred, finally, to the court of experience.[56] Croly therefore approved the rule enunciated by "the wisest of modern educators" that " 'the only way to prepare for social life is to engage in social life.' " Dewey's rule, Croly believed, "applies to society conceived as a school no less than to the school conceived as a society. Men and women will become better citizens by participating in those political and social activities which liberate and intensify the human will."[57]

Nor can any student of modern American thought read Croly's final chapter, significantly entitled "Social Education," without noticing the direct impact of Dewey's ideas on *Progressive Democracy*. The thesis of the chapter was that "whatever else society must do to preserve and promote its own integrity, the creation of an adequate system of educating men and women for disinterested service is a necessary condition both of social amelioration and social conservation. . . ." According to Croly, moreover, the sort of education appropriate to a democracy "must accomplish for the mass of the peo-

---

[54] Ibid., 358.

[55] See, for example, James's famous essays "The Will to Believe" and "The Sentiment of Rationality," both in *The Will to Believe and Other Essays in Popular Philosophy* (New York, 1897). James began the former lecture by describing it as "an essay in justification *of* faith, a defence of our right to adopt a believing attitude in religious matters, in spite of the fact that our merely logical intellect may not have been coerced." Compare to HC's justification of "the creative power of the will, which insists, even though its brother, the reason, cannot ascertain" (*PD*, 424).

[56] Dykhuizen, *Life and Mind of John Dewey*, 82–85. See also H. Heath Bawden, *The Principles of Pragmatism: A Philosophical Interpretation of Experience* (Boston, 1910), chs. v and vi.

[57] *PD*, 423–24.

ple a work of intellectual and moral emancipation similar to that which the traditional system of humane culture has been supposed to accomplish for a minority."[58] Both of these requirements—that education must be democratized and that it must be placed in the service of a society's social purposes—were, of course, fundamental to Dewey's teachings.[59]

Croly's work, then, reveals a considerable debt to the pragmatic philosophers. His condemnation of inherited creeds and his determination to avoid creating a fresh one; his view of ideas as instruments designed to accomplish specific and limited purposes; his reliance on faith and will; his insistence that thought and action were parts of a single process; and his confidence in the possibilities of social education indicate the extent to which he was influenced. The question to consider, however, is the extent to which the new element of pragmatism constituted a rejection of Herbert Croly's bedrock foundation in the positivism of Auguste Comte.

The pragmatists themselves thought they were uprooting positivism and replacing its sterility with a living and fruitful body of ideas. But, in retrospect, it seems clear that they were overestimating their revolt. Like the positivists, they denounced "metaphysics" and praised empiricism. Like the positivists, they placed great faith in "science" and regarded inherited formulations as pernicious.[60] And at those points where the two schools were in strongest agreement, Herbert Croly made his strongest, his most confident points. The Constitution of the United States, for example, could be attacked by a positivist as a prime example of the philosophy of the "metaphysical stage" of political speculation—after all, David Goodman Croly had launched a full attack on it in the 1880s;[61] likewise, exaggerated reverence for the Constitution could be condemned by pragmatists (Charles A. Beard or Oliver Wendell Holmes, for example) as a dangerous in-

---

[58] Ibid., 408, 417.

[59] Although Dewey's monumental *Democracy and Education* would not appear until 1916, he put forward his ideas in dozens of articles and books before 1914. See George E. Axtelle and Joe R. Burnett, "Dewey on Education and Schooling," in Jo Ann Boydston, ed., *Guide to the Works of John Dewey* (Carbondale, Ill., 1970), 257–305; and Arthur G. Wirth, *John Dewey as Educator: His Design for Work in Education (1894–1904)* (New York, 1966).

[60] For the relationship between Comtean positivism and pragmatism, see Ralph Barton Perry, *The Thought and Character of William James* (Boston, 1935), chs. xxvii and xxxi; Thayer, *Meaning and Action*, 328; Dykhuizen, *Life and Mind of John Dewey*, 71; and H. Stuart Hughes, *Consciousness and Society: The Reorientation of European Social Thought, 1890–1930* (New York, 1958).

[61] See above, p. 41.

flexibility, which hampered the national task of dealing with the new industrial environment.[62] Similarly, the reliance on administrative and scientific expertise and the faith in thoroughgoing education could be applauded with equal conviction by an adherent of Auguste Comte or an adherent of John Dewey.

Yet there were obvious differences between the positivists and the pragmatists, and in at least two matters Croly abandoned the faith of his father. There was no credence given, in *Progressive Democracy*, to the orderly and inevitable laws of development that Comte had promulgated. Indeed, Croly went out of his way to compose a brief attack upon such laws, and it is possible to detect in that paragraph a significant movement in his intellectual life. "The brand of intellectualism which sought to prescribe authoritative or necessary forms of social behavior," Croly announced, "was never really reasonable. It consisted in an attempt to impose permanent rules and laws upon a social process which was too complicated and too wilful to submit to any such dictation." When Karl Marx made the laws specific, social development had a way of falsifying them. And "whenever they were made extremely vague, as they were by the earlier sociologists, their very generality and vagueness deprived them of significance and fertility."[63] Croly never specified which "earlier sociologists" he had in mind, but probably it was just as well that David Goodman Croly was not alive to read that paragraph.

Another way in which the pragmatic element in *Progressive Democracy* signalled a partial rejection of Comtean positivism was in the triumphantly democratic tone of the entire book. Gone was the appeal to a few, sensitive, idealistic Americans to provide moral examples for their backward countrymen. That message of the final chapter of *The Promise of American Life* was replaced by a ringing vindication of the ability of all citizens to weigh alternatives, decide wisely, and shape the nation's future. Thus it was entirely appropriate that this book should have placed much more confidence in the mechanisms of direct democracy than had the earlier one. In 1909, Croly had believed that the central tension in American life was between a commitment to democracy and a commitment to nationalism (symbolized by the figures of Jefferson and Hamilton). In 1909,

---

[62] Richard Hofstadter, "Charles Beard and the Constitution," in Howard K. Beale, ed., *Charles A. Beard: An Appraisal* (Lexington, 1954), 75–92; Felix Frankfurter, *Mr. Justice Holmes and the Constitution: A Review of His Twenty-Five Years on the Supreme Court* (Cambridge, Mass., 1927). See also Morton White, *The Revolt Against Formalism*, ch. viii.

[63] *PD*, 178.

the future success of the United States depended upon a vigorous assertion of nationalism and a redefinition of democracy to give it national purpose and scope. In 1914, Croly argued that the central tension was between a commitment to the democratic impulse and a commitment to a restricting and oppressive Law. In 1914, success depended upon freeing democracy from the chains that bound it.

Thus the impact of pragmatism upon *Progressive Democracy* was in the direction of providing a larger field for human freedom. Like William James and John Dewey, two of the most eloquent proponents of democratic freedom in modern times, Croly too had come to believe that men must be free if they are to solve their problems.[64] To whatever extent Auguste Comte seemed to restrict men's sense of possibility—whether through iron laws of social development or through passive reliance on an artistocracy of heroes and saints—to that extent (but, it is important to remember, only to that extent) Comte's social teachings, like his strictly religious ones before, had to be left behind.

V

Herbert Croly was astute enough to recognize that the argument of his book depended on a view of human nature. Free people from legal restraints, he had contended, and they will be worthy of the trust. Even in *The Promise of American Life* he had acknowledged that any theory of democracy rested on a belief in human potentiality; but in that book, Americans would still be regulated by their allegiance to a national ideal, which would effectively encourage some behavior and discourage other. In *Progressive Democracy* that sort of qualification had largely disappeared. The democratic society he was advocating, Croly was frank to state, "assumes the ability of the human will, both in its individual and its collective aspects, to make an effective contribution to the work of fulfilment. It assumes the ability of the human intelligence to frame temporary programs which will provide a sufficient foundation for significant and fruitful action."[65] In short, "Democracy must risk its success on the integrity of human nature."[66]

For Croly, therefore, the critical difference between a modern con-

[64] Merle Curti, *The Social Ideas of American Educators* (New York, 1935), chs. xiii and xv; Henry Steele Commager, *The American Mind: An Interpretation of American Thought and Character Since the 1880* (New Haven, 1950), ch. v.

[65] *PD*, 378.

[66] Ibid., 27.

servative and a modern progressive was the difference in how each perceived human beings. Conservatives feared an unrestrained human impulse and could be counted on to oppose any weakening of constitutional or other restrictions. Progressives had outgrown that timidity. Croly acknowledged the possibility that the conservatives might be correct; but in a passage that was to be significant for his later mental development, he recoiled from the implications:

> Of course, if human nature is so essentially erring that it will certainly go astray unless it continues to be personally conducted along the highroad to civilization, then the Law and the schoolmaster constitute our only hope of salvation; but in that case the less said about the character of the American people the better. A political system based upon such a conception of human nature would imply an essential and permanent lack of character on the part of its beneficiaries.[67]

The reason for Croly's optimism about human nature, the reason why the pragmatic faith in freedom sounded such a sympathetic note is not hard to guess. Everywhere they looked, in 1914, men of Herbert Croly's persuasion were convinced that the American people were performing with astonishing nobility. The election of Wilson had been followed by a flood of progressive legislation, and while one might choose to quarrel with Wilson's doctrine, one could scarcely object to the thrust of his program. Progressivism in Washington, D.C., moreover, was being echoed in dozens of states and hundreds of cities and towns all over the country. The people were every day vindicating the faith upon which democracy rested and quieting the doubts about whether humanity would be worthy of its freedom.

Unfortunately for Croly, and for the others too, they were being exhilarated and assured and emboldened by what Robert H. Wiebe has called "the illusion of fulfillment."[68] Between the time that Croly submitted his manuscript to Macmillan and its appearance in October, 1914, Archduke Francis Ferdinand had announced plans for a visit to Sarajevo. Some very serious trouble ensued. It was exactly the sort of trouble, moreover, calculated to throw into gravest doubt the assumptions about human nature upon which so much of progressivism rested. Many progressives, Croly among them, were furnished with unmistakable evidence that the human beings who were

---

[67] Ibid., 170.

[68] Robert H. Wiebe, *The Search for Order, 1877–1920* (New York, 1967), ch. viii. See also Eric F. Goldman, *Rendezvous with Destiny: A History of Modern American Reform* (New York, 1952), ch. x.

capable of making "an effective contribution to the work of fulfilment," were also ready to exhibit incredible destructiveness, mindless brutality, and narrow intolerance.

No one could have seen that, of course; and in the meantime there
was, as William Allen White had happily written to Roosevelt, "so
much to be done." At the same time that Croly was seeing his book
safely through to publication, he was busily involved in another project—one that would make his ideas far more influential than either
one of his books of political philosophy.

1. Herbert Croly
(1869–1930)

2. Jane Cunningham Croly
(1829–1901)

3. David Goodman Croly
(1829–1889)

4. Learned Hand (1872–1961)

5. Felix Frankfurter
(1882–1965)

6. Willard and Dorothy Straight

7. Walter Lippmann
(1889–1974)

8. Walter Weyl
(1873–1919)

9. Francis Hackett
(1883–1962)

10. Randolph Bourne
(1886–1918)

11. Edmund Wilson
(1895–1972)

12. Bruce Bliven
(1889–1977)

SEVEN

A Journal of Opinion

WILLARD STRAIGHT'S life was of the sort that inspired boys' stories. His parents, two itinerent science teachers, died before he was eleven, and he was raised by friends of the family in Oswego, New York. After Cornell, he shipped out to China and before long had mastered the language and was an authority on Asian political and economic life. He worked briefly for the Chinese, and during the Russo-Japanese War he became a correspondent for Reuter's. After the war he was with the United States State Department in various Asian posts and, for a short time, in Washington, but he left government service in order to negotiate for railroad concessions in Manchuria on behalf of a group of powerful United States bankers. "He took his orders from the prompting of a lively and versatile imagination," Herbert Croly later wrote. "He could never refrain from deserting the less for the greater adventure."[1] Handsome, energetic, youthful, before he was thirty he had charmed and cultivated E. H. Harriman, Theodore Roosevelt, Elihu Root and Jacob H. Schiff. Soon he was working as J. P. Morgan's expert on Asian affairs.[2]

Willard Straight was a superb example of that special combination of progressive sentiment and imperialist impulse. He had no moral qualms about the economic penetration of the Orient by American capital. Not only did such activity uplift backward peoples, it also vindicated America's sacred mission and spread the blessings of democracy and freedom. For Straight—as for Roosevelt and Croly— the connection between progressivism and imperialism was the ideal

---

[1] HC, *Willard Straight* (New York, 1924), xii.

[2] HC's biography is the best source for the details of Willard Straight's life. The Willard Straight mss. at Cornell University are also rich with revealing diaries and letters. For his career in the Orient, see Louis Graves, "An American in Asia," *Asia* (September, 1920–May, 1921); Charles Vevier, *The United States and China, 1906–1913: A Study of Finance and Diplomacy* (New Brunswick, N.J., 1955); and Helen Dodson Kahn, "Willard D. Straight and the Great Game of Empire," in Frank J. Merli and Theodore A. Wilson, eds., *Makers of American Diplomacy* (New York, 1974), 29–54.

of patriotic nationalism.[3] Insofar as he had systematically thought it through at all, Straight had come to believe that an active and energetic nation had important work to accomplish—both at home and abroad. Perhaps it was inevitable that Willard Straight and Herbert Croly should be drawn to each other.

In the meantime, however, he married a fairy princess. Dorothy Whitney was the youngest daughter of William C. Whitney, a traction magnate, Wall Street financier, and leader of Washington social life during Grover Cleveland's first administration. Miss Whitney was strikingly beautiful. She was also high-spirited, vivacious, and intelligent. At seventeen she inherited a huge fortune and, with it, a sense of guilt, which she attempted to relieve through social work. Active in the Working Women's Trade Union League and in the suffrage movement, Dorothy Whitney considered it her special duty to "keep alive in the privileged members of society the sense of responsibility for those less fortunate than themselves."[4] In September 1911, when he was thirty-one and she was twenty-four, she married the dashing Willard Straight and they went to live out their fairy tale in Peking.

The couple read *The Promise of American Life* while in China, and they were captivated by Croly's message. No doubt the author's fervent assertion of a reawakened nationalism appealed to the Straights. And the book's obvious sympathy with the disadvantaged and its call for the leadership of a new and dedicated élite must also have struck sympathetic chords. Moreover, the extravagant praise of their friend Theodore Roosevelt (perhaps it was even the Colonel himself who had put Croly's book into their hands)[5] indicated to the couple that here was a writer of genuine insight. But what really convinced them—and especially Willard—that Herbert Croly was a major prophet of American life was the writer's comments on foreign policy. Croly's tenth chapter, "A National Foreign Policy," could have been written by young Willard Straight himself. "Americans have claimed and still claim a large degree of national aloofness and independence,"

[3] William E. Leuchtenburg, "Progressivism and Imperialism: The Progressive Movement and American Foreign Policy, 1898–1916," *Mississippi Valley Historical Review*, 39 (1952): 483–504. Leuchtenburg uses both Straight and HC as examples, in this article, to make his point about the connection between the Theodore Roosevelt brand of domestic progressivism and American imperialism.

[4] W. A. Swanberg, *Whitney Father, Whitney Heiress* (New York, 1980). See also her obituary, *New York Times*, December 16, 1968. For her father, see Mark D. Hirsch, *William C. Whitney, Modern Warwick* (New York, 1948).

[5] For evidence that the couple's son, Michael Straight, believed that TR had given "his copy" to the couple, see "A Journal of Opinion, and the Challenge of 1953," *NR*, 118 (March 16, 1953): 50.

Croly had written, "but such a claim could have been better defended several generations ago than it can to-day." Croly had called for "an increasingly complicated group of international ties and duties," and he had explicitly linked the willingness to become involved in world politics to the success of American domestic hopes:

> The American nation, just in so far as it believes in its nationality and is ready to become more of a nation, must assume a more definite and a more responsible place in the international system. It will have an increasingly important and an increasingly specific part to play in the political affairs of the world; and, in spite of 'old-fashioned democratic' scruples and prejudices, the will to play that part for all it is worth will constitute a beneficial and a necessary stimulus to the better realization of the Promise of our domestic life.

Croly had also touched upon China in a way certain to impress Willard Straight. "The future of China raises questions of American foreign policy second only in importance to the establishment of a stable American international organization. . . . During the life of the coming generation there will be brought home clearly to the American people how much it will cost to assert its own essential interests in China." Croly predicted that before it was over the United States would need its colonial outpost in the Philippines, a vastly strengthened Pacific fleet, and a far more serious attitude about Asian diplomacy.[6] Obviously this Croly fellow was a man of considerable vision, and the Straights determined to look him up when they got back home.

They left China forever in the summer of 1912, and after settling in New York City, contacted Croly through his publisher. Straight commissioned Croly to prepare a report "on the kind of social education which would be most fruitful in a democracy."[7] The initial discussion led to a series of meetings, usually at the Straights' Long Island estate. And during one of those encounters, probably at the end of the summer of 1913, the conversation took a turn that changed Croly's career and fixed the remainder of his life.

The conversation centered on Norman Hapgood, Croly's classmate at Harvard and summertime neighbor at Cornish. Hapgood had edited *Collier's Weekly* through most of the campaign of 1912. He had, however, fallen completely under the influence of Louis Bran-

---

[6] HC, *The Promise of American Life* (New York, 1909), 289, 309–10.
[7] HC, *Willard Straight*, 472; Swanberg, *Whitney Father, Whitney Heiress*, 341.

deis, one of his closest friends, and the pages and editorial columns of *Collier's* constituted a continuing denunciation of Roosevelt and an open and unrestrained plea for the election of Woodrow Wilson. In mid-October, shortly after Roosevelt was wounded by a fanatic in Milwaukee, Robert Collier came out personally for his friend Roosevelt, apologized to his readers for the bias in the magazine and summarily fired Hapgood. Within a few months, and with the help of Brandeis and Wilson's friend, Charles R. Crane, Hapgood took over *Harper's Weekly*.[8]

Hapgood, who began the new venture with a private letter to President Wilson ("possibly . . . you may be able to make a suggestion from time to time about desirable points for us to emphasize"),[9] quickly converted *Harper's* into an interpreter and defender of "the New Freedom." By the late summer of 1913, Hapgood was running a series of articles by Brandeis, which were later compiled into the famous *Other People's Money and How the Bankers Use It*. The articles, which ran through January 1914, touched all of Brandeis's most common themes: the evils of large business, the inefficiency of "our financial oligarchy," the dangers of bigness to American democracy. In short, *Harper's Weekly* had become the chief mouthpiece for that very brand of progressive reform that Herbert Croly most detested. No wonder, therefore, that he indulged himself, in front of Dorothy and Willard Straight, in a thorough denunciation of what Hapgood's journal had become.

Dorothy Straight said, "Why don't you get out a weekly yourself, Herbert?" "Where would I find the money?" Croly replied. "I will find it," she answered. Croly, who once told Oswald Villard that he had dreamed of running a weekly magazine of political opinion since the 1890s, was stunned.[10] "It would take a lot of money," he warned. "About a hundred thousand for the first year. The next year should show a smaller deficit and the third year still less. It might take five

---

[8] *New York Times*, October 19 and 20, 1912; *Collier's Weekly*, November 2, 1912; and Melvin I. Urofsky and David W. Levy, eds., *The Letters of Louis D. Brandeis* (Albany, 1971–1978), 2: 704–706, 711–15, 719–20; and 3: 4, 20.

[9] Norman Hapgood to Woodrow Wilson, May 20, 1913, Wilson mss., Library of Congress. Wilson replied on May 22: "You may be sure that I shall not be slow to send you any suggestions, such as you so kindly ask for, that may occur to me. I shall have you very much in mind. . . ." Ibid. See also Wilson to Hapgood, February 4, 1914, ibid.

[10] HC to Oswald G. Villard, October 6, 1915, Villard mss., Houghton Library, Harvard University. In 1911, HC had told Learned Hand that he had an ambition to edit a weekly magazine of opinion. Learned Hand's interview with Charles Forcey, April 14, 1956, in the possession of Forcey.

years to make the paper self-supporting." Dorothy Straight said, "Yes, I understand. It may take longer, much longer. But let's go ahead."[11]

If Croly harbored any serious reservations about the offer, he managed to suppress them. By the end of 1913 he was deep into plans for the new journal. And the first step was to gather together a proper staff.

I

Croly knew enough about himself to understand that, while he could bring valuable training and interests to the new enterprise, his strengths would have to be supplemented by others. From the start, no doubt, he saw himself as the journal's "philosopher," the grand strategist, the elucidator of policy in its largest outlines. The journal's success, however, would require the talents of others experienced in the ways of political journalism, who knew economics and sociology and who possessed greater sensitivity about modern literature. In short, he needed a group of talented writers—men more skilled and graceful with their pens than he was—who could provide expertise in areas where he was weak.

Walter E. Weyl offered at least two of those skills. He was a superbly trained economist, having earned a Ph.D. at the Wharton School under the great Simon N. Patten. And he had, by 1913, been free-lancing around muckrake journalism for more than a decade. On September 27, Weyl opened a letter from Herbert Croly explaining his hopes for the new magazine and asking Weyl to serve as one of the editors. "I am in entire accord," Weyl wrote in his diary. "Meeting to be held with Willard Straight et al about middle of November."[12]

Weyl was forty in 1913, only four years younger than Croly. He

---

[11] This version of the conversation may be found in Alvin S. Johnson, *Pioneer's Progess, An Autobiography* (New York, 1952), 233. Johnson writes: "This was the conversation as Herbert Croly related it to me." But he quickly adds, "I doubt the accuracy of the reporting. Nobody has ever reported a miracle accurately." See also Felix Frankfurter, "Herbert Croly and American Political Opinion," *NR*, 63 (July 16, 1930): 249; Harlan B. Phillips, ed., *Felix Frankfurter Reminisces* (New York, 1960), 91; Bruce Bliven, "The First Forty Years," *NR*, 113 (November 22, 1954): 6; Swanberg, *Whitney Father, Whitney Heiress*, 341–42; and Charles Forcey, *The Crossroads of Liberalism: Croly, Weyl, Lippmann and the Progressive Era, 1900–1925* (New York, 1961), 169–74.

[12] Quoted by Forcey, *Crossroads of Liberalism*, 52. The meeting referred to took place at the Straights' estate on Sunday, November 16, 1913 (Swanberg, *Whitney Father, Whitney Heiress*, 342).

had grown up in a large family and won a scholarship to Wharton in a national competition when he was only seventeen.[13] He turned in an impressive record there and was encouraged by Patten to study in Europe. After three years of study and travel, Weyl returned to America in 1896, finished his degree, and proceeded to drift aimlessly for the next five years. He traveled, worked for the government in the Bureau of Labor Statistics, tried to find himself in the settlement house movement. In 1902, Weyl attached himself to the dramatic and effective leader of the United Mine Workers, John Mitchell; he got deeply involved in the gigantic anthracite strike of that year and for the next three years worked for and with Mitchell on the problems of American labor.

In 1907, Weyl married Bertha Poole and the couple settled in Woodstock, New York, and tried to make ends meet through free-lance writing. By 1913, they had published articles in the most important magazines in the country. He was an acknowledged authority on railroads (his dissertation had been on passenger traffic), and he was also well trained in labor and immigration questions. Weyl was one of those uncommon reformers who did not blanch at statistics. One colleague thought him "by far the best trained economist in the progressive movement," a man who believed that progressivism "could be justified by statistics of the social facts as well as by moral denunciation." His devotion to numerical "probabilities" became the raw material for jokes about him.[14]

Weyl's systematic discussion of American progressivism, *The New Democracy*, appeared in 1912. The book was sophisticated and thoughtful, and it established Weyl as more than a facile magazine reporter and more than a highly competent technical economist. *The Nation*, despite some reservations, called the book "a noteworthy contribution to the literature of 'social unrest,' " and *The Survey* agreed that *The New Democracy* was "still another book which none of us can afford not to read."[15] In its strategy and scope it resembled Croly's own work, and at least one reviewer compared them: "Each gives an illuminated panoramic view of the growth of democracy in America. But, whereas Mr. Croly makes a searching analysis of the

[13] The best discussion of Weyl's life and thought is Forcey, *Crossroads of Liberalism*, 52–87; see also Forcey's introduction to the 1964 edition of *The New Democracy*, vii–xix. A memorial book of personal reminiscences is also valuable: Howard Brubaker, ed., *Walter Weyl: An Appreciation* (n.p., 1922).

[14] Walter Lippmann, "As a New Republic Editor," in Brubaker, ed., *Walter Weyl*, 87, 89–91.

[15] *Nation*, 94 (April 25, 1912): 412; *Survey*, 28 (August 10, 1912): 634.

ideas of liberty and equality . . . , Dr. Weyl adopts the democratic assumptions and narrates how they are gradually receiving new political, social and intellectual expression. . . . He is an expositor, not prophet nor philosopher. He does not unfold a continuous argument; he makes a survey."[16] Nevertheless, there were sufficient affinities between the ideas of the two men to make Weyl an attractive prospect for the new journal.[17]

Like Croly, Walter Weyl had set out to provide guidance to the progressive movement. And, like Croly, he argued that some old traditions would have to be smashed—in particular, the excessive adulation of the "individual" and the excessive worship of the Constitution and the excessive devotion to the untrammeled right to private property. Weyl agreed with Croly that the hope lay in charting a middle course between Adam Smith and Karl Marx, and he agreed that such a direction would require a more active and resolute central government. Weyl thought that the creation of "a social surplus," a level of material prosperity well above subsistence, offered democracy a fair chance of success. If he placed more faith in direct participation by the masses and less reliance on an élite of saints and heroes, Weyl agreed with Croly about trusts, efficiency, consumerism, conservation, and, in general, the labor movement. Weyl was more optimistic than Croly (one reviewer believed he was "almost too secure in his feeling that things will work of themselves toward the desired goal"),[18] and more willing to blame America's ills on a conspiracy of the powerful (*The Nation* thought him "too much obsessed by the spectre of a highly organized, class-conscious, malignant plutocracy poisoning the wells of law and government.").[19] But none could doubt that the two men were committed spokesmen for identical tendencies in American life.

For a statistician and a muckraker, Weyl was a man of unusual gentleness: "I have never known him to hate, or even dislike anyone," his brother wrote. A co-worker on Croly's journal believed that "he had no enemies. He had no, literally no, abiding hatreds." He shared his ideas with anyone who wanted to hear them, and "would make suggestions faster than you could steal them."[20] "He told one

[16] *Independent*, 72 (May 2, 1912): 957.

[17] For a comparison of Weyl's book with Croly's *PAL*, see Forcey, *Crossroads of Liberalism*, 75–87.

[18] Frances F. Bernard in *American Journal of Sociology*, 18 (September 1912): 263.

[19] *Nation*, 94 (April 25, 1912): 412.

[20] Maurice Weyl, "In the Family," in Brubaker, ed., *Walter Weyl*, 9; and Lippmann, "As a New Republic Editor," ibid., 91, 94.

the truth, even the pleasant truth," said another friend. "And he tried to help, as if the world were a place where one had obligations to something besides one's brain."[21] Weyl loved leisurely talk and bad jokes and bad movies. He was pathetically human—regularly resolv-ing to give up smoking or to get more exercise or to learn Latin. And he felt other people's injustices deeply; even far-away suffering touched him intimately and caused him pain. According to a colleague, "he was personally gentle and humble and extraordinarily easy to get on with. He liked to sit near the fire of friendship and kindness. But his mind was incorruptible."[22] A younger economist, who joined Croly's staff soon after the journal began publication, thought Walter Weyl "looked like a saint and fundamentally was one."[23]

No one would ever have talked about Herbert Croly's next prospective editor that way. By the time Walter Lippmann was twenty-six, Theodore Roosevelt could describe him as "on the whole the most brilliant young man of his age in all the United States," and Roosevelt was not alone in that judgment.[24] Lippmann was born in 1889 into a comfortable New York City home. He entered Harvard in 1906 and quickly distinguished himself as one of the brightest students in a class distinguished for its stars. Many knew the story about William James, who had read a review of Lippmann's in *The Crimson* and walked over to the student's room to introduce himself; and about the visiting lecturer Graham Wallas, a pioneering Fabian Socialist, who was so impressed by the young student that he dedicated his next book to him. Lippmann breezed through Harvard's requirements in three years, but decided to stay a fourth as George Santayana's assistant.[25] His classmate, John Reed, who helped Lippmann found the Socialist Club at Harvard, left a famous poetic portrait:

> . . . LIPPMANN,—calm, inscrutable,
> Thinking and writing clearly, soundly, well;
> All snarls of falseness swiftly piercing through.
> His keen mind leaps like lightning to the True;
> His face is almost placid,—but his eye,—

[21] Francis Hackett, "Publicist and Radical," ibid., 101.

[22] Ibid., 106.

[23] Johnson, *Pioneer's Progress*, 234.

[24] Theodore Roosevelt to Romulo S. Naon, January 6, 1915, in Elting E. Morison et al., eds., *The Letters of Theodore Roosevelt* (Cambridge, Mass., 1951–1954), 8: 872.

[25] For Lippmann's early life, see Ronald Steel, *Walter Lippmann and the American Century* (Boston, 1980), chs. i–vi; Forcey, *Crossroads of Liberalism*, 88–118; and William E. Leuchtenburg's introduction to *Drift and Mastery* (Englewood Cliffs, N.J., 1961).

> There is a vision born to prophecy!
> He sits in silence, as one who has said;
> "I waste not living words among the dead!"
> Our all-unchallenged Chief![26]

And if the young man was widely respected for his intellectual power, he was also well known for his ability to write. One class-mate remembered him as "a Manhattan Zeus, steady, massive, impassive, hurling his thunderbolts judiciously among the herds of humankind."[27] Walter Weyl, soon to be working with him on Croly's journal, confided to his diary: "Walter Lippmann is my ideal of a man who writes easily, because he is big and strong and full. He gives the sense of giving merely his overflow. . . . He does not hammer it out; it comes (or seems to come) out automatically by mere gravity."[28]

When Lincoln Steffens went to Cambridge looking for a young reporter to work with him on *Everybody's Magazine*, he asked students and professors for "the ablest mind that could express itself in writing." It was little wonder that everyone agreed on Walter Lippmann. Steffens found him to be "keen, quiet, industrious," a man who "understood the meaning of all that he learned." He brought him to New York, taught him many things about urban politics and magazine journalism, and introduced him around to the older generation of muckrakers and the rising young radicals who gathered at Mabel Dodge's salon in Greenwich Village.[29] In January 1912, Lippmann left *Everybody's* to serve as an assistant to George R. Lunn, newly elected Socialist mayor of Schenectady. The Socialists' victory was thought to be the great opportunity to show how well the party could govern a sizable American city; but the experience was enough to convince Lippmann that he wanted no part of practical politics. He left Schenectady with serious questions about socialism and with a firm determination to devote his life to writing and thinking. By the time he went to talk to Herbert Croly about the new magazine, Lippmann had published one book and finished a second.

A Preface to Politics appeared in 1913. It was an astounding performance for a young man of twenty-three, two years out of college. The *Boston Transcript* called it "in many respects . . . the ablest brief

---

[26] John Reed, *The Day in Bohemia* (New York, 1913), 42.

[27] Edward E. Hunt, quoted in Granville Hicks, *John Reed: The Making of a Revolutionary* (New York, 1936), 48.

[28] Quoted in Forcey, *Crossroads of Liberalism*, 55.

[29] Lincoln Steffens, *The Autobiography of Lincoln Steffens* (New York, 1931), 592–97.

book of its kind published during the last ten years."[30] The book treated various aspects of current political ferment within the context of the latest developments of European thought. Lippmann was trying to respond to Graham Wallas's call for a better understanding of human nature among political analysts,[31] and had immersed himself in Bergson, Sorel, Nietzsche, and above all, in Sigmund Freud. *A Preface to Politics* was Lippmann's bold attempt to force reformers to acknowledge the dark elements of human irrationality—will, impulse, drive, taboo—before they announced grand schemes for the betterment of the world. To Lippmann, for example, the Chicago Vice Commission's report on prostitution was "well meaning but unmeaning" because "what the Commission advocates is . . . repression," the naïvely moralistic commissioners had simply failed to "face the sexual impulse squarely."[32]

His second book, *Drift and Mastery* (1914), was the one which had called forth such unrestrained praise from Roosevelt when he reviewed it jointly with Croly's own *Progessive Democracy*. To young Randolph Bourne (who knew Lippmann slightly through the Intercollegiate Socialist Society), *Drift and Mastery* was "a book one would have given one's soul to have written."[33] The argument of the work was simple: Modern man had to choose between "drift," mindless trust in the huge forces of the world, the fatalist's confidence that everything would, somehow, end well, and "mastery," the "substitution of conscious intention," the brave and willful effort to think and plan and act upon society's problems. Abandoning much of the anti-intellectualism of his first book, Lippmann now insisted that the scientific method, the patient pursuit of facts coupled with a willingness to experiment, offered mankind limitless promise for a better future. That message, of course, was congenial to Herbert Croly; and so were Lippmann's views on labor, democracy, consumers' power, and half a dozen other topics. But it was undoubtedly the way in which Lippmann handled the trust question that persuaded Croly that he had encountered a kindred spirit.

[30] Quoted in Forcey, *Crossroads of Liberalism*, 110.

[31] Graham Wallas, *Human Nature and Politics* (London, 1908).

[32] Lippmann, *A Preface to Politics* (New York, 1913), 124, 135–36. For excellent discussions of the book, see Forcey, *Crossroads of Liberalism*, 109–18; Benjamin F. Wright, *Five Public Philosophies of Walter Lippmann* (Austin, Texas, 1973), 17–25; and Steel, *Walter Lippmann*, 45–49.

[33] Randolph Bourne to Dorothy Teall, June 14, 1915, Bourne mss., Columbia University. For discussions of *Drift and Mastery*, see Forcey, *Crossroads of Liberalism*, 163–69; Wright, *Five Public Philosophies*, 26–37; and Leuchtenburg's introduction to the 1961 edition.

In his eloquent chapter "A Nation of Villagers," Lippmann echoed Croly's views precisely—and, unlike Croly, he expressed those views in sparkling prose:

> If the anti-trust people really grasped the full meaning of what they said, and if they really had the power or the courage to do what they propose, they would be engaged in one of the most destructive agitations that America has known. They would be breaking up the beginning of a collective organization, thwarting the possibility of cooperation, and insisting upon submitting industry to the wasteful, the planless scramble of little profiteers. They would make impossible any deliberate and constructive use of our natural resources, they would thwart any effort to form the great industries into coordinated services, they would preserve commercialism as the undisputed master of our lives, they would lay a premium on the strategy of industrial war— they would, if they could. For these anti-trust people have never seen the possibilities of organized industries. They have seen only the obvious evils, the birthpains, the undisciplined strut of youth, the bad manners, the greed, and the trickery.

"I should not like to answer before a just tribunal," Lippmann wrote, "for the harm done this country in the last twenty-five years by the stupid hostility of the anti-trust laws."

From that perspective, it was a simple step to a devastating denunciation of Woodrow Wilson: "Nowhere in his speeches will you find any sense that it may be possible to organize the fundamental industries on some deliberate plan for national service. He is thinking always about somebody's chance to build up a profitable business. . . ." Wilson's "New Freedom" was nothing more than the desperate attempt of small businessmen to use government against the modern world. To Walter Lippmann it was crass: "I submit that it is an unworthy dream. I submit that the intelligent men of my generation can find a better outlet for their energies than in making themselves masters of little businesses. They have the vast opportunity of introducing order and purpose into the business world, of devising administrative methods by which the great resources of the country can be operated on some thought-out plan." Repeating the central thrust of Croly's treatment of the trust problem, Lippmann concluded that "we don't imagine that the trusts are going to drift naturally into the service of human life. We think they can be made to serve it if the American people compel them." And if the country proved unwilling to assert its will, then "we shall drift along at the mercy of economic forces that we are unable to master."[34]

Uncompromisingly intellectual and strikingly self-confident, Lippmann bore little resemblance to Walter Weyl. He often appeared arrogant, Olympian, prematurely jaded, oddly detached for one so young. He might get into a fight now and then, Mabel Dodge thought, "but he will never lose an eye."[35] John Reed saw it too:

> But were there one
> Who builds a world, and leaves out all the fun,—
> Who dreams a pageant, gorgeous, infinite,
> And then leaves all the color out of it,—Who wants to
> make the human race, and me,
> March to a geometric Q. E. D.—
> Who but must laugh, if such a man there be?
> Who would not weep, if WALTER L. were he?[36]

Early in January 1914, Croly invited Lippmann down to Washington for a few days, and "tested him out all along the line." "He does not know quite as much as he might," Croly reported to Learned Hand, "but he knows a lot and his general sense of values is excellent. He has enough real feeling, conviction, and knowledge to give a certain assurance, almost a certain dignity to his impertinence, and, of course, the ability to get away with impertinence is almost the best quality a political journalist can have." Croly was sold: "I consider him as a gift from Heaven. . . . I don't know where I could find a substitute with so much innocence of conviction united with so much critical versatility."[37]

Besides Weyl and Lippmann, Croly hired three additional editors before the first issue of the new journal appeared. To handle literary matters, Croly chose a gifted and lively Irishman named Francis Hackett. Oliver Wendell Holmes thought Hackett was the only authentic "genius" on Croly's staff, a writer who could "express the inexpressible."[38] A brilliant conversationalist, a superb stylist of sure tastes, Hackett was an invaluable addition. He had come to the United States in 1901, at the age of seventeen, and was soon working for the *Chicago Evening Post* as an editorial writer; in 1909, he took over the paper's *Friday Literary Review* and developed it into what Felix

[34] Walter Lippmann, *Drift and Mastery* (New York, 1914), ch. vii.

[35] Mabel Dodge Luhan, *Movers and Shakers* (New York, 1936), 119.

[36] Reed, *Day in Bohemia*, 42.

[37] HC to Learned Hand, January 5, 1914, Hand mss., Law School Library, Harvard University.

[38] Phillips, ed., *Felix Frankfurter Reminisces*, 92.

Frankfurter regarded as "the best book review page of any in the land."[39] Hackett already enjoyed a national reputation as a literary critic by 1913, but Croly's interest in him was undoubtedly strengthened by his memory of the enthusiastic review of *The Promise of American Life*, which Hackett had written back in 1910. "In the long list of political books," Hackett had said, "his stands out for breadth of vision, sanity of judgment, and inspiration." Late in 1913, Croly journeyed to Chicago to interview him. Even though Hackett was out of the city, Croly met many who testified to his abilities; and when he returned to New York, Croly wrote, offering Hackett a job and letting him name his own salary. Hackett promptly accepted and asked for sixty dollars a week.[40]

The only editor Croly had known before 1913 was Philip Littell. His grandfather had founded *Littell's Living Age* in 1844 and passed that prominent national weekly on to his son. It is unlikely that young Phil ever seriously considered any career outside of literature and journalism. He entered Harvard with Croly in 1886, but did not remember his solitary and silent classmate.[41] Littell's great friend in Cambridge was George Rublee, and, after graduation, he went to work for Rublee's father, the owner of the *Milwaukee Sentinel*. In 1900 he moved to Cornish, a house adjoining Rublee's, and it was there that he and Croly became neighbors, business associates in one or two minor undertakings, and close friends.[42]

Littell tried to write plays in Europe for a while, but discovered that he had no talent for it. He returned to the United States and, in 1910, took a job with the *New York Globe*. Croly hired him to write the only regular column for the new journal, a full page each week (the editors agreed that Littell's column should occupy no more nor less than one full page), and he called it "Books and Things." Writing came hard to Littell and he labored manfully over his 1,134 words each week, consuming pipe tobacco in huge quantities. His writing was elegant and lucid—it reminded Malcolm Cowley of the graceful and flashing conversation that was no longer popular in the modern world.[43] Littell was intensely loyal to Croly, and a man of mild and tolerant spirit who often served as a peacemaker among the others.[44]

---

[39] Ibid., 91.

[40] Francis Hackett, *American Rainbow: Early Reminiscences* (New York, 1971), 286–87.

[41] Philip Littell, "As a Friend," *NR*, 63 (July 16, 1930): 243.

[42] George Rublee, "Oral History," Columbia University Oral History Project, 47–48.

[43] Malcolm Cowley, "Books and People," *NR*, 109 (November 15, 1943): 689.

[44] Forcey, *Crossroads of Liberalism*, 181.

Charlotte Rudyard graduated from Vassar in 1904 and went directly into editorial work. After a short apprenticeship on the *Brooklyn Daily Eagle*, she worked for Harper & Brothers and then became an associate editor of *Harper's Weekly*. Croly put her on the staff (she had copy-edited *The Promise of American Life*) in charge of make-up and technical editing. She was "an exquisite stylist," one co-worker remarked, "but with a fatal disposition to take favorite pedantic expressions out of an editor's living hide."[45]

Business affairs and bookkeeping became the responsibility of Robert Hallowell, who, in 1916, was to marry Charlotte Rudyard. A classmate of Lippmann and John Reed at Harvard, Hallowell was a curious mixture of quiet charm, social idealism, practical business sense and aesthetic sensibility. He was in charge of paying the bills, designing the format, arranging contracts, making collections and selling advertising. And although not given full editorial status, Hallowell also served as the art editor for the magazine. In 1925, he divorced his wife, left the journal, and devoted himself to becoming a painter.[46]

By any standard, the original group that Herbert Croly had taken a full year to gather ("the way a producer of a play looks around and asks for suggestions in filling the roles," Frankfurter thought)[47] was a distinguished one. Willard Straight, for one, was entirely satisfied with Croly's choices: "He has a rattling good staff collected," the young financier wrote to a friend. "In fact, it is by far the best crowd that has been brought together in New York for many a day and I think that we are really going to be able to pull something off."[48]

II

If Croly had been granted his first choice, he would have called the new journal *The Nation*. That name would have succinctly signalled the grand aspirations of the enterprise, and would also have effectively announced Croly's intention to advocate, whenever possible in its pages, the active centralization of American life, the assumption of new responsibilities by the federal government in the pursuit of

[45] Johnson, *Pioneer's Progress*, 234. See also Johnson, "Oral History," Columbia University Oral History Project, 117; and Rudyard's entry in *Who's Who in America, 1950–1951* (New York, 1950).

[46] See Hallowell's own autobiographical sketch in *Harvard College Class of 1910, Twenty-fifth Anniversary Report (Report VII)* (Cambridge, Mass., 1935), 329–32; and the affectionate obituary by Edward E. Hunt in ibid. (*Report VIII* [1940]), 102–107.

[47] Phillips, ed., *Felix Frankfurter Reminisces*, 91.

[48] Willard Straight to Henry P. Fletcher, April 6, 1914, Straight mss.

his well-known vision of genuine, national, progressive democracy. Unfortunately, the name had been taken by E. L. Godkin in 1865. The second choice was *The Republic*, and the editors quickly agreed upon it. Early publicity for the journal and early references to it in private correspondence used that name. But during the summer of 1914 another *Republic* surfaced—an obscure Boston magazine read by followers of John "Honey-Fitz" Fitzgerald—and its editor vigorously protested. Finally, with what Lippmann remembered as "a positive dislike for the suggestion of utopianism," they decided to call it *The New Republic*.[49]

Headquarters were set up in an old and elegant brownstone at 421 West Twenty-first Street, a property owned by Croly and purchased from him by the Straights. The ground floor consisted of a large reception area and a spacious dining room. Croly, Lippmann, and Weyl occupied offices on the second floor, and Hackett and Alvin Johnson on the third. The house was connected by a passageway to the neighboring one at 419, and there Bob Hallowell, together with secretaries and typists, managed the business affairs of *The New Republic*. Croly was a man of exacting tastes—in cigars and coffee, in architecture, furniture and décor. It took a long time to get things to his liking. The same trait accounted for the fact that it took months to decide on the proper format and lettering for *The New Republic*.[50]

One of the first things Croly did was to bring to the offices a couple from the Italian Riviera. They lived in the basement and Lucy, the wife, prepared exquisite daily lunches for the staff, while her husband, Étienne, took care of the property and served the food. All the editors ate together on Tuesday, but at least some of the group were there on any given day. More important, they could invite to lunch whomever they wanted; and before long the lunches at *The New Republic* had become famous for their fine food and their intense, unrestrained, brilliant conversation. Writers, artists, reformers, jurists, statesmen, foreign visitors—anyone with ideas who happened to be in New York City sooner or later turned up for lunch at 421 West Twenty-first Street. "Croly had a marvelous net out for notables," one staff member recalled, "and a genius for drawing out their opinions."[51] Croly supplemented the informal luncheons with

---

[49] Walter Lippmann, "Notes for a Biography," *NR*, 63 (July 16, 1930): 251.

[50] Forcey, *Crossroads of Liberalism*, 184; Phillips, ed., *Felix Frankfurter Reminisces*, 92. The layout of the building and the locations of offices may be reconstructed from a bill for "Repairs and Alterations" in the Dorothy Straight Elmhirst mss., Cornell University (Folder #3725: 12–11).

[51] Johnson, *Pioneer's Progress*, 242–43. There are many descriptions and reminis-

regular dinners, usually twice each month, and then the staff and selected friends of the magazine gathered to hear distinguished speakers present their views and respond to the lively comments of the group.[52]

After careful consideration, the editors agreed to delay publication until after the congressional elections of November 1914. They were fearful that if their first pronouncements were issued shortly before the election, they would promptly be labelled and dismissed as narrow partisans, and make enemies in the process. Instead it seemed more prudent to note the results, summarize them as objectively as possible, and, as Willard Straight put it, "be ready for the fight in 1916."[53] The decision to wait gave the editors months in which to prepare themselves for the work ahead. And there was plenty to do.

There was, for example, the matter of getting people to subscribe. The subsidy from the Straights, of course, relieved much of the pressure in that regard, but from the beginning Croly wanted to make the journal self-supporting. He believed that *The New Republic*'s ability to maintain itself through subscriptions would be the surest measure of its influence. "Within five years I want to make it pay," he wrote his old Harvard friend John Jay Chapman. "That is I want it supported, not by its contributors, its advertisers, or by an opulent angel, but by its readers. It is they who ought to pay for it; and if they don't it will either be our fault or theirs. If I can help it, I don't want it to be our fault. . . . I should suspect the vitality of a publication which would need" an indefinite subsidy.[54] Croly was also

---

cences of the *New Republic* luncheons and of the illustrious men and women who attended them. See, for examples, Francis Hackett, *I Chose Denmark* (New York, 1940), 1–2; Malcolm Cowley, "The Old House in Chelsea," *Carleton Miscellany*, 6 (1965): 40–41; Robert Morss Lovett, *All Our Years* (New York, 1948), 174; George Soule, interview with the author, October 7, 1963, in the possession of the author; Norman Angell, "Oral History," Columbia University Oral History Project, 132; Bruce Bliven, "Oral History," Columbia University Oral History Project. In contrast to Johnson's view that HC had a talent for drawing out his guests, compare Frankfurter's memory: "There were these luncheons, Croly . . . could hardly open his mouth. Somebody else had to do the inciting and the interchanges that keep a dinner table going, if it goes. If it had depended on Croly, there would have been an eternal frost. But he would then take his guests upstairs and talk to them tete-a-tete, and that was a very different story." Phillips, ed., *Felix Frankfurter Reminisces*, 92–93.

[52] HC to Learned Hand, June 29, 1914, January 15 and February 18, 1915, Hand mss.; HC to Henry Stimson, September 24 and October 7, 1915, and April 24, 1916, Stimson mss., Yale University.

[53] Willard Straight to Henry P. Fletcher, April 6, 1914, Straight mss.; Bruce Bliven, "The First Forty Years," 6.

[54] HC to John Jay Chapman, June 21, 1914, Autograph File, Houghton Library,

wise enough to understand that the project he was inaugurating could expect neither large newsstand sales nor significant income from advertisers.

In early August, therefore, the editors prepared a circular to be sent to "a selected list of people who should be antecedently well inclined toward the weekly."[55] The list was gathered by borrowing other promising mailing lists, by having the editors compile the names of acquaintances who might subscribe, and by soliciting similar lists from friends.[56] "It does not seem to me wise," Croly admitted to Hand, ". . . to go too much into detail." Revealing in advance all of the "specific economic and political reforms which will constitute our program," he thought, would only create "both illusory friends and unnecessary enemies." Therefore, "we have confined ourselves pretty much to generalities."[57]

In September, after revision, the circular was sent out. It was every bit as bland as Croly desired. The editors were introduced, and a solemn pledge registered that *The New Republic* would "stir the intellectual imagination of its readers, and create in them an attitude of mind productive of sound and determined action in the face of our national needs." Prospective subscribers were assured that "the New Republic will respect no taboos; it will play no favorites; it will be confined to no set creed and tied to no political party. Its philosophy will be a faith rather than a dogma. Its editorial attitude will be good-natured, open-minded, eager to find and accept facts."[58] On the basis

---

Harvard University. HC continued: "Being a good socialist, I have to be conscientious about money-matters—that is about the money matters of other people. The money with which to start The Republic is being supplied by an angelic lady who spends some hundreds of thousands of dollars every year upon many different philanthropies. I imagine that she regards The Republic as chiefly philanthropy, which while it appears to be doing good, she would be willing to continue to support. . . . If we succeed in conquering a paying following and can become economically self-supporting, so much the better. But if we fail, I shall not ask a perpetual subsidy; neither shall I seek to cultivate popularity. I shall quit. In this particular instance I would rather be a quitter than a sucker. Neither do I want to put angel Dorothy in the position of herself being either a quitter or a sucker." See also HC to Learned Hand, February 25, 1915, Hand mss.

[55] HC to Learned Hand, August 10, 1914, Hand mss.

[56] For examples, see HC's arrangement with the National Civic Federation, HC to Ralph Easley, August 17, 1914, National Civic Federation mss., New York Public Library; and HC to Learned Hand, August 7, 1914, Hand mss.

[57] HC to Learned Hand, August 17, 1914, Hand mss.

[58] For a copy of the circular, see HC to Albert J. Beveridge, September 19, 1914, Beveridge mss., Library of Congress.

of this decidedly noncommittal plea, 875 people sent in their four dollars for a year's subscription.[59]

The New Republic's format, it was agreed, was to consist of five elements. Each issue would open with a series of short editorial paragraphs called leaders. They were to be written by the editors and appear anonymously, each of them offering a brief comment about some aspect of the week's events. The leaders were to be followed by longer editorial statements, generally running a little more than a full page. They were also to be written by the editors and were to appear anonymously, but they were to have titles. The third section of the journal was to consist of longer articles of around 1,500 words, written by the editors or by contributors, and signed by the authors; included in this section was to be Phil Littell's column, "Books and Things." Next came a page or two of "Correspondence" from readers. And, finally, reviews of new fiction and nonfiction, the theater, art and poetry, signed—or at least initialled—by the editors or by the contributors who were solicited to write them. The format owed a considerable (and a conscious) debt to the English journal, *The New Statesman*, and placed a high value on anonymous contributions.[60] But as Lippmann wrote to Mabel Dodge, "one of the best tests of a man's interest in his work as distinguished from his interest in his ego was the readiness to do fine things anonymously."[61]

The staff gathered every Monday or Tuesday in Croly's large upstairs office for the weekly conference. There, with Croly sitting behind his desk and the others ranged in a semicircle of chairs, the serious talk began. The content of the next issue was determined and responsibility for the various leaders and editorials was assigned. In addition, the staff criticized the contents and quality of the current number and discussed the details of editorial management. The weekly conference also hammered out the editorial policy of the journal and decided which of the received articles should be accepted and which of the already-accepted articles should be published next. Opinions were freely exchanged and sometimes acrimonious debate erupted, but almost always a consensus emerged and became *The New Republic*'s policy.[62] All work, whether done by the editors themselves or

---

[59] Forcey, *Crossroads of Liberalism*, 190.

[60] HC to Randolph Bourne, June 3, 1914, Bourne mss.

[61] Lippmann to Mabel Dodge, December 14 [?], Dodge mss., Yale University.

[62] HC to Learned Hand, June 29, 1914, Hand mss.; Johnson, *Pioneer's Progress*, 241–42 and also his "Oral History," 103–104, 120–21; Weyl, *Diary*, October 11, 1917; HC to Randolph Bourne, October 5, 1914, Bourne mss.; Soule, interview with the author, October 7, 1963.

by others, was passed around the office and commented on by the staff. Occasionally articles were sent to outside readers for their opinions.[63]

In the planning stages, before the first issue actually appeared, the editors intended that all matters of interest would be passed on by the entire group. But when the actual rush of publication, week after week, became an overwhelming reality, an informal division of responsibilities evolved.[64] Usually the literary criticism was supervised by Littell and Hackett, and the political, social, and economic commentary was the province of Croly, Weyl, and Lippmann—but there were many exceptions to the rule and the weekly conferences occurred for as long as Herbert Croly was associated with the journal.

The editors were equals and felt themselves such, and there were many times when Croly was overruled by the others. In 1918, for example, Brandeis sent Croly a passage from Euripides, which the Justice thought eloquently summarized American feeling at the end of World War I. "I myself was very much in favor of using it," Croly reported back, "and did my best to obtain the consent of my associates on the editorial staff of the paper, but, unfortunately, I did not succeed."[65] Amy Lowell once suggested that she be given two pages each month in order to edit a poetry department. Croly's reply indicates some of the internal workings of the journal:

> The proposal that you made to the New Republic has been the occasion of a great deal of discussion in our office, and I have been unable to write to you sooner because it took us such a long time to reach our decision. . . . I myself am quite willing to admit that you know a good deal more about poetry than anybody else in this office, and are much more likely to add an original and vital department of poetry than we could ourselves; but in spite of all these things in favour of your plan, the edi-

[63] For examples, see HC to Charles McCarthy, January 13, 1915, McCarthy mss., Wisconsin State Historical Society, Madison, Wis.; Weyl, *Diary*, June 15, 1919; HC to Learned Hand, February 25 and November 9, 1915, Hand mss.; and HC to Randolph Bourne, October 28, 1914, Bourne mss. See also Soule, interview with the author, October 7, 1963.

[64] Lippmann, "Notes for a Biography," 250.

[65] HC to Louis D. Brandeis, November 15, 1918, Brandeis mss., University of Louisville Law School Library. See also Urofsky and Levy, eds., *Letters of Louis D. Brandeis*, 4: 362–63. So that it will not be thought that HC hid behind "my associates," and lacked the courage himself to refuse Brandeis's suggestion, it should be noted that HC incorporated the Euripides passage in his own unpublished book (HC, *The Breach in Civilization*, 75).

torial board of the paper has decided to reject it. They are not willing to give up their control of two pages of the paper, even once a month. I think it is quite probable that we are making a mistake in rejecting your offer, and if I were an autocratic editor and had the decision to make myself, I should almost certainly accept it as I like to take a chance of this kind and I believe in you, but I cannot act in the matter against the practically unanimous decision of my associates.[66]

Despite the forms of democracy and the freedom of discussion and the assertions of editorial equality, despite even the occasional overriding of Croly's own views, it was clear to everyone that he was the guiding spirit and the controlling influence of *The New Republic*. "All editors were to be free and equal," Lippmann recalled, "though in fact Croly was the editor-in-chief." Malcolm Cowley, who was to join the staff in the late 1920s, agreed: "Although Croly sometimes made the pretense of running a soviet of equal editors, there was little question that he was the editor-in-chief."[67] He had gathered the staff. He conducted the weekly conferences. He handled the voluminous correspondence with outside contributors. He met with each of the editors individually to explore approaches to their work and to offer suggestions.

There were several reasons for Croly's ascendancy. In the first place, he, more than the others, had the confidence and the support of the Straights. And being closest to the source of the money invested his opinions with a certain power that the others recognized and to which

[66] HC to Amy Lowell, December 12, 1914, Amy Lowell Correspondence, Houghton Library, Harvard University. As it turned out, the debates over poetry caused the most internal division in the early days of the journal. HC was frankly bewildered by "the present anarchy in critical standards in respect not merely to poetry but to all the arts," and saw that it was causing hopeless disruption among the staff. (See the long and sometimes painful exchanges between HC and Amy Lowell in late 1914 and early 1915, ibid.) Finally, within the first year, the editors simply assigned one of their number the responsibility for selecting poetry. HC wrote to one would-be contributor that he had not even read the submitted poem, "because it would not make any difference under the circumstances whether I approved of it or not." HC to Donald R. Richberg, May 19, 1915, Richberg mss., Library of Congress. For further comments on his managerial style, see HC to Dorothy Straight, May 31, 1918, Dorothy Straight Elmhirst mss.

[67] Lippmann, "Notes for a Biography," 250; Malcolm Cowley, interview with the author, November 12, 1966. See also Johnson, "Oral History," 103–105; Maxwell Anderson to Upton Sinclair, September 24, 1919, in Laurence G. Avery, ed., *Dramatist in America: Letters of Maxwell Anderson* (Chapel Hill, 1977), 14; and Soule, interview with the author, October 7, 1963.

they deferred. In addition, he, more than the others, came into the enterprise with a coherent general vision of what the journal ought to be; he had a sense of purpose for it, a firmly grounded philosophy for it, which the other editors respected. They might write more gracefully and persuasively, but none of them (with the possible exception of Lippmann) possessed as thoughtful and as comprehensive a view of American life as a whole and of the role a progressive journal of opinion should play in bringing that view to the public.

Finally, it soon became clear that Herbert Croly was willing to invest a larger portion of his intellectual effort in the enterprise than were any of the others. The other editors were able to muster only a partial loyalty to *The New Republic*. They were forever coming and going, accepting government service, leaving to write one or another "big" book. In 1922, Lippmann, who had himself already left the journal twice, observed that "the organization of 'The New Republic' was based on the theory that none of its editors wished to do much editing, that none of them would remain at a desk very long, and that there would be a place on the board for men who were not wholly organizable."[68] Croly, who in the early stages shared the disposition to make the commitment tentative, soon changed his tune. He emerged quickly as the symbol of the journal's continuity. He hated watching the others leave. And the fullness of his commitment also strengthened his ascendancy over the others: "We often overruled Croly on minor things," one editor remembered, "but we wouldn't fight it out with him on major things."[69]

Undoubtedly the most delicate matter that had to be settled before the first issue ever went to press was the precise relationship of Dorothy and Willard Straight to the venture. On the face of it, a liberal journal bankrolled by a Wall Street financier and his socialite wife was bound to be suspect, and special care had to be taken at the outset to define their prerogatives and assure the editors of their own editorial independence. Francis Hackett recalled a meeting with the Straights, during which Walter Weyl spoke of his misgivings "with simplicity and fairness and force," and Straight made "a thoroughly satisfactory response."[70] Either at that meeting or at a subsequent one, the parties arrived at an understanding: the Straights were to have, together, a single vote at weekly conferences, and they were to have no veto power over editorial decisions. For the purpose of

---

[68] Lippmann, "As a New Republic Editor," 84–85.
[69] Johnson, interview with the author, October 21, 1963.
[70] Hackett, "Publicist and Radical," 96.

preventing the Straights from bringing along friends whose views Croly mistrusted, Croly made it a rule to exclude from the conferences all visitors. Finally, the couple agreed to put up enough money to keep the journal afloat for at least four years.[71]

In practice the Straights were everything that the editors could have hoped for. Their financial support of *The New Republic* was unstinting—indeed, despite Croly's intense embarrassment, Dorothy Straight dutifully sent in her check for four dollars in response to the September circular for subscribers. Usually, in fact, it was Croly who resisted extra expenses and Willard or Dorothy Straight who insisted upon them. Their insistence, moreover, was so lighthearted and informal that no one could doubt their sincerity. "I know you want to keep down expenses for the paper," Willard wrote Croly in 1916, "but Dorothy and I want to see the paper succeed. . . . Please consider seriously again the question of taking on more help. It needn't go into the budget at all. In this we are both very much in earnest. Go into Gath and the haunts of the Philistines, did they live in Gath? and gather rosebuds and chase butterflies, bring the wordlings into the sanctuary at 421." Ten days later he repeated the message: "I know that Dorothy feels that this is the time when you should not be perturbed by any fear of extra expense. The paper has done so much already and has made a position which will enable it to do so much more that you ought to drive pretty hard at the present time, even if you must increase your overhead very considerably. It seems to me that it should be done."[72]

Their attitude regarding financial matters was more than a mere perfunctory readiness to let Croly spend more money. Private letters between Willard and Dorothy, letters none of the editors would ever see, revealed the extent of their generosity. In February 1918, for example, Willard, in Europe, wrote his wife: "Now you must not let Herbert get the Economy Bee. It's rot. The paper is just coming into its great usefulness. . . . This is no time to count pennies. I'm sure you agree. I don't mean they should blow cash but they must keep up their standard. This is no moment to count costs if results can be gained." Two weeks later Straight instructed his wife to make Croly "stop worrying about finances. He's so terribly conscientious that it's always on his mind the fact that he's using your money.

---

[71] Forcey, *Crossroads of Liberalism*, 175–76; HC to Learned Hand, June 29, 1914, Hand mss.; HC, *Willard Straight*, 473–74; and *New York Times*, April 20, 1914, p. 11.

[72] Willard Straight to HC, March 5 and 16, 1915, Straight mss. For Dorothy Straight's insistence on paying for her subscription, see Swanberg, *Whitney Father, Whitney Heiress*, 346.

Talk to him and tell him to go to it."[73] Croly had virtually a blank check from his patrons. Between 1914 and the end of 1924, *The New Republic* received more than $800,000 in subsidies, an average of more than $80,000 each year, and Dorothy continued her support into the 1950s.[74]

The Straights were also ideal as far as editorial policy was concerned. Phil Littell, for one, doubted in the beginning whether a man with opinions as strong as Willard Straight's could keep his hands off the journal's policy decisions. As time passed, however, and as the inevitable differences between the editors and their patrons surfaced, those doubts were quieted. Straight was vitally interested in the paper and he wrote long critiques of each of the early issues and sent innumerable suggestions to Croly; but he never questioned the process by which the final decisions were made. In February 1915, for example, Straight sent in some ideas, which Croly did not use in his editorial. Straight hastened to set the editor's mind at ease:

> As I've told you many times you need have no thought that I have any feeling about suggestions turned down. If you don't like 'em say so and that's enough, or do so which is the same thing. You'll remember that you more or less apologized for not using some of my bright thoughts in this particular case. On reading it in print I'm glad you didn't use most of them. There are one or two that I mourn, but Herbert about this thing which is nothing and not worth writing about, save to clear it off the slate, my only regret was that you—or didn't you?—tried to save my feelings by talking of the expense of making changes in the proof. It was very kind, in your thought, but I would have felt better if you'd said Willard Go to Blazes, I don't like and won't use you[r] brilliant but undigestible suggestions.[75]

Next month, on shipboard, Straight sent in two leaders for Croly to consider. "Please use either or both of these things as you see fit.

[73] Willard Straight to Dorothy Straight, February 10 and 26, 1918, Straight mss.

[74] The most concise and accurate summary of the Straights' financial support (through 1924) is to be found in the memorandum dated October 25, 1924, preparatory to the *NR*'s filing for bankruptcy, in the Dorothy Straight Elmhirst mss., Folder 3725: 12–14. See also Beulah Amidon, "The Nation and the New Republic," *Survey Graphic*, 29 (1940): 24; Forcey, *Crossroads of Liberalism*, 334; Michael Straight, "A Journal of Opinion and the Challenge of 1953," 5–6; and Bliven, "Oral History," 29. A complete file of *NR* requests and of affirmative answers from Dorothy Straight's accountants, through 1924, can be found in the Dorothy Straight Elmhirst mss.

[75] Willard Straight to HC, March 1, 1915, Straight mss. See also HC to Straight, November 29, 1914, ibid.

Scrap them, amend them, print them. They are grist sent to your mill, and having travailled all I care is that the brats be kindly treated. The effort at least passed the time on this ship and brought bread to the mouth of the lady typist on board."[76]

Some people, outside *The New Republic* group, insisted that the relationship with the Straights put clear boundaries around the freedom of the editors. H. L. Mencken once called them all "kept idealists," and William J. Ghent, the Socialist, believed the paper's policy to be "polluted" and "determined" by the financial arrangement which had given it birth.[77] But nobody connected with *The New Republic* ever expressed that view. The subsidy from Dorothy Straight, on the contrary, was thought to be a liberating rather than a confining factor; it freed the journal from a cowering dependence on wealthy advertisers, from the debasing necessity to attract mass audiences by pandering to popular tastes, from the debilitating fear of taking an editorial position that might cost subscribers and sink the enterprise. The editors were shamelessly unrestrained in their praise. One of them wrote in his autobiography, "How could it have happened that Fate should have placed an immense fortune in the hands of a woman so brave, so true, so beautiful as Dorothy Straight? A real angel: in the years I was associated with *The New Republic* I heard hundreds of persons speak of her and I have heard hundreds more since. I have never heard one voice of criticism of Dorothy Straight. Not one person ever detected the faintest blot on the white purity of her spirit."[78] Littell, once skeptical, came to admit "how utterly mistaken" he had been. Getting to know Willard Straight "and seeing his relation to Herbert and the rest of us through difficult hours, has changed my notions of human nature. Never had I suspected that one man could unite such fighting force with such a deep-seated tolerance."[79]

So, by November 1914, the new journal, on the brink of its first public appearance, was equipped with an editorial staff, a name, an office, a format, a set of editorial procedures, close to a thousand subscribers, and an understanding with its financial benefactors. "I really have a vision of the New Republic in my head," Croly wrote Hand. "The vision will I fear, set angel Dorothy back some hundreds of thousands of dollars and may never be realized at that; but she

[76] Willard Straight to HC, March 5, 1915, ibid.

[77] The Mencken remark is reported in Eric F. Goldman, *Rendezvous with Destiny: A History of Modern American Reform* (New York, 1952), 316; William Ghent's views are quoted in Forcey, *Crossroads of Liberalism*, 176.

[78] Johnson, *Pioneer's Progress*, 233–34.

[79] Philip Littell to Dorothy Straight, December 10, 1918, Straight mss.

will get a little education for her money and so will I and so, I hope, will you and the others."[80]

III

The kind of "education" that Croly proposed to deliver—not only to Dorothy Straight and Learned Hand, but to the American people as a whole—could not be delivered, week after week, by the editors alone. A typical issue of *The New Republic* required approximately twenty-five thousand words; and even if each of the five writing editors could somehow manage to produce three thousand words each week, that would account for only three-fifths of the magazine.[81] It was obvious that Croly would need more help, and he set out to find additional contributors. Within the first months of publication, he had secured the cooperation of three talented writers.

Randolph Bourne was only twenty-eight in 1914, but he was already regarded as a highly promising writer and critic.[82] A tragic accident at birth and a crippling childhood disease had left him grotesquely deformed—to Theodore Dreiser, Bourne was "that frightening dwarf,"[83] and many others who were later to become his friends recalled how "startled" they were by their first encounter. Nevertheless, Bourne steadfastly refused to permit his physical appearance to embitter his disposition or obstruct his career. In 1913 he graduated from Columbia and published his first book, *Youth and Life*, a collection of enthusiastic essays celebrating the potential of the younger generation to change American civilization. A fellowship enabled him to spend a year in Europe, and he was traveling in Italy in May 1914, when two of his patrons back home independently called Herbert Croly's proposed journal to his attention. Both Ellery Sedgwick, whose *Atlantic Monthly* had been publishing Bourne's articles since 1911, and Charles Beard, one of Bourne's favorite professors at Columbia, wrote to say that the young man might be able to find an outlet and a steady income with *The New Republic*. Beard went further and secured from Croly an agreement to guarantee the writer at least $1,000 a year.[84]

[80] HC to Learned Hand, March 7, 1914, Hand mss.

[81] Johnson, *Pioneer's Progress*, 234.

[82] Louis Filler, *Randolph Bourne* (Washington, D.C., 1943); John A. Moreau, *Randolph Bourne, Legend and Reality* (Washington, D.C., 1966).

[83] Quoted in Carl Resek, introduction to *War and the Intellectuals: Essays by Randolph S. Bourne, 1915–1919* (New York, 1964), viii.

[84] Ellery Sedgwick to Bourne, May 9, 1914, Bourne mss.; and Charles Beard to Bourne, May 15, 1914, ibid.

"It seems like just the opportunity that I have wanted to get myself expressed," Bourne wrote to a friend, "and I am only hoping to be able to be really big enough for the opportunity." After reading some of Bourne's previous work, Croly told him that he thought the journal was "exceptionally fortunate" in hiring him.[85]

Bourne was an intellectual of wide-ranging interests. Unlike many critics of his day, he was unwilling to treat American culture—the productions of artists and writers—apart from the social, economic, and political struggles which shaped that culture.[86] Hence there were few topics that failed to engage his intelligence; his friend, Van Wyck Brooks believed that his interests were "almost universal," and that "no other of our younger critics had cast so wide a net."[87] Croly set Bourne to work writing about recent trends in education (what better topic for a recent student of John Dewey?) and city planning. But Randolph Bourne also wrote about and reviewed everything from Maeterlinck to modern music. Hardly an issue appeared without some signed or unsigned piece by Bourne—he made at least nineteen contributions to the first twenty-five issues of the magazine.[88]

Croly's second recruit, Alvin S. Johnson, was an economics professor at Cornell in 1914.[89] He had just written a defense of capitalism for Henry Holt's *Unpopular Review*, which caught Croly's eye and resulted in an invitation for lunch next time Johnson was in New York City. Croly asked him for occasional contributions on economic topics, but Johnson, who wrote with graceful ease, also ended up submitting something for nearly every issue, much of it published in the form of anonymous leaders. Johnson was a Nebraskan, schooled in midwestern agrarian progressivism—he had always suspected Roosevelt and admired La Follette, and he had the temerity to vote for Wilson in 1912 and to describe himself as a Jeffersonian in the hotbed of *New Republic* Hamiltonianism.[90] Despite the obvious possibilities for disagreement, however, Johnson got along well with the

[85] Bourne to Alyse Gregory, September 28, 1914, ibid.; HC to Bourne, October 5, 1914, ibid.

[86] On Bourne's thought, see Christopher Lasch, *The New Radicalism in America (1889–1963): The Intellectual as a Social Type* (New York, 1965), ch. iii; Sherman Paul, *Randolph Bourne* (Minneapolis, 1966); and Olaf Hansen, introduction to *The Radical Will: Randolph Bourne, Selected Writings, 1911–1918* (New York, 1977): 17–62.

[87] Van Wyck Brooks, introduction to *The History of a Literary Radical and Other Papers by Randolph Bourne* (New York, 1956), 2.

[88] The best bibliography is in Hansen, ed., *The Radical Will*, 541–45.

[89] Johnson, *Pioneer's Progress* is the best source for his life; see also his "Oral History."

[90] Johnson, *Pioneer's Progress*, 63, 86–87, and 272; Johnson, "Oral History," 107–10.

others, at least at first, and before the end of the journal's first year, Croly made him *The New Republic*'s seventh editor.[91]

George Soule joined the staff in December. He had gone from Yale, where his interests were largely literary, to the publishing house of Frederick A. Stokes. There he and another young manuscript reader named Sinclair Lewis urged the cautious Stokes to publish Dreiser and H. G. Wells and Soule was fired. The publisher's assistant, William Morrow, knew Herbert Croly and got Soule a job in the office, working on the journal's make-up and proofreading copy. As Croly's confidence in Soule grew, so did Soule's responsibilities. He soon moved from occasional reviews and leaders to enlisting writers on the arts. Gradually his own interests turned to economic questions and before long he, like Bourne and Johnson, was making regular contributions to the journal.[92]

Even the addition of these three regulars—Bourne, Johnson, and Soule—failed to satisfy *The New Republic*'s enormous appetite for copy, and Croly doggedly pursued other talented and progressive intellectuals. He concluded arrangements with two of Lippmann's Harvard friends: Alfred Booth Kuttner, whose early translation of Freud influenced Lippmann's *Preface to Politics*, agreed to submit articles on psychology; and Lee Simonson, on the threshold of his distinguished career in theatrical art and stage design, wrote on art and the theater. In addition, Croly solicited contributions from Brandeis, Henry Stimson, Amy Lowell, John Jay Chapman, Finley Peter Dunne, Robert Grant, Donald Richberg, Chester Rowell, William Allen White and dozens of others—sometimes issuing a general invitation to write for the journal, sometimes making specific suggestions for a particular article.[93]

Although many of those Croly enlisted were willing to donate their work in the name of the progressive cause, Croly always preferred paying his writers. At the same time, he felt apologetic about

---

[91] Johnson's name first appeared as an editor in the issue of September 4, 1915.

[92] Soule, interview with the author, October 7, 1963.

[93] HC to Louis D. Brandeis, October 5, 1914, Brandeis mss.; HC to Henry Stimson, December 10, 1914, Stimson mss.; various letters between HC and Amy Lowell in late 1914 and early 1915, Amy Lowell Correspondence; HC to John Jay Chapman, June 21, 1914, Autograph File, Houghton Library, Harvard University; HC to Finley Peter Dunne, April 18, 1916, Finley Peter Dunne mss., Library of Congress; HC to Robert Grant, December 3, 1914, Robert Grant mss., Houghton Library, Harvard University; HC to Chester Rowell, September 10, 1914, November 17, 1914, July 20, 1920, September 7, 1920, Chester H. Rowell mss., Bancroft Library, University of California, Berkeley; HC to William Allen White, November 23, 1914, and October 6, 1915, William Allen White mss., Library of Congress.

the low rates *The New Republic* had to offer. "I am aware that this is very inadequate compensation. . . ." Croly wrote to Stimson after accepting an article on Charles Evans Hughes. "I am sorry to say The New Republic cannot afford to compete with the monthly magazines in paying large prices for contributed matter." Usually the magazine paid about two cents a word for contributions—anywhere from thirty to eighty dollars for an article, depending upon its length.[94]

Nevertheless, the results were extremely impressive. Despite the modest compensation, Herbert Croly was able to attract to the pages of *The New Republic* the most illustrious intellectuals in the English-speaking world. In the first twenty-five issues of the magazine, for example, Croly published articles, reviews, or communications from a host of such prominent academic intellectuals as John Dewey, George Santayana, Josiah Royce, Horace M. Kallen, Charles Beard, Morris R. Cohen, James Harvey Robinson, Edward A. Ross, Edward S. Corwin, Simon Patten and Albert Bushnell Hart. From the world of literature and criticism, Croly printed work by Robert Frost, Amy Lowell, Van Wyck Brooks, Floyd Dell, Ford Madox Ford, Percy Boynton, Paul Claudel, Padraic Colum, and Robert Herrick. Among those associated with progressive reform and muckrake journalism were Ray Stannard Baker, Donald Richberg, John B. Andrews, Clyde King, George Creel, John Graham Brooks, W. J. Ghent, and Frank Colby. From England came contributions by Rebecca West, H. N. Brailsford, Henry Nevinson, Graham Wallas, S. K. Ratcliffe, and Alfred Zimmern.

In the following twenty-five issues, Croly was able to add other spectacular names. Readers of *The New Republic* were soon regularly encountering the views of such important writers as H. G. Wells, Roscoe Pound, Lewis Mumford, Theodore Dreiser, Norman Angell, Arthur O. Lovejoy, Ralph Barton Perry, Gertrude Atherton, Max Eastman, Conrad Aiken, Harold Laski, John A. Hobson, and many others. It will be recalled that nearly half a century before, when Herbert was only two years old, David Goodman Croly had promised subscribers to *his* journal of opinion, the abortive *Modern Thinker*, that he would "employ the best minds of his age as contributors."[95]

[94] HC to Henry Stimson, October 20, 1916, Stimson mss. For other comments, over the years, on the *NR*'s rates of payment, see HC to Robert Grant, December 3, 1914, Grant mss.; HC to Amy Lowell, February 24, 1915, Amy Lowell Correspondence; HC to William Allen White, February 25 and March 10, 1921, White mss.; Edmund Wilson to John Peale Bishop, October 20, 1925, John Peale Bishop mss., Princeton University.

[95] David G. Croly, "Egotisms," *Modern Thinker*, No. 1, 1–7. See above, pp. 14–15.

But in this, as in so many other matters, the son was to achieve the ambitions of the father.

In two instances, however, Croly was deeply disappointed. He could never quite persuade Learned Hand to "discard the dignity of being a judge" and join *The New Republic*; nor could he convince Felix Frankfurter to turn down the offer from Harvard Law School, though Croly assured him that "the Lord" intended Frankfurter to be a journalist and it was only "perversity" that had carried him off into the law.[96] Croly was closer to these two men than to any others, and he pleaded with them both, repeatedly, but both resisted his efforts. A month before the appearance of the first issue, Hand wrote Frankfurter a note, which, beneath its lighthearted tone, revealed the depth of Croly's feeling:

> Poor old H.C. is deeply cast down by your coerced defection. To be deprived of him "who more than any one else understands his point of view and shares his conviction," was hard indeed. . . . I was incontinently, unsympathetically joyous. I suppressed mirth which would have been too unfriendly, but I was unconcealedly glad. . . . Thereby I showed that I was, besides a tyrant, 1. a truant to the faith in ideas as the final director of life; 2. a jealous mole who wanted other men to be kept out of the light, just because I have got a life sentence myself; 3. an obscurantist, a believer in factory life without "Normal Rules of Industry," a dullard, a grind, a dryasdust, a soul-quencher, a German pedant, a blear-eyed, soulless, plodding, son of Caliban without faith, vision, trust in life. . . .[97]

Both Hand and Frankfurter were to remain close to *The New Republic*, attending its luncheons and dinners, occasionally even responding to Croly's insistent requests for contributions.[98] But despite Croly's continual urgings, each kept some distance from the enterprise and remained faithful to his calling in the law.

It would be hard to argue that the group Herbert Croly had gath-

[96] HC to Learned Hand, June 29, 1914, Hand mss.; Phillips, ed., *Felix Frankfurter Reminisces*, 92.

[97] Learned Hand to Felix Frankfurter, October 9, 1914, Frankfurter mss., Library of Congress.

[98] Both men made contributions to the *NR*. Hand's were usually anonymous—see for examples HC to Hand, January 20, February 25, and November 9, 1915, Hand mss. Frankfurter's contributions were both signed and unsigned, during HC's editorship, Frankfurter contributed dozens of pieces to the journal. He also agreed to serve as a trustee of the company, together with HC and Willard Straight. See Forcey, *Crossroads of Liberalism*, 181–82.

ered together was, in any way, representative of the American people as a whole.[99] They were upper-middle-class intellectuals, by and large; and although Weyl, Lippmann, and Bourne had once flirted with the Socialists, and Hackett and Bourne had once struggled to earn their livings, the group had few firsthand contacts with farmers or factory workers.[100] All of them, excepting Hackett, had earned college degrees—Johnson from Nebraska, Rudyard from Vassar, all the rest of them from the Ivy League. Only Hackett and Johnson knew anything about the Midwest. All the others were easterners. There was no one connected with the journal who pretended to know much at all about the South or the West. Although Croly tried to remedy the narrowness, attempting, for example, to get William Allen White to write about Kansas and Chester Rowell to handle California, the limitations of *The New Republic* group were to be more or less permanent because they were more or less written into the sociology of the American intellectual community. It was simply the case that the best literary, philosophic, artistic talent in America came from precisely those places, social classes, and colleges where Herbert Croly had found them.

If, among American intellectuals, *The New Republic* group had any special characteristic, it was youthfulness. Phil Littell and Croly, at forty-six and forty-five, were the eldest members of the staff; Weyl and Johnson had just turned forty. But Hackett, Bourne, Soule, Lippmann, Rudyard, Hallowell, Simonson, and Kuttner were all between twenty-five and thirty-one. And yet, despite their youth, Croly's staff possessed very little either of youthful exuberance or of that cautious modesty, that intellectual deference toward their elders, sometimes associated with being young. They were bold beyond their years, they were filled with confidence in their vision and in themselves, and, notwithstanding those luncheons of studied informality or those regularly spaced dinners of studied gaiety, they were deadly serious. To Ellery Sedgwick, up at the Boston offices of *The Atlantic Monthly*, they looked like "the solemnest procession that ever marched. . . ."[101]

IV

For months after his crucial conversation with Dorothy and Willard Straight, Croly was assailed by personal misgivings about the new

[99] Forcey, *Crossroads of Liberalism*, 182–83.

[100] Hackett, *American Rainbow, passim*; Randolph Bourne, "What is Exploitation," *NR*, 9 (November 4, 1916): 12–14.

[101] Ellery Sedgwick to Randolph Bourne, May 9, 1914, Bourne mss.

enterprise. A few weeks after the bargain had been struck with the Straights, Croly sent Learned Hand a note from Cornish. He was "plugging away" at *Progressive Democracy*, he wrote, and "having a thoroughly good time—as I always do, when I lock myself up with my work." For Croly, the man of anguished seriousness and painful shyness, the calm and cloistered life of the scholar was, in some ways, an ideal one. "Every once in a while I think I'm a damned fool to surrender it even for a few years, and when such thoughts occur I never know whether they are prompted by the devil of sloth and indolence or by some protective divinity."[102] Five months later and the same doubts persisted: "The hour has arrived to cease talking about the Republic and begin building the actual structure. Now that the time has come I am very much depressed at the idea of abandoning the quiet contemplative life of the last eight years. It has been thoughtful and it has been satisfying. I am much better fitted for it than I am for editing a weekly paper." And yet, he could already detect in himself a growing enthusiasm: ". . . in spite of my regrets at what I am abandoning, I am in a queer contradictory kind of way exhilarated at the prospect of the new work."[103]

There were, after all, important considerations pushing Croly toward the experiment, and the precarious state of his personal finances was a factor not to be underestimated. "Probably I never would have the courage to hitch myself to a desk in New York again if my money matters were in better shape," he confided to Hand. "It is a solace to know that I shall be actually earning during the next few years our expenses."[104] But there were other influences as well. Journalism, of course, was practically a family tradition—both his mother and his father had been not only outstanding practitioners but also warm defenders of the art. Most decisive perhaps were Croly's own views of American life and the high role he assigned to "critics" in shaping and improving public opinion. In *The Promise of American Life*, Croly compared the critic to "the lantern which illuminates the path," one of that élite company of heroes and saints destined to direct the future progress of the nation. And *Progressive Democracy*, written at the very moment when Croly was preparing to launch *The New Republic*, contained an entire chapter on "Majority Rule and Public Opinion." In a democracy, Croly argued, "Public opinion requires to be aroused, elicited, informed, developed, concentrated

---

[102] HC to Learned Hand, October 13, 1913, Hand mss.

[103] HC to Learned Hand, March 7, 1914, Hand mss.

[104] HC to Learned Hand, October 13, 1913, Hand mss. For HC's financial condition, see Forcey, *Crossroads of Liberalism*, 179–80; and Swanberg, *Whitney Father, Whitney Heiress*, 343.

and brought to an understanding of its own dominant purposes."[105] Obviously there was noble and worthy work for those willing to arouse, elicit, and inform.

In any case, as the time for beginning drew near, and as the editor-in-chief immersed himself increasingly in the necessary preparations, doubts and hesitations began to slip away. By the spring of 1914, Croly was ready to invest in *The New Republic* his highest ambitions and ideals. Sometime in the spring or early summer, he gave a dinner for the staff, potential contributors, the Straights, friends of the magazine. And after the meal was over, Herbert Croly rose and spoke to them for thirty or forty minutes, summarizing his hopes.[106]

"We are assembled here tonight," he began, "in order to anticipate and after a modest fashion to celebrate the prospective foundation of a new periodical review. We propose to publish a weekly vehicle of artistic, literary, business, political and social criticism; and we justify our hardihood in adding to the long list of existing periodical publications by claiming for our enterprise a certain flavor of novelty." One by one, then, he criticized the shortcomings of the competition: *The Nation, The Outlook, The Independent, Harper's, Collier's*—they all, to be sure, served a useful public purpose, but "none of them is furnishing the needed stimulus and corrective to our national thought and practice."

What was to make this new journal of opinion different, Croly suggested, was its devotion to the attainment of progressive and national fulfillment. Avoiding the dogma of eighteenth-century individualism and the dogma of modern socialism, even criticizing much that called itself progressive, the new weekly would dedicate itself to the intelligent criticism and analysis of our national life. The journal must "vindicate the dignity of American thought," and point the way to constructive democratic reform. Croly closed his little speech with the hope that a social critic who diligently pursued the elusive purpose would be "entitled to the sympathetic assistance of all those who believe that Truth has an essential contribution to make to the work of human emancipation and fulfillment."

His listeners could have few doubts about the direction Croly wanted to go. It was obvious that he intended to pursue, in *The New Repub-*

[105] HC, *PAL*, 450–52; HC, *Progressive Democracy* (New York, 1914), 229, 304.

[106] An undated copy of HC's eighteen-page speech, with editorial emendations in HC's handwriting, can be found in the Willard Straight mss., Box 32. The speech is impossible to date with certainty. Since HC calls the new journal "The Republic," however, it seems likely that the speech was given before the end of the summer of 1914.

lic, the purposes set forth in his books—the creation of a national community, the strengthening of the federal government, the achievement of basic structural and social reforms to enhance national efficiency and create a climate of social and economic justice in the United States. *The New Republic*, in short, would vigorously advocate the program that was associated with Theodore Roosevelt and his Bull Moose party.

If any of those listeners, a few weeks later, had bothered to remember Herbert Croly's little speech, or to think about his efforts to prepare for the entrance of *The New Republic* onto the national scene, they might have been struck by a momentous, by an almost incredible omission. Nowhere in his after-dinner remarks did he make any reference to international affairs or to America's role in the international community. And nobody in that distinguished, youthful, brilliant, solemn staff knew the first thing about the world outside the United States. "We started on the assumption that we were enlisted as loyal, though we hoped critical, members of the Progressive movement," Walter Lippmann later remembered. "We thought that the movement was established. We thought that Roosevelt would continue to lead it. We never dreamed that there would be a World War before our first issue was printed." But on the very day that *The New Republic* office on West Twenty-first Street opened for business, the war began in Europe. By November, when the first issue was published, the old world of the Bull Moose was destroyed forever.[107]

[107] Lippmann, "Notes for a Biography," 250, and Lippmann, "As a New Republic Editor," 87.

EIGHT

Years of "Rare Opportunity"
1914–1918

FROM LONDON, on August 2, 1914, a distraught Walter Lippmann dashed off a note to Felix Frankfurter. "This isn't a very cheerful day to be writing to you. It's an hour since we learned that Germany has declared war against Russia. We shall hear of France later in the day, no doubt." Lippmann was with a group of British intellectuals—Wallas, Murray, Hobhouse, Thomson—and they were all stunned by events ("we sit and stare at each other and make idiotically cheerful remarks"). They plotted foolish schemes to keep England out of the conflagration, but they knew it was hopeless. "Nothing can stop the awful disintegration now. Nor is there any way of looking beyond it; ideas, books seem too utterly trivial, and all the public opinion, democratic hope & what not, where is it today? Like a flower in the path of a plough."[1]

Two days later, Herbert Croly, Walter Weyl, and Frankfurter caught the morning train to Oyster Bay. Weeks earlier, well before the European explosion, Roosevelt had summoned these three of his followers for the purpose of discussing the current state of the American labor movement. "Needless to say," Frankfurter remembered the day, "when we got out at Sagamore Hill, we didn't talk about the American labor movement or American industrial problems, we talked about the war."[2] There was a world of bitterly symbolic foreshadowing for Herbert Croly in that otherwise unimportant episode. He had journeyed to this point in his life, eager to talk about the problems and opportunities, the dangers and hopeful promises of American life. He was brimming with plans and ideas. He had been provided, almost miraculously, with precisely the vehicle he needed, a weekly journal of opinion. And now that the time had come and the preparations carefully completed, had the time also fled?

Croly thought not. So profound was the quality of his optimism and so powerful was his faith in the power of constructive thought

[1] Walter Lippmann to Felix Frankfurter, August 2, 1914, Frankfurter mss., Library of Congress.

[2] Harlan B. Phillips, ed., *Felix Frankfurter Reminisces* (New York, 1960), 89; Hermann Hagedorn, *The Roosevelt Family of Sagamore Hill* (New York, 1954), 341–42.

that he saw, even in the horror of war, not the "awful disintegration" that Lippmann saw, but new opportunities for the cool pragmatist to improve the world. Two weeks after the pilgrimage to Sagamore Hill, Croly excitedly shared his vision with Learned Hand. The war, he thought, might "prove in the end an actual help to the 'New Republic.' It will tend to dislocate conventional ways of looking at things and to stimulate public thinking. . . . It will create, that is, a state of mind in which a formal political and social agitation will find its words more influential and more effective in modifying public opinion."[3] Both James and Dewey, after all, had taught that creative intelligence was awakened by the intrusion of new problems. Far from being "too utterly trivial," ideas, now more than ever, would have their chance to exert genuine influence. Herbert Croly clung to this hope for a very long time.

I

The first issue of *The New Republic* was filled with observations about the war. From Roland Usher's speculative article, "The War and the Future of Civilization," to Frank Simonds's analysis, "Has German Strategy Failed?", that first issue was obsessed by the three-month-old conflict. Rebecca West pleaded that the war not be permitted to interrupt the duty of penetrating criticism; H. N. Brailsford discussed the likely effects of the war on Turkey and the Balkans; Hugh Walpole described the nervous calm of neutral Stockholm. But it was in two unsigned editorials in that historic issue, one by Lippmann and one by Croly, that the editors revealed some of their most poignant and prophetic convictions.

Lippmann's editorial, "Force and Ideas," appeared first. It was a brave and moving plea that constructive thought not be abandoned during the months of slaughter that lay ahead. "Every sane person knows that it is a greater thing to build a city than to bombard it, to plough a field than to trample it, to serve mankind than to conquer it," Lippmann began. "And yet once the armies get loose, the terrific noise and shock of war make all that was valuable seem pale and dull and sentimental. . . . Who cares to paint a picture now, or to write any poetry but war poetry, or to search the meaning of language, or speculate about the constitution of matter? It seems like fiddling when Rome burns. Or to edit a magazine—to cover paper with ink, to care about hopes that have gone stale, to launch phrases that are lost in the uproar? What is the good now of thinking?"

[3] HC to Learned Hand, August 17, 1914, Hand mss., Harvard Law School Library.

It was obvious, if only from Lippmann's last example, that the editors were thinking about themselves and about their fragile new enterprise. Was a journal of ideas in the middle of a raging war nothing more than "a flower in the path of a plough?" Lippmann, calmer and more confident now than he had been on that momentous day three months earlier, made the only response possible. At once a touching declaration of faith in reason and a solemn promise about how the journal would cover the war, his answer was unequivocal: "Yet the fact remains that the final argument against cannon is ideas. . . . We cannot abandon the labor of thought. However crude and weak it may be, it is the only force that can pierce the agglomerated passion and wrongheadedness of this disaster. . . . There is only one way to break the vicious circle of action, and that is by subjecting it endlessly to the most ruthless criticism of which we are capable."

Stirring pronouncements about the importance of thought, however, did not take readers of the new journal very far. All the parties to the wartime debates—from the most eager belligerents to the most extreme pacifists—were appealing to their own species of reasonability. What was required was some indication of the basic assumptions of thought and the general purposes toward which it would be directed. Lippmann's first editorial offered one vague hint: "It is not enough to hate war and waste, to launch one unanalyzed passion against another, to make the world a vast debating ground in which tremendous accusations are directed against the Kaiser and the financiers, the diplomatists and the gun manufacturers," he warned. But except for revealing the view that clichés and simple-minded sloganeering would not satisfy the demands of detached analysis, Lippmann left the major questions about the policy and direction of *The New Republic* unanswered.

It was Croly's editorial that presented, in embryonic form, the central policy positions that were to govern *The New Republic*'s treatment of World War I. The editorial's title, "The End of American Isolation," served to register the first contention. "The self-complacent isolation of a great people has never received a ruder shock than that which was dealt to the American nation by the outbreak of the European war," Croly wrote. Our sense of freedom from European politics and economics has turned out to be "a delusion" and it must be consigned to the "accumulating scrapheap" of our misconceptions.[4]

---

[4] This idea HC had held at least since 1909. In *The Promise of American Life* (New York, 1909), 331, he had argued that "the isolation which has meant so much to the United States, and still means so much, cannot persist in its present form."

Croly was not content, however, merely to announce that the period of independence from Europe was over. The first weeks of the war, he thought, brought another lesson. They had revealed the pressing need for a more active and centralized American government—just the sort of government Croly had advocated in *The Promise of American Life*. "The American nation was wholly unprepared to cope with such a serious political and economic emergency. It possessed no organization and no equipment with which to protect its citizens against the loss and the suffering caused by the war." The crisis had already demonstrated that "there was no adequate political and business machinery" directing the affairs of the nation. But as awareness grew under the continuing pressure of domestic and international demands, it "should bring with it a political and economic organization better able to redeem its obligations" at home and abroad.

Finally, Croly asserted, Americans had a direct and vital interest in the outcome of Europe's war and in the nature of the settlement that would eventually conclude the hostilities: "No matter who is victorious, the United States will be indirectly compromised by the treaty of peace. If the treaty is one which makes for international stability and justice, this country will have an interest in maintaining it. If the treaty is one which makes militarism even more ominously threatening, this country will have an interest in seeking a better substitute."

In the years ahead, *The New Republic* would be required to face and to explicate the complex issues of war and peace—the intricacies of defense, the rights of neutrals, the nature of contraband, the role of the military, the mechanics of a settlement. But throughout that tortured journey, the journal decided its policies in the light of those principles that Croly and Lippmann had enunciated in the first issue: the necessity for pragmatic thought detached from the blind passions of the hour; the favorable opportunity the war offered for a more centralized and active national community; and the American stake in a peace settlement that assured stability and justice.

From the very outset, moreover, the editors began their consideration of the wartime issues on the basis of a pair of assumptions, which they shared with most Americans and which carried enormous implications for editorial policy. The first assumption was that it would be the greatest folly for the United States to rule out absolutely the possibility of fighting. In an important editorial, "Pacifism vs. Passivism," in the sixth issue of the journal, Croly himself put the matter succinctly: "A nation does not commit the great sin when it fights. It commits the great sin when it fights for a bad cause or when it is

221

afraid to fight for a good cause. . . . A modern nation which wants the world to live in peace . . . must be willing and ready, whenever a clear case can be made out against a disturber of the peace, to join with other nations in taking up arms against the malefactor."[5] It would be many months before *The New Republic* was ready to acknowledge that "a clear case" had been made; but the journal's ultimate advocacy of intervention was in some measure foreordained by Croly's argument. This assumption—that Americans might someday have to fight—also accounted for one of the clearest and most consistent editorial positions, which pervaded the magazine throughout the war years: the relentless and bitter denunciation of "dogmatic pacifism."[6]

The second of *The New Republic*'s basic assumptions was that American interests, hopes, and affections were more closely tied to the Allied cause than to that of the Central Powers. Despite conscientious attempts to retain a fair-minded balance, and despite genuine anguish over the inclusion of the despotic Czar ("Any misgivings we may have entertained about the cause of the Allies," the editors wrote in February 1916, "have always turned upon the contribution that Russia has made to the Alliance"),[7] the editors, like most Americans, hoped that the Allies would fare well in the contest. In part, no doubt, this leaning reflected the social and cultural biases of the editors. But even those who might have been expected to harbor reservations, supported the Allies—both Walter Weyl, whose father was a German immigrant and who had completed a part of his own education in Germany, and Francis Hackett, a militant Irish nationalist with little love for the English, favored the Allies.[8] Willard Straight, mean-

[5] "Pacifism vs. Passivism," *NR*, 1 (December 12, 1914): 6–7. In this case, as in some others, the authorship of anonymous editorials is ascribed to HC on the basis of distinctive style.

[6] For early expressions of the view that America might eventually be compelled to join the conflict, see "Security for Neutrals," *NR*, 1 (January 2, 1915): 7–9; "The Minute-Men Myth," ibid. (January 9, 1915): 9–10; ibid. (January 30, 1915): 3–4; "Getting it Both Ways," ibid., 2 (February 27, 1915): 86–87; "Are We Militarists?" ibid. (March 20, 1915): 166; ibid., 3 (May 15, 1915): 24; "Not Our War," ibid. (June 5, 1915): 108–10; ibid. (July 3, 1915): 212–13. For early criticism of the pacifists, see "Pacifism vs. Passivism," ibid., 1 (December 12, 1914): 6–7; ibid. (December 19, 1914): 3; "Peace and Publicity," ibid. (December 26, 1914): 7–8; "Security for Neutrals," ibid. (January 2, 1915): 7–9; "The Minute-Men Myth," ibid. (January 9, 1915): 9–10; ibid. (January 30, 1915): 3–4; ibid., 2 (March 6, 1915): 110–11; "Are We Militarists?" ibid. (March 20, 1915): 166–67.

[7] "The War As We See It," *NR* 6 (February 26, 1916): 103.

[8] Charles Forcey, *The Crossroads of Liberalism: Croly, Weyl, Lippmann and the Progressive Era, 1900–1924* (New York, 1961), 228–29. For Weyl, see ibid.; for Hackett, see his *I Chose Denmark* (New York, 1940), 12, and Alvin S. Johnson, *Pioneer's Progress, An Autobiography* (New York, 1952), 241–42.

while, was unrestrained by any pretense of moderation: "I detest the German, personally, politically, socially . . . ," he wrote Croly in March 1915. "I have never been able to walk down the Unter den Linden without a terrible desire to commit manslaughter, nor can I hear that gutteral tongue without inward revolt." By 1918, Straight would be calling wildly for the "extermination" of German leadership and the total destruction of the German people.[9]

Reinforcing the natural bent of the editors was the group of English intellectuals that Croly had gathered around *The New Republic*. Norman Angell was particularly close to the journal, attending editorial meetings, writing "constantly for it, both unsigned leaders and signed articles."[10] Other Englishmen—Brailsford, Laski, Zimmern, Ratcliffe, Murray and others—made numerous contributions during the period of American neutrality. Although these writers were often radical critics of English policy, particularly of English imperialism, they manifested sufficient loyalty to England's cause to impart to the journal a tone generally (though not always and never blindly) sympathetic to the Allies. Evidently some Englishmen had no doubts about the magazine's direction: after Croly's opening editorial, "The End of American Isolation," a distinguished English publisher walked into the office and offered to buy fifty thousand copies of the journal every week, if he could be assured that each issue would contain such an article. Lippmann later recalled that the bizarre episode provided his only taste of "what it feels like to be offered a bribe."[11]

Over the years, *The New Republic*'s wartime editorials have been studied by numerous historians.[12] Many of them have been able to

[9] Willard Straight to HC, March 1, 1915, Straight mss., Cornell University. The wartime letters from Straight to his wife were filled with violent anti-German language; see especially, letters of March 2, April 29, May 12, and May 19, 1918. ". . . the more I see and think of this thing, the more I am convinced that bar the upheaval in Germany, which I don't believe will come, we must destroy that people. If they wont destroy their Government we must destroy them with the Government they have tolerated and crush them and their poisonous breed for all time" (April 29, 1918).

[10] Norman Angell, "Oral History," Columbia Oral History Project, 129; see also Angell, *After All: The Autobiography of Norman Angell* (New York, 1951), 202–204.

[11] Walter Lippmann, "Notes for a Biography," *NR*, 63 (July 16, 1930): 251.

[12] For examples, see Forcey, *Crossroads of Liberalism*, 221–91; William H. Atwood, "Pathfinders of American Liberalism: The Story of *The New Republic*" (unpublished senior thesis, Princeton University, 1941); Robert E. Osgood, *Ideals and Self-Interest in America's Foreign Relations: The Great Transformation of the Twentieth Century* (Chicago, 1953), 115–30; David Noble, *The Paradox of Progressive Thought* (Minneapolis, 1958), 34–54; Christopher Lasch, *The New Radicalism in America (1889–1963): The Intellectual as a Social Type* (New York, 1965), 181–250; Eric F. Goldman, *Rendezvous with Destiny: A History of Modern American Reform* (New York, 1952), 233, 251–53; Frank Luther Mott, *A History of American Magazines* (Cambridge, Mass., 1968), V: 200–209;

subscribe, at least in part, to the verdict of George Kennan. "In point of sheer literary excellence alone, these men had no superiors among their American contemporaries," Kennan wrote. "In addition, they were able to muster among them a catholicity of interest, a depth of perception, a seriousness of concept, a tolerance, and a good taste that placed their collective effort in the foremost ranks of English-language journalism of all time."[13] Others have rightly praised *The New Republic*'s exemplary moderation, its freedom from hysteria, its lucid and thoughtful approach. But none has been able to argue that the journal served as a beacon of consistent and creative intellectual leadership, guiding Americans wisely through the morass of international politics. Reading those old articles and editorials two generations after they were written forces the historian to the conclusion that the editors, like virtually everyone else in America, were swept along by gigantic forces and tripped up by unexpected episodes. It has been a simple matter to point out obvious fluctuations, even stunning inconsistencies in the magazine's positions on the war. And, in retrospect, it is clear that Croly and his associates were moved along roughly the same path, and moved along at roughly the same speed, as many other Americans. Indeed, they were in general harmony with the course of the administration of Woodrow Wilson—sometimes a few weeks ahead, sometimes a few weeks behind, but in general harmony.[14]

II

The journal's position on the emotional issue of "preparedness" was virtually dictated by the editors' assumption that the country might someday have to fight. For a time *The New Republic* tried to mediate the issue of increasing armaments, seeing itself as walking the rational middle way between the extremism of the militarists and the extrem-

---

Paul F. Bourke, "The Status of Politics, 1909–1919: *The New Republic*, Randolph Bourne and Van Wyck Brooks," *Journal of American Studies*, 8 (1974): 171–208; Clarence Karier, "Making the World Safe for Democracy: An Historical Critique of John Dewey's Pragmatic Liberal Philosophy in the Warfare State," *Educational Theory*, 27 (1977): 12–47. James A. Neuchterlein, "The Dream of Scientific Liberalism. *The New Republic* and American Progressive Thought, 1914–1920," *Review of Politics*, 42 (April 1980): 167–90.

[13] Cited in Neuchterlein, "The Dream of Scientific Liberalism," 168.

[14] For Wilson's path to war, see the three volumes by Arthur S. Link, *Wilson: The Struggle for Neutrality, 1914–1915* (Princeton, 1960), *Wilson: Confusions and Crises, 1915–1916* (Princeton, 1964), and *Wilson: Campaigns for Progressivism and Peace, 1916–1917* (Princeton, 1965).

ism of the pacifists. Through the midsummer of 1915 (despite the sinking of the *Lusitania* in May), the journal insisted that while some strengthening of the army and navy was obviously necessary, both sets of "agitators" failed to discern that armaments were merely tools— and that what was desperately required was constructive national discussion of America's purposes and interests in the world. "The army and the navy are not ready to do the work which may be eventually imposed upon them; but they are far better prepared than are the mind and will of the American nation."[15]

Pious calls for deeper thought (which had become nearly a substitute for taking a position in the early issues of *The New Republic*) could not serve for very long. And by the end of August 1915 (a week after the sinking of the *Arabic*), the editors had chosen preparedness. "The only safe course is what looks like the dangerous one: to let Germany understand now that the United States is preparing to act, and that only a disavowal, which means a guarantee for the future, can stop the carrying out of our intention to isolate and boycott and mobilize." The nation was not yet ready for unlimited entanglement with the Allies, but there was much that might be done immediately. "We can prepare complete non-intercourse with Germany; stoppage of mails, wireless, imports, exports; seizure of German property and patents. We can increase our output of munitions, we can open up the American money markets to the enemies of Germany."[16] Clearly, *The New Republic*, under the pressure of events on the high seas, had abandoned the role of mediator between pacifists and militarists and, despite an occasional rebuke at their excesses, had opted for the latter. President Wilson, who had brooded over the preparedness question all summer, announced a similar policy five days after *The New Republic*'s editorial.[17]

Croly and the others were moved toward preparation only in part by the pressure of events. They had an additional reason, one that did not enter into the thinking of the president. It was precisely the vehicle of preparedness that would carry the country toward Herbert

[15] "Preparedness for What?" *NR*, 3 (June 26, 1915): 189. For similar early expressions on preparedness, see ibid., 1 (December 12, 1914): 3–4; ibid. (December 19, 1914): 3; "The Minute-Men Myth," ibid. (January 9, 1915): 9–10; ibid. (January 30, 1915): 4; ibid., 2 (February 27, 1915): 84; "Are We Militarists?" ibid. (March 20, 1915): 166–67; "The Deeper Preparedness," ibid. (July 3, 1915): 218–19; ibid., 5 (November 6, 1915): 3; ibid. (January 1, 1916): 206.

[16] *NR*, 4 (August 28, 1915): 82–83.

[17] For Wilson's "reversal of position," see Link, *Wilson: Struggle for Neutrality*, 588–93.

Croly's dream of a centralized and activist federal government—in effect, "social reform may be attached as a rider to military preparedness." In a candid editorial entitled "Preparedness—A Trojan Horse," *The New Republic* argued that a nation cannot prepare for a war, much less fight one, if it "clings to a *laissez-faire* policy about property, business, labor, and social organization." While admitting that war and social reform were "contradictory purposes," the journal insisted that getting ready for the possibility of conflict provided a golden opportunity to enact the social and economic program of *The Promise of American Life*:

> Modern war implies a concerted use of the railroad, telegraph, telephone, postal, and wireless services. Are our systems of communications capable of coordination at short notice? Is anyone preparing a plan by which the constitutional difficulties can be circumvented and a powerful national control imposed? Modern war requires the commandeering of much private property. Is anyone studying what property would have to be taken, what the terms would be, what the procedure, and what the administrative technique? Modern war requires a very flexible factory system with men adaptable enough to turn quickly from one kind of work to another. Is the government planning to make a survey of our industrial assets so that they can be mobilized effectively? Modern war is a relentless test of organization. The transition from a peace basis means temporary unemployment, malemployment, destitution, food scarcity. The raising of armies means the creation of large numbers of dependent women and children who require pensions and relief. These needs can be handled only by a large administrative machine composed of men with expert knowledge. Our present method of foozling with unemployment, sickness, age, and infancy, would break down utterly in a war that really tested the nation.[18]

Since the advocacy of preparation took place against the background of German provocation, it resulted in a certain amount of anti-German commentary. But neither *The New Republic* nor President Wilson was ready to suggest that there was any necessary connection between rearming and the abandoning of the official Amer-

---

[18] "Preparedness—A Trojan Horse," *NR*, 5 (November 6, 1915): 6. For similar expressions, see ibid., 1 (November 14, 1914): 4; S. K. Ratcliffe, "How England Organised at Home," ibid. (December 12, 1914): 15–16; "The Landslide into Collectivism," ibid., 2 (April 10, 1915): 253–55; "The Plattsburg Idea," ibid., 4 (October 9, 1915): 247–49; "The Reality of Peace," ibid. (October 30, 1915): 322–23.

ican policy of neutrality. The country might be forced to strengthen its military, but that did not mean that it had to rush into the arms of one or another set of belligerents.

At the outbreak of the war, of course, Wilson had called upon Americans to be neutral "in fact as well as in name. . . . impartial in thought as well as action."[19] That sort of neutrality, however, must have involved considerable psychological strain for Herbert Croly—and not merely because he quietly shared the general American sympathy for the Allies.[20] Since 1909, after all, Croly had enjoyed the reputation of being the foremost advocate of activism, of Rooseveltian action, of determined commitment in the conduct of national affairs. To whatever extent the policy of neutrality implied passivity, impotence, fatalism, standing aloof in the confidence that things would work themselves out for the best—to that extent neutrality was at war with everything Croly had come to symbolize. Neutrality in foreign relations must have seemed uncomfortably similar to the pernicious American faith in that "automatic fulfillment" (what Croly's associate Walter Lippmann had contemptuously called "drift") that so bedeviled the conduct of domestic affairs. Therefore, although Croly and his colleagues started editorializing from the position of strictest Wilsonian neutrality, they took special pains to insist that *their* neutrality was neither cowardice nor drift. On the contrary, they maintained, their neutrality was the product of pragmatic analysis, the desire to avoid blind fanaticism, and the hope of contributing to peace in the most useful way possible.

The scrupulous neutrality of the early issues of *The New Republic* was based on the editors' analysis of what was at stake in the European war. They consistently refused to tie their position to any abstract moral balance sheet, to favor one side over the other because one was "right" and the other "wrong"—the editors found plenty of instances of "wrong" on both sides. Instead, they concluded early in the war that a total victory by either side would be disastrous. As the victor imposed his harsh terms on the vanquished, the seeds of international instability would be sown and the fruit of that mistake would be new wars and fresh dislocations. British control of the seas must not be endangered by a too decisive German victory; and the German check upon Russian ambitions must not be endangered by a too decisive Allied one. Hence Croly and the others were led to es-

[19] Link, *Wilson: Struggle for Neutrality*, 65–66.

[20] In *The Promise of American Life*, five years earlier, HC had called for a formal treaty between Canada, the United States, and Great Britain (306–307). For his remarks on England, France, and Germany, see *PAL*, ch. viii.

pousing two positions, which they were to maintain long after the sinking of the *Lusitania*: an inconclusive war and a peace that would not be punitive.[21]

The opening of the submarine campaign in the spring of 1915 not only found *The New Republic* decisively behind preparedness, it also brought a new definition of "neutrality." The "cruel violence" of submarine warfare provoked the editors to some momentarily harsh language—they sought, for example, a way to demonstrate the conviction that Germany was "unfit for the society of nations. . . ." But the journal carefully enumerated English sins as well ("England has stretched the list of contraband, has blockaded neutral ports, has exerted to its full capacity her dominion of the seas. She has treated us politely and humanely, but she has taken away our rights upon the highways of Europe."). Nevertheless, the crimes were unequal and, morality quite aside, so were the dangers to the future of Europe being posed by the belligerents. Germany's abuses were "infinitely greater" than England's. What America needed was a way to express its resistance to German practices and policies while at the same time "declining responsibility" for the aims of the Allies.[22]

By November, with Germany showing no signs of limiting her submarine strategy, *The New Republic* was advocating a policy far removed from the impartiality originally called for by Wilson. In an editorial advising against an embargo on British goods, despite British provocations, Croly himself defined the new neutrality:

> The threat of an embargo on exports might bring Great Britain to terms, but the threat will not and should not be made; and whatever reason may be given officially for not making it, the essential reason is simple and decisive. Great Britain and the United States are to a very exceptional extent interdependent countries. They cannot afford to quarrel. They have every reason to cooperate. In relation to the issues raised by the war, American sympathies are, on the balance, pro-Ally. The United States is

---

[21] For some early expressions of these views, see "Chesterton-Viereck," *NR*, 1 (January 23, 1915): 7–8; "Contraband and Common Sense," ibid. (January 30, 1915): 7–8; ibid., 2 (March 20, 1915): 163–64; "Futile War Indemnities," ibid. (April 17, 1915): 276–77; HC, "The Meaning of It," ibid., 4 (August 7, 1915): 10–11; "A Congress of Neutrals," ibid. (October 23, 1915): 296–97; "Pro-German," ibid., 5 (December 4, 1915): 107–108; "Playing Germany's Game," ibid. (December 4, 1915): 108–10; "Germany Stands Pat," ibid. (December 18, 1915): 160–61; "Are We Pro-German?" ibid. (December 18, 1915): 161–62; "A Negligible Germany," ibid. (December 25, 1915): 184–86; ibid. (January 8, 1916): 235.

[22] "The Next Step," *NR*, 3 (July 31, 1915): 322–23.

neutral, but it is benevolently neutral. So far as we have any discretion, we do not propose to embarrass Great Britain and France during their desperate contest with a ruthless and terrifying enemy.[23]

The policy of "benevolent neutrality"—asserting American rights against all belligerents, but tacitly refusing to do anything that would impede the Allied war effort—became the posture of *The New Republic* until the spring of 1916.

In their issue of April 22, 1916 (the Germans had torpedoed the *Sussex* on March 24), in a specially printed "Appeal to the President," the editors unequivocally announced that "we must abolish the old doctrine of neutrality. . . . [W]e must say that from now on the United States is not neutral. It intends to use its moral power, its economic resources, and in some cases its military force against the aggressor." The journal then proceeded to lay down a series of demands on Germany, which the editors must have realized were impossible. We must announce to Germany "that we shall not only break off negotiations but aid her enemies until she agrees to abandon submarine warfare against commerce, until she agrees to evacuate Belgium, France, and Serbia, to indemnify Belgium and to accept the principle that in the future all nations shall use their resources against the Power which refuses to submit its quarrel to international inquiry."[24]

The "*Sussex* pledge"—Germany's promise to refrain from torpedoing merchant ships without warning—was accepted by the administration in early May. It opened the way for eight months of more relaxed German-American relations and rekindled the flickering hope for peace without American entry. Both *The New Republic* and Wilson, who was now in the midst of a closely contested election, seized on the possibility of peace, and the journal pressed the president for

[23] *NR*, 5 (November 13, 1915): 27. In defining their own position, in a long response to a critical letter from George Santayana ("The War As We See It," *NR*, 6 [February 26, 1916]: 102), the editors wrote: "THE NEW REPUBLIC has argued in favor of stretching that neutrality in the direction of benevolence towards the Allies. The policy of benevolent neutrality did not require or even permit the surrender of the rights of American citizens under international law. . . . While still asserting the legal rights of American citizens under the law of nations as the clearest evidence of that international order for which the Allies claim to be fighting, the American government could use its own discretion in pushing its protests home. . . . THE NEW REPUBLIC has argued in favor of a benevolently neutral policy towards the Allies on the ground of national interests as well as of international. . . ."

[24] "An Appeal to the President," *NR*, 6 (April 22, 1916): 303–305.

a serious attempt to guide the belligerents toward a settlement.[25] The fact remained, however, that back in April, *The New Republic* had practically declared war on Germany, a full year before the United States Congress.

Throughout their long and tortured march toward advocating American entry, Croly and his colleagues never lost sight of their twin objectives of battlefield stalemate and lenient peace terms. Even in November 1915, while first defining their policy of "benevolent neutrality," the journal reported with satisfaction that "at the beginning of a second winter's campaign everything indicates that the subjugation of their enemies will constitute a task beyond the military strength of either group." Under the circumstances, therefore, peace discussions should begin immediately. And the Allies would do well to remember that "an inconclusive ending to the war and a treaty of compromise and adjustment has a much better chance of contributing to the ultimate peace of Europe than has the ruthless subjugation of Germany."[26] And a year later, with Wilson safely reelected and the peace effort obviously failing to produce any hopeful movement whatsoever, *The New Republic* reasserted its program in a single, memorable phrase: "Peace without Victory."[27]

The first three months of 1917 saw the nation slide helplessly toward involvement in the war. A combination of anger, frustration, and fear drove many Americans, hitherto neutral, to clamor for decisive action from the government, whatever the cost. *The New Republic* was not immune to these currents of popular feeling. The editors, like many other Americans, were particularly moved by two international developments. The German resumption of unrestricted submarine warfare (January 31) and Wilson's immediate breaking of diplomatic relations (February 3) convinced them that all the previous attempts to "pocket pride" and calmly negotiate, however justifiable they might have been in the past, were now beside the point. "We are now in a twilight zone between peace and war," the editors declared on February 10. "How long we shall stay in it no human being in America knows. It is nevertheless perfectly clear that the period of suspense must be devoted to increasing the pressure on Germany.

---

[25] See for examples, "Mr. Wilson's Great Utterance," *NR*, 7 (June 3, 1916): 102–104; "Terms of Peace," ibid., 8 (September 9, 1916): 131–32; ibid., 9 (November 4, 1916): 1; "Honor and Election Returns," ibid. (November 18, 1916): 62; "The Note as Americanism," ibid. (December 30, 1916): 228–30.

[26] "War At Any Price," *NR*, 5 (November 27, 1915): 84–85.

[27] "Peace Without Victory," *NR*, 9 (December 23, 1916): 201–202.

The only course of action now is to assume that there will be war.
. . ."[28]

Then, in mid-March, the incredible news came filtering in from
Russia. *The New Republic* spoke of it in almost religious tones: "In a
period like the present, of agony and foreboding, let us be humbly
thankful for a great event which is also a great victory. The most
corrupt government, the most detestable despotism, which has survived among the nations of the modern world, is by way of perish-
ing. . . ."[29] The Russian government (which "befouled the political
atmosphere of modern Europe" and "tainted or revolted every decent human being who was cast within the circle of its influence")
was no longer to stand as an obstacle to full-hearted support of the
Allied cause. Now at last all the enemies of Germany were more or
less democratic.[30]

Herbert Croly had quite a special reason, however, for joining in
the clamor for war in early 1917. On January 22, President Wilson
appeared before the United States Senate to define the principles of
an eventual peace settlement. In point after point (with the exception
of a single quibble over the meaning of freedom of the seas),[31] Wilson
expressed views that were in harmony with those of *The New Republic*. And when the President of the United States actually used the
phrase "peace without victory," a phrase the journal had launched
only a month before, the editors were beside themselves.[32]

That night, Croly hurried over to East Fifty-third Street to see
Colonel Edward M. House, the president's closest confidant and adviser. Wilson's speech, Croly told House, was "the greatest event of
his own life."[33] The next day Croly wrote directly to the president.
"It seems to me that in that address you marshal with great lucidity
and eloquence every important fact which has been brought up by

[28] "America's Part in the War," *NR*, 10 (February 10, 1917): 33.

[29] "War and Revolution," *NR*, 10 (March 24, 1917): 212.

[30] "German Political Strategy," *NR*, 10 (April 7, 1917): 281–82. For additional commentary on developments in Russia, see "Liberal Russia and the Peace of the World,"
ibid. (March 24, 1917): 214–15; ibid. (April 21, 1917): 332. In general, see Christopher
Lasch, *The American Liberals and the Russian Revolution* (New York, 1962).

[31] "America Speaks," *NR*, 9 (January 27, 1917): 341. The editors argued that "the
passage referring to the freedom of the seas appears to contradict the idea of a league
to enforce peace. In an organized world freedom of the seas would certainly not exist
for the aggressor."

[32] For the text of Wilson's address, see Arthur S. Link et al., eds., *The Papers of
Woodrow Wilson* (Princeton, 1966–), 40: 533–39.

[33] Edward M. House to Woodrow Wilson, January 22, 1917, Wilson mss., Library
of Congress, published in Link et al., *Papers of Woodrow Wilson*, 40: 539.

231

the two and a half years of world warfare, and every important principle which the experience of that two and a half years has made authoritative and real. It is a document which will leave a permanent mark on the moral consciousness of, and I hope in the actual institutions of the American people, and which will reverberate throughout history."[34] Wilson lost no time in responding. "I was interested and encouraged when preparing my recent address to the Senate to find an editorial in the New Republic which was not only written along the same lines but which served to clarify and strengthen my thought not a little. In that, as in many other matters, I am your debtor." The president closed the letter "with warmest appreciation, cordially and sincerely yours."[35]

Herbert Croly's response to Wilson's speech was, on the face of it, astonishingly unrestrained—calling *any* political speech "the greatest event" of his life was a remarkable thing for Croly to have done. Even discounting his enthusiasm by attributing some of it to the euphoria of having his magazine quoted by the president in a major speech, it is clear that the ecstatic reaction exposed some of the editor's deepest feelings and needs. The central ambition of Croly's life, after all, was to influence public affairs, to serve as a guide and a philosopher, pointing the way to sounder and more thoughtful national policies. His books had been written and his journal founded with precisely that aim in mind. Achieving his purpose, however, required gaining the ear of those in power—Croly always understood that shrill shouting from the "outside" would be easily dismissed as mere carping. It was natural, therefore, that he should find in President Wilson's quotation confirmation that he was, at last, being heard by those in authority. And Wilson's letter, tactfully worded so as to encourage the feeling that influence was indeed being wielded, must have reminded Croly of that other momentous letter, written seven years before by Theodore Roosevelt, that praised Croly's ideas and launched his career. In view of what he had personally at stake, Croly's unrestrained satisfaction is not hard to understand.

The president's speech to the Senate did more than gratify Herbert Croly, however. It also confirmed, in the minds of many who watched national affairs, what had long been suspected—that Croly's *New*

[34] HC to Woodrow Wilson, January 23, 1917, Wilson mss., published in Link et al., eds., *Papers of Woodrow Wilson*, 40: 559. See also Ray Stannard Baker to Walter Lippmann, August 31, 1932, Ray Stannard Baker mss., Library of Congress, and Lippmann's reply, September 14, ibid.

[35] Woodrow Wilson to HC, January 25, 1917, Wilson mss., published in Link et al., eds., *Papers of Woodrow Wilson*, 41: 13.

Republic enjoyed a special relationship with the Wilson administration, that officials in Washington were, in some measure, being tutored by the cluster of intellectuals that Croly had gathered in New York City. The legend of the journal's influence had been growing since the election of 1916, and on the strength of its suspected importance subscriptions came in steadily. Lippmann believed that on one occasion the stock market fell because of a *New Republic* editorial, and Oswald Garrison Villard remembered that "it was considered bad form in some official circles to be seen without" *The New Republic*.[36] Woodrow Wilson's speech, of course, did very little to discourage the notion that the magazine was what Norman Angell later called it, "a mouthpiece for the White House," and that Croly and the others were "insiders."[37]

III

In reality, *The New Republic*'s relation to the administration was more subtle and complex. Croly and the Straights had started the journal, after all, in order to advocate a particular brand of domestic progressivism, the brand associated with Wilson's archenemy, Theodore Roosevelt. To Croly, the principles of the Bull Moose progressivism of the Colonel—nationalism, centralization, scientific efficiency, sympathy for large units of production—were filled with hopeful promise; the progressivism of Wilson—Jeffersonian, moralistic, eager to restore primitive competition between small entrepreneurs—was retrograde and potentially disastrous. By the fall of 1914, when the first issue of *The New Republic* appeared, Herbert Croly was widely recognized as one of the foremost critics of the president. How could the man who had written *Progressive Democracy*, that strident denunciation of Wilson's "New Freedom," have hoped to have his counsel taken seriously by the White House?

At the same time, because he wanted so profoundly to shape domestic policy, and because he had such deep faith in the magic of

[36] Lippmann, "Notes for a Biography," 251; and Oswald Garrison Villard, *Fighting Years: Memoirs of a Liberal Editor* (New York, 1938), 361. In his *Dictionary of American Biography* article on HC (supplement 1), Villard repeats the stock market story. As far as the influence of the *NR* is concerned, Villard writes: "That the publicaton played a great part in getting the United States into the First World War admits of no doubt. . . ." See also Bruce Bliven, "Oral History," Columbia University Oral History Project, 29–31.

[37] Angell, *After All*, 203; Villard's *DAB* article (see preceding note) also mentioned "the spreading belief that *The New Republic* was the mouthpiece of Woodrow Wilson."

executive leadership, reaching some sort of an intellectual accommodation with Wilsonianism must have been a high temptation for Croly. The task was a delicate one, requiring a careful balance of praise and instruction, but the attempt constituted the underlying theme of *The New Republic*'s treatment of domestic issues.

The journal's coverage of American life, of course, went far beyond the rivalry between Roosevelt and Wilson, and the split between progressives, which that rivalry symbolized. Week after week, Croly published leaders, editorials and articles having little or nothing to do with such matters. The magazine took up the Leo Frank case in Georgia, the Senate's rejection of George Rublee for the Federal Trade Commission, and La Follette's Seamen's Bill.[38] It campaigned for women's suffrage, the dissemination of birth control information, the rights of Negroes.[39] The editors printed numerous articles advocating progressive education and the academic freedom of teachers.[40] They examined major trends in literature and the arts, philanthropy and agriculture, immigration and religion. In short,

[38] On Leo Frank, see *NR*, 1 (November 28, 1914): 5; ibid., 2 (April 24, 1915): 290; "Leo Frank," ibid., 3 (July 24, 1915): 300; and "Georgia and the Nation," ibid., 4 (September 4, 1915): 112–14. On Rublee, see ibid., 2 (February 27, 1915): 83; "Personally Offensive," ibid., 6 (February 26, 1916): 89–90; ibid., 7 (May 20, 1916): 49; ibid., 8 (September 2, 1916): 101; and ibid. (October 21, 1916): 280. On the Seamen's Bill, see ibid., 2 (February 27, 1915): 85–86; Gerard Henderson, "The Seamen's Law and World Wages," ibid., 4 (October 9, 1915): 254–56, and Henderson, "The Seamen's Law on Safety at Sea," ibid. (October 16, 1915): 279–81.

[39] On women's suffrage, see *NR*, 1 (November 7, 1914): 4–5; ibid. (November 21, 1914): 4; ibid. (January 16, 1915): 4; "Chivalry in Congress," ibid. (January 23, 1915): 8–9; ibid., 2 (February 13, 1915): 30; ibid., 3 (July 3, 1915): 213; and a special supplement, "Votes for Women," ibid., 4 (October 9, 1915): 1–16. For the journal's position on birth control, see "The Control of Births," ibid., 2 (March 6, 1915): 114–15; "The Control of Births," ibid. (April 17, 1915): 273–75; ibid., 4 (September 18, 1915): 164; and "The Age of Birth Control," ibid. (September 25, 1915): 195–97. On the race problem, see ibid., 1 (November 21, 1914): 5; ibid., (January 9, 1915): 5; Francis Hackett, "Brotherly Love," ibid., 2 (March 20, 1915): 185; ibid. (April 24, 1915): 291–92; ibid., 3 (June 5, 1915): 105; ibid. (June 26, 1915): 186; ibid., 5 (November 13, 1915): 28; and "A Leader of Humanity," ibid. (November 20, 1915): 60–61.

[40] For the numerous articles on education by Randolph Bourne and John Dewey, see Olaf Hansen, ed., *The Radical Will: Randolph Bourne, Selected Writings, 1911-1918* (New York, 1977), 541–45; and Milton H. Thomas, *John Dewey: A Centennial Bibliography* (Chicago, 1962), 42ff. See also "Puzzle Education," *NR*, 1 (January 2, 1915): 10–11; "The Schools from the Outside," ibid. (January 30, 1915): 10–11; and ibid., 2 (February 13, 1915): 31. On academic freedom, see "Academic Freedom—A Confession," ibid., 1 (January 2, 1915): 17–18; and "Academic Feedom in Utah," ibid., 4 (October 16, 1915): 274–75. In general, see Steven Jay Turner, "The New Education in *The New Republic* Magazine: 1914–1930" (unpublished D.Ed. dissertation, University of Oklahoma, 1983).

readers were given wide-ranging, if fleeting, observations on the whole array of American cultural, political, economic, and social life; and there is probably no better way to grasp both the particular concerns and the general spirit of American progressivism than to explore the pages of *The New Republic* during these years. It is hardly an exaggeration to say that no major issue was fully defined and clarified, as far as American liberals were concerned, until Herbert Croly's journal of opinion had spoken.

Although an effort was made to present a catholic coverage of domestic affairs, from the start the whole program of nationalist progressivism was the undeniable message of *The New Republic*. The journal left no doubt, for example, about the need for the federal government to assume drastic and far-reaching new responsibilities. The central government had to take firmer hold of the problem of immigration,[41] adequately fund the Children's Bureau,[42] establish a respectable merchant marine,[43] and provide a system of agricultural credits.[44] Washington had the responsibility for creating federal labor exchanges to find work for the unemployed,[45] and, if that failed, to consider putting the unemployed to work on worthy federal projects.[46] American railroads should be nationalized immediately.[47] Federal conservation and water-power projects should be undertaken at once.[48]

Accomplishing these new tasks required that government itself be refashioned. *The New Republic* insisted that state authority be streamlined and rationalized,[49] and that the Constitution be rendered simpler to amend.[50] Congress should recognize its limitations;[51] and

[41] *NR*, 1 (November 14, 1914): 4; "Wanted—An Immigration Policy," ibid. (December 26, 1914): 10–11.

[42] *NR*, 2 (February 13, 1915): 30.

[43] *NR*, 3 (May 29, 1915): 79; and ibid. (June 19, 1915): 159.

[44] "Agricultural Credit," *NR*, 1 (December 19, 1914): 6–8.

[45] *NR*, 1 (December 5, 1914): 4; supplement to ibid. (December 26, 1914): 1–8, by John B. Andrews.

[46] "Federal Use of the Unemployed," *NR*, 2 (April 10, 1915): 250–51.

[47] "The Railroads and the Nation," *NR*, 1 (November 21, 1914): 11–12; "Railroad Regulation on Trial," ibid. (December 19, 1914): 8–9; Edward S. Corwin, "Making Railroad Regulation National," ibid., 2 (February 27, 1915): 94–96.

[48] "Conservation in Water Power," *NR*, 1 (January 23, 1915): 10–11.

[49] "Sessions in Texas," *NR*, 1 (November 14, 1914): 9; "The Republicans and the State Constitution," ibid. (November 28, 1914): 7–8; ibid. (January 23, 1915): 4–5; "A Decline of Legicide," ibid., 2 (March 6, 1915): 116–17.

[50] *NR*, 1 (January 23, 1915): 3–4.

[51] *NR*, 1 (November 7, 1914): 5; ibid. (November 14, 1914): 4–5; "The Spoken Message," ibid. (December 5, 1914): 11–12; ibid. (December 26, 1914): 3–4; ibid. (January 23, 1915): 3.

the public business should be directed by scientific experts, working through federal commissions or advising decision-makers.[52] Above all, the powers of the presidency should be increased: "[T]here is manifest need for the adjustment of the political structure to the representative function of the President," the journal argued in its very first issue. For example, "the president should have the right to introduce bills and bring them to a vote."[53]

No one familiar with Croly's economic views could have been much surprised by the editorial positions of *The New Republic* in that sphere. The journal was unabashedly pro-labor. In addition to urging the federal government to solve the unemployment problem, the journal regularly praised the unions,[54] called attention to particularly wretched working conditions and unfair wages,[55] and pressed upon state governments and judicial authorities alike, the desperate need for laws establishing—for both men and women workers—maximum hours and minimum wages.[56] (In the fall of 1919, Croly had the chance to practice what he had preached for so long, and *The New Republic* suspended publication for four issues during a printers' strike rather than have the journal printed by a non-union shop.)[57] As far as business was concerned, the journal advocated the same sort of scientific efficiency in management as it advocated for government.[58] And on the crucial question of the "trusts," Croly's magazine argued, as might have been expected, that the proper test of any corporation's abuse of power was the damage it did to the public,

[52] *NR*, 1 (December 19, 1914): 405; Edward Fitzpatrick, "Municipal Research—A Criticism," ibid. (January 2, 1915): 19–21; ibid. (January 23, 1915): 4–5; "The Utilities Bureau," ibid., 2 (March 6, 1915): 117; and ibid. (April 3, 1915): 217.

[53] *NR*, 1 (November 7, 1914): 5.

[54] "The Tolerated Unions," *NR*, 1 (November 7, 1914): 11–12; ibid. (November 14, 1914): 6; ibid. (January 16, 1915): 4; "Economic Statesmanship," ibid., 2 (February 6, 1915): 11-13.

[55] *NR*, 1 (December 26, 1914): 4, 5–6; ibid. (January 9, 1915): 3–4; ibid. (January 30, 1915): 3; "So-Called Industrial Peace," ibid. (January 30, 1915): 6–7; "Sidetracking Labor," ibid., 2 (March 27, 1915): 196–97; Walter Lippmann, "The Campaign Against Sweating," ibid. (March 27, 1915): supplement, 1–8.

[56] *NR*, 1 (November 7, 1914): 5–6; ibid. (November 28, 1914): 4; ibid. (January 30, 1915): 10; ibid., 2 (February 27, 1915): 85; "Sidetracking Labor," ibid. (March 27, 1915): 196–97; Walter Lippmann, "The Campaign Against Sweating," ibid. (March 27, 1915): supplement, 1–8; "Eight Hours for Work," ibid., 4 (September 18, 1915): 170–71.

[57] "The Printing Trade Dispute and the New Republic," *NR*, 20 (November 12, 1919): 313–14.

[58] *NR*, 1 (January 2, 1915): 3–4; Melvin T. Copeland, "Scientific Business," ibid. (January 2, 1915): 21–22.

not its mere "bigness" or the percentage of the market it happened to control.[59] In short, the positions espoused by *The New Republic*, were, in general, the familiar positions of the "New Nationalism."

But to the astonishment of the editors, the Wilson administration was not performing as poorly as had been anticipated on this economic, social, and political agenda. During their first eighteen months in power, Wilson and the Democrats had lowered the tariff, instituted an income tax, created the Federal Reserve System and the Federal Trade Commission, and addressed the trust problem in the Clayton Act.[60] Predictably, *The New Republic* had reservations about the antitrust program ("The Clayton Bill will probably do more harm than good, but the final draft constituted such a marked improvement upon the earlier versions that . . . it can at least be considered an example of successful destructive legislation").[61] But on the whole, the journal reported that the Democrats' record was "surprisingly good."[62] By January 1915, the editors were prepared to agree with Wilson that "the present Congress should be credited with the most remarkable record of any Congress since the Civil War. . . ." Even more, "the credit is largely due to Mr. Wilson."[63]

Despite Wilson's accomplishments, however, the editors found it hard to warm to him. Partly, it was the president's style, his annoying tendency to appear so "unequivocally righteous."[64] The editors detected in Wilson (as have many historians since) "a mind which is fully convinced of the everlasting righteousness of its own performances and which surrounds this conviction with a halo of shimmering rhetoric." But it was more than irritation with the president's moralism that kept the editors cool; they could not forgive him his philosophy. Woodrow Wilson "utterly misconceived the meaning and the task of American progressivism," they charged. He was, therefore, "a dangerous and unsound thinker upon contemporary political and social problems."[65] This discrepancy between his admirable acts and his inadequate political philosophy continued to gnaw at Croly and the others and they continued to punctuate their praise with snip-

---

[59] "Restraint of Trade," *NR*, 1 (November 21, 1914): 9–10; ibid. (December 5, 1914): 4; "An Unseen Reversal," ibid. (January 9, 1915): 7–8; ibid. (January 30, 1915): 5; ibid., 2 (April 3, 1915): 216.

[60] Arthur S. Link, *Wilson: The New Freedom* (Princeton, 1956).

[61] "A Narrow Escape for the Democrats," *NR*, 1 (November 7, 1914): 8.

[62] Ibid.

[63] *NR*, 1 (January 16, 1915): 3.

[64] "The Other-Worldliness of Wilson," *NR*, 2 (March 27, 1915): 194.

[65] "Presidential Complacency," *NR*, 1 (November 21, 1914): 7.

ing commentary. The editors approved of the Federal Trade Commission, for example, but they could not resist pointing out that it "represents a totally different approach, a spirit strangely contradictory to the campaign theories of the President."[66]

By 1914, Wilson had, in fact, edged away from his campaign theories. There were several reasons for the gradual shift. In the first place, the differences between the "New Freedom" and the "New Nationalism" had been badly exaggerated in the campaign of 1912. Both schools of progressive ideology addressed similar problems and saw similar dangers in American life—and whether one "regulated" the trusts or "busted" them, it turned out that it would require an activist, bureaucratic, and interventionist federal government, the sort of government advocated by Croly and typified by Wilsonian institutions such as the Federal Trade Commission or the Federal Reserve Board. In addition, the tense international scene after August 1914, required a prudent modification of any philosophy of rampant and thoroughgoing fragmentation of heavy industry. Finally, Wilson was enough of a political realist, despite the rhetoric of morality, to understand his electoral problem. He had received only forty-two percent of the vote in 1912. And he knew that his chances in 1916 depended on capturing the loyalties of a sizable portion of the four million supporters of Theodore Roosevelt.

In early and mid-1916, with the election approaching, Wilson embarked upon a series of domestic moves designed to win the support of progressives.[67] The nomination of Brandeis to the Supreme Court on January 28, gratified even those reformers who disagreed with some of the views of "the people's attorney," and convinced many people of the sincerity of the president's progressive instincts. Wilson's successful fights for a tariff commission, for the establishment of a system of rural credits, and for the Keating-Owen Child Labor Act (all of which positions could be interpreted as abandonments of aspects of the "New Freedom" of 1912) also helped to win over many. His handling of the threatened railroad strike during the summer of 1916, by imposing a mandatory eight-hour day, further endeared him to progressives of all stripes. These domestic measures, as well as Wilson's toughening stance on preparedness and certain "nationalistic" elements in his conduct of foreign relations, were all dutifully praised by The New Republic.[68] But whether the president's

[66] "An Unseen Reversal," NR, 1 (January 9, 1915): 7–8.

[67] Link, Wilson: Confusions and Crises, ch. xi.

[68] For the full-throated support of Wilson's nomination of Brandeis, see the numerous leaders and editorials published between February 5 (NR, 6: 4) and June 10, 1916

new flexibility would be sufficient to win over the likes of Herbert Croly (even given the latter's undoubted desire to reach an accommodation) remained to be seen.

At the same time that Wilson was demonstrating flexibility, Theodore Roosevelt was alienating the editors by his blustering intolerance. The break came quickly and decisively. In the *New York Times Magazine* of December 6, 1914, Roosevelt unleashed an unrestrained attack on Wilson's Mexican policy. Because of the president's "officious and mischievous intermeddling," he argued, the American nation was partly responsible for the brutal atrocities taking place in that country.[69] *The New Republic* promptly denounced Roosevelt: the ex-president's fulmination "was an example of the kind of fighting which has turned so many of his natural admirers into bitter enemies. . . . Where his profound knowledge of foreign affairs and his very realistic judgment might have made [a] contribution to the Mexican puzzle, he has kicked up so much dust to gain a petty end. . . . [S]omewhat driven by his prejudice against Mr. Wilson, he struck blindly and unfairly."[70]

It was not the sort of talk that Theodore Roosevelt expected from his followers, and he told Francis Hackett that he thought Croly and Weyl were "disloyal." Croly responded immediately:

> In writing and publishing that critical paragraph, we all of us considered it merely as the same kind of criticism which candid friends continually pass upon one another, and we had no idea that any question of loyalty or disloyalty could be raised by it. I

(ibid., 7: 134–35). On the Tariff Commission, see "A Tariff Board," ibid., 6 (February 12, 1916): 31–32; and "The Democrats as Legislators," ibid., 8 (September 2, 1916): 103–104. On rural credits, see ibid., 6 (April 8, 1916): 250; ibid., 7 (May 20, 1916): 51; and ibid. (July 22, 1916): 288–89. On child labor and the Keating–Owen Act, see "Devil's Advocates," ibid., 6 (February 5, 1916): 8–9; "The Child Labor Bill," ibid. (March 18, 1916): 171–72; and the exchange in the same issue, "Child Labor Under the Constitution," 182–84; and ibid., 8 (September 30, 1916): 203. For praise of Wilson's handling of the railroad labor difficulties, see "The Railroad Crisis and After," ibid. (August 26, 1916): 80–81; ibid. (September 2, 1916): 100–101; "Mr. Hughes's Rebuttal," ibid. (September 30, 1916): 208–209; and ibid. (October 7, 1916): 233. For the journal's approval of Wilson's military and foreign policies, see ibid., 7 (May 13, 1916): 26; "Mr. Wilson's Great Utterance," ibid. (June 3, 1916): 102–104; ibid. (June 17, 1916): 156; "Mr. Hughes and the Task Ahead," ibid.: 158–59; Walter Lippmann, "The Case for Wilson," ibid., 8 (October 14, 1916): 263–64; and HC, "The Two Parties in 1916," ibid. (October 21, 1916): 289–91.

[69] Theodore Roosevelt, "Our Responsibility to Mexico," *New York Times Magazine* (December 6, 1914): 1.

[70] *NR*, 1 (December 12, 1914): 5.

can understand that a criticism of that kind would be disloyal in case you were still President and we were subordinate administrative officials under you, or in case you were running for the Presidency upon a party ticket which we were supporting, but I do not see that at the present time we were under any obligation not to express our opinions such as they were upon any public utterance by you. The New Republic has never pretended to be a party organ, and its whole future success in life depends upon the impression which it makes upon its readers of being able to think disinterestedly and independently. . . .

In conclusion, I can only say that I myself possess a very deep and firm sense of personal loyalty to you, and I am more grateful to you for everything which you have done for me in the past than I am ever likely to have an opportunity of expressing.[71]

Roosevelt replied coolly:

There was the distinct implication in the editorial . . . that I was actuated by an unworthy motive. Now, I need not point out to you that the ascription of an unworthy motive by a man who is intimate with another carries very much more weight than if it comes from a stranger or from a political opponent. I absolutely agree with you that you are under no obligation whatever to not express any opinions you have as regards any public utterance by me. I also absolutely agree with you that the usefulness of "The New Republic" depends upon impressing its readers with its ability to think disinterestedly and independently. Moreover, my dear sir, I have done nothing for you. You are not under the least possible obligation to me of any kind. My sole feeling about you is that you have rendered a very great service to the republic. . . . It merely shows that we can't work together, which would be important if we were active party associates, but is not important as between an independent editor and an independent politician. . . .[72]

Personal relations between Croly and Roosevelt were ended forever by that exchange, and it is hard to escape the conclusion that Roosevelt was at fault. His denunciations of *The New Republic* grew ever more violent as he helplessly watched Wilson cutting deeper into his former support. The journal was being run, he said, by "three ane-

[71] HC to Theodore Roosevelt, January 11, 1915, Theodore Roosevelt mss., Library of Congress.

[72] Theodore Roosevelt to HC, January 15, 1915, Theodore Roosevelt mss.

mic gentiles and three international Jews."[73] The editors, he said, were "well-meaning geese—early Victorian geese" and "nice old ladies," who were "sinning against the light."[74] In March 1916, the editors discovered to their considerable embarrassment, that they had been ascribing to Roosevelt a position on the invasion of Belgium that he had not actually held at the time, and their revelation (together with an apology to Wilson) made Roosevelt appear to be something of a hypocritical opportunist.[75] By September 1916, Roosevelt was describing *The New Republic* as having "played a cur's part," and in a ranting letter to a friend he managed to misspell the names of all three chief editors.[76]

For their part, the editors felt with some justice that they had been entirely fair to Roosevelt. He received far more praise than criticism in the journal, and Lippmann confessed to Willard Straight after the Belgian exposé that "if my conscience troubled me about our attitude towards him it would be that we have not been as candid about Roosevelt as we have been about Wilson."[77] Roosevelt, after all, retained the ideological purity that meant so much to Croly and his associates; for all his flaws, he was the veritable symbol of vigorous, nationalist reform. If he had won the Republican nomination in 1916, there is little doubt that *The New Republic* would have supported him. Lippmann, speculating about that very possibility, wrote Straight that "if Roosevelt is nominated this campaign is going to be the most crucial test of our independence that has ever been presented to us because as I see it we have got to do two things. We have got to lean towards Roosevelt and we have got to keep a running fire of criticism about him. . . . We are bound to be the most troublesome friend he has."[78] When the Republicans chose Charles Evans Hughes, they relieved *The New Republic* of that responsibility. The journal politely suggested that Roosevelt have a try for the New York Senate seat.[79]

---

[73] Johnson, *Pioneer's Progress*, 245. To account for the "three international Jews," Roosevelt must have included Felix Frankfurter. While Frankfurter was active in the Zionist movement, neither Weyl nor Lippmann ever showed much interest in Jewish affairs.

[74] Theodore Roosevelt to Willard Straight, February 8, 1916, in E. E. Morison et al., eds., *The Letters of Theodore Roosevelt* (Cambridge, Mass., 1951–1954; 8 vols.): 8, 1019–21.

[75] "Mr. Roosevelt's Afterthought," *NR*, 6 (March 25, 1916): 204.

[76] Cited by Forcey as Roosevelt to Dan Wister, September 28, 1916, Roosevelt mss. Roosevelt referred to "Albert" Croly, Walter "Lippman" and Walter "Weil."

[77] Walter Lippmann to Willard Straight, April 6, 1916, Straight mss.

[78] Ibid.

[79] *NR*, 7 (June 17, 1916): 155.

For Croly the choice between Hughes and Wilson was a difficult one, and he wavered a long time before announcing his decision. He was tugged toward Wilson by his admiration for the president's progressive record and by the influence of former Bull Moose allies who flocked over to Wilson during the summer of 1916; in *The New Republic* office, Lippmann had come out for Wilson in July and Weyl did so in late September. On the other hand, Croly's friends were by no means unanimous—Willard Straight was for Hughes and so was Henry Stimson. In addition, Croly had been a Republican for so long and had so low a view of the party of Jefferson and Jackson (the Democratic party, he once wrote, "has the vitality of a low organism"),[80] that supporting Wilson would have required a wrenching break with his past. Above all, there was the lingering suspicion that the president was incapable of that heroic national leadership—either in domestic or foreign affairs—that Croly longed for.

In the end, Croly went for Wilson. But he waited until the October 21 issue and explained himself in one of the longest articles *The New Republic* had ever published. The tone hardly constituted a ringing endorsement:

> I shall vote for the reelection of President Wilson on November 7th chiefly for a reason which if its decisive effect had been predicted a few years ago would have seemed to me incredible. I shall vote for him chiefly because he has succeeded, at least for the time being, in transforming the Democracy into the more promising of the two major party organizations. To be entirely frank, the decision has been reached reluctantly and only after prolonged hesitation.

Croly's article—balanced, judicious, even-handed, and one of the best short pieces he ever wrote—denounced the Republicans soundly: they "have degenerated into a negative alternative to the Democrats. . . . [T]he moral integrity of the Republican party was destroyed by the schism of 1912." There were two factions in the party, and in trying to lead a unified effort, Hughes seemed incapable of developing a program acceptable to both. All that the Republicans could agree about was how much they despised Woodrow Wilson. Meanwhile, the president, for all his timidity, incompetence, and ideological unsoundness, had grown steadily in the office. In foreign affairs, after August 1915, he had developed a consistent and sound national policy. In domestic life, "Mr. Wilson and the Democratic party have

---

[80] *NR*, 1 (January 16, 1915): 3. Lippmann attributes the anonymously published remark to HC in *Newsweek*, 64 (July 6, 1964): 13.

begun to perform that work of national reconstruction which the Progressive party declared indispensable to the welfare of the commonwealth. . . . They have not gone very far, but they have at least started to fasten on the popular consciousness a new and better meaning for the American idea."[81]

In a private letter to Stimson, Croly admitted that he had originally intended to vote for Hughes but was disgusted by the campaign. Nevertheless, Croly told Stimson, he had no sharp preference between the two men: "It is a case with me of a comparatively small percentage." Weighing everything, and "in spite of the distrust of Mr. Wilson it seems to me that on record the balance tips in his favor. . . . As a result, I am perhaps 55% for Mr. Wilson at the present time. I shall vote for him without enthusiasm but still with the full conviction that the case for him is a little bit better than the case against him."[82] *The New Republic* attempted to maintain its reputation for fairness by publishing an article by Stimson, "Why I Shall Vote for Mr. Hughes," emphasizing mostly foreign affairs. And it solved what could have been an extremely delicate family squabble by giving a generous introduction to an equally generous expression of support for Hughes by Willard Straight.[83]

Thus had a certain amity been established between the editor and the administration. Each side harbored reservations, but each needed the other for the attainment of private purposes. The president wanted reelection and was persuaded that *The New Republic*, with its undoubted influence among progressives, could help. Croly, cut adrift by Roosevelt, wanted to make his ideas count and was persuaded that an accommodation with Wilson was the path to wielding influence. In the process, no doubt, principles were relaxed on both sides, but the editors were probably right in believing that the president had given more ground than they had.[84] Once America entered the war, the reverse was to be the case.

IV

The New Republic's support of Wilson's reelection, no matter how qualified and hesitant, opened the way for closer relations; and the

[81] HC, "The Two Parties in 1916," *NR*, 8 (October 21, 1916): 289–91.

[82] HC to Henry L. Stimson, October 5, 1916, Stimson mss., Yale University.

[83] Stimson, "Why I Shall Vote for Mr. Hughes," *NR*, 8 (October 28, 1916): 317–19; and "A Letter from Mr. Straight," ibid. (October 28, 1916): 313–14.

[84] Cf. Forcey's contention that the editors came around to Wilson because "the bright light of power held more allure for them than firm principle." *Crossroads of Liberalism*, 250–63.

praise-filled editorials of the closing days of the campaign continued into the fall and winter. The president's attempts to bring the belligerents to terms, his flattering use of the "peace without victory" editorial in January 1917, his dignified and decisive response to renewed submarine warfare, all encouraged hearty applause from Croly and the others.[85] By the time America declared war in April, the president of the United States could count on the warm sympathy of *The New Republic*. Because he saw the issues so clearly and addressed them so wisely, the editors proclaimed in the issue following the American declaration, "our debt and the world's debt to Woodrow Wilson is immeasurable."

> Only a statesman who will be called great could have made America's intervention mean so much to the generous forces of the world, could have lifted the inevitable horror of war into a deed so full of meaning. . . . No other statesman has ever so clearly identified the glory of his country with the peace and liberty of the world. . . . He can mean more to the happiness of mankind than any one who ever addressed the world. Through force of circumstances and through his own genius he has made it a practical possibility that he is to be the first great statesman to begin the better organization of the world. . . . Mr. Wilson is to-day the most liberal statesman in high office, and before long he is likely to be the most powerful. He represents the best hope in the whole world. He can go ahead exultingly with the blessings of men and women upon him.[86]

The editors did not confine their support to inflated rhetoric; they enlisted their services in a variety of more dramatic ways as well. Lippmann's activities were the most spectacular. Converted to Wilson in the summer of 1916, he consulted with the candidate, tried to persuade the others at the magazine, even took to the stump on Wilson's behalf. He fired off policy suggestions to Wilson and House and was granted personal interviews at the White House. When America entered the war, Lippmann volunteered his talents, left *The New Republic*, and became Newton Baker's assistant in the War Department. He soon attracted Colonel House's eye and was appointed secretary to the Inquiry, the extensive and prestigious organization of distinguished American academics charged with preparing detailed

[85] See for examples "The Note as Americanism," *NR*, 9 (December 30, 1916): 228–30; "The Power of the Pen," ibid. (January 20, 1917): 313–15; "America Speaks," ibid. (January 27, 1917): 340–42; and ibid., 10 (March 24, 1917): 210–11.

[86] "The Great Decision," *NR*, 10 (April 7, 1917): 279–80.

information for eventual use at the peace conference. Lippmann ended the war as a captain, in Military Intelligence, producing war propaganda. He went to Paris a trusted member of House's personal staff.[87] While Lippmann's wartime service was the most notable, he was not the only one of Croly's associates affected by the upheaval. Felix Frankfurter left Harvard for numerous and important official duties. Walter Weyl, who temporarily deserted the magazine in order to write a book, worked for the War Department and also on the Inquiry project. Robert Hallowell wrote patriotic tracts for the secretary of the treasury, and Alvin Johnson joined the mobilization effort as a dollar-a-year man under Wesley Mitchell. George Soule enlisted and rose from private to second lieutenant in seven months; and Willard Straight went in as a major.[88] Herbert Croly, meanwhile, remained steadfastly at his post—the editorial offices of *The New Republic* on West Twenty-first Street.

It is probable that Croly never met President Wilson face-to-face. Lippmann believed he did not;[89] and certainly Norman Angell's assertion that Croly "had access to the White House" is at best misleading.[90] But if Woodrow Wilson maintained his distance from Croly, Colonel House did not. The contacts between House and Croly, begun before the election of 1916, grew increasingly frequent and intimate afterwards. Years later, Lippmann, who was often a participant in the meetings, took special pains to insist that nothing improper had taken place: "He never told us what the President was going to do. We never knew anything that hadn't appeared in the newspapers. . . . The paper was never the organ of the Wilson administration. We never knew any secrets, we never had a request to publish or not to publish anything, and we were not in a confidential relationship. Colonel House made it his business to see all kinds of people, and we were among the people he saw."[91]

[87] Ronald Steel, *Walter Lippmann and the American Century* (Boston, 1980), chs. x–xii.

[88] Liva Baker, *Felix Frankfurter* (New York, 1969), 58–83; Michael Parrish, *Felix Frankfurter and His Times: The Reform Years* (New York, 1982), chs. v and vi; Forcey, *Crossroads of Liberalism*, 284; "Robert Canby Hallowell," *Harvard Class of 1910* (Report VII, 1935): 329–31; Johnson, *Pioneer's Progress*, 248–58; "George Soule," *Who's Who in America* (Chicago, 1920), 11: 2655; and HC, *Willard Straight* (New York, 1924), 478–79.

[89] Lippmann, "Notes for a Biography," 251. President Wilson spent several summer vacations in Cornish, and he and HC might have encountered one another there, but no record of such an encounter survives. Professor Link believes that the two men never met.

[90] Norman Angell, "Oral History," 132.

[91] Lippmann, "Notes for a Biography," 251.

Lippmann's assurances notwithstanding, the relationship between House and the two *New Republic* editors was so close to confidentiality as practically to reduce the journal to an arm of the Wilson administration. "I hope that we can see you at frequent intervals in the near future," Croly wrote to the Colonel in December 1916. "Both Mr. Lippmann and I are more interested in doing what little we can to back the President in his work than in anything else we have ever tried to do through The New Republic, and we are only too glad to give whatever ability we have and whatever influence the paper may have to presenting to our public the underlying purposes of the President's policy." By itself that pledge came perilously near to compromising the impartiality of *The New Republic*—a journal that had once boldly asserted that "an editor too friendly with a politician has mortgaged his integrity."[92] But Croly went even further: "In case you read anything we write upon the matter I should be very much obliged if you would occasionally let us know whether or not we are misinterpreting what the President is trying to do, or whether we are under-stating or over-stating the real motives of his policy. We merely want to back him up on his work and be the faithful and helpful interpreter of what seems to us to be one of the greatest enterprises ever undertaken by an American president."[93]

With the coming of the war in April 1917, Croly and Lippmann met with House almost every week. On April 17, House confided to his diary, "Lippmann and Croly and Miss Ida Tarbell came to lunch. Lippmann and Croly arrived a half hour in advance in order to have their weekly talk. . . . I outlined to all of them the things I thought they should do to help best."[94] On July 26, "Herbert Croly took lunch with me to talk over New Republic affairs. . . . He also wished to talk of the future policy of the New Republic, and to get an outline of the foreign situation, so that he and his staff might write intelligently and not conflict with the purposes of the Government."[95] The editor also tried to arrange meetings for friends and acquaintances, including John Dewey, who wanted to present some idea or information for House's consideration.[96]

Herbert Croly was confident enough of House's good will to make

[92] "Blinders," *NR*, 2 (February 13, 1915): 34.

[93] HC to Edward M. House, December 26, 1916, House mss., Yale University, published in Link et al., eds., *Papers of Woodrow Wilson*, 40: 359–60.

[94] Edward M. House, *Diary* (April 17, 1917), 10: 110, House mss.

[95] Ibid. (July 26, 1917), 11: 227.

[96] See HC to Edward M. House, May 9, 1917; March 6, 1918; March 13, 1918; July 25, 1918; August 3, 1918; and May 14, 1919, all in the House mss.

personal requests of him. A week after American entry, he suggested that House elevate Willard Straight to "a staff appointment with the Quartermaster's department," and a week after that he asked House to expedite Norman Angell's passport difficulties so that the English liberal could return to work for *The New Republic*.[97] The special relationship between Croly and House was unmistakably revealed after Lippmann's resignation from the magazine: "Mr. Lippmann's severance of his connection with the paper in order to go into the government's service has been a great blow to me," Croly wrote House, "and before the arrangement hardens down into an accomplished fact I should like to have a talk with you about the effect of his withdrawal upon The New Republic and the safeguards which can be provided against making the consequences of that withdrawal too serious for us." Croly made clear his request three days later. In the event that Croly's health prevented him from carrying on his duties at the magazine, he wondered if the Colonel could get Lippmann released from the War Department so that he could return to *The New Republic*.[98] Three months later, Croly offered another suggestion to House touching upon Lippmann:

> The idea that I am working up to is this. I should like to send Mr. Lippmann to Berne nominally as a correspondent of The New Republic, we paying all of his expenses. After he got there he would, of course, do a certain amount of writing for us, but his real purpose in going there would be to write reports that would be confidential both for you and for us upon the general situation as he could pick it up from the various diplomats who are living in Berne, or who are passing through. While his nominal status would be only that of a correspondent, he would through the help of letters which you might give him have access to very valuable information. . . . Of course, any such information would be entirely confidential, and in case there was any doubt about it would not be used for journalistic purposes except with your express[ed] approval.[99]

In 1918, Croly and House concluded a somewhat similar arrangement with Ray Stannard Baker—the former muckraker was sent to Europe by House on a special mission (to report on liberal opinion

[97] HC to Edward M. House, April 10 and April 17, 1917, House mss. The latter is published in Link et al., *Papers of Woodrow Wilson*, 42: 89–90.
[98] HC to Edward M. House, June 4 and June 7, 1917, House. mss.
[99] HC to Edward M. House, September 7, 1917, House mss.

in England); but to disguise his purposes, he went as a representative of *The New Republic*.[100]

With *The New Republic* safely co-opted, House and Wilson weighed Croly's requests with cool deliberation. Naturally, the president was in no rush to gratify Willard Straight, who had broken with his editors and announced his support for Hughes; and the young major languished in Oklahoma for seven months after Croly's request, until he was finally called to Washington at the end of October.[101] On the matter of Norman Angell, Wilson was unequivocal. In a note to House, three days after Croly's appeal that Angell be permitted into the United States, Wilson wrote:

> I do not think that we ought to have Mr. NORMAN ANGELL in this country just now as his activities would be likely to be embarrassing to the Administration. He would try to show that the real feeling in England is for an early peace, which is being controlled by a military censorship. This is a line which I am afraid the "New Republic" generally are [*sic.*] going to take, i.e. that of "the smothered opposition to the war which exists in England."[102]

And, ironically, at the very moment that Croly was angling with House to have Lippmann returned to *The New Republic*, the Colonel had his own designs on the brilliant publicist; on September 21, two weeks after Croly suggested assigning him to Berne, House told Lippmann that he wanted him to help organize the Inquiry.[103]

Croly's most important wartime service, the closest he was ever to come to an official assignment, was also in connection with House's Inquiry. On the same day House approached Lippmann, he also asked for Croly's help in drafting a plan of action for the organization. House wanted nothing less than the mobilization of the intellectual resources of the country, preparatory to any peace conference. The Inquiry would gather supporting data on all war-related questions and define the aims of American policy.[104] Characteristically, Croly

[100] Ray Stannard Baker to HC, February 18, 1918, Ray Stannard Baker mss.; Baker to Frank Polk, April 11, 1918, and to HC, September 30, 1918, ibid. See also John E. Semonche, *Ray Stannard Baker: A Quest for Democracy in Modern America, 1870–1918* (Chapel Hill, 1969), 313–14.

[101] HC, *Willard Straight*, 479.

[102] Woodrow Wilson to Edward M. House, April 20, 1917, House mss.

[103] House, *Diary* (September 21, 1917), 11: 287.

[104] Ibid (September 21, 1917), 11: 286, and HC to Edward M. House, September 28, 1917, House mss. On the Inquiry project, see Lawrence E. Gelfand, *The Inquiry: American Preparations for Peace, 1917–1919* (New Haven, 1963).

had most difficulty with the latter task. After only a few hours of work on the general plan, Croly told House that "the most difficult part of the work consists in a constructive analysis of the principles which should guide the policy of the American government at the conference. The collection of data to which these principles have to be concretely applied is a laborious and exacting job; but it will be plain sailing compared to the difficulties which will come up in relation to the principles themselves, their relative importance, their relation one to another, and the form in which they can be put in order to be of the utmost diplomatic use."[105] In addition to soliciting Croly's ideas on the Inquiry's purposes and organization, House also wanted suggestions about personnel. Croly offered several names (again including Willard Straight), but pushed especially for James T. Shotwell, the Columbia University historian. Croly acted as House's go-between with Shotwell, and the professor eventually accepted an important position with the Inquiry.[106]

V

On one occasion, shortly after Congress declared war on Germany, Herbert Croly, in a private note to Straight, permitted himself a brief moment of cosmic optimism. "But what a rare opportunity is now opened up, my dear Willard! During the next few years, under the stimulus of the war & its consequences there will be a chance to focus the thought & will of the country on high and fruitful purposes such as occurs only once in many hundred years. We must all try humbly and indefatigably and resolutely to make good use of it."[107]

In their very last issue before the American declaration, the editors outlined "A War Program for Liberals," a list of eight principles, which, in general, defined the wartime editorial policies of the magazine. There were no surprises—many of the principles had been advocated from the beginning and had been thoroughly explored in previous issues. The list naturally began by urging a renewed commitment to constructive intelligence: "The real danger of the war psychology is to forget where you are going but to go furiously on your way. This is the path that leads to disastrous entanglement and to merely blind fighting. It is the business of liberalism to insist by the most drastic criticism that 'defense' shall not become the mask

[105] HC to Edward M. House, September 28, 1917, House mss.

[106] James T. Shotwell, *At the Paris Peace Conference* (New York, 1937), 3; or Shotwell, *The Autobiography of James T. Shotwell* (Indianapolis, 1961), 76.

[107] HC to Willard Straight, n.d., Straight mss.

for a mere process of running amuck and refusing to think." In addition to insisting that Americans think, liberals had to see to it that the army was democratized, labor fully unionized, and programs of education and social amelioration expanded.[108]

But what Croly really had closest to heart when he wrote to Willard Straight about the rare opportunity ahead, what he really meant by using the war "to focus the thought & will of the country on high and fruitful purposes" was the chance to centralize American life. *The New Republic* ceaselessly urged the nationalization of all important economic resources ("By nationalization we mean government regulation of output, prices, profits, and labor conditions").[109] This campaign for centralization was the most persistent domestic policy espoused by the journal during the war, and Croly wasted no opportunity to pound the message home. He hired William Hard, a talented and prolific young Washington reporter, to chronicle the progress of nationalization, and by the end of the war Hard had written dozens of articles, adding his pen to those of Croly and the others, pushing the message relentlessly forward.[110]

While the primary domestic thrust of *The New Republic* was the attempt to sneak nationalization into the camp under cover of war, the main concern in foreign affairs was the demand, as old as the journal itself, for a lenient and constructive peace. In issue after issue, the editors advocated a settlement short of unconditional surrender, based on a policy of no annexations or indemnities, and resulting in a permanent league of nations to insure peace.[111] The editors could view with satisfaction, therefore, both the trend toward consolidation at home, a trend necessitated, in their view, by the inexorable demands of war, and the constant reassurances from President Wilson about the liberal and lenient peace settlement to which the United States was committed. No doubt the editors did more than take satisfaction from the direction that American affairs seemed to be taking—no doubt they quietly took some of the credit as well.

On one matter, however, they felt profound misgivings. The growing evidence of wartime hysteria, acts of brutal repression and

[108] "A War Program for Liberals," *NR*, 10 (March 31, 1917): 249–50.

[109] Ibid.

[110] *NR*, 10 (March 31, 1917): 243–44.

[111] The *NR* had always supported the establishment of a league of nations to preserve peace. For some early examples, see "Pacifism vs. Passivism," *NR*, 1 (December 12, 1914): 6–7; "A League of Peace," ibid., 3 (June 26, 1915): 190–91; "International Security," ibid., 9 (November 11, 1916): 35–37. For the view that Germany must be a part of such a league, see "Germany and the League of Peace," ibid. (November 18, 1916): 60–62.

intolerance, the callous suppression of constitutional rights, affected them deeply. And when, to this display of democratic ill-feeling and fanaticism there was added the specter of federal censorship, the journal moved into opposition. Croly and his colleagues had always recognized that "a censorship will be necessary" and "a certain minimum of secrecy will be required." But they demanded that "political discussion must under no circumstances be suppressed even though some of it is inconvenient. The nation can not do its work if it depends merely upon a 'patriotic' press."[112] Consequently, *The New Republic* expressed increasing uneasiness over the various vigilante groups that prowled the nation, over the Creel Committee—Wilson's attempt to propagandize for a favorable public opinion toward the war—and over the Espionage Act of June 1917, which placed controls over the dissemination of printed matter in the hands of Postmaster General Albert S. Burleson.[113]

Croly was widely respected for his devotion to the maintenance of basic civil liberties. At the start of the war, the radicals and pacifists of the American Union Against Militarism decided to form a defense league to protect political prisoners during the war. Lillian Wald, the New York social worker and president of the union, suggested that "since the NEW REPUBLIC stood for the right of free speech and individual liberty," the editors should be approached about organizing such a committee. At Norman Thomas's suggestion, Miss Wald and Max Eastman went to explore the possibility with Croly. However, since he was still trying to maintain some middle ground between the pacifists and the militarists, Croly gave the group a prompt refusal.[114] Even at the end of the war, the antiwar radical Oswald Garrison Villard of *The Nation* proposed a special government board assigned to protect freedom of the press, and "consisting of men like Albert Shaw, William Allen White and Herbert Croly."[115]

The New Republic's initial strategy to combat hysteria and censor-

[112] "A War Program for Liberals," *NR*, 10 (March 31, 1917): 250. For a general discussion of wartime suppression and censorship, see H. C. Peterson and Gilbert Fite, *Opponents of War, 1917–1918* (Madison, Wis., 1957).

[113] For some examples, see *NR*, 11 (May 12, 1917): 32; ibid. (June 2, 1917): 119; ibid. (July 21, 1917): 316; ibid., 12 (September 29, 1917): 228; ibid. (October 6, 1917): 255; "The Bigelow Incident," ibid., 13 (November 10, 1917): 35–37; "The President's Commission at Bisbee," ibid. (December 8, 1917): 140–41; "Lynching: An American Kultur?" ibid., 14 (April 13, 1918): 311–12; "America Tested by War," ibid., 15 (June 22, 1918): 220–21; and "Mob Violence and War Psychology," ibid., 16 (August 3, 1918): 5–7.

[114] Minutes of the Executive Committee of the American Union Against Militarism, April 4 and April 16, 1917, in Amos Pinchot mss., Library of Congress.

[115] "The Nation and the Post Office," *Nation*, 107 (September 28, 1918): 337.

ship was to try to drive a wedge between Wilson and the fanatics by arguing that such "malignant and venomous passions" endangered the noble and enlightened war aims enunciated by the president. The continual barrage of "rancor and intolerance" undermined the attempt to achieve a restrained and moderate settlement; by "classing the whole German nation together as assassins and Huns," for example, the propagandists were only alienating reasonable elements within Germany and dismaying liberal Americans who agreed to support the war because they believed in its democratic and internationalist aims. Even the Creel Committee "has done nothing to assist the President's diplomacy by disseminating its spirit, and by explaining its purposes and its consequences. . . . Its notion of information and propaganda has been a poor survival of the muckraking magazine."[116]

By mid-October 1917, however, it was hard to pretend that the unreasoning propaganda and coercive censorship could be entirely divorced from administration policy. When Postmaster Burleson began a ruthless campaign to suppress the Socialist press, Croly appealed directly to the president himself. In a careful, seven-page letter, Croly tried to point out to Wilson that censorship gave credence to the Socialist position, cost Wilson some of "the best element in your following," and divided the country along a line dangerous for the future:

> The policy pursued by the government in relation to public opinion seems to me to incur the danger at the present time of dividing the body of public opinion into two irreconcilable classes. It tends to create on the one hand irreconcilable pacifists and socialists who oppose the war and all its works, and a group of equally irreconcilable pro-war enthusiasts who allow themselves to be possessed by a fighting spirit and who tend to lose all sight of the objects for which America actually went into the war.[117]

These developments, Croly told the president, made it extremely difficult for someone like himself, who believed in Wilson and in the war's announced purposes, but who rejected the hysteria and fevered intolerance of the militarists.

Wilson's response to Croly's "thoughtful and important letter" was nothing more than a perfunctory, if polite, defense of government policy. He too was worried about censorship, he assured the editor,

[116] "War Propaganda," *NR*, 12 (October 6, 1917): 255–57.
[117] HC to Woodrow Wilson, October 19, 1917, Wilson mss.

but "after frequent conferences with the Postmaster General," Wilson was convinced that Burleson's pronouncements were "misunderstood." Indeed, the president wrote—with an irony that no doubt escaped him—"he is inclined to be most conservative in his exercise of these great and dangerous powers." Wilson closed with the pious hope that once the "processes of censorship work out and the results become visible," Croly's apprehensions would be "relieved."[118] The president was under pressure from many journalists and intellectuals on the censorship question, and his method for dealing with the problem was to simultaneously soothe the uneasy while quietly supporting Creel and Burleson. Two weeks after Wilson's reply to Croly, George Creel asked the president if he would care to receive a delegation to discuss the free speech issue. Wilson's reply—"it would be extremely difficult to state correctly and wisely my views about free speech just now, and I think I had better seek a later occasion"—spoke volumes.[119]

The climate of ugliness was brought home to *The New Republic* in more personal ways, as its advocacy of a lenient peace was interpreted in some circles as being "pro-German." Alvin Johnson was followed by the police and told, at his club, that if this country had a "real President," the editors of the journal "would be shot at sunrise." Norman Angell, finally admitted into the country, was arrested and interrogated about Johnson, Lippmann, and Croly.[120] In November 1917, William English Walling, a Socialist who broke with the party over its pacifism, denounced *The New Republic* in a lengthy and vitriolic diatribe in the *New York Globe* (reading *The New Republic*, Walling exclaimed, was to "find repeated again and again the familiar arguments of the German propagandist").[121] Finally, in 1918,

[118] Woodrow Wilson to HC, October 22, 1917, ibid.

[119] Woodrow Wilson to George Creel, November 5, 1917, George Creel mss., Library of Congress. For examples of the distress of intellectuals over the free speech issue, see Amos Pinchot to Joseph P. Tumulty, July 14, 1917, Wilson mss. (published in Link et al., eds., *Papers of Woodrow Wilson*, 43: 175–76); Walter Lippmann to Edward M. House, October 17, 1917, Newton D. Baker mss., Library of Congress; Upton Sinclair to Woodrow Wilson, October 22, 1917, Wilson mss.; Oswald Garrison Villard to Joseph P. Tumulty, November 8, 1918, Wilson mss. For attitudes within the administration, see Albert S. Burleson to Woodrow Wilson, October 16, 1917, Wilson mss.; George Creel to Woodrow Wilson, October 26, 1917, Creel mss.; Woodrow Wilson to Breckinridge Long, November 20, 1917, Creel mss.; and Woodrow Wilson to George Creel, January 14, 1918, Creel mss.

[120] Johnson, *Pioneer's Progress*, 264–66; and Angell, "Oral History," 144–46.

[121] *New York Globe and Commercial Advertiser*, November 24, 1917. On November 28, Creel sent a copy of the Walling letter to President Wilson with a complaint of his own about the NR and specifically about Lippmann. No doubt the editors would have

Burleson actually considered suppressing *The New Republic* in the same way he had suppressed so many radical and pacifist papers.[122]

The New Republic fought the hysteria forthrightly, consistently, and right up to the Armistice. But to Croly and the other editors, reviewing the experience of the war at its conclusion, the social insanity wrought by the conflict was merely an aberration. (Not until later did they regard it as a challenge to fundamental beliefs.) "We have been working under great difficulties during the last four or five months owing to the intemperate condition of American public opinion," Croly wrote Jane Addams four months before the shooting stopped, "but I think the worst is over. . . ."[123] The bigotry of the populace was dangerous, of course—there was no blinking at that, and *The New Republic* had never blinked at it. But to Croly the ugliness had not been the chief characteristic of the war years. The chief characteristic was the hopefulness, the "rare opportunity" to achieve better domestic and international arrangements.

Everywhere one looked in November 1918, after all, one saw the American nation, at long last, assuming its political, economic, and social responsibilities, fashioning a government capable of directing the destinies of the nation, not only through the duration of the conflict, but for the long future beyond the conflict. And everywhere the air was filled with talk of lasting peace—the establishment of a set of principles and an institutional framework for mediating the future international quarrels of the civilized world. In their first issue after the Armistice, the editors solemnly warned against dismantling the mechanisms of social and economic centralization that had worked so satisfactorily during the war;[124] and in the issue after that one, they praised the president for his decision to go to the Peace Conference himself.[125]

---

been astonished by Wilson's reply: "Walling seems to me to have a great deal of sense, and certainly your attitude towards what Lippman [*sic*] and others have suggested to you is entirely correct." Creel to Wilson, November 28, 1917, and Wilson to Creel, November 30, 1917, Wilson mss.

[122] The *NR*'s offense was to publish a controversial advertisement in the issue of June 22, 1918. The advertisement appealed for funds to secure a fair trial for 110 I.W.W. leaders. The appeal was signed by eleven well-known intellectuals and reformers, among them John Dewey, Walter Weyl, Helen Keller, James Harvey Robinson, and Thorstein Veblen. See Lippmann, "Notes for a Biography," 252, and for HC's comments on the incident, HC to Dorothy Straight, June 25, 1918, Dorothy Straight Elmhirst mss., Cornell University.

[123] HC to Jane Addams, July 26, 1918, Jane Addams mss., Swarthmore College.

[124] "The Uses of an Armistice," *NR*, 17 (November 16, 1918): 59–61; see also the earlier statement, "After the War—Reaction or Reconstruction," ibid., 13 (January 19, 1918): 331–33.

[125] *NR*, 17 (November 23, 1918): 82.

The man in the White House, recently converted to the need for consolidation at home, was going to Paris firmly, irrevocably committed to a generous peace abroad. And firmly supporting him—wielding its enormous influence, having the ear of the president's chief adviser, helping to define the principles of peace and reform, recognized everywhere as being close to the centers of power—was Herbert Croly's journal of opinion. Despite the flurry of hysteria, there was ample ground for a little cosmic optimism.

VI

One of the most gratifying signs of success was the growth in circulation. By the time the seventh issue appeared, the original list of 875 subscribers had grown to 3,000, and another 7,000 copies were sold at newsstands. ("I never expected to get an immediate circulation of 10,000 a week," Croly boasted; after all, that was "more than the Nation has obtained after fifty-five years.")[126] By 1915, *The New Republic* was selling around 15,000 copies of each issue. And once the rumors of the special relationship with President Wilson gained credence, the circulation quickly doubled—between 1917 and 1920, around 30,000 copies were sold, and sometimes as many as 45,000.[127] By existing standards this was a relatively modest circulation for a magazine pretending to be national—in 1917 *Collier's, Hearst's, McClure's,* and *Everybody's* sold more than half a million copies of each of their issues, and *Harper's* and *The Outlook* each sold more than 100,000.[128] Nevertheless, Croly, who had always intended that his magazine be aimed at the superior few, had good reason to be satisfied with the steady growth. Revenue from advertising also increased; the first issue contained three advertisements, but by the end of the war each carried ten or fifteen.

There were other indications that the magazine was being given serious attention. Prominent politicians, intellectuals, jurists, and reformers praised *The New Republic* lavishly from the beginning. Wilson clipped and filed particular editorials.[129] Albert Beveridge thought

[126] HC to Willard Straight, December 17, 1914, Straight mss.

[127] For *NR* circulation figures, see the reports in the Dorothy Straight Elmhirst mss., Folders 3725: 12–1 to 12–7. See also Mott, *History of American Magazines,* 5: 201. For analyses of the economic and geographic appeal of the magazine, see C. Wright Mills, *Sociology and Pragmatism: The Higher Learning in America* (New York, 1964), 325–32; and Forcey, *Crossroads of Liberalism,* 338–39.

[128] *N. W. Ayer & Son's American Newspaper Annual & Directory: A Catalogue of American Newspapers,* 59 (1917): 1192.

[129] Ray Stannard Baker to Walter Lippmann, October 25, 1928, Ray Stannard Baker mss.

the journal was "wonderfully keen and brilliant."[130] Justices Holmes and Brandeis made regular comments and suggestions, funneling them through Laski or Frankfurter.[131] Roger Baldwin, founder of the American Civil Liberties Union, thought *The New Republic* was a "powerhouse of liberalism," Charles McCarthy, the Wisconsin progressive, told Croly it was "a crackerjack paper," and from Kansas, William Allen White kept up a constant stream of fulsome praise.[132] Ray Stannard Baker reported from England that the journal was "widely read among the people who count in the Liberal and Labour movement."[133] According to George Soule, "author after author would tell us that when an article was published in *The Saturday Evening Post* or in *Collier's*, that would be the end of it. But when something was published in *The New Republic* it would stimulate considerable debate and discussion in the author's personal correspondence."[134] Croly traded on just such praise: "Of course, you could obtain a larger audience by using some other medium than the New Republic," he wrote to Stimson, soliciting an article on preparedness, "but the paper has already a circulation of about twelve hundred, and, while it is not large, it certainly includes an unusually large proportion of people who are capable of giving the important matter of national defense its serious and candid consideration."[135]

It was precisely this sense of speaking to an élite, the tone of calm surety, which sometimes seemed like arrogance, that provided *The New Republic*'s critics their most consistent complaint. Horace Kallen talked about "the over-sophisticated staff of that lofty periodical,"

[130] Albert J. Beveridge to HC, August 21, 1920, Beveridge mss., Library of Congress. See also Beveridge to *NR*, March 4, 1918, ibid.

[131] For Holmes, see the many references to the *NR* in Mark A. DeWolfe Howe, ed., *Holmes-Laski Letters: The Correspondence of Mr. Justice Holmes and Harold J. Laski, 1916–1935* (Cambridge, Mass., 1953), 2 vols. For the relationship between Brandeis and the journal, see David W. Levy and Bruce A. Murphy, "Preserving the Progressive Spirit in a Conservative Time: The Joint Reform Efforts of Justice Brandeis and Professor Frankfurter, 1916–1933," *Michigan Law Review*, 78 (1980): 1281–85, and HC to Brandeis, February 4, 1918, Louis D. Brandeis mss., University of Louisville Law School Library.

[132] Roger Baldwin, "Oral History," Columbia University Oral History Project, 349; Charles McCarthy to HC, January 2, 1915, McCarthy mss., Wisconsin State Historical Society, Madison, Wis.; William Allen White to HC, November 18, 1914; to Robert Hallowell, December 21, 1914; to *NR*, January 1, 1916; to HC, November 16, 1918, William Allen White mss., Library of Congress.

[133] Ray Stannard Baker to HC, April 13, 1918, Ray Stannard Baker mss.

[134] Interview with George Soule, October 7, 1963.

[135] HC to Henry L. Stimson, December 10, 1914, Stimson mss. HC strikes the same note in another letter to Stimson, October 5, 1916, ibid.

and Paul Rosenfeld ridiculed "the gospel of polite liberalism without tears."[136] *The Catholic World* noted the "intellectual dilettanteism" of the journal,[137] and the *New York Tribune* published a satirical poem entitled "On Reading *The New Republic*":

> Ah, pause, Appreciation here
>   Sophistication doubly nice is,
> See polished paragraphs appear
>   Anent some cataclysmic crisis.
>
> . . . .
>
> And here beyond the stir of strife,
>   Where distant drones the blatant babble
> Ah, tread the promenade of life,
>   A pace behind the vulgar rabble.[138]

On the score of obscure superiority, the chief editor was particularly vulnerable. Albert Jay Nock of *The Freeman* (who probably coined the phrase "Crolier than thou") was willing to "give ten to one that Mr. Herbert Croly was trained under John of Scotland."[139] Commenting on one article, Robert Herrick wrote that it "must be a left over from Croly it is so cotton wooly in thought. . . . The few who wade through to its sad end will be more fuddled minded [*sic*] than before."[140]

Grumbling about *The New Republic*'s style and tone was never limited to critics—some of Croly's closest friends and admirers made the same point. "That part of the N.R. that shapes our destinies I generally skip," Justice Holmes informed Laski.[141] William Allen White, after reading the first issue, broached the topic as delicately as he could: "I wonder if you would let a friend, who wishes you well, suggest that the tone and character . . . is too deadly; too deadly serious. . . . [I]t is often necessary to back the dose with a little humor, with a little sprightliness. It is better it seems to me to have one's ideas carry, even if they have to be carried somewhat frivolously now and then, rather than to have them fall because they are

[136] Horace M. Kallen to Randolph Bourne, May 15, 1917, and Paul Rosenfeld to Randolph Bourne, July 7, 1918, both in the Randolph Bourne mss., Columbia University.

[137] Cited in Mott, *A History of American Magazines*, 5: 202.

[138] Ibid.

[139] Albert Jay Nock to Newton D. Baker, January 27, 1917, Newton D. Baker mss. See also, Robert Morss Lovett, *All Our Years* (New York, 1948), 179.

[140] Robert Herrick to Robert M. Lovett, n.d., Herrick mss., University of Chicago.

[141] Oliver Wendell Holmes to Harold Laski, September 6, 1917, in Howe, ed., *Holmes-Laski Letters*, 1: 99.

too heavy. I know you will take these suggestions as they are meant."[142] Even Learned Hand was impatient: "Herbert's remarks about [Herbert Hoover] in one issue partook of the most typical Herbertian inscrutability: they left me wholly at sea as to what he meant, with a general sense,—which I own I have found quite commonly,—that if you could not square to the Esoteric standards of N. Republican rectitude you needn't come around."[143] One reason Willard Straight insisted that Croly keep William Hard on the staff was that "all the rest of you are too high-brow, and you have got to have someone to lighten up the tone of the paper and give a sugar-coating to get it across even with the semi-intelligent reader."[144]

Criticism of *The New Republic*, however, extended far beyond matters of style. The journal was regularly denounced by conservatives for its radicalism and by radicals for its conservatism. Thus Charles W. Eliot, staid former president of Harvard who had known some of the editors since their undergraduate days, reported that he "used to read the New Republic; but found so many unjust and dangerous suggestions in it for the destruction of existing social structures—mostly covert—that I found reading it a disagreeable experience." Eliot particularly objected to the theory that in order to produce a better society, "the first step is to destroy the present social and industrial structure."[145] At the same time, the radical Amos Pinchot denounced the magazine for its timidity. *The New Republic*, as far as Pinchot was concerned, "concentrates attention on symptoms and incidentals, and maintains silence in regard to the foundations upon which the whole fabric of social injustice rests." To Pinchot, it seemed that the editors suffered from "an impregnable virtue, already cast in the mould of respectable middle age."[146] And if *The New Republic* suffered the blows of diverse critics on its handling of domestic problems, the onslaught was even more bitter when it came to questions of foreign policy. Every month the paper was found to be too militaristic for the pacifists and too lukewarm for the patriots. It was always too pro-Allied for the German-Americans and the Irish, too pro-German for those who sympathized with the Allies.

The editors enjoyed publishing letters from their critics. It was a

[142] William Allen White to HC, November 18, 1914, White mss.

[143] Learned Hand to Felix Frankfurter, June 6, 1920, Felix Frankfurter mss., Library of Congress.

[144] Willard Straight to HC, February 10, 1918, Straight mss.

[145] Charles W. Eliot to Robert M. Lovett, October 8, 1921, Robert M. Lovett mss., University of Chicago.

[146] "Criticism from Mr. Amos Pinchot," *NR*, 3 (May 29, 1915): 95–97.

rare issue of *The New Republic*, therefore, that did not contain at least
one denunciation from a subscriber on some aspect of the journal's
domestic or foreign editorial positions; and if the critic was well known
or dangerously plausible, the editors allowed themselves the treat of
a reply—cool, reasoned, devastating, the special province (one sus-
pects) of Walter Lippmann. This exercise served several purposes. It
demonstrated that the journal was open and tolerant—even of error.
It proved that *The New Republic* was at the storm center of vital
national discussion, as befitted a journal of national importance, and
that its utterances were felt to be an important part of that discussion.
Perhaps above all, by printing their opponents' letters and then re-
plying to them, Croly and the others had the chance to vindicate
their pragmatic approach to the country's problems, their admirable
freedom from "doctrinaire" solutions. Thus, "Mr. Pinchot must forgive us if we cannot imitate his simplicity. We are puzzled about
these complex issues; we don't pretend to know the answers to very
many of them, and we have tried at all times to avoid the delusion
which finds the answer easy because the problem itself has never been
thoroughly understood. . . . Mr. Pinchot with fine feeling is devoted
to the task of saying with no precision at all what he would like to
see come to pass. The labor of finding means to his end, the task of
appraising methods, are drudgeries which he has been able to spare
himself."[147] How easy it would be, the editors repeated again and
again in replies to their critics, if *The New Republic* could give up the
duty of constructive thought and fly into the arms of some comfortable dogma. Alas, the road of the pragmatist was not so easy.

VII

In the case of one troublesome critic, however, the formula of superiority masked as humility was inadequate—and the fact that this
critic spoke from within *The New Republic*'s walls did not make his
points any the less telling or any the more palatable. Almost from
the beginning, Randolph Bourne (the young man who originally had
hoped he was only "really big enough for the opportunity") felt res-
tive under Croly's leadership. He soon saw himself as an outsider at
the magazine, "a very insignificant retainer of its staff," paid "star-
vation wages," having nothing to say about policy, watching help-

[147] Ibid., 97–98.

lessly as much of his work was rejected.[148] Before long he was complaining about the "vapid, sure New Republic" and the editors who were "too busy interpreting America to each other and to America" to care about running the enterprise efficiently.[149] The magazine suffered from "priggishness," Bourne wrote to his friend Van Wyck Brooks in March 1918: "The New Republic's sense of leadership— the limited but influential class—is obnoxious because it comes not from youthful violence, but from a middle-aged dignity, that not only presents no clear program of values, but chooses for its first large enterprise a hateful and futile war."[150]

In a series of brilliant articles written for *The Seven Arts*, Randolph Bourne condemned that hateful and futile war, and in the process, levelled a penetrating critique of *The New Republic* intellectuals who had so eagerly supported Wilson.[151] "We have had to watch . . . the coalescence of the intellectual classes in support of the military programme," Bourne wrote, and he wondered how it could have happened that society's thinkers so easily joined "the greased slide toward war." In part, no doubt, it was the unwillingness of the intellectuals to remain aloof any longer, to continue the duty to think clearly, to resist the allure of "quick, simplified action." Thus "it is not so much what they thought as how they felt that explains our intellectual class."

But Bourne struck even harder and he struck directly at the pragmatism the editors flaunted with such self-assurance. The abdication of responsibility by American intellectuals, their transformation into willing propagandists and servants for the war machine, was to be explained by their devotion to the philosophic stance of John Dewey

[148] For Bourne's dissatisfaction with his life at the *NR*, see Bourne to Alyse Gregory, December 1, 1914; HC to Bourne, December 10, 1914; Bourne to Alyse Gregory, December ?, 1914; to Alyse Gregory, [Winter, 1915]; to Prudence Winterrowds, January 19, 1915; to Elizabeth Shepley Sergeant, June 25, 1915; to Alyse Gregory, July 24, 1915; to Elizabeth Shepley Sergeant, August 24, 1916, all in the Bourne mss. See also, Agnes DeLima to Dorothy Teall, n.d., ibid.

[149] Bourne to Alyse Gregory, [Winter, 1915], and to Simon P. Barr, December 13, 1914, both in ibid.

[150] Bourne to Van Wyck Brooks, March 27, 1918, ibid.

[151] See particularly "The War and the Intellectuals," *Seven Arts*, 2 (June, 1917): 133–46, and "Twilight of Idols," ibid. (October, 1917): 688–702. The following quotations, unless otherwise indicated, come from these two important articles. See also, "Below the Battle," ibid. (July, 1917): 270–77; "The Collapse of American Strategy," ibid. (August, 1917): 409–24; and "A War Diary," ibid. (September, 1917): 535–47. The conflict between Bourne and the *NR* group is discussed in Forcey, *Crossroads of Liberalism*, 279–81; Bourke, "The Status of Politics," 187–94; Lasch, *New Radicalism*, 205–13; and Hansen, introduction to *The Radical Will*, 25–62.

and *The New Republic* (that "organ of applied pragmatic realism").[152] Bourne readily admitted that he had been one of those "who have taken Dewey's philosophy almost as our American religion," and that breaking with it was not easy: "What I come to is a sense of suddenly being left in the lurch, of suddenly finding that a philosophy upon which I had relied to carry us through no longer works." The war had uncovered a double inadequacy in the pragmatic approach.

First, the crisis exposed the extent to which pragmatism was a philosophy of means rather than one of ends. It was a philosophy of intelligent control, scientific method, the manipulation of brute matter and the expert weighing of facts.

> The war has revealed a younger intelligentsia, trained up in the pragmatic dispensation, immensely ready for the executive ordering of events, pitifully unprepared for the intellectual interpretation or the idealistic focussing of ends. . . . They have absorbed the secret of scientific method as applied to political administration. They are liberal, enlightened, aware. They are touched with creative intelligence toward the solution of political and industrial problems. . . . Practically all this element, one would say, is lined up in service of the war-technique. There seems to have been a peculiar congeniality between the war and these men. It is as if the war and they had been waiting for each other.

Unfortunately, these intellectuals, adept in the technical side of the war, were at sea when it came to the interpretative side. "The formulation of values and ideals, the production of articulate and suggestive thinking, had not, in their education, kept pace, to any extent whatever, with their technical aptitude. . . . [T]hey have never learned not to subordinate idea to technique. . . . They have, in short, no clear philosophy of life except that of intelligent service, the admirable adaptation of means to ends. They are vague as to what kind of a society they want, or what kind of society America needs, but they are equipped with all the administrative attitudes and talents necessary to attain it."

Croly might have been uncomfortable at Bourne's first charge against pragmatism, but he might also have presented a credible defense—*The New Republic*, after all, had consistently emphasized ends and taken pains to make its war aims explicit and clear. Bourne's second

---

[152] Bourne, "A War Diary," 539.

charge, however, was not so easy to dismiss. The pragmatists, he argued, were infatuated by their notions of social control and mastery. "It is only on the craft, in the stream, they say, that one has any chance of controlling the current forces for liberal purposes. If we obstruct, we surrender all power for influence. If we responsibly approve, we then retain our power for guiding." To Bourne, such a strategy represented a sort of intellectual suicide. Intellectuals who went along in the hope of exercising control, in the hope of managing the war for noble purposes, counted for nothing; they were "swallowed in the mass and great incalculable forces" carry them helplessly on. They have joined the most reactionary elements in American society; but "only in a world where irony was dead could an intellectual class enter war at the head of such illiberal cohorts in the avowed cause of world-liberalism and world-democracy."

What had happened was not hard to understand. Intellectuals, under the spell of John Dewey's pragmatism, had overestimated their ability to control and had underestimated the unmanagable power of the vast forces released by the war. "The realist thinks he at least can control events by linking himself to the forces that are moving. Perhaps he can. But if it is a question of controlling war, it is difficult to see how the child on the back of a mad elephant is to be any more effective in stopping the beast than is the child who tries to stop him from the ground."

Herbert Croly, who never attempted to answer Bourne's arguments directly, had seen the war as a "rare opportunity" to improve America by exercising mastery. Not even domestic hysteria and the suppression accompanying it could quench his pragmatist and progressive faith in the ability of constructive intelligence to guide human affairs. It would take the news from Versailles to shock him into the recognition that he had been a little like the overconfident child on the back of a mad elephant. Walter Lippmann's first instinct, expressed on that fateful day in August 1914 (in a metaphor remarkably like Bourne's), proved to be prophetic. Ideas, public opinion, influence, democratic hope, cosmic optimism, even the ear of those in authority, had proved, all of them, to be less like instruments for carving out a better world than like flowers in the path of a plough.

NINE

Years of Despair
1919–1930

THE EDITORIAL meeting that Croly called early in the second week of May 1919, was an exceedingly grim one. Filing into his office that day were Lippmann and Weyl, both recently returned to the journal, Alvin Johnson, Francis Hackett, Phil Littell and Bob Hallowell. Croly sat in his usual place behind the big desk and led the discussion.[1]

From the beginning of the peace negotiations, *The New Republic* had approached the conference as if it had been a morality play, a vast drama in which the forces of good contended against the forces of evil:

> There are at present two great international parties. One of these looks forward to a peace of reconciliation, to be perpetuated by a solidly established League of Nations, under which every state, great or small, shall enjoy security, justice and equality of economic opportunity. The other party would impose a punitive peace. . . . The former party, predominantly liberal and labor, has come to regard President Wilson as its natural leader. It believes that his presence at the Peace Conference will place an effective check upon the machinations of the Tories, the imperialists and the exponents of an international order founded on power instead of justice and good faith.[2]

Now the time had come, in the tense meeting in Croly's office, to pay the price for placing so much faith in a single man and so much hope in a single moment of history.

For weeks, disturbing rumors had been issuing from Paris, hints of general compromise, intimations of a retreat from the noble principles of the Fourteen Points. During that anxious time of waiting,

---

[1] Alvin S. Johnson, interview with the author, October 21, 1963; Walter Lippmann, "Notes for a Biography," *NR*, 63 (July 16, 1930): 252; Ronald Steel, *Walter Lippmann and the American Century* (Boston, 1980), 158–59; Charles Forcey, *The Crossroads of Liberalism: Croly, Weyl, Lippmann and the Progressive Era, 1900–1925* (New York, 1961), 289–91.

[2] *NR*, 17 (December 7, 1918): 146.

Croly and the other editors had been reduced to insubstantial speculation, impotent repetition of the Wilsonian program, and increasingly shrill calls for unity behind the president. All the editors could
do, of course, was to hope that Wilson would be firm. And up until
the last issue before the treaty's terms were published, they had remained cautiously optimistic. Despite the persistent rumors that "too
much has been conceded," *The New Republic* had argued in the last
minutes of suspense, "there is a strong presumption in favor of accepting the peace." Surely the people of the world could "correct
errors that may have been made at Paris and complete what Paris has
left undone."[3]

Until the end of her life Louise Croly remembered the moment
when her husband learned the actual terms of the Treaty of Versailles. Croly returned home from work on Wednesday evening, May
7, to discover that the provisions were published in the *New York
Evening Post*. Louise read aloud and Herbert "walked up & down &
up & down as I read." Ten years later she could still recall his "concentrated, undeviated attention."[4] The outcome was far worse than
Croly had dreamed possible, and he was shattered. Germany was
severely punished by the loss of Alsace-Lorraine and her colonial
possessions; the treaty contained a clause blaming Germany for the
war; she was saddled with a tremendous indemnity and the promise
that huge reparations, still to be negotiated, would be required of
her. While the principle of self-determination was honored in some
instances, in many others it was not. The Italians, frustrated in their
desire to have some of Yugoslavia, were rewarded with some of
Austria; the Japanese won the former German rights in China's Shan-
tung province. The Allies, in short, had written a settlement so removed from the hopeful notions of enlightened international statesmanship, so harsh to the defeated, so remindful of the worst excesses
of traditional diplomacy, that it instantly dispirited those who had
hoped that the war might bring a new order to the world. Lippmann's
remark to Ray Stannard Baker ("For the life of me I can't see peace
in this document") summarized the acute disappointment and anger
of many American liberals.[5] The next day Croly went into seclusion
and for three days he walked the floor.[6] He wrote Brandeis asking

---

[3] "The Treaty is Ready," *NR*, 19 (May 10, 1919): 35.

[4] Louise Croly to Dorothy Straight Elmhirst, June 22, 1930, and to Leonard Elmhirst, September 20, [1938?], Dorothy Straight Elmhirst mss., Cornell University.

[5] Cited in Steel, *Walter Lippmann*, 158.

[6] Malcolm Cowley, "The Old House in Chelsea," *Carleton Miscellany*, 6 (1965): 44.

for his confidential opinion of the treaty, but frankly indicated that "my own mind is pretty well made up."[7]

And now, at the meeting with his editorial staff, Croly discovered that they had all reached roughly similar conclusions.[8] One by one they expressed their horror and outrage, Croly among the most vehement. He felt obliged to point out to them that breaking with Wilson would cost the journal dearly—credibility, influence, subscriptions had all been tied to the popular belief that the magazine spoke for the president. But he, who had the most to lose, saw no way to maintain integrity and still endorse the Treaty of Versailles. They all agreed to publish Alvin Johnson's editorial "A Punic Peace," drafted before the editorial conference, and to come out fighting. Croly summarized his feelings in a second letter to Brandeis:

> After much searching of heart and prolonged discussion we felt obliged in the New Republic this week to write ourselves out from under the Treaty. It is a bitter decision to make because it is practically a confession of failure, so far as our work during the last few years is concerned, but it was unanimous and we shall have to take whatever loss follows from adopting it.[9]

By any standard it was a courageous act. Robert Morss Lovett was not far wrong when he called it "one of the bravest things in the history of American journalism." For Croly, the decision meant "the failure of hopes and plans for which his life had been a preparation, and for the realization of which public support was necessary."[10] Opposing the treaty served to reveal that, however deeply ingrained his pragmatism, Croly saw certain principles as inviolable. The decision was at once an admission that Randolph Bourne had been right about

[7] HC to Louis D. Brandeis, May 8, 1919, Brandeis mss., University of Louisville Law School.

[8] In 1930, Lippmann claimed that "the decision to oppose ratification was Croly's. I followed him, though I was not then, and am not now, convinced that it was the wise thing to do. . . . If I had to do it all over again I would take the other side; we supplied the Battalion of Death with too much ammunition." ("Notes for a Biography," 252.) There can be no doubt, however, that at the time Lippmann was among the most unrestrained opponents of the Treaty of Versailles. See for example, his long letter to Newton D. Baker, June 9, 1919, Newton D. Baker mss., Library of Congress. Ronald Steel, whose discussion of the matter is definitive, quite rightly concludes that "At the time, . . . he was in the front ranks, leading the charge." (Steel, *Walter Lippmann*, 157–66.)

[9] HC to Louis D. Brandeis, May 13, 1919, Brandeis mss.

[10] Robert Morss Lovett, "Herbert Croly's Contribution to American Life," NR, 63 (July 16, 1930): 246.

the helplessness of the intellectuals in the path of forces too strong for them to control, and wrong about the inability of *The New Republic* intellectuals to remove themselves from the seductive mainstream of power, wrong about their supposed incapacity to maintain the distinction between means and ends.

Reacting as much to the utter disappointment of the hopes that Wilson had awakened as they were to the actual provisions of the treaty itself, the editors of *The New Republic* savaged the document over the next two months with all the unrestraint characteristic of those who feel a personal betrayal. The treaty was an "inhuman monster" and those who wrote it "have acted either cynically, hypocritically or vindictively, and their handwork will breed cynicism, hypocrisy or vindictiveness in the minds of future generations."[11] In one editorial the editors listed each of the Fourteen Points and proceeded to show how far the treaty had strayed from the promise— the editors thought it was "abundantly plain that if this treaty is to be defended every candid man must preface his argument by saying: 'It is not the peace which the President speaking for the Allied and Associated governments promised to make.' "[12] Not even the League could redeem the treaty; under the circumstances it would function merely to solidify the rule of the victors. And the final verdict on the president was terse and bitter: "Wilson for lack of courage and knowledge and administrative capacity has yielded to a settlement which means a Europe of wars and revolution and agony." Vindicative men of small vision "are entitled to their laugh. They were right about Mr. Wilson. We were wrong. We hoped and lost. They did not hope and did not lose."[13]

I

The years after the signing of the armistice were catastrophic for Herbert Croly. The Treaty of Versailles was merely the chief tragedy in a period when everything else went wrong too.

On December 1, 1918, three weeks after the armistice, Willard Straight died in Paris of influenza and pneumonia. He was thirty-eight years old. "There was warmth in his heart; there was light in his eyes," wrote the editors in the next issue of the magazine he had made possible. "During his brief life he did not achieve as much as

---

[11] "Peace at Any Price," *NR*, 19 (May 24, 1919): 100.
[12] "Mr. Wilson and His Promises," *NR*, 19 (May 24, 1919): 104–106.
[13] "Joy Among the Philistines," *NR*, 19 (June 7, 1919): 170.

his qualities entitled him to achieve, but he did achieve the confidence and the affection of those who knew him best to an extent which must surely constitute the final test and vindication of a man's life."[14] To his widow Croly explained that the editors were people "whose personal fulfillment depends on their ability to communicate fully and completely to others. . . ." Straight, by providing them "the perfect opportunity," rendered them all a service of incomparable value.[15] Naturally, Croly acceded to Dorothy Straight's request that he write her husband's biography and he began immediately to collect the materials. Willard Straight's death, however, threw into temporary uncertainty Croly's whole financial and professional future.

Three weeks after Straight's death, Randolph Bourne died in the same flu epidemic. Bourne was only thirty-two. The acrimony of 1917 seemingly behind them, the editors published an affectionate memorial to him, written by his friend Floyd Dell.[16] A month after Bourne's death, Theodore Roosevelt died at sixty-one. On November 9, 1919, Walter Weyl died of cancer at forty-six. "His method was to comprehend, no matter where it led him," wrote his former colleagues. "He asked questions and explained, and always when he honestly could, he gave the benefit of the doubt. That is what we who were his friends are remembering to-day."[17]

Croly's relations with each of these four men were different but close; and their deaths provided unmistakable intimations of his own mortality. Croly turned fifty on January 23, 1919, and the deaths of his friends—three of them younger than he was—must certainly have provoked solemn reflections about the course of his own life, the extent of his accomplishment, the amount of time left to him. By the early 1920s, his letters were filled with references to the fact that his time was running out and that so much remained to be done.[18] His father had died at sixty, after all, and like his father's, Herbert's health had been precarious, even in the best of times.

The war had put a tremendous strain on him. Not only had more of the editorial chores fallen on him as the others entered government service, but he also was involved with a number of public associa-

[14] "Willard D. Straight," NR, 17 (December 7, 1918): 164.

[15] HC to Dorothy Straight, December 23, 1918, Willard Straight mss., Cornell University.

[16] Floyd Dell, "Randolph Bourne," NR, 17 (January 4, 1919): 276. The editors' own tribute can be found in ibid. (December 28, 1918): 233.

[17] "Walter E. Weyl, 1873–1919," NR, 20 (November 19, 1919): 335.

[18] See for examples, letters to Dorothy Straight on August 2, 1921, May 31 and December 23, 1922, and November 18, 1924, Dorothy Straight Elmhirst mss.

tions: the "Committee for Immigrants in America," the "National Americanization Committee," and the "League of Free Nations Association." Probably his duties were not heavy, but he had joined, in 1918, with Winston Churchill, Norman Angell, Paul Kellogg, Norman Hapgood, and Charles Beard to draft some preliminary principles for the League of Nations.[19] In addition to the increased responsibilities in connection with the journal, his work for the Inquiry, and these voluntary organizations, the heightened pressures and excitement of the war years had drained and weakened him. By the end of February 1918, Willard Straight had been urgently concerned about Croly's mental and physical condition. The editor's letters, Straight had observed to his wife from France, seemed "terribly depressed and tired" and "as if he lacked confidence in his own power."[20] "Herbert is tired out and must have a rest at once," Willard wrote Dorothy in May, "even if the paper has to shut up for a week or two."[21] It was no wonder that Croly had attempted to provide, through Colonel House, for the future of *The New Republic* should he be unable to carry on his duties. The end of the war did not restore Croly's strength very much; indeed, it merely inaugurated the long decline that ended only with his death in 1930.

The agitation over the treaty was also responsible, at least in part, for the interruption of one of Croly's oldest and most intimate friendships. Learned Hand supported the treaty with reservations ("I seldom have been surer that I was right about a public matter than about the ratification," he wrote to Frankfurter).[22] But Hand found *The New Republic* ill-tempered on the whole question. "Herbert was so quite intolerable in June that I have found it hard to be as forgiving as proper magnanimity required. I have given up much talk w. him on public questions, which in his case means a decided limitation of intercourse."[23] Hand often felt "like a little boy with his teacher" when he was with him, but this time Croly and the other editors seemed especially irritating. "Their continued hostility to Wilson, full of personal feeling, has bred in me feelings I don't like to have

[19] Allen T. Burns to Louis D. Brandeis, November 9, 1918, Brandeis mss. The full text of their proposal can be found, together with a list of distinguished signers, in "League of Free Nations Association: Statement of Principles," *NR*, 17 (November 30, 1918): 134–37.

[20] Willard D. Straight to Dorothy Straight, February 26 and March 2, 1918, Willard Straight mss.

[21] Willard D. Straight to Dorothy Straight, May 12, 1918, Willard Straight mss.

[22] Learned Hand to Felix Frankfurter, December 3, 1919, Felix Frankfurter mss., Library of Congress.

[23] Learned Hand to Felix Frankfurter, November 8, 1919, Frankfurter mss.

toward my initmate friends."[24] Later, when the break had been smoothed over by time, Croly wrote Hand about "a rather forlorn feeling of recent years that the N.R. was making a difference between me & the friendship of some of the people I most loved, and it made me wish to give up the New Republic."[25] When Croly died, Hand admitted to Frankfurter that he had "hurt him deeply eleven years ago in ways that he could not understand. . . ."[26] No doubt it was the break with Hand to which Phil Littell referred (all three were neighbors in Cornish) when he recalled how Croly "saw old friendships die suddenly, saw them dwindle into estrangements, and these things must have tasted bitter."[27]

Another episode during these dark years was particularly symbolic of Croly's descent into frustration and despair. The New School for Social Research had its origins in discussions held in *The New Republic* offices. Beginning in 1918, a small group of intellectuals, dissatisfied with the state of American higher education, met regularly to hammer out plans for an exciting new departure. They were intrigued by the London School of Economics and the *École Libre des Sciences Politiques*, and wanted to create an institution "not handicapped by mobs of beef-devouring alumni, passionate about football and contemptuous of scholarship."[28] They listened as Harold Laski explained how the London School had weathered the war without infringing academic freedom—a dramatic contrast to the record of American higher education, tarnished by witch-hunting and the dismissal of controversial and "unpatriotic" professors. Even Columbia University suffered at the hands of the orthodox—one distinguished professor was fired for "sedition" and "treason," others (including the eminent historian Charles Beard) resigned.

[24] Learned Hand to Felix Frankfurter, February 12 and December 3, 1919, Frankfurter mss.

[25] HC to Learned Hand, [?], 1922, Hand mss., Harvard Law School Library. Another old friend, George Rublee, also quarreled with HC over the treaty. See his letter, "President Wilson and Article X," *NR*, 20 (September 17, 1919): 206, wherein he calls the editors "unfair." The editors reply in "Mr. Rublee and Article X," ibid. (September 24, 1919): 218–20.

[26] Learned Hand to Felix Frankfurter, May 19, 1930, Frankfurter mss. See also Hand, "Oral History," Columbia University Oral History Project, 48–50.

[27] Philip Littell, "As a Friend," *NR*, 63 (July 16, 1930): 244.

[28] Alvin S. Johnson, *Pioneer's Progress, An Autobiography* (New York, 1952), 272. For useful discussions of the origins and early history of the New School for Social Research, see ibid., 271–88; James Harvey Robinson, "The New School," *School and Society*, 11 (January 31, 1920): 129–32; Luther V. Hendricks, "James Harvey Robinson and the New School for Social Research," *Journal of Higher Education*, 20 (1949): 1–11, 58; Beulah Amidon, "New Schoolman," *Survey Graphic*, 25 (1936): 188–89.

Croly, who had urged a school for the training of social experts since 1910,[29] plunged enthusiastically into the discussions—another energy-consuming activity of the hectic war years. At the center of the project were some of the Columbia exiles—Beard, James Harvey Robinson, Wesley C. Mitchell—and John Dewey, who retained his Columbia connection, Alvin Johnson, Croly, and others. They envisioned a school run by its teachers, with no degrees, departments, or president. The school was to serve mature adults, center on the social sciences broadly conceived, and conduct research into the pressing social and economic problems facing the United States. By June 1918, Croly was confident enough about the progress of the deliberations to discuss its purposes and aims in a long article. The school, as he imagined it, would "make social research of immediate assistance to a bewildered and groping American democracy." It would train social experts, particularly labor experts, public administrators and managers, and enter into the life of the society as an active participant: "Thus a school of social science becomes above everything else an instrumentality both of social purpose and of social research."[30]

Croly was not only an eager participant in the theoretical discussions leading to the New School, he was also active in raising the necessary funds for the project, enlisting Dorothy Straight and other philanthropists. He also tried, in vain, to attach Frankfurter to the project as chairman of the faculty, and conducted negotiations with Graham Wallas for a series of lectures in the first year of the school's program.[31] Before long, modest but attractive facilities had been obtained down Twenty-first Street from *The New Republic*. A remarkable faculty was soon gathered—Thorstein Veblen, Horace Kallen, Emily James Putnam, Harry Elmer Barnes, the Columbia group, and others. Wallas, Dewey, Laski, and Roscoe Pound agreed to give lecture courses. Full of optimism and courage, the New School for Social Research opened its doors to about one hundred students in the fall of 1919.

Within two years, the experiment, from Croly's perspective, was in shambles. There were the expected attacks from the conservatives,

---

[29] HC, "A Great School of Political Science," *World's Work*, 20 (May, 1910): 12887–88.

[30] HC, "A School of Social Research," *NR*, 15 (June 8, 1918): 167–71.

[31] HC to Felix Frankfurter, December 4, 1918, and Frankfuter's undated reply, detailing his reasons for not accepting the offer, are in the Frankfurter mss.; HC to Graham Wallas, March 29, May 16, June 28 and September 10, 1919, Graham Wallas mss., London School of Economics. The author wishes to thank Professor Kugwon Sang for calling the Wallas negotiations to his attention.

of course. Even before the New School opened, *The National Civic Federation Review* warned its readers about the dangerous men plotting to establish the new institution. Denouncing specifically Croly, Johnson, Beard, and Robinson for their lukewarm, pro-German and "internationalist" proclivities, the article alerted Americans to the awful danger that German propaganda "has been simply converted into another yet no less definite and inimical form, the propaganda of social discontent, revolution and civil strife. . . ."[32] Later, when Dorothy Straight innocently suggested that fellow-members of the Junior League might profit, as she was profiting, by taking courses at the New School, a faction of the organization presented a resolution proclaiming that certain members of the school's faculty were not fit teachers for League members.[33]

It was not the attacks of conservatives, however, but the incessant internal bickering that ruined the undertaking for Croly. The New School's mission had never been defined with much precision; and the founders, it soon turned out, were interested in accomplishing different things. Some of them wanted adult education, others wanted an informal center where cultivated professors could talk to one another, still others wanted to emphasize research. Croly's aims were twofold—to encourage advanced research into social problems and to provide labor unions with experts. He set out to attach to the school a Labor Research Bureau organized by himself and Robert Bruere, an experienced social worker interested in labor problems. The tensions soon became impossible to contain. Croly developed a hearty dislike of James Harvey Robinson, and he proposed diverting more and more of the New School's funds into the Labor Research Bureau. After a stormy board meeting, during which Croly's faction voted against all proposals, he and his supporters resigned from the board and left the experiment.[34] The New School, crippled and impoverished, was taken over in 1923 by Alvin Johnson, who turned it into an institution for adult education and nursed it back to health. To Croly, who placed so much importance on social education, the fact that a group of the country's leading progressives could not carry off harmoniously an experiment in advanced education for progressive purposes was a tragedy heavy with depressing implications.

Meanwhile, business affairs at *The New Republic* were in rather steady decline. Dorothy Straight quickly assumed the financial re-

---

[32] Quoted in Hendricks, "Robinson and the New School," 10–11.

[33] Ibid., 9; and W. A. Swanberg, *Whitney Father, Whitney Heiress* (New York, 1980), 450–51.

[34] Johnson, *Pioneer's Progress*, 274–81.

sponsibility for the paper and gave assurances of her commitment to its continuation. But Croly, who had hoped that the paper could be self-supporting, watched helplessly as subscriptions declined and calls upon Mrs. Straight for assistance became more frequent. In 1920, for example, *The New Republic* received ten separate infusions from Dorothy Straight of $5,000 each and six of $10,000 each.[35] On Armistice Day, *The New Republic* claimed 27,750 subscribers. By the end of 1919, that figure was down to 23,912. By the end of 1920, to 21,477; and two years later to 19,384. Finally, in October 1924, with debts to Dorothy Straight in excess of $800,000 and subscriptions down to 13,970, *The New Republic* filed for bankruptcy, in order to resolve Dorothy's tax problems, and was reorganized.[36] Croly's warning of disaster, made at the editorial meeting after the Treaty of Versailles was published, had come stunningly, depressingly true.

Relations between the editors had also soured. Lippmann returned to the magazine in March 1919, charged by Harold Laski to perform "the great human service of bringing to maturity the ideas and hopes which struggle for expression in Herbert's mind."[37] But somehow Lippmann seemed unable to throw himself into that task with unalloyed enthusiasm. He stayed away from the office and cultivated a deep hatred for Francis Hackett, which the latter returned. In April 1921, Lippmann asked for a leave of six months to write a book, but instead of returning to the journal he accepted a job with the *New York World*. "Herbert and I no longer learn from each other, and for two years our intellectual relationship has been a good natured accommodation rather than an inspiring adventure," he explained to Frankfurter. "We've done our work together, and it's just as well to recognize it."[38] For Croly, the loss of Lippmann, with his range, his incomparable prose, his deepening maturity, was a staggering blow.

In 1916, Croly had hired Charles Merz, a brilliant and versatile young journalist who had been the managing editor of *Harper's Weekly*

---

[35] For a record of Dorothy Straight's contributions to the *NR*, see Dorothy Straight Elmhirst mss., Folder 3725: 12–12.

[36] For *NR* circulation figures, see the reports in ibid., Folder 3725: 12–1 to 12–7; the papers relating to the bankruptcy and reorganization are in Folder 3725: 12–14.

[37] Quoted in Steel, *Walter Lippmann*, 155.

[38] Walter Lippmann to Felix Frankfurter, June 24, 1921, Frankfurter mss. Lippmann added: "Among the sub-reasons for going is, of course, F[rancis].H[ackett]. One's feeling that it takes all sorts of people to make a world is alright where the density of population is 2 per square mile, but in a flat it breaks down. He has made the intellectual tone steadily more uncharitable, more querulous, more rasping. He has taken the department which deals with the freer life of the mind and made it more factious than the political part."

at the age of twenty-two—Bourne had once called him a "wizard
. . . who can do everything from writing advertisements, running
the business department, editing the magazine to doing articles far
cleverer than any of us can do."[39] After two years as *The New Republic's* Washington correspondent, Merz joined the army and went
to Paris for the negotiations. He returned to the journal in 1919, and
Croly probably hoped that Merz would help to fill the gap left by
Lippmann's departure. That hope was dashed, however, when Merz
left with Lippmann for the *World*. Less than a year after the loss of
Lippmann and Merz, Francis Hackett and his bride, Signe Toksvig,
another *New Republic* editor, quit and moved to Denmark.[40] In August 1923, Phil Littell, in poor health and almost never at the office
anymore, also quit. In 1925, Robert Hallowell resigned and moved
to Paris. Alvin Johnson remained, but the tensions between him and
Croly over the direction of the New School increased. In the fall of
1926, as Johnson later remembered it, "I picked a quarrel with Croly—
a quarrel in which I was in the wrong—and resigned."[41] Of that
hopeful company that had started the experiment in 1914, only Croly
now remained.

The editors had long since ceased being a community of friendship
and mutual respect. They were torn by private animosities and differences of doctrine. In February 1921, at Lippmann's urging, Croly
had hired Edmund Wilson, still in his mid-twenties, as managing
editor. "When you become a regular editor of the N.R.," Wilson
wrote to a friend, "you draw a large salary and never go near the
office, but stay at home and write books." He thought that the editors had grown "respectable to the point of stodginess." Lippmann
was the "livest of the lot," but Wilson found even him conventional—"nothing more correct could be imagined than the home life
of the Lippmanns, and when I tell you that the Lippmanns regard
the Crolys as old-fashioned and dull, you will be able to form some
idea of what your poor friend Dr. Wilson is going to be in for. . . ."
There was also the pettiness. The editors, Wilson reported, were "very
much at odds with each other. Each one had taken me aside and told
me confidentially that the rest of the staff were timid old maids."[42]

[39] Randolph Bourne to Elizabeth Shepley Sergeant, August 24, 1916, Bourne mss.,
Columbia University. Merz became the editor of the *New York Times* in 1938.

[40] Bruce Bliven asserted that HC fired Hackett when the latter requested time off to
write a popular history of Ireland. Bruce Bliven, *Five Million Words Later, An Autobiography* (New York, 1970), 156.

[41] Johnson, *Pioneer's Progress*, 284.

[42] Edmund Wilson to Stanley Dell, February 19, 1921, in Elena Wilson, ed., *Edmund*

To Croly, who had always invested more in the enterprise than anyone else and who regarded *The New Republic* group almost as a family, the breakdown of community was a personal tragedy. He hated the bickering and tried desperately to contain it. And when one or another of his colleagues left, he thought of it as being akin to desertion. In 1924, when friends suggested a celebration dinner commemorating the tenth anniversary of *The New Republic*, Croly killed the idea: "There have been so many casualties on the editorial board of the New Republic since we started ten years ago, and these casualties have left so many scars on my own feelings that I don't see how I could get through a celebration of that kind," he explained to Brandeis.[43] To Dorothy Straight he confessed, "It makes me feel lonely."[44]

Nor could Croly have derived much comfort from the events of the day. He was horrified as he watched the postwar world taking form during the two years following the armistice. The hope that the war would inevitably lead to greater nationalization of American life, a hope so central to his advocacy of American entry, was quickly crushed. The promising agencies of nationalization erected during the war were rapidly dismantled, even the railroads, which had been rather successfully nationalized, were hurriedly returned to private ownership. More ominously, the country seemed to be indulging itself in an orgy of reaction, ugliness, and greed—the very antithesis of the spirit Croly had hoped to see established. The race riots and lynchings in the closing months of 1919 and the rise of the Klan were symptomatic and sufficiently alarming. Civil rights and free speech seemed everywhere on the defensive; five Socialists were expelled from the New York legislature and Debs languished in prison; anti-immigrant sentiment ran rampant. Especially troubling to Croly and *The New Republic* was the labor unrest and the uncompromising attitudes exhibited by employers. In the Boston police strike, in the labor troubles in steel mills and coal fields, Americans demonstrated how far they really were from achieving national unity under just social arrangements.

Wilson: Letters on Literature and Politics, 1912–1972 (New York, 1977), 56. Later, Wilson himself was at the center of office politics and internal power struggles—principally against Bruce Bliven. One editor remembered, HC "was the only fellow who could keep that backbiting staff together at all. They got along like cats and dogs but they all revered Croly." T. S. Matthews, "Oral History," Columbia University Oral History Project, 4.

[43] HC to Louis D. Brandeis, November 13, 1924, Brandeis mss.

[44] HC to Dorothy Straight, November 18, 1924, Dorothy Straight Elmhirst mss.

If there were any doubts about the mood of America, they were set to rest by the "red scare" raids and deportations, which began in the fall of 1919 and continued through the spring of 1920. The persecution of radicals ordered by Attorney General A. Mitchell Palmer left *The New Republic* editors torn between feelings of furious anger and impotent despair. "So ends a chapter in American history," they began the last issue of 1919. "On December 21, 1919, one hundred and thirty years after the foundation of the American government, the right of asylum was abolished, and the ancient institutions of banishment and exile reestablished. . . . Of those who applaud or acquiesce today, many will in later years think back to this and feel the humiliation of it."[45] *The New Republic* attempted to counter the hysteria with reasoned argument, constitutional explication, withering satire, the examination of individual cases of injustice.[46] Years later, Lippmann recalled the resistance of *The New Republic* to the "idiotic intolerance" of the red scare and gave Croly the credit for the journal's valiant stand: "He had the cold courage of a man who does not enjoy martyrdom."[47]

The presidential campaign of 1920 revealed how deeply submerged were the once progressive instincts of the American people. *The New Republic* launched a brief campaign for Herbert Hoover, but after the parties chose Warren Harding and James Cox, the editors resigned themselves to impotent ridicule.[48] ("Governor Cox, with all his shallowness and febrile excursions into hysteria and theology, is by several shades the superior of Senator Harding," they wrote in the last issue before the election.)[49] Croly helplessly cast his own vote for Parley P. Christensen, the Farmer-Labor candidate.[50] Since writing his biography of Mark Hanna, Croly had been an expert in Ohio Republican politics, and the election of Harding was worse than a

[45] *NR*, 21 (December 31, 1919): 127.

[46] For examples, see "The Anarchist Deportations," *NR*, 21 (December 24, 1919): 96–98; "Deporting a Political Party," ibid. (January 14, 1920): 186; "Speaker Sweet Does His Bit," ibid. (January 21, 1920): 210–12; "The Red Hysteria," ibid. (January 28, 1920): 249–52; and "Bringing the Constitution into Disrepute," ibid. (February 18, 1920): 330–31. For the general temper, see Robert K. Murray, *Red Scare: A Study in National Hysteria* (Minneapolis, 1955).

[47] Lippmann, "Notes for a Biography," 252.

[48] "Hoover as President," *NR*, 21 (January 21, 1920): 207–208; "Hoover and the Issues," ibid. (February 4, 1920): 281–83; "The Meaning of Hoover's Candidacy," ibid. (February 18, 1920): 329–30; "Fighting for Hoover," ibid., 22 (March 3, 1920): 4–6; and "Hoover's Chances," ibid. (April 14, 1920): 196–98.

[49] *NR*, 24 (November 3, 1920): 225.

[50] HC, "The Eclipse of Progressivism," *NR*, 24 (October 27, 1920): 210–16.

tragedy for him. Theodore Roosevelt and Woodrow Wilson had left much to be desired, but at the very least they were men of high intelligence and an undoubted capacity for constructive leadership. Harding was a hopeless mediocrity, and the size of his victory could only signal the start of a long period of bland, lusterless, and reactionary politics.

Thus the years after the armistice were heavy ones for Herbert Croly and hard to bear. The deaths of some of his friends and the estrangement of others, the failure of health, the disappointment at the direction of the New School, the decline of *The New Republic*'s strength and influence, the loss of his colleagues—all combined with the dashing of his hopes by the Treaty of Versailles and the sour turn in American political life to create an atmosphere of despair and bitterness. Croly made two responses to the new circumstances. First, he carried on, as best he could, fighting manfully against the popular current on behalf of the old articles of the progressive creed. And second, he searched for some measure of private solace in religious faith.

II

Her husband's sudden death had left Dorothy Straight so deeply affected that she resorted to a medium in order to reestablish communication with him. During the second of the nine séances, on Sunday morning, October 19, 1919, she put the following question to her husband's spirit: "Is there anything valuable the N[ew]. R[epublic]. can do?" According to the medium, the answer from the Beyond was "Do not become too rabid. . . ."[51] As it happened, the ghost of Willard Straight need not have worried. Nothing in Herbert Croly's temperament lent itself to becoming too rabid. The climate of opinion in the United States during the 1920s may have led a few intellectuals to extreme statement, desperate action, or blind fanaticism. But the effect on Croly and *The New Republic* was not so dramatic. They persevered.

The first task had been to assure the continuing support of Dorothy Straight. The money had always come from her, of course, but the business details were handled between Croly and Willard. In his will, Straight had urged his widow to continue to provide a subsidy

---

[51] The transcription of the series of séances can be found in the Willard Straight mss. For the details of Dorothy's resort to a medium, see Swanberg, *Whitney Father, Whitney Heiress*, 451–52.

for *The New Republic*, and she willingly acceded to the request. In the process of writing Willard's biography, however, Croly spent countless hours with Dorothy and a profound mutual respect grew up between the two of them. Herbert and his wife, it is not too much to say, loved Dorothy as a daughter, and their letters to her were filled with the most intimate expressions of deep affection and solicitude. No doubt the fact that the Crolys were entirely dependent upon her largess played its part in their relations, but that motive cannot completely account for the depth of the couple's regard for her. Croly seemed genuinely to respect her critical intelligence and repeatedly urged her to join the magazine as an editor and to take over its business affairs after he died.[52] In 1925, Dorothy married Leonard Elmhirst, an Englishman studying agriculture at Cornell, and the couple, to Croly's consternation, moved to England to pursue Elmhirst's reform schemes in scientific agriculture and education.[53] But there were regular reunions between the Elmhirsts and the Crolys, and the distance did not dim Dorothy's interest in or support for *The New Republic*.

Croly's biography, *Willard Straight*, was published by Macmillan in April 1924. Despite Brandeis's advice that he keep the work brief, the book ran to 596 pages.[54] Much of it consisted of long quotations from Straight's diaries and letters, and it was illustrated by sketches drawn by Straight. Croly included almost nothing about his own relationship to his subject. It was, of course, a generous and sympathetic assessment—the text was examined and approved before publication by Dorothy and several of Willard's friends.[55] Most reviewers contented themselves with discussing Straight's life rather than the merits or demerits of Croly's craftsmanship. But those who did comment were complimentary, and several praised Croly's mastery of Asian affairs in the early chapters.[56] The reviewer in *The Outlook*,

---

[52] HC to Dorothy Straight, May 10 and November 18, 1924, June 23, 1925, n.d. [1924–25], all in the Dorothy Straight Elmhirst mss.

[53] HC earnestly urged Dorothy to remain in the United States after her marriage. See letters to her on February 10, February 27, and n.d., 1925. The couple opened an experimental school associated with a farm and some light industry on two thousand acres around Dartington Hall, Devon. Swanberg, *Whitney Father, Whitney Heiress*, 463–68.

[54] Louis D. Brandeis to Felix Frankfurter, March 2, 1921, in Melvin I. Urofsky and David W. Levy, eds., *The Letters of Louis D. Brandeis* (Albany, 1971–1978), 4: 538.

[55] HC to Dorothy Straight, September 8, 1923, Dorothy Straight Elmhirst mss. Willard's one-time friend and Dorothy's one-time suitor, George Marvin, also examined the text.

[56] See for examples, Nathaniel Peffer's review in the *Nation*, 119 (October 29, 1924):

however, hit closest to the mark: "This careful biography is a work of friendship; and we get the impression that Mr. Croly has been in some sense deputed to the task by the whole body of Willard Straight's friends." The reviewer also ventured the usual criticism of Croly. "He takes matters, as always, a little heavily. A more flexible sense of humor would have eliminated detail here and there. . . ."[57] *Willard Straight* was, for Croly, the discharging of a duty to the memory of his friend and to the continuing friendship and support of his friend's widow. But the central arena for Croly's sense of duty was, and always would be, the editorial offices of *The New Republic*.

If his first task was to cement personal and financial relations with Dorothy Straight, the second was to lure fresh writers and intellectuals as talented as those who had deserted the enterprise. Somehow Croly succeeded in that effort and succeeded brilliantly—it was his best achievement, perhaps the only real achievement of his last ten years. He was able to attract to *The New Republic* some of the most sparkling writers of the younger generation and he was able to maintain a rapport with young intellectuals, which few men of his years would have attempted. T. S. Matthews, whom Croly hired in 1925, had been nine years old when *The Promise of American Life* appeared. "Different generations seem, if not hostile to each other, at least irrelevant," Matthews observed; but "of all the men of his generation, he talked to me most like one of mine."[58] It was this trait that enabled Croly to replenish the staff with young minds as good as those who had gone.

In March 1923, Croly hired Bruce Bliven as the journal's managing editor—the post formerly held by Charles Merz. The two had met when they jointly covered the Washington Naval Conference in 1921,

471–72; William Adams Brown's review in the *Survey*, 53 (December 1, 1924): 287; and the review in the *Christian Science Monitor*, September 3, 1924. For other reviews of Croly's biography of Straight, see *New York Times Book Review*, September 7, 1924 (by Nicholas Roosevelt); *Far Eastern Review* (July, 1924): 307ff; *Boston Transcript*, September 20, 1924 (by Straight's friend, Martin Egan); and the *New York World*, April 19, 1925 (by Charles Merz).

[57] H. W. Boynton, "One of Ours," *Outlook*, 138 (October 8, 1924): 212.

[58] T. S. Matthews, "One Generation to Another," *NR*, 63 (July 16, 1930): 270. For the same sentiment, see Matthews, *Name and Address, An Autobiography* (New York, 1960), 209–10; and Philip Littell, "As a Friend," *NR*, 63 (July 16, 1930): 244–45. Littell wrote: "It makes one happier about Herbert to know that while some old friends were going, new friends came, good friends whom his faith and his battles for his faith brought to his office and his house. To find new friends when you are past forty-five . . . is a reward which does not come to most men. . . . More and more, as he grew older, he found younger men coming to him because of their interest in his ideas and remaining his friends because they prized his companionship."

and Croly took an instant liking to the informal and easygoing Bliven. Only thirty-four at the time he joined *The New Republic*, Bliven brought almost fifteen years of journalistic experience with him and was the only newspaperman on the staff.[59] His usefulness to the magazine was not due to any flashing brilliance but rather to his steadiness, fluency, competence, and integrity. "His editorial work lacks intellectual distinction and drive," Croly reported to Dorothy in 1926, "but his signed articles are sometimes very good and he is a trustworthy and able managing editor. He is one of the most thoroughly kind, considerate, and good people I have ever known."[60] Gradually Bliven and Croly came to divide the journal's political writing and Bliven took over the affairs of the magazine whenever Croly was away from the office. Bliven was to stay with *The New Republic* until 1955. To cover economic topics, Croly relied on Alvin Johnson during the first half of the decade and then on George Soule, who returned to *The New Republic* as an editor in January 1925.

Supplementing the editorial staff on political and economic matters were half a dozen prolific and talented "regulars" whom Croly enlisted. The notable English economist, John Maynard Keynes, whose controversial *Economic Consequences of the Peace* was serialized in *The New Republic* before publication,[61] contributed more than forty signed articles during the decade. John Dewey wrote nearly a hundred, covering a wide variety of topics. William Hard had an article in almost every issue of the early 1920s, nearly fifty altogether. Later, Croly published frequent contributions from Stuart Chase, David Friday, Rexford Tugwell, Leo Wolman, and Gerard Henderson. Felix Frankfurter continued to write (mostly anonymously) on legal and judicial matters. These were distinguished names and there were many others; and they provided *The New Republic* with a steady stream of provocative and intelligent political and economic commentary.

If the political-economic side of the paper was distinguished during the 1920s, the literary-cultural side was illustrious. In addition to Francis Hackett (until 1922) and Phil Littell (until 1923), Croly gathered an extremely impressive group of critics during the decade. Robert Morss

[59] Bliven, *Five Million Words Later*, and Bliven, "Oral History," Columbia University Oral History Project.

[60] HC to Dorothy Straight Elmhirst, December 4, 1926, Dorothy Straight Elmhirst mss.

[61] The *NR* reprinted Keynes's third chapter as "When the Big Four Met," 21 (December 24, 1919): 103–109; his sixth chapter as "Europe After the Treaty" (January 14, 1920): 189–95; and his final chapter as "How to Mend the Treaty" (January 21, 1920): 215–24.

Lovett, a sensitive and versatile professor of English literature, was hired to run the book pages, and he turned them into a consistently exciting forum for the leading ideas of the era.[62] T. S. Matthews, a gifted young critic with a graceful style and a talent for satire, added even more depth on the literary side. Matthews left in 1929 to manage the book section of *Time* magazine, finally becoming *Time*'s general manager.[63] Undoubtedly the best critic on the staff, however, was Edmund Wilson. He maintained a loose connection with *The New Republic* until he became a full editor in November 1926. "Of all the younger men who have been associated with the paper of late years he has grown most consistently and most importantly," Croly wrote to Dorothy. "There is every prospect that before long he will take his place as the soundest and most trustworthy critic in this country."[64] Wilson, who amply fulfilled Croly's confidence in him, remained with *The New Republic* until 1931. In 1928, Wilson brought his friend Malcolm Cowley into the office and Cowley's name went officially onto the editors' list a few weeks before Croly's death.[65] The drama criticism was shared by Stark Young, a softspoken southerner who wrote numerous plays himself, and Robert Littell, Phil's son, who remained with *The New Republic* until 1927 and ended his career as editor of the popular *Reader's Digest*.

In addition to the critics attached directly to the journal, Croly was able to attract reviews from leading writers and intellectuals. In philosophy, he published Dewey, Horace Kallen, Morris R. Cohen, and Bertrand Russell; in literature and poetry, Virginia Woolf, Allen Tate, Conrad Aiken, Babette Deutsch, and Robert Herrick; in history, Charles Beard, Samuel Eliot Morison, Harry Elmer Barnes, and William Langer.

Three other specialists in cultural criticism made significant contributions to *The New Republic* during the 1920s. Lewis Mumford wrote on a variety of topics but concentrated on urban affairs, architecture, and the impact of technology on modern sensibilities. He wrote three-dozen articles for the magazine and many reviews. Waldo

[62] Robert Morss Lovett, *All Our Years* (New York, 1948), ch. xi. Lovett also wrote on political topics for the *NR*. For a description of him, see Hutchins Hapgood, *A Victorian in the Modern World* (New York, 1939), 76.

[63] Matthews, *Name and Address*, 186–215; Matthews, "Oral History."

[64] HC to Dorothy Straight Elmhirst, December 4, 1926, Dorothy Straight Elmhirst mss. For a more critical comment on Wilson, see HC to Felix Frankfurter, June 23, [1927], Frankfurter mss. For a description of Wilson at the *NR*, see Matthews, *Name and Address*, 192–204.

[65] Cowley, "The Old House in Chelsea," 40–49.

Frank, a veteran (with Bourne) of *The Seven Arts*, became a close friend of Croly's, the two sharing a number of religious ideas. Out of that friendship, and against the advice of the other editors, Croly decided to publish Frank's *The Re-discovery of America*, a book dedicated to Croly himself, in twenty-one interminable installments. "The serialization," Bruce Bliven recalled, "went on forever, amid scores of letters of complaint from the readers, and canceled subscriptions."[66] Finally there was Eduard C. Lindeman, Croly's closest intellectual companion during the last years of his life. A sensitive young man of frail health, Lindeman was interested in everything—social philosophy, adult education, public housing, family relations, recreation, social work, and much besides. Croly was captivated by his sincerity and his earnest attempts to apply religious insights to social problems, and he persuaded Dorothy Elmhirst to contribute to Lindeman's support so that he could devote himself entirely to his writing. Croly summarized their relationship in a letter to Dorothy in 1924: "He and I are more closely allied intellectually than I have ever been with any previous friend. He is not as suggestive as Walter [Lippmann] used to be, and he is not as stimulating to me, but I have more confidence in him and affection for him."[67]

And so Herbert Croly, his journal once more financially secure and brilliantly staffed, went forth to do battle against the temper of the era. That temper did not improve much, by Croly's lights, after the red scare and the election of Harding. It was largely a thankless effort, therefore, and one with few compensations; but *The New Republic* steadfastly tried to keep the liberal program alive in a time discouragingly indifferent to the old appeals. The editors continued their battles for academic freedom and for freedom of speech. They were jealous advocates of the rights of women, Negroes, and immigrants—and they opposed restrictive immigration laws. They fought to put Harry Daugherty and the Teapot Dome conspirators in jail and to get Eugene Debs and Tom Mooney out. Throughout the decade, Croly and the others continued to champion the cause of labor, and they pointed with alarm to the abuses of unrestrained capitalism. *The New Republic* condemned the Klan, high tariffs, industrial espionage, and the persecutors of John T. Scopes; it urged the vigorous conservation of natural resources, genuine agricultural reform, and the public production and ownership of electric power.

[66] Bliven, *Five Million Words Later*, 162–63; see also Cowley, "Old House in Chelsea," 44.

[67] HC to Dorothy Straight, June 23, 1924, Dorothy Straight Elmhirst mss.

Week after week it heaped ridicule and abuse on Warren Harding and Calvin Coolidge—and, like everyone else in America, it praised Lindbergh.

The prohibition question placed Croly in a dilemma. At first he was not disposed to take the issue very seriously, and he limited *The New Republic*'s consideration of it to a few scattered comments. Unfortunately, the utter breakdown of law enforcement, which characterized the experiment, raised an entirely new set of problems; and, by 1926, the journal was describing prohibition as "the most irrepressible and significant of all domestic political issues."[68] Croly regarded prohibition as an excessive interference with the rights of individuals and a product of narrow-minded fanaticism. At the same time, however, the experiment had acquired the status of a national responsibility, the assumption of a new sort of authority by the central government. Croly, the foremost advocate of an active and energetic central government, was torn between disliking the policy yet wanting the government to demonstrate its capabilities. In an early attempt to discuss the issue—an attempt which Brandeis rightly called "weak, wooly, apologetic, ineffective"[69]—the journal reluctantly suggested leaving enforcement to the states. "It will be charged that this is a confession of failure on the part of the national government. It is," the editors admitted.[70] *The New Republic*'s eventual position was suggested by Brandeis, who passed the message through Felix Frankfurter.[71] The federal government should be responsible for preventing liquor from entering the United States from foreign countries and should assume the responsibility for stopping the traffic across state lines. But the states should be given the immense task of controlling violations within their own boundaries. This assignment to state governments of a vast new power must have been a bitter pill for Croly, but given the ambiguities of the experiment and the impossibility of the federal government's adequately discharging the responsibility, Croly decided that the effort to enforce prohibition was discrediting and retarding genuine progressive reform. The Brandeis suggestion became *The New Republic*'s position until the possibility of actual repeal emerged.[72]

[68] *NR*, 47 (June 9, 1926): 70.

[69] Louis D. Brandeis to Felix Frankfurter, September 25, 1922, in Urofsky and Levy, eds., *Letters of Louis D. Brandeis*, 5: 65.

[70] "The Enforcement of Prohibition," *NR*, 32 (September 13, 1922): 60.

[71] Louis D. Brandeis to Felix Frankfurter, September 25, 1922, in Urofsky and Levy, eds., *Letters of Louis D. Brandeis*, 5: 65.

[72] For representative early statements of the journal's policy on prohibition, see *NR*,

The period was not without brief and flickering moments of optimism. The two chief instances, for Croly, were the presidential elections of 1924 and 1928. Since the end of the war he had hoped for a third political party, a union of farmers and workers dedicated to progressive principles, and he provided the various embryonic efforts in that direction with full and sympathetic coverage in *The New Republic*.[73] He joined the prestigious "Committee of Forty-Eight," a group largely composed of intellectuals anxious to help form such a party, and he attended the well-publicized Washington dinner, in December 1922, which served as a rallying point for the newly formed Conference for Progressive Political Action and a preliminary for the Progressive party movement of 1924.[74]

When the time came, Croly supported La Follette to the fullest, running a seven-part series in which such distinguished progressives as Jane Addams, Norman Hapgood and Felix Frankfurter explained "Why I Shall Vote for La Follette."[75] The last installment he reserved for himself, and, in it, he denounced Coolidge's complacency about America as "almost incredible in its fatuous ignorance and its essential absurdity." The program of Democrat John W. Davis, a well-

---

35 (June 13, 1923): 55–56; ibid., 36 (October 24, 1923): 214; "Shall We Have Prohibition," ibid., 44 (September 23, 1925): 109–11; "Politics and Prohibition," ibid., 45 (January 6, 1926): 178–79; "The Prohibition Muddle," ibid. (February 3, 1926): 280–82; "Progressivism and Prohibition," ibid., 46 (April 21, 1926): 261–63; "Irrepressible Prohibition," ibid., 48 (October 20, 1926): 232–34.

[73] See for examples, C. R. Johnson, "The Conviction of Townley," *NR*, 20 (August 6, 1919): 18–20; "Towards a New Party," ibid. (August 13, 1919): 41–43; "New York Labor's First Campaign," ibid. (September 3, 1919): 138–39; C. R. Johnson, "Minnesota and the Nonpartisan League," ibid. (October 8, 1919): 290–98; "Labor in Politics," ibid. (November 19, 1919): 335–37; Charles Merz, "Enter the Labor Party," ibid., 21 (December 10, 1919): 53–55; Robert Bruere, "The New Alliance—Farm and Factory," ibid., 22 (March 10, 1920): 53–56; William Hard, "Third Party Happenings," ibid., 23 (July 28, 1920): 246–47; Hard, "Farmer-Labor: The Project," ibid., 24 (October 27, 1920): 218–19; Arthur Fisher, "A Farmer-Labor Party for 1924?" ibid., 35 (July 11, 1923): 169–70; and "Why a Third Party," ibid., 37 (February 20, 1924): 324–25.

[74] For the "Committee of Forty-Eight" (which took its name from the number of states, not the number of its membership), see "A New Political Alignment," *Nation*, 108 (March 29, 1919): 460–61; Lincoln Colcord, "The Committee of Forty-Eight," *Nation*, 109 (December 27, 1919): 821–22; and Oscar Leonard, "The Forty-Eighters," *Survey*, 43 (December 20, 1919): 255–56. For the general movement toward a third party, culminating in the La Follette campaign of 1924, see Kenneth C. MacKay, *The Progressive Movement of 1924* (New York, 1947), ch. iv; D. Joy Humes, *Oswald Garrison Villard, Liberal of the 1920s* (Syracuse, 1960), ch. vi; and Robert Morss Lovett, "A Party in Embryo," *NR*, 83 (July 24, 1935): 295–97.

[75] The series ran between September 10 and October 29, 1924.

paid Wall Street lawyer, Croly argued, consisted of compromises and evasions.[76] (In the final issue before the election, he called Davis "the man whose recent private and professional life most completely disqualified him from dealing thoroughly with the economic issue," of all those candidates whom the Democrats might have chosen.)[77] Nevertheless, Croly had to swallow hard to support La Follette: the senator's vague statements on foreign affairs reiterated the platitudes of prewar, midwestern isolationism, and his discussion of big business sounded like the simplistic trust-busting rhetoric of 1912, both positions anathema to Croly. That he supported La Follette at all was a measure of his faith in the ability of a new party eventually to define better programs. That he supported La Follette with such unrestrained enthusiasm was a measure of the desperation he felt at the state of American politics in the 1920s.

Croly's enthusiasm for La Follette's movement lasted until the November election revealed that only one out of seven voters shared his vision of America.[78] The enthusiasm for Al Smith's movement, in 1928, did not survive even through July. Croly, who did virtually all of the early political writing on the campaign of 1928, initially felt encouraged by the prospect of Smith's candidacy.[79] "For the first time in a great many years," he wrote Waldo Frank more than a year before the campaign, "I look forward to the future, if not with confidence, at least with a certain amount of exhilaration." He thought the debate between Smith and the Republicans (he still presumed that Coolidge would be the Republican nominee) would provide "an opportunity of saying things that have more significance to them than anything we have had to say about politics in the last few years."[80]

[76] HC, "Why I Shall Vote for La Follette," NR, 40 (October 29, 1924): 221–24. The same issue contained an article on behalf of Coolidge by Chester Rowell, a California progressive, and one on behalf of Davis by Walter Lippmann.

[77] "Barriers to Progressivism," NR, 40 (November 5, 1924): 241. Although appearing anonymously, the editorial is obviously by HC.

[78] Shortly after the election, HC wrote to Dorothy Straight, "I have been thinking a great deal since last Tuesday about the results of the election. Quite apart from its public significance it raises serious questions about the future policy of the New Republic. I had hoped that hereafter the paper could act as the interpreter of a practical progressive political agitation. It now looks as if we would remain without any political shelter or corroboration for another four or eight years. What shall we do? Shall we quit or shall we alter our policy and pay less attention to politics and seek compensation in writing about education, art and religion?" HC to Dorothy Straight, November [?], 1924, Dorothy Straight Elmhirst mss.

[79] HC to Leonard Elmhirst, July 27, 1928, Dorothy Straight Elmhirst mss.

[80] HC to Waldo Frank, April 29, 1927, Waldo Frank mss., University of Pennsylvania.

Indeed, Governor Smith's speech accepting the Democratic nomination was based, in part, on memos written for him by various *New Republic* editors.[81] And when the Republicans nominated Herbert Hoover, Croly was even more confident of a stimulating and useful national discussion. Hoover had shown as secretary of commerce that he believed in subordinating government to business and was, therefore, a true Republican; but he was well-qualified to assume the presidency, imbued with the engineer's mentality for solving problems, and many cuts above Coolidge and the typical Republican reactionary.[82]

For weeks Croly waited in increasing impatience for the great debate to begin. To his dismay it never materialized. At the end of July, he poured out his frustration to Leonard Elmhirst:

> Hoover and Al Smith are not really engaged in any clash. They are merely manoevring at arms length and are saying and doing as little as they can. It is almost impossible, consequently, to place them side by side and institute any really significant political comparison. I am afraid that as the campaign develops they will continue to spar and manoevre rather than engage in any really hard or close fight. Al Smith, is, I think, afraid of attacking Hoover because he does not wish to be attacked himself, and Mr. Hoover, of course, occupying as he does, a much stronger strategic position than his rival, will not need to attack if Al Smith lets him alone.[83]

In the same week as his letter to Elmhirst, Croly wrote an angry article, "The Progressive Voter: He Wants to Know!" Progressives should demand forthright statements from the candidates on the social and economic issues of the hour. If they do not receive adequate answers, he wrote, they should vote for Norman Thomas, the Socialist.[84]

If any single episode of the 1920s was symbolic of the general feelings of outrage, bitterness, and frustration that Croly and the other editors experienced, it was the battle on behalf of Sacco and Vanzetti. *The New Republic* followed the case from the start and poured every

[81] HC to Dorothy Straight Elmhirst, August 23, 1928, Dorothy Straight Elmhirst mss.

[82] See HC's anonymous editorial, "Herbert Hoover and the Republican Party," and his signed article, "How Is Hoover?" both in *NR*, 45 (June 27, 1928): 138–40.

[83] HC to Leonard Elmhirst, July 27, 1928, Dorothy Straight Elmhirst mss.

[84] HC, "The Progressive Voter: He Wants to Know!" *NR*, 45 (July 25, 1928): 242–47.

resource it had into the effort to get a new trial for the two condemned radicals. The journal's first comment, astonishingly, was a
full-length article on Vanzetti written by John N. Beffel even before
the pair's murder trial started.[85] Thereafter, down through the seven
years leading to the execution, the editors reported each new disclo-
sure, each new development, each fresh disappointment. Before the
affair ended, *The New Republic* had published more than forty editorials and better than two-dozen articles about the case. Alongside
these were poems, appeals for funds, notices of protest meetings,
reviews, documents important to the case, letters from frantic readers. The whole staff had their say about the matter: Stark Young,
Robert Morss Lovett, Phil Littell, Edmund Wilson, Croly himself.
Bruce Bliven visited the two condemned men in prison and returned
to New York to write a moving article.[86] In addition to the staff
contributions, the journal published opinion on the case from such
luminaries as John Dewey, Babette Deutsch, and Alexander Meikeljohn, and from Sacco and Vanzetti activists such as Frankfurter, Elizabeth Glendower Evans, Gardner Jackson, and defense attorney William G. Thompson. The editors even published one of their articles
in the *New York Times* as a paid advertisement.[87] It is not surprising
that a month after the execution the journal ran three editorial paragraphs justifying, somewhat defensively, their handling of the case.[88]
Another evidence of the traumatic effect of the episode on the magazine's editors was their apparent inability to put the matter aside. In
the twenty-eight months between the execution and the end of the
decade, the journal printed more than twenty editorials and better
than fifteen articles on the case. They reviewed the evidence endlessly
and seized on scattered shreds of new information. In various articles—with titles such as "Vanzetti Was Innocent" or "President Lowell and the Sacco Alibi"—they renewed the old charges and the, by
then, useless arguments.

In a sense, the vain attempt to save Sacco and Vanzetti summarized
a good deal of what had happened to progressivism during the 1920s.

[85] John N. Beffel, "Eels and the Electric Chair," *NR*, 25 (December 29, 1920): 127–
29.

[86] Bruce Bliven, "In Dedham Jail," *NR*, 51 (June 22, 1927): 120–21; see also Bliven,
Five Million Words Later, 183–87.

[87] The advertisement appeared in the *New York Times*, August 19, 1927. It cost
$1,900 to publish. Some of the money was raised in the *NR* offices, some came from
friends, and some from Mrs. Elmhirst. The article, "A Letter to President Lowell,"
appeared in *NR*, 52 (August 24, 1927): 6–8.

[88] *NR*, 52 (September 21, 1927): 108.

The most obvious thing about the case, of course, was the fact that the combined, aroused, militant forces of American liberalism had not been able to prevent the execution of two Italian radicals. John Dos Passos expressed perfectly the feelings of defeat: "all right you have won you will kill the brave men our friends tonight there is nothing left to do we are beaten."[89] But it was not only the powerlessness that was demonstrated by the failure to save Sacco and Vanzetti (that had already been amply demonstrated by the disastrous results of the election of 1924). The case also showed the extent to which the energies of American liberalism had been diverted away from the large questions of social and economic reform. *The New Republic* had been founded, in 1914, to direct the momentous forces dedicated to social change—the early issues leave the impression of a group of intellectuals trying to formulate vast and thoughtful proposals for the general reformation of American life. The issues of the 1920s leave the impression of a group of harried volunteers frantically trying to stamp out brush fires of reaction and injustice. The situation afforded little opportunity for thoroughgoing, radical, courageous analysis. Had Croly heard it, the advice of Willard Straight's anxious wraith—"Do not become too rabid"—might have provided a little needed amusement.

As it was, Croly was far from amused about America and positively glum about the day-to-day operation of *The New Republic*. His life fell into a pattern. Dorothy Straight had provided money for the Crolys to remodel their apartment on Seventy-first Street, and Herbert, for the first time in his life, had his own study.[90] He worked there every morning, usually on next week's leader or editorial. Around noon he brought his handwritten notes to the typist at the office and, at one, lunched with those staff members and guests who happened to be present. He then retired to his office on the second floor and took a nap on his couch—he had installed a special "vita glass" in the windows because he had been persuaded that it would screen out actinic rays and preserve health.[91] The evenings were devoted to reading, socializing, concerts, and the theater. He tried to break the routine by travel: to London in the summer of 1921; to Mexico in the winter of 1926–1927; to Hawaii (as a delegate to the Conference of the Institute of Pacific Relations) and back through the Canadian

[89] John Dos Passos, *U.S.A.* (New York, 1937 edition), 462.

[90] HC to Dorothy Straight, December 25, 1923, Dorothy Straight Elmhirst mss.

[91] George Soule, interview with the author, October 7, 1963; Bliven, *Five Million Words Later*, 165–66; T. S. Matthews, "Oral History," 10.

Rockies in the summer of 1927; and to Italy and a visit with the Elmhirsts in England in the spring of 1928.

He thought frequently about "killing" *The New Republic*, and, after Dorothy's second marriage, he certainly had little expectation of the journal's surviving him. Despite a short-lived flurry of new subscriptions during the 1924 campaign (which made the failure of such a flurry to materialize in 1928 doubly disappointing) and a slight rise in circulation at the height of the Sacco and Vanzetti agitation, the magazine seemed unable to make itself more attractive to the American public.[92] "The New Republic plods along without either gaining or losing," Croly wrote Dorothy out of the depths of the Coolidge administration, ". . . [I]t is not easy to keep the point of one's spear sharp and keen. I feel sometimes as if my own future career would and should run more in the direction of silence."[93] In mid-1925, with subscriptions numbering around 14,500 (more than ten thousand less than on Armistice Day), Croly blamed the "unfavorable atmosphere" for the poor circulation figures. "And there is no telling how long we can keep it up. . . . My vitality is ebbing slowly but inexorably."[94] Eighteen months later he sent a report to Dorothy Elmhirst, which unmistakably revealed his discouragement and feelings of impotence:

> The New Republic seems to be doing about as well as we had any right to expect. . . . There is no evidence of an increasing public demand for it, but we seem to succeed in holding our old readers better than we have done of late years. The New Republic seems indeed to have carved out a niche in the public mind for itself which is not as important a place as it occupied at one time but which is not unimportant and which is relatively secure. I do not think that I am capable of making the New Republic a more positive factor than it is in American opinion unless there is a change in our favor of the general atmosphere. If there were a revival of progressivism in politics, we probably could double our circulation. But without such a revival there is nothing which the present staff can do very much to improve its position.[95]

[92] HC to Dorothy Straight Elmhirst, December 1, 1927; and to Leonard Elmhirst, July 27, 1928, both in the Dorothy Straight Elmhirst mss.

[93] HC to Dorothy Straight Elmhirst, February 10, 1925, Dorothy Straight Elmhirst mss. See also HC to Waldo Frank, June 23, 1927, Frank mss.

[94] HC to Dorothy Straight Elmhirst, June 23, 1925, Dorothy Straight Elmhirst mss.

[95] HC to Dorothy Straight Elmhirst, December 4, 1926, Dorothy Straight Elmhirst mss.

Insofar as Croly evolved any conscious strategy to cope with the "unfavorable atmosphere" of the 1920s, it was the most obvious one. From the Treaty of Versailles until Croly's death, *The New Republic* subtly but noticeably de-emphasized its coverage of political and legislative affairs and pointedly increased its attention to general cultural developments. It was no accident that the literary-cultural side of the staff required so many and such gifted writers; indeed, in 1929, Croly called Malcolm Cowley to his apartment and startled him by proposing that all the editors be fired except Cowley and Edmund Wilson and that *The New Republic* be converted to a literary journal.[96] Through the decade, Croly devoted more and more space to science and art, to philosophy and education, to architecture, music and drama. And also to religion. The changed emphasis was partly a product of the hostile climate of the 1920s, but it also reflected—and especially in its religious aspect—the changed views and preoccupations of the anguished chief editor.

III

"When a young man," Croly reminisced in September 1920, "I possessed for a few months a vision of religious truth as a part of my personal business, which subsequently for many years became dim & almost expired. It is only recently that I fully began to believe again."[97] Louise always considered her husband's "conversion," as she called it, to be the product of that very night in their apartment when she read to him the provisions of the Treaty of Versailles: "From that time on he turned to religion."[98] Whether it all happened with such dramatic suddenness is impossible to determine.[99] But only eight months after the treaty, Harold Laski would report to Justice Holmes that "Croly has the religious bug very badly."[100] And in 1926, Croly would write feelingly about the need "to reconstruct the personal

[96] Malcolm Cowley, interview with the author, November 12, 1966; and Cowley, "Old House in Chelsea," 44.

[97] HC to Dorothy Straight, September 11, 1920, Dorothy Straight Elmhirst mss.

[98] Louise Croly to Dorothy Straight Elmhirst, [August 1923], and June 22, 1930, Dorothy Straight Elmhirst mss.

[99] For evidence that HC was heading in that direction already, see the conclusion of his article, a week before the Versailles incident, "The Obstacle to Peace," *NR*, 18 (April 26, 1919): 403–407.

[100] Harold Laski to Oliver Wendell Holmes, January 4, 1920, in Mark A. DeWolfe Howe, ed., *Holmes-Laski Letters: The Correspondence of Mr. Justice Holmes and Harold J. Laski, 1916–1935* (Cambridge, Mass., 1953), 1: 231. Laski was reporting the observation of Walter Lippmann.

intellectual architecture which the war destroyed and which I have been trying ever since to recover."[101]

Questions of ultimate meaning had never been far removed from Croly's mind. Raised by his parents in Comte's "Religion of Humanity," discovering Christianity at college, Croly had distinguished himself from his fellow-progressives by his willingness to deal with matters many of them would have dismissed as "religious" or even as "mystical." Both the final chapter of *The Promise of American Life*, with its emphasis on altruism, regeneration, and human brotherhood and the utopian passage in *Progressive Democracy*, with its evocation of "the faith of St. Paul" and "a love which is . . . at bottom a spiritual expression of the mystical unity of human nature," indicate that Croly had always felt the need to range beyond the standard progressive preoccupation with better laws and improved institutions.[102] But until the war, he tended to entrust the moral improvement of mankind to what he called "social education." Now he demanded another basis.

A new book, *The Breach in Civilization*, was in production early in 1920. In it Croly tried to embody his views on the role of religion in the past and in the future of human society. Macmillan had begun to set the text into page proofs and was planning to publish it in the fall, but Croly, acting on the earnest advice of Felix Frankfurter, suddenly decided to reimburse the publisher's expenses and to withdraw the book from publication.[103] The manuscript, only part of which still survives, bore some marks of haste and disorganization.[104] Nevertheless, Croly presented in it another stimulating and, in this case, personally revealing argument.

His two previous books on current affairs had demonstrated a characteristic mental habit. Croly's method was to reach backward to some important historic moment and to explain how a crucial intellectual conflict had been born, how it developed through time,

---

[101] HC to Dorothy Straight Elmhirst, September 14, 1926, Dorothy Straight Elmhirst mss.

[102] HC, *Progressive Democracy* (New York, 1914), 427.

[103] Originally, the book was to have appeared in March 1920 (see *NR*, 22 [March 3, 1920]: 35). When HC published a chapter of the book, "Regeneration," in *NR* (23 [June 9, 1920]: 40–47), an introductory statement announced that the entire book would be published early in the fall. For the decision to withdraw the manuscript, see Felix Frankfurter to Louise Croly, March 15, 1945, Autograph File, Houghton Library, Harvard University, and HC to Learned Hand, January 27, 1930, Hand mss.

[104] The only known fragment is the 151 pages of proof deposited at Houghton Library, Harvard University. It is impossible to tell how long the entire book was to have been or what additional topics HC proposed to discuss in it.

and how the elements in that conflict must now be reconciled. In *The Promise of American Life*, he had traced the tension between nationalism and democracy in America from the battles between Hamilton and Jefferson in the 1790s. In *Progressive Democracy*, he had elaborated on the opposition between the faith in democratic freedom and the simultaneous faith in the sacred constitutional limitations on democratic freedom, an opposition written into the American fabric at the nation's birth. This time, Croly left America completely (there is, in fact, surprisingly little about the United States in the surviving section of *The Breach in Civilization*) and found the crucial historic moment to have been the Protestant Reformation of the sixteenth century.

Not only did the Reformation shatter the political and religious unity of Europe, it destroyed the vision of a single community, which was inherent in Catholicism. Under the dominion of the Church, society had been informed by a unified moral system, which served as the basis of political, economic, and intellectual arrangements. The emergence of Protestantism, however, changed everything. It provided the impulses for all the central features of modern society. By authorizing dissent the Reformation "started a fumbling experiment in the building of an essentially secular civilization," Croly proclaimed, and it accomplished a disastrous division between the moral and the intellectual life of Christendom. The evils that plagued modern life (the anarchy of standards, the blind faith in science, the rampant and destructive greed, the chaos of international relations) stemmed from the introduction of Protestant subjectivism, materialism, and individualism at the expense of a unified and authoritative moral system.[105]

The solution to this momentous breach in civilization, with its moral life on one side and its intellectual, scientific, and political life on the other, was obvious: truly progressive men and women "will have to resurrect the mediaeval vision of a single catholic community." They must restore "the social ideal of Catholicism," and if they fail to do it, "their civilization will remain divided against itself and will drift helplessly to its own destruction."[106] Naturally, safeguards had to be provided to prevent a recurrence of the abuses of medieval Catholicism; but the only hope of mankind was to recover the moral and religious vision, the "authoritative knowledge" that Catholicism had once symbolized.

[105] HC, *The Breach in Civilization*, 9–16.
[106] Ibid., 15.

It is not difficult to understand why Frankfurter advised his friend to withdraw the manuscript from publication. *The Breach in Civilization* was practically a confession of defeat on Croly's part, a discouraged and disheartened admission that so much of what he had advocated in the past had proved useless. Social legislation to correct economic abuses, disinterested scientific expertise, constitutional democracy—all were unimportant in the absence of an accepted body of moral doctrine. Croly even challenged the old belief with which he was most often associated in the public mind, the role of the central government in bringing about human amelioration. Progressivism, he declared, had been content "to fall back uncritically on the state as the conscious agency of individual and social liberation. It failed to understand that in falling back upon the existing moral anarchy, it was playing into the hands of the enemies of liberalism."[107]

Croly's manuscript is also notable for the opinions he expressed on other current matters. His most definitive denunciation of the war ("the most consummate tragedy in the sombre annals of human catastrophe") was contained in the introduction. His most thorough dissection of the Treaty of Versailles, item by item, including the League of Nations, was offered in the fifth chapter, and the sixth carried his mature reflections on bolshevism. He agreed with the popular assessment that bolshevism was a menace, arguing that it constituted merely a grab for power on behalf of a particular class without presenting a significant moral and human vision for society. But he insisted that capitalism had to take the Bolshevik indictment seriously and move to correct its abuses if it hoped to defeat the danger. What made the red scare so frightening was the misguided hope that once the agitators were silenced, happiness would follow. "The way to render a capitalist society immune from revolutionary socialism," Croly thought, "is to treat revolutionary agitation not as itself the removable cause of social insecurity, but as the natural effect of social irresponsibility, helplessness and impiety."[108] Unfortunately, Croly's opinions on the treaty and bolshevism, as well as his chapter on Germany, were poorly integrated into the central argument of the book. This is probably what Frankfurter objected to when he complained about Croly's "mode of execution."[109]

Despite the fact that Croly offered a brief criticism of Auguste Comte (he and the other early sociologists were too confident of their

[107] Ibid., 54.

[108] Ibid., 123.

[109] Felix Frankfurter to Louise Croly, March 15, 1945, Autograph File, Houghton Library, Harvard University.

ability to predict the future, Croly alleged),[110] *The Breach in Civilization* marked a return to the French philosopher's distinctive approach to historical analysis, the approach that had contributed so much to *The Promise of American Life*. Comte, too, had seen in the Protestant Reformation an event of signal significance. For the Frenchman, the Reformation was the start of the breakdown of the theological polity—a step necessary for the progress of mankind, but destined to be erected into the crippling orthodoxy of the metaphysical stage. "Protestantism," Comte had written, "must be charged with having seriously impaired the fundamental principles of morality, both domestic and social, which Catholicism had established. . . ." Subordinating spiritual authority to secular individualism was natural, Comte argued; the metaphysical polity would always unthinkingly seize the weapons best calculated to destroy the theological. But it was a grave and mischievous error. Not least because it led men "to seek the satisfaction of social needs in changes of legal institutions; whereas, in general, the thing wanted is a preparatory reformation of principles and manners."[111] Comte and Croly agreed that the solution was some combination, in the future, of progress and order, of moral stability and scientific knowledge, of personal regeneration and social altruism.

Although Croly borrowed again from Comte's law of the three stages, he did not succumb to the "Religion of Humanity." The tone of the book, with its emphasis on the necessity for spiritual regeneration, may have sounded like a recurrence of the religious beliefs of Comte and of Croly's father, but it was not.[112] Herbert Croly's rejection of the "Religion of Humanity" three decades before, had been permanent. And in a series of articles and editorials in *The New Republic*, interspersed among the normal political and economic commentary, Croly made it clear that he was investing his hopes for spiritual rebirth in a reawakened Christianity.[113] "The effective testimony in favor of human regeneracy must come from the affirmation by a renascent Christianity of the saving virtue of the imitation of

[110] HC, *The Breach in Civilization*, 128.

[111] Auguste Comte, *The Positive Philosophy, Freely Translated and Condensed by Harriet Martineau* (London, 1896), 3: 154–82. The quotations are at 179 and 178.

[112] Cf. Forcey, *Crossroads of Liberalism*, 304–305: "He turned once more to the faith of his father, to that 'religion of humanity' that had made his youth a mystic orgy."

[113] HC, "Disordered Christianity," *NR*, 21 (December 31, 1919): 136–39; "A Modern Instance," ibid., 23 (July 14, 1920): 194–95; HC, "Behaviorism in Religion," ibid., 29 (February 22, 1922): 367–70; HC, "The Reconstruction of Religion," ibid., 31 (June 21, 1922): 100–102; "The New Christianity," ibid., 32 (October 11, 1922): 159–61; "Methodism vs. Intellectual Honesty," ibid. (November 1, 1922): 237–39; and HC, "Surely Good Americanism," ibid. (November 15, 1922): 294–96.

Christ," he declared in the last issue of 1919. "The love and reverence for human life born of the imitation of Christ constitute the substance of a truth which in so far as it is acknowledged really has some chance of setting mankind free."[114]

Croly assigned a double mission to a renascent Christianity. The first responsibility was to make its principles more effective in the conduct of social life. He joined the "Christian Way of Life Committee" and prepared a questionnaire for its members. Arguing that "a clear and flagrant discrepancy now exists" between Christ's teachings and modern practices, Croly suggested "a study of what these discrepancies are, whether or not they can be overcome, and if so how. . . ."[115] For himself, Croly asserted, "I see no way out of this morass except through the new affirmation of Christian truth as a way of life and the solemn belief in it by Christian peoples as more formative and sacred than any of the special gods of natural science, politics, economics and the world."[116]

But reborn Christianity had another task as well. Its fundamental concern should be making "the religion of Jesus Christ more creative of liberated, invigorated and integrated human beings."[117] The mission of individual regeneration, of freeing men and women to achieve their human potential in this life—that sacred undertaking was the basis of all else that Christianity might hope to accomplish. The enormous work of regeneration would require tremendous effort. But a promising institutional beginning would be to set up Christian schools. And a promising philosophic start would be to abandon the old (and to Croly's mind, the harmful and entirely unwarranted) view of human depravity propagated in traditional Christianity; instead Christians should borrow from the new psychology and emphasize the human potential for change and improvement.[118]

[114] HC, "Disordered Christianity," NR, 21 (December 31, 1919): 139.

[115] A copy of the questionnaire and HC's introduction to it can be found in the Eduard C. Lindeman mss., Columbia University Library. For examples of HC's attempt to reconcile Christianity and modern capitalism, see "Christian Ethics and Pittsburgh Employees," NR, 25 (February 16, 1921): 335–37; "Dr. Manning's Social Creed," ibid., 26 (May 4, 1921): 276–78; "Social Creeds and Christian Truth," ibid., 27 (June 8, 1921): 37–39; and "War and Christian Ethics," ibid., 29 (January 11, 1922): 166–69.

[116] HC, "Behaviorism in Religion," NR, 29 (February 22, 1922): 368.

[117] HC, "Christianity as a Way of Life," NR, 39 (July 23, 1924): 234.

[118] For HC's advocacy of Christian schools, see ibid., 233. For comments on the Christian view of human nature and how it must be modified, see HC, "Disordered Christianity," ibid., 21 (December 31, 1919): 138–39; HC, "Regeneration," ibid., 23 (June 9, 1920): 40–47; "War and Christian Ethics," ibid., 29 (January 11, 1922): 166–69; HC, "Behaviorism in Religion," ibid. (February 22, 1922): 367–70; and HC "The Reconstruction of Religion," ibid., 31 (June 21, 1922): 101–102.

More and more, however, Croly came to advocate, as a way to apply religious truth to the liberation of individual men and women, the discovery of some sort of "method." Christians must "realize how completely destitute they are of a method which will enable them to unfold their lives in the light of any authentic knowledge of themselves."[119] Soon the concept of a method became, for Croly, an obsession—the key to joining religion to the process of improving individuals. "Science thrives as compared to religion because it consists . . . of an activity directed and tempered by method. The religious life, also, can only grow by subordinating institutions and dogmas to an activity which is no less methodical."[120] Croly's emphasis on method was not an accident—it had come from his personal involvement with two extraordinary religious teachers.

Georges Ivanovitch Gurdjieff was one of a long line of mystics who sought to bring the wisdom of the East to Europe and America.[121] Much of his life is shrouded in mystery, but as a young man he spent twenty years in Asia, searching out occult knowledge. He returned to teach "the System" and eventually established his "Institute for the Harmonious Development of Man" in a château near Fontainebleau—financed by "breathless English ladies," Waldo Frank remarked.[122] He held a particular attraction for intellectuals, and his reputation blossomed after the English writer, Katherine Mansfield, moved to the Institute and died there in 1923. Gurdjieff was a man of enormous energy and charm; *Time* magazine once characterized him as "a remarkable blend of P. T. Barnum, Rasputin, Freud, Groucho Marx and everybody's grandfather."[123] And in January 1924, he arrived in the United States with his troupe of musicians, dancers, and disciples. His New York demonstrations attracted many, and his enigmatic and magnetic personality, the hints of prophetic wisdom

[119] HC, "Christianity as a Way of Life," *NR*, 39 (July 23, 1924): 235. For other expressions of the need for Christianity to develop a "method," see "Why the Church?" ibid., 43 (July 22, 1925): 224; "More—and Better Religion," ibid., 44 (November 4, 1925): 268–70; "Challenging the Church," ibid., 45 (December 30, 1925): 152; HC, "Consciousness and the Religious Life," ibid. (January 27, 1926): 262–65; "Christianity and Business," ibid., 46 (May 12, 1926): 245–46; and HC, "Religion as Method," ibid., 47 (June 30, 1926): 174–77.

[120] HC, "Religion as Method," *NR*, 47 (June 30, 1926): 176.

[121] Robert S. Ellwood, Jr., *Alternative Altars: Unconventional and Eastern Spiritualism in America* (Chicago, 1979).

[122] Waldo Frank, *The Rediscovery of Man: A Memoir and a Methodology of Modern Life* (New York, 1958), 425. For an excellent study of the Gurdjieff movement, see James Webb, *The Harmonious Circle: The Lives and Work of G. I. Gurdjieff, P. D. Ouspensky and Their Followers* (New York, 1980).

[123] "Wise Man from the East," *Time*, 59 (January 28, 1952): 100.

and surety that he gave off, drew numerous searching intellectuals of the 1920s to consider his message.

Unfortunately, his message was almost entirely incomprehensible. Gurdjieff was the mystic seer who spoke with mysterious osbcurity and who inspired by his overpowering presence—what he needed was an effective and articulate interpreter who could make "the System" seem rational and approachable. In America, his interpreter was a fascinating man, A. R. Orage. Former editor of the English periodical *The New Age*, Orage had given up everything to follow Gurdjieff. The Master sent him to the United States to propagate the teaching, and he could not have sent a better man. Orage was a spellbinding talker, brilliant and lucid; Margaret Anderson, founder of *The Little Review*, called him "the most persuasive man I have ever known."[124] He gave classes in Gurdjieff's ideas to curious New Yorkers and succeeded in interesting some of the country's most important writers and thinkers: Hart Crane, Kenneth Burke, Waldo Frank, Jean Toomer, Amos Pinchot, T. S. Matthews, Zona Gale, and many others.

Gurdjieff and his disciples sought to liberate the individual by helping followers to awaken the higher consciousness, which slumbered under the stale habits of life. What Orage contributed to this endeavor was the elucidation of the means for accomplishing it, a means always referred to by the initiated as the "Method." The cornerstone of the Method was the most rigorous and exhaustive self-observation. Initiates were required to concentrate their whole effort to contemplating their breathing, for example, or their movements or emotions or appearances. In addition to self-observation, Orage taught the liberation of consciousness through gymnastic exercises, diet, and, eventually, attempts to modify the very conduct of life itself.[125]

Herbert Croly always claimed to have maintained some intellectual distance from Gurdjieff, even to not knowing enough of the Master's system to express a definite opinion (although Robert Morss Lovett remembered the evening Croly tried to explain to him Gurdjieff's central teachings, and Croly probably also attempted to instruct Dorothy Straight as well).[126] It was different with Orage. For a time

[124] Quoted by Webb, *Harmonious Circle*, 281.

[125] The best description of "the Method," is ibid., 305–10. See also the personal reminiscence, Matthews, *Name and Address*, 204–207.

[126] HC to Waldo Frank, December 1, 1927, Frank mss.; Lovett, *All Our Years*, 192 (Lovett theorizes that HC's death was hastened by his following the rigorous regime of Gurdjieff); HC to Dorothy Straight, [early 1925], Dorothy Straight Elmhirst mss. ("I am thankful that you seem to be getting something out of a trial of the method of self-observation.")

Croly came quite close to falling completely under his captivating spell. He gave a dinner in Orage's honor in March 1925, and a series of weekly classes and discussions were held at the Crolys' apartment.[127] After one evening with Orage, Croly wrote Dorothy ecstatically, "He is becoming, in a sense which would be like [that] of no other person I know, a religious teacher; and although my own efforts to profit by his teachings are up to date nothing much, I am more than ever convinced that all our present knowledge of human motive and religious experience points in the direction of his method."[128]

For Croly, the effort to follow the Method took the form of a dedicated and concerted program of self-observation. In an unpublished paper of the mid-1920s, he explained and advocated the exercise:

> Believing as I do, that the existing estate of moral education is wholly and even perilously unsatisfactory and that there ought to be some way of improving it which will satisfy both religious and scientific requirements, I am at a loss to know in what alternative direction to seek a way out. Assuming that what we need is a Christian education, the individual must act as the agent of his own regeneration. . . . If the individual is to find any fulfilment for his life, he must discover what some of those [nonscientific] possibilities are with respect to himself. I do not see how he can uncover them save by systematically using his consciousness to explore his own behavior and by exploration to learn how it may be transformed for the better.

"I am submitting these suggestions," Croly cautioned, "with a frankly and honestly experimental intention. I would not submit them at all if I had not tried the proposed method for a year or more and have been sufficiently encouraged by the result to continue. . . ."[129]

Louise joined her husband in the experiment and was quite sure that it was doing both of them worlds of good. After his return from a vacation in Mexico, in 1927, Croly was persuaded to speak to a group about conditions in that country. Public speaking was such an excrutiatingly painful experience for the bashful Croly that, as he had

[127] HC to Eduard C. Lindeman, March 13, 1925, Lindeman mss.; Alan Trachtenberg, ed., *Memoirs of Waldo Frank* (Amherst, 1973), 196; HC to Dorothy Straight, February 10, 1925, Dorothy Straight Elmhirst mss.

[128] HC to Dorothy Straight, February 10, 1925, Dorothy Straight Elmhirst mss.

[129] The forty-page paper, "Religion in Life," with HC's handwritten corrections, is deposited in Houghton Library, Harvard University. The quotations are found at 37–38.

confessed to Leonard Elmhirst, he tried it only about once every five years.[130] But this time, Louise noted, Herbert spoke with rare confidence, "without embarrassment & fairly freely." She was amazed: "I have never seen Herbert do anything like it before. I believe I have a right to think something is breaking down inside him which entangled and confused him—some nervous psychosis of some sort or other. . . . It gives one so much hope that really profound habits, with multitudinous associations which cause pain & a sense of futility & hopelessness, may be removed." Louise Croly was certain about what had caused the transformation: "It all comes from Orage's method," she advised Dorothy. "It's really delivering both of us from some of the handicaps all human beings have in one form or another."[131] The Crolys encouraged Dorothy to undertake the program of self-observation for herself. "I am more interested at present in living my own personal religious experiment than I am in writing about it," Herbert wrote her. "I am more sceptical than I used to be about the good that one can accomplish by writing books—unless they be really great books."[132]

Nevertheless, Croly did not surrender himself without reserve to the teachings of Orage. Even at the height of his infatuation with the Method he took pains to make his doubts explicit. Thus, while recommending self-observation to his hearers on the basis of his own promising preliminary results, he was careful "unequivocally to disclaim the idea that my own experience substantiates even a small part of the claim which a trustworthy method of life must make for itself."[133] As late as 1927, after at least two years of experimenting with the Method, Croly was still unable to become a wholehearted adherent. After describing to Waldo Frank a series of "extraordinarily brilliant expositions" by Orage ("the most exhilarating and impressive intellectual performance that he has attempted since he has been in New York"), and after acknowledging that "I myself have derived more benefit from it than from any other episode in my association with it," Croly carefully drew back a step: "I am not able to follow Orage any more completely than I was before, but I find it a wonderful exercise to try to imagine the world in coherent terms irrespective of my own agreement with that particular picture of the universe."[134] By the beginning of 1928, Croly had probably given up

[130] HC to Leonard Elmhirst, August 10, 1927, Dorothy Straight Elmhirst mss.

[131] Louise Croly to Dorothy Straight Elmhirst, January 30, 1927, Dorothy Straight Elmhirst mss.

[132] HC to Dorothy Straight Elmhirst, [1926], Dorothy Straight Elmhirst mss.

[133] HC, "Religion in Life," 38.

[134] HC to Waldo Frank, March 24, 1927, Frank mss.

on Gurdjieff and Orage, moving closer to a position advocated by Frank, who had had an explosive break with Gurdjieff in 1927.[135]

It was no accident that Croly's flirtation with mysticism occurred during the administration of Calvin Coolidge, that bleak period when so much of what he had hoped for in America seemed unattainable. And it is not surprising that mysticism's hold upon him should have weakened at that very moment when the rise of Al Smith and the prospect of reinvigorated national politics reasserted its old magnetic appeal. By the end of the summer of 1928, Croly was still deeply interested in religious questions and occasionally even spoke in the phraseology of the Method. But his omnivorous attention was once again drifting back to those perennial fascinations of his, presidential politics and the chances for a renewal of progressive reform.

IV

Herbert Croly's long search for individual regeneration through religious mysticism and his long search for national regeneration through progressive politics both came to a sudden and final end one night in the early autumn of 1928. He was awakened by severe pain, made his way to the bathroom of his apartment, and collapsed on the floor, where his wife found him in the morning.[136] He had suffered a massive stroke—his right arm and leg were impaired and his power of speech greatly affected. From the start it was apparent that he would require a long convalescence, complete inactivity, and a radical change of scene. Dorothy Elmhirst immediately cabled $10,000 to cover medical and moving expenses.[137]

For the next twenty months he fought a desperate battle to regain his strength. In New York, in Warm Springs, in Cornish and, finally, after November 1929, in Santa Barbara, California, Croly and his wife devoted themselves to his recovery. Each painful advance was reported to friends, and each laborious gain in the ability to think was seized upon with pitiful optimism.[138] But there were setbacks too, and the conclusion was inevitable. It came on May 17, 1930,

---

[135] Webb, *Harmonious Circle*, 352–53; for Frank's reflections on Gurdjieff and the "Eastern Method," see his *Rediscovery of Man*, 420–27.

[136] Bliven, *Five Million Words Later*, 177.

[137] Louise Croly to Dorothy Straight Elmhirst, October 7, 1928, Dorothy Straight Elmhirst mss.

[138] For examples, see HC to Waldo Frank, September 6 and December 31, 1929, Frank mss.; to Felix Frankfurter, October 30, 1929, and February 2, 1930, Frankfurter mss.; to Learned Hand, October 9, 1929, and January 27, 1930, Hand mss.; and the letters from HC and Louise Croly to Leonard and Dorothy Elmhirst, between September 1928 and May 1930, Dorothy Straight Elmhirst mss.

and the reaction of Learned Hand must have summarized the feelings of many of his friends. "Herbert's death," he wrote to Frankfurter two days later, "I was glad to hear; the thought of another agonizing pull back to the only sort of life he could hope to have, always threatened with a new blow, seemed to me too atrocious even in a world where suffering is so much the inevitable consequence of existence. I shall always think of him with admiration and tenderness."[139] His body was taken back to Cornish, the place he loved best of all, and buried high on a hill overlooking a pine forest and beneath two giant trees. Fifteen years later, after a life of wandering with her sister between New York, Georgia, Cornish, and California, growing progressively blind, Louise died and was buried at his side.[140]

News of Croly's death was received at the offices of *The New Republic* without surprise. The Elmhirsts quickly indicated their intention to continue supporting the magazine, and after a brief power struggle, Bruce Bliven assumed the editorship. It was probably Bliven's idea to compile the moving thirty-page supplement to the issue of July 16.[141] Croly's friends and co-workers tried, in those sorrowful pages, to encapsulate his contribution and delineate his character, to leave behind a record, to preserve for the future their memories of his life and work.

None of the writers, of course, had been present at the start, at that quaint and prophetic ceremony when the infant had been dedicated to the goddess Humanity and admonished to live for others. But Felix Frankfurter, who always had a remarkable talent for summarizing the lives of his friends, might almost have been rendering a final accounting to those who had gathered sixty years before to pray that the child would muster the courage to live a life of unselfish service. "In fair weather and foul he lived his faith with extraordinary fidelity," Frankfurter wrote. "Though highly sensitive and strong-willed, he maintained his intellectual and emotional rectitude with unruffled serenity. . . . He was as far removed from a prig as the poles are asunder; nothing therefore could have been farther from his mind than to serve as an exemplar. But if he had been consciously designed as a model of brave and sincere and generous living, he could not have been fashioned more appropriately."[142]

[139] Learned Hand to Felix Frankfurter, May 19, 1930, Frankfurter mss.

[140] For her obituary, see *New York Times*, October 1, 1945. It is possible to trace her wanderings and health from the letters to the Elmhirsts, 1930–1945, in the Dorothy Straight Elmhirst mss.

[141] *NR*, 63 (July 16, 1930): 243–71.

[142] Felix Frankfurter, "Herbert Croly and American Political Opinion," *NR*, 63 (July 16, 1930): 250.

TEN

Conclusion

ONE OF the things that Orage liked his followers to do was to write autobiographies. What better way, the teacher of the Method reasoned, to stimulate the process of self-examination and bring to consciousness new discoveries of self-revelation?[1] So, perhaps it was partly as a religious exercise that Herbert Croly set down, sometime in the mid-1920s, some reflections on the course of his life. He didn't get very far with the enterprise, and the fragment that survives was obviously not intended for public scrutiny.[2] Nevertheless, the first few pages of the document reveal very well the state of his mind near the end of his life, the extent to which he thought it all to have been rather a waste. The first four sentences fix the tone.

> The following essay is partly an obituary of a past world of opinion and aspiration and partly the project of a new world. Twenty-five years ago the vast and apparently fertile estate of political democracy looked bright with the promise of abundant harvests. I among others imputed to the thoroughly democratic commonwealth the power to contribute enormously and speedily to human welfare. It was a mistake.

The past world of progressive optimism, of faith in the efficacy of human effort to reform society and enhance the quality of life, had been thoroughly discredited, Croly thought, by events since 1914. The failure was general. Democratic leaders (he was obviously thinking of Roosevelt and Wilson) "proved impotent to deal with the recent exigencies of war, industry, politics and education." Demo-

[1] James Webb, *The Harmonious Circle: The Lives and Work of G. I. Gurdjieff, P. D. Ouspensky and Their Followers* (New York, 1980), 30.

[2] See chapter 1, n. 1, above. The completed autobiography was to have consisted of three sections. The first was to have described the intellectual suppositions of HC's *Promise of American Life* and why HC came to feel those suppositions were invalid. The second part was to have been an attempt to reconstruct the traditional religious approach so as to make it more serviceable. And the third was probably to have been devoted to applying religious values to contemporary problems. HC apparently gave up on the project very early into the first section—the last page of the manuscript ends abruptly in the middle of summarizing the historical section of *PAL*. For this outline, see "Fragment," 3–4.

cratic intellectuals (he was obviously thinking of himself) "were not mentally prepared for the surprises, the disappointments and the disasters of the last ten years." And the democratic rank and file (he was obviously thinking of the orgies of repression, intolerance, and greed, which had sullied America since the start of the war) "did not behave under the strain any better or any worse than the rank and file in the less democratic states." That time of hope and youth, of confidence in the possibilities of political and economic reform was now gone; it had been destroyed by "a lack of vision on top and good will underneath."[3]

Yet, Croly insisted, with a doggedness little short of heroic, the destruction of the false hopes of progressive reform did not necessarily imply the need to surrender to hopelessness. On the contrary, "the diminished prestige of the old democratic ideology has created a vacancy which needs to be filled" by a better vision, and he thought he knew what that better vision would be. "The direction in which I am searching for a substitute," he wrote, ". . . is the old path of conscious and methodical self-realization." After all, "if the shortcomings of democracy are traceable to the personal inadequacy of individual democrats, it is the business of democratic pioneers to seek a more trustworthy method of creating a high quality of individual human being." Other thinkers, similarly disillusioned by events, had also turned to the attempt to create high quality individual human beings; but Croly quickly separated their efforts from his own. They saw the process as a social, cultural, and educational one; but "it seems to me to be rather a matter of individual self-discipline which requires . . . an essentially religious motive. Its precursors are the millions of people who have spared themselves no sacrifice and suffering in the effort to overcome the apparent obstacles to personal communion with God." Croly was no fool, and he knew that most modern Americans would think his notion "a silly or a shocking idea." His new direction, he fully realized, condemned him to an almost certain intellectual isolation. "I shared my interest in the old ideology with a large group of alert contemporaries. Scarcely any of them sympathize with my interest in this new project."[4] Thus Croly's autobiographical reflections, despite the brave attempt to discover fresh purposes in religion, conveyed a tone of frustration, disappointment, and loneliness as the writer surveyed the wreckage of early hopes.

[3] HC, "Fragment," 1.
[4] Ibid., 2.

Perhaps inevitably, one is reminded of another, far greater auto-biographer. With infinitely superior insight and artistry, Henry Adams, at the close of *his* life, described in unforgettable terms his own sense of disappointment, his own career of failure and waste, his own isolation from the main currents of his time. He had also come to his maturity indoctrinated by an unusually engaging father to a set of assumptions and expectations.[5] He, too, had flung his father's ideas and standards against a world that turned out to be hostile or indifferent. Whereas Croly sought solace in religion, Adams sought it in the creation of a scientific, deterministic theory of history. But each man considered his life to be a failed quest, a tale of hopeless fluctuation and useless, mistaken effort.

I

Historians are not obliged, of course, to accept uncritically the self-evaluations of the dead—indeed, our responsibilities pull us in exactly the opposite direction. Normally this means the delicious duty of revising downward the self-important claims of those unable to imagine how history could have unfolded without the benefit of their own unique contributions. But the duty does not *always* lie in that direction. Three generations of commentators have been at pains, for example, to convince us that Henry Adams had too low an opinion of his achievements—measured by any standard less exacting than his own, they assure us, his life was very far from being a failure and a waste. In the case of Herbert Croly, similarly, the revision of his own estimate must be upward. The negative judgment he rendered on his career was too harsh, and probably his gloomy self-evaluation can be largely explained on the basis of three factors.

The first reason for Croly's low estimate of himself, no doubt, was temperamental. "Among your shortcomings," David Goodman Croly had cautioned four decades before, "I think lack of self-confidence is one." He pleaded with his son again and again to resist his

[5] Henry Adams described his relation to his father in terms quite similar to HC's account: ". . . his education was chiefly inheritance, and during the next five or six years, his father alone counted for much. If he were to worry successfully through life's quicksands, he must depend chiefly on his father's pilotage. . . . His father's character was therefore the larger part of his education, as far as any single person affected it, and for that reason, if for no other, the son was always a much interested critic of his father's mind and temper. . . . To his son Henry . . . Charles Francis Adams possessed the only perfectly balanced mind that ever existed in the name." *The Education of Henry Adams* (New York, 1931 edition), 26–27.

"feelings of morbid self-deprecation," and Herbert labored hard to do it. His valiant efforts to socialize, his relentless endeavors to cultivate friendships, his brave daily appearances at *The New Republic* luncheons were attempts to compensate for, almost to exorcise, the suspicions of his inadequacy. The very assertiveness and confidence of his writings, the very surety with which he prescribed for America, maybe even the very boldness and mastery he so often urged upon the nation, may owe something to the nagging conviction that he was, himself, perhaps, just a little too timid. And when things were going well—his fame established, his health good, his journal thriving and influential—he even knew some success: he wanted "another whack" at the Insurgents; he was ready to tell off Roosevelt (*"Me Big Injun"*); he was able to press his claims face-to-face with Colonel House. But when things were going badly, when disasters cascaded upon him without relief as they did in the 1920s, the old self-doubts surfaced, and in the end they conquered. Maybe it was not surprising that a man who stared in panic at the top of his desk when strangers half his age entered the room, who regarded speaking in public with dread, who, at the last minute, withdrew from publication his final book of social commentary, would come to feel that the bulk of his early life had been spent in pursuit of "a mistake."

A second reason for his dissatisfaction at the end was this: he looked back over his career and it seemed to him (as it had also seemed to Henry Adams) that his life had been characterized by hopeless fluctuations and changes of course. He saw massive shifts in his opinions and was filled with the special despair reserved for those who think that they have been inconstant. But Herbert Croly almost certainly overestimated the extent and the importance of his various shifts. Looked at from other angles, his thought was remarkably constant, both in its purpose and in its content. Not only did his faith in the efficacy of ideas to ameliorate the human condition never waver, and not only did his trust in dozens of particular ideas hold steady, but the central thrust of his intellectual effort remained the same over all the years.

His main inheritance from his father and from Auguste Comte— more important even than those dozens of smaller articles of belief upon which so much of his reputation rested—was the particular compulsion to link together better social, political, and economic arrangements with what Croly called individual regeneration and emancipation. The effort to make a place in his social philosophy for both the "practical" and the "religious" elements (an effort, which in the case of Comte himself led to two almost entirely distinct careers) occupied Croly's mind throughout his active life.

His first book of social commentary, *The Promise of American Life*, succeeded in combining those two concerns most smoothly. The book presented a penetrating diagnosis of American life and a persuasive set of political and economic suggestions for adjusting American practice in the twentieth century; but the important concluding chapter contained Croly's earnest plea for a new kind of American personality, a regenerated individual whose purified aspirations and awakened altruism would make a more appropriate citizen of the modern world than had been the "pioneer democrat" who preceded him. The optimistic *Progressive Democracy*, published five years later, was devoted to political and economic policy and was clearly written under the delusion that the progressive impulses of the American people had come to maturity and permanence and that all that remained was to guide those impulses into the proper political channels. But even in that notably practical guidebook, Croly did not turn away from the vision of human regeneration that lay at the heart of his inheritance. The long section in *Progressive Democracy* devoted to explaining the moral reasons for democratic reform and the brief concluding passage, heavy with utopian speculation about the changes in the human character that might be expected in the wake of social change, indicate that even at the height of his reformist enthusiasm, Croly had not forgotten the other half of his lifelong concern.

By the 1920s—as can be seen in his unpublished manuscript, *The Breach in Civilization*, in his articles on religion in *The New Republic*, and in his autobiographical fragment—the experiences of the war years and after had convinced him that he had overemphasized his political and economic concerns and that he had slighted his moral and religious ones. He wrote to Waldo Frank in October 1927, that he was eager to rewrite *The Promise of American Life*. "As I look back upon the book I find its omissions and stupidities very depressing. I was moving in the right direction, but I was altogether too much hypnotized by politics and the supposed possibility of social fulfillment by means of legislation, and I fell down almost completely in my last chapter, which should, of course, have shown much more in detail than it did the direction in which we must search for the real synthesis."[6]

It is not hard to see how Croly, reviewing in his own mind these

[6] HC to Waldo Frank, October 25, 1927, Waldo Frank mss., University of Pennsylvania.

various shifts, could have concluded that too much time and effort had been wasted chasing down blind alleys, and how that conclusion could have reinforced his personal view that his life might have been spent to better purpose. Nevertheless, it should be remembered that his decision to emphasize his religious beliefs during the mid-1920s did not mean the abandonment of his political and economic liberalism—no more than his emphasis on practical schemes in *Progressive Democracy* meant abandoning his moral and religious assumptions. Even in the mid-1920s, Herbert Croly still went to the office every day to work out some editorial about the McNary-Haugen bill or tariff reform or the public production of water power. His heart still fluttered its hopeful response to the hopeful songs of Robert La Follette and Al Smith. Even in the most otherworldly of his writings, the autobiography, he managed to reassert the old political faith: "In my opinion it is essential to the promised future of the American commonwealth that its citizens should now and always keep up the search for an ideal synthesis which is both national and democratic."[7] Thus what seemed to him like massive and depressing changes in direction, might more properly be viewed as a kind of fine-tuning of his consistent central purpose, shifting, perceptibly but hardly radically, the attention and the emphasis he gave to its elements.

Finally, Croly pronounced that negative verdict upon his early life because he fundamentally misread the American experience in the twentieth century. This is a particularly impudent charge, I realize, against one whose life was spent in such close and careful analysis of his country's past and present, and whose cogent and often brilliant insights have established him as one of the soundest social observers in our history. Nevertheless, he looked backward to the end of the Civil War and came to the conclusion that the era of social experimentation and reform (which he dated from 1901 to 1917) had been an aberration and that since the end of World War I, Americans "have apparently reverted to the self-satisfaction which was characteristic of their forbears from 1870 to 1901."[8] It was almost as if Croly believed that Harding's election really *did* represent a "return to normalcy" and that the progressive movement had been a sort of inexplicable break in the regular preoccupations of the American people—blind greed, narrow intolerance, stolid indifference to the cries for social justice and human brotherhood. That is why, when he wrote about those stirring days of progressive energy, he felt as

[7] HC, "Fragment," 22.
[8] Ibid., 21.

though he were composing an obituary of a past world of opinion and aspiration. And that is why, when he remembered how much of his own work had gone into explicating and guiding that dead world, he concluded that it had been a mistake.

II

More than half a century has passed since Croly's death, and we now know better. The 1920s were, in fact, the aberration—a strange interlude in a century that has otherwise largely devoted itself to social experimentation, creation of the welfare state, steady nationalization of American life at the expense of states and localities, organization of workers, expansion of executive authority, attempts to control the economically powerful through government action, aggressive initiatives in international relations, and many other things for which Herbert Croly argued as the century opened.

It is idle, of course, to ponder for very long over what he would have thought about the events of the 1930s. The administration of Franklin Roosevelt brought to prominence precisely those men and women most likely to have been readers of *The New Republic*; and to have seen so many of his friends and colleagues return in triumph to power and influence—Frankfurter, Tugwell, Brandeis, Landis, Wolman, Richberg, and a host of others—would have certainly filled him with pleasure. No doubt he would have roundly condemned many New Deal measures. But to whatever extent Roosevelt's program represented a genuine and vital exercise in the centralization of authority, to whatever extent it established a national commitment to social amelioration and to better standards of justice, to whatever extent it demonstrated the enormous potential for presidential leadership, to that degree Herbert Croly would have warmly applauded and, in some measure perhaps, felt a gratifying personal vindication of his lifelong views. At the same time, it is scarcely conceivable that he could have believed, after a decade of vigorous federal activity in the name of progressive democracy, that the New Deal had contributed in any significant way to the creation of truly regenerated and emancipated human beings. Most disturbing of all, surely, would have been the fearful rise, in Italy and Germany, of a monstrous perversion of what Croly had intended when he advocated the transference of "loyalty" to the nation and the necessity for strong executive leadership. At the very least, European fascism would have required him to have given more thought than he had in *The Promise of American Life* to providing safeguards against the eventuality of a nation-state gone mad.[9]

Yet, despite the momentous dilemmas and dangers of the 1930s, Herbert Croly would have relished the excitement. How easy it is to picture him laboring, as before, over some thoughtful and even-tempered commentary on the resurgence of national reform—trying, as before, to serve as a guide to his countrymen as they stumbled forward in pursuit of the promise. And if he had lived longer, it is probable that his evaluation of the meaning of his life would have been both happier and more accurate. As it turned out, Herbert Croly had not wasted his life on a dead world of opinion and aspiration. He had, instead, been one of the pioneer explorers and one of the genuinely perceptive interpreters of the most critical and enduring issues of the twentieth century.

[9] HC and the *NR* did comment extensively on Italian fascism during the 1920s. See the intelligent and balanced discussion of the *NR*'s attitude in John P. Diggins, *Mussolini and Fascism: The View from America* (Princeton, 1972), 227–34. Diggins explores HC's affinities for certain Fascist ideas and his willingness to give the experiment time to work itself out. He also points out that the *NR* published many articles that "blasted Fascism's suppression of free speech, Il Duce's cult of personality . . . and the regime's imperialism and 'obstreperous, jingoistic glorification of war.' " Diggins also writes: "As the decade drew to a close, the freshness of Fascism waned and *The New Republic* grew wary of the Italian government, commenting critically on the increasing 'archaic imperialism' of Mussolini, his 'perilous' attempt at autarchy, and his sustained suppression of liberty." Once HC was gone, Diggins writes, the journal was freer to move into direct opposition.

SELECTED BIBLIOGRAPHY

THIS listing is not intended to be exhaustive—readers are referred to the appropriate footnotes for the fullest accounting of my sources. What follows is merely a selective recording of those primary materials and secondary studies that I have found most useful in the completion of this work.

Manuscript Sources[1]

Jane Addams papers, Friends Historical Library, Swarthmore College
Autograph File, Houghton Library, Harvard University
Newton D. Baker papers, Library of Congress, Washington, D.C.
Ray Stannard Baker papers, Library of Congress, Washington, D.C.
Albert J. Beveridge papers, Library of Congress, Washington, D.C.
John Peale Bishop papers, Princeton University Library
Randolph S. Bourne papers, Columbia University Library
Louis D. Brandeis papers, Law School Library, University of Louisville
Malcolm Cowley papers, Newberry Library, Chicago
George Creel papers, Library of Congress, Washington, D.C.
Finley Peter Dunne papers, Library of Congress, Washington, D.C.
Dorothy Straight Elmhirst papers, Cornell University Library
Waldo Frank papers, University of Pennsylvania Library
Felix Frankfurter papers, Library of Congress, Washington, D.C.
Robert Grant papers, Houghton Library, Harvard University
Learned Hand papers, Law School Library, Harvard University
Robert Herrick papers, University of Chicago Library
Edward M. House papers, Sterling Library, Yale University
Robert Morss Lovett papers, University of Chicago Library
Amy Lowell Correspondence, Houghton Library, Harvard University
Charles McCarthy papers, Wisconsin State Historical Society, Madison
Amos Pinchot papers, Library of Congress, Washington, D.C.

---

[1] There is no central depository of Herbert Croly materials. Gathering his letters, therefore, has involved the search of dozens of manuscript collections. Those listed here proved to be the ones that contained the most valuable letters written by him.

Gifford Pinchot papers, Library of Congress, Washington, D.C.
Donald R. Richberg papers, Library of Congress, Washington, D.C.
Theodore Roosevelt papers, Library of Congress, Washington, D.C.
Chester H. Rowell papers, Bancroft Library, University of California (Berkeley)
Henry L. Stimson papers, Sterling Library, Yale University
Willard Straight papers, Cornell University Library
Oswald Garrison Villard papers, Houghton Library, Harvard University
William Allen White papers, Library of Congress, Washington, D.C.
Woodrow Wilson papers, Library of Congress, Washington, D.C.

The Works of Herbert Croly in Chronological Order[2]

1889–1891, Unsigned editorials in *The Real Estate Record and Builders' Guide*

October–December 1891, "Art and Life," *AR*, 1: 219–27.

1900–1906, Unsigned editorials in *AR*

February 1901, "American Artists and Their Public," *AR*, 10: 256–62.

April 1901, "Criticism that Counts," *AR*, 10: 398–405

October 1901, "The Pan-American Exposition," *AR*, 11: 590–614.

May 1902, "Rich Men and Their Houses," *AR*, 12: 27–32.

June 1902, "The New World and the New Art," *AR*, 12: 134–53.

December 1902, "A Contemporary New York Residence," *AR* 12: 704–22.

1903, *Stately Homes in America from Colonial Times to the Present Day*, with Harry William Desmond. New York.

January 1903, ★"New York's Great Commercial Institution," *AR*, 13: 55–69.

February 1903, ★"Recent Brickwork in New York Architecture," *AR*, 13: 144–56.

March 1903, "New York as the American Metropolis," *AR*, 13: 193–206.

April 1903, ★"English Pleasure Gardens," *AR*, 13: 335–48.

June 1903, "Renovation of the New York Brownstone District," *AR*, 13: 555–71.

July 1903, "Some Really Historical Novels," *Lamp*, 26: 509–13.

---

[2] The following abbreviations are used in this chronological listing: *AR, The Architectural Record*; ★, articles signed with the pseudonym A. C. David; *NR, The New Republic*.

July 1903, ★"Private Residences for Banking Firms," *AR*, 14: 13–27.

October 1903, ★"Co-operative Studio Building," *AR*, 14: 233–54.

December 1903, "American Architecture of Today," *AR*, 14: 413–35.

January 1904, ★"New Theatres of New York," *AR*, 15: 39–54.

February 1904, "Henry James and His Countrymen," *Lamp*, 28: 47–53.

March 1904, "The Architectural Work of Charles A. Platt," *AR*, 15: 181–244.

April 1904, ★"The Architecture of Ideas," *AR*, 15: 361–84.

June 1904, ★"The St. Regis—The Best Type of Metropolitan Hotel," *AR*, 15: 552–600.

July 1904, "The American Farmer," *Lamp*, 28: 477–78.

July 1904, "What is Civic Art?" *AR*, 16: 47–52.

September 1904, "The New York Rapid Transit Railway," *Review of Reviews*, 30: 306–11.

December 1904, "Lay-Out of a Large Estate," *AR*, 16: 531–55.

January 1905, ★"The Finest Store in the World," *AR*, 17: 17–42.

February 1905, "The Art Ascetic," *AR*, 17: 148–49.

February 1905, "The Architect in Recent Fiction," *AR*, 17: 137–39.

March 1905, ★"Three New Hotels," *AR*, 17: 167–88.

April 1905, "The New Use of Old Forms," *AR*, 17: 271–93.

April 1905, ★"A Modern Instance of Colonial Architecture," *AR*, 17: 305–17.

July 1905, "An American Country Estate," *AR*, 18: 1–7.

July 1905, "The Use of Terra-Cotta in the United States," *AR*, 18: 86–94.

October 1905, ★"The Residence of Samuel Cabot," *AR*, 18: 263–72.

January 1906, ★"The Building of the First National Bank of Chicago," *AR*, 19: 48–59.

January 1906, "The Proper Use of Terra-Cotta," *AR*, 19: 73–81.

February 1906, ★"Houses by Howard Shaw," *AR*, 19: 104–22.

February 1906, ★"An Architectural Oasis," *AR*, 19: 135–44.

March 1906, "The New Harvard Club-House," *AR*, 19: 195–98.

April 1906, "Glazed and Colored Terra-Cotta," *AR*, 19: 313–23.

April 1906, "Harmonie Club House," *AR* 19: 237–43.

June 1906, "The Promised City of San Francisco," *AR*, 19: 425–36.

July 1906, "Architect of Residences in San Francisco," *AR*, 20: 47–62.

October 1906, "Houses by Myron Hunt and Elmer Grey," *AR*, 20: 281–95.

October 1906, ★"An Architect of Bungalows in California," *AR*, 20: 306–15.

November 1906, "A California Country House," *Sunset Magazine*, 19: 50–65.

1907, *Houses for Town or Country*, under the pseudonym William Herbert. New York.

January 1907, "The Knickerbocker Hotel," *AR*, 21: 1–17.

May 1907, "Civic Improvements," *AR*, 21: 347–52.

June 1907, "What is Indigenous Architecture?" *AR*, 21: 434–42.

July 1907, ★"The New Fifth Avenue," *AR*, 22: 1–14.

October 1907, "The House of Colonel Frank O. Lowden," under the pseudonym William Herbert, *AR*, 22: 299–310.

December 1907, "Recent Work of Mr. Howard Shaw," *AR*, 22: 421–52.

February 1908, "American Architecture," *AR*, 23: 111–22.

March 1908, ★"An Intimate Auditorium," *AR*, 23: 223–27.

April 1908, "The New University of California," *AR*, 23: 269–93.

May 1908, "Business Buildings in St. Louis," *AR*, 23: 391–96.

July 1908, ★"Co-operative Apartment House in New York," *AR*, 24: 1–18.

August 1908, ★"Innovations in the Street Architecture of Paris," *AR*, 24: 109–28.

October 1908, "College Theatre in Chicago," *AR*, 24: 271–76.

1909, *The Promise of American Life*. New York.

April 1909, "How to Get a Well Designed House," *AR*, 25: 221–34.

May 1909, ★"The Advent of the Fireproofed Dwelling," *AR*, 25: 309–14.

November 1909, ★"New Phases of American Domestic Architecture," *AR*, 26: 309–12.

April 1910, ★"A Contemporary German Architect," *AR*, 27: 299–310.

May 1910, "Democratic Factions and Insurgent Republicans," *North American Review*, 191: 626–35.

May 1910, "A Great School of Political Science," *World's Work*, 20: 12,887–88.

June 1910, "My Aim in *The Promise of American Life*: Why I Wrote My Latest Book," *World's Work*, 20: 13,086.

September 1910, ★"The New York Public Library," *AR*, 28: 144–72.

December 1910, ★"New Architecture," *AR*, 28: 388–403.

March 1911, "The United States Post Office, Custom House, and Court House, Cleveland, Ohio," *AR*, 29: 192–213.

March–April 1911, Ten articles on contemporary politics for the *Cleveland Leader*.

June 1911, "The Recent Works of John Russell Pope," *AR* 29: 441–511.

1912, *Marcus Alonzo Hanna: His Life and Work*. New York.

January 1912, ★"The New San Francisco," *AR*, 31: 1–26.

February 1912, "State Political Re-organization," *American Political Science Review*, 6: supplement, 122–35.

February 1912, "The Work of Kilham and Hopkins," *AR*, 31: 97–128.

June 1912, "Portland, Oregon: The Transformation of the City from an Architectural and Social Viewpoint," *AR*, 31: 591–607.

July 1912, "Building of Seattle," *AR*, 32: 1–21.

November 1912, "A Test of Faith in Democrary," *American Magazine*, 75: 21–23.

April 1913, "The Recent Work of Howard Shaw," *AR*, 33: 285–307.

August 1913, "The Work of Parker, Thomas, and Rice," *AR*, 34: 96–167.

December 1913, "A Country House in California," *AR*, 34: 483–519.

1914, *Progressive Democracy*. New York.

August 1914, "English Renaissance at Its Best," *AR*, 36: 81–97.

October 1914, "Local Feeling in Western Country Houses," *AR*, 36: 342–58.

December 1914, "Water Front Villa," *AR*, 36: 481–99.

1914–1928, Unsigned leaders and editorials in *NR*.

May 1915, "Examples of the Work of Otis and Clark," *AR*, 37: 385–409.

August 7, 1915, "The Meaning of It," *NR*, 4: 10–11.

September 1915, "Stuart Duncan Residence at Newport," *AR*, 38: 288–309.

October 9, 1915, "The Obligation of the Vote," *NR*, 4: supplement, 5–10.

February 5, 1916, "Unregenerate Democracy," *NR*, 6: 17–19.

July 1916, "The Effect on American Institutions of a Powerful Military and Naval Establishment," *Annals of the American Academy of Political and Social Science*, 66: 157–72.

July 22, 1916, "Commonwealth of Greater Britain," *NR*, 7: 309–12.

October 21, 1916, "The Two Parties in 1916," *NR*, 8: 286–91.

January 13, 1917, "The Structure of Peace," *NR*, 9: 287–91.

September 15, 1917, "The Future of the State," *NR*, 12: 179–83.

December 15, 1917, "The Counsel of Humility," *NR*, 13: 173–76.

June 8, 1918, "A School of Social Research," *NR*, 15: 167-71.

January 11, 1919, "Victory without Peace," *NR*, 17: 301–303.

April 26, 1919, "The Obstacle to Peace," *NR*, 18: 403-407.

December 31, 1919, "Disordered Christianity," *NR*, 21: 136–39.

1920, *The Breach in Civilization* (151-page section of an unpublished mss., Houghton Library, Harvard University).

February 18, 1920, "The Paradox of Lincoln," *NR*, 21: 350–53.

March 1920, "The Residence of the Late F. W. Woolworth," *AR*, 47: 195–213.

September 1920, "Pidgeon Hill: Residence of Meredith Hare, Huntington, Long Island," *AR*, 48: 178–91.

October 27, 1920, "The Eclipse of Progressivism," *NR*, 24: 210-16.

December 8, 1920, "Liberalism vs. War," *NR*, 25: 35–39.

August 24, 1921, "Better Prospect," *NR*, 27: 244–49.

November 30, 1921, "Hope, History, and H. G. Wells," *NR*, 29: 10–12.

December 21, 1921, "In Memoriam, Willard Straight," *NR*, 29: 94–96.

February 22, 1922, "Behaviorism in Religion," *NR*, 29: 367–70.

June 21, 1922, "Reconstruction of Religion," *NR*, 31: 100–102.

November 15, 1922, "Surely Good Americanism," *NR*, 32: 294–96.

December 6, 1922, "The *New Republic* Idea," *NR*, 33: supplement, 1–16.

February 28, 1923, "Naturalism and Christianity," *NR*, 34: 9–11.

September 12, 1923, "American Withdrawal from Europe," *NR*, 36: 65–68.

December 1923, "Reclamation of a Business Slum," *AR*, 54: 587–88.

December 12, 1923, "Education for Grown-Ups," *NR*, 37: 59–61.

1924, *Willard Straight*. New York.

February 1924, "Skyscraper in the Service of Religion," *AR*, 55: 203–204.

February 27, 1924, "Economics and Statesmanship," *NR*, 38: 17–19.

March 1924, "The Architect's Interest in Low Rent Dwellings," *AR*, 55: 307–308.

May 28, 1924, "Social Discovery," *NR*, 39: 18–20.

July 23, 1924, "Christianity as a Way of Life," *NR*, 39: 230–37.

August 1924, "Controlling Economic Factors in Current Building," *AR*, 56: 185–86.

October 29, 1924, "Why I Shall Vote for La Follette," *NR*, 40: 221–24.

December 10, 1924, "The Outlook for Progressivism in Politics," *NR*, 41: 60–64.

January 1925, "A New Dimension in Architectural Effects," *AR*, 57: 93–94.

February 11, 1925, "What Ails American Youth," *NR*, 41: 301–303.

August 1925, "Architectural Response to Social Change," *AR*, 58: 186–87.

September 1925, "A New Era of Building," *AR*, 58: 289–90.

November 25, 1925, "Christians Beware!" *NR*, 45: 12–14.

Mid-1920s (?), Autobiographical Fragment (unpublished typescript in the Felix Frankfurter mss., Library of Congress, Container 215, 44 pp).

January 1926, "Work of Richard Morris Hunt," *AR*, 59: 88–89.

January 27, 1926, "Consciousness and the Religious Life," *NR*, 45: 262–65.

March 1926, "Architects and State Aid to Housing," *AR*, 59: 293–94.

May 1926, "Architectural Counterpoint," *AR*, 59: 489–90.

September 1926, "Traffic Congestion in Manhattan," *AR*, 60: 279–80.

January 1927, "The Traffic Problem," *AR*, 61: 86–87.

March 30, 1927, "Mexico and the United States," *NR*, 50: 159–64.

April 1927, "New York's Skyscrapers," *AR*, 61: 374–75.

October 5, 1927, "The Human Potential in the Politics of the Pacific," *NR*, 52: 164–72.

January 1928, "The Scenic Function of the Skyscraper," *AR*, 63: 77.

February 22, 1928, "Smith of New York," *NR* 54: 9–14.

May 1928, "The Modern Problem in Architectural Education," *AR*, 63: 469–70.

June 1928, "Willard Straight Hall," *AR*, 63: 545–54.

June 27, 1928, "How is Hoover?" *NR*, 55: 138–40.

July 25, 1928, "The Progressive Voter: He Wants to Know!" *NR*, 55: 242–47.

December 10, 1928, "Mexico's Renascence," *World Review*, 7: 177.

Interviews and Oral Histories

Norman Angell, "Oral History," Columbia University Oral History Project, 1951.

Frances Arnold, Interview with the author, October 15, 1963, Cornish, N.H.

Roger Baldwin, "Oral History," Columbia University Oral History Project, 1954.

Bruce Bliven, "Oral History," Columbia University Oral History Project, 1964.

Carter Burnham, Interview with the author, October 15, 1963, Cornish, N.H.

Malcolm Cowley, Interview with the author, November 12, 1966, Columbus, Ohio.

Learned Hand, "Notes of an Interview with Learned Hand, April 5, 1956," in the possession of Professor Charles Forcey.

———, "Oral History," Columbia University Oral History Project, 1957.

Alvin S. Johnson, Interview with the author, October 21, 1963, New York, N.Y.

———, "Oral History," Columbia University Oral History Project, 1960.

Walter Lippmann, "Oral History," Columbia University Oral History Project, 1956.

T. S. Matthews, "Oral History," Columbia University Oral History Project, 1959.

George Rublee, "Oral History," Columbia University Oral History Project, 1951.

George Soule, Interview with the author, October 7, 1963, Cambridge, Mass.

Autobiographies, Reminiscences, and Published Primary Sources

Adams, Henry, *The Education of Henry Adams* (New York, 1931 edition).

Angell, Norman, *After All: The Autobiography of Norman Angell* (New York, 1951).

Baker, Ray Stannard, *American Chronicle* (New York, 1945).

Bliven, Bruce, "The First Forty Years," *NR*, 113 (November 22, 1954): 6.

———, *Five Million Words Later, An Autobiography* (New York, 1970).

———, "Herbert Croly and Journalism," *NR*, 63 (July 16, 1930): 258–60.

Bourne, Randolph S., *War and the Intellectuals: Essays 1915–1919* (New York, 1964).

Brown, Rollo W., *Harvard Yard in the Golden Age* (New York, 1948).

Brubaker, Howard, ed., *Walter Weyl: An Appreciation* (n.p., 1922).

Chapman, John Jay, *Memories and Milestones* (New York, 1915).

———, "Portrait of Royce," *Outlook*, 122 (July 2, 1919): 372ff.

Comte, Auguste, *A General View of Positivism*, trans. by J. H. Bridges (Stanford, 1953 edition).

———, *The Positive Philosophy, Freely Translated and Condensed by Harriet Martineau* (New York, 1856).

———, *System of Positive Polity*, trans. by J. H. Bridges and others (London, 1875–1877), 4 vols.

Cowley, Malcolm, "The Old House in Chelsea," *Carleton Miscellany*, 6 (1965): 40–49.

Croly, David Goodman, *Glimpses of the Future: Suggestions as to the Drift of Things (To Be Read Now and Judged in the Year 2000)* (New York, 1888).

———, *Miscegenation: The Theory of the Blending of the Races Applied to the American White and Negro*, (New York, 1864).

———, ed., *The Modern Thinker: An Organ for the Most Advanced Speculations in Philosophy, Science, Sociology and Religion* (1870, 1873).

———, *A Positivist Primer: Being a Series of Familiar Conversations on the Religion of Humanity* (New York, 1871).

———, ed., *The Real Estate Record and Builders' Guide*, 1869–1889.

———, *The Truth about Love: A Proposed Sexual Morality Based Upon the Doctrine of Evolution, and Recent Discoveries in Medical Science* (New York, 1871).

———, "What to Do with Wealth," *Galaxy*, 8 (November 1869), 706–708. Signed "An American Positivist."

Croly, Jane Cunningham, *Demorest's Illustrated Monthly Magazine*, 1860–1887.

———, *For Better or Worse: A Book for Some Men and All Women* (Boston, 1875).

———, *History of the Women's Club Movement in America* (New York, 1898).

———, *Jennie Juneiana: Talks on Women's Topics* (Boston, 1869).

———, *Thrown on Her Own Resources; or, What Girls Can Do* (New York, 1891).

Day, Haryot Holt, "Jennie June Croly, the Mother of Clubs," *New York Post*, May 10, 1916.

DuBois, W.E.B. *Dusk of Dawn: An Essay Toward an Autobiography of a Race Concept* (New York, 1940).

———, "A Negro Student at Harvard at the End of the Nineteenth Century," *Massachusetts Review*, 1 (Spring 1960): 439–58.

Elmhirst, Dorothy, "Herbert Croly," *NR*, 63 (July 16, 1930): 243.

Ely, Richard T., *Ground Under Our Feet* (New York, 1938).

Frank, Waldo, "The Promise of Herbert Croly," *NR*, 63 (July 16, 1930): 260–63.

————, *The Rediscovery of Man: A Memoir and a Methodology of Modern Life* (New York, 1958).

Frankfurter, Felix, "Herbert Croly and American Political Opinion," *NR*, 63 (July 16, 1930): 247–50.

Garraty, John A., ed., "The Correspondence of George A. Myers and James Ford Rhodes, 1910–1923," *Ohio Historical Quarterly*, 64 (1955): 1–29.

Grant, Robert, *Fourscore: An Autobiography* (Boston, 1934).

————, *Unleavened Bread* (New York, 1900).

Hackett, Francis, *American Rainbow: Early Reminiscences* (New York, 1971).

————, *I Chose Denmark* (New York, 1940).

Hansen, Olaf, ed., *The Radical Will: Randolph Bourne, Selected Writings, 1911–1918* (New York, 1977).

Hapgood, Hutchins, *A Victorian in the Modern World* (New York, 1939).

Hapgood, Norman, *The Changing Years* (New York, 1930).

Howe, Mark A. DeWolfe, ed., *The Holmes-Laski Letters: The Correspondence of Mr. Justice Holmes and Harold J. Laski, 1916–1935* (Cambridge, Mass., 1953), 2 vols.

"In Memoriam. David Goodman Croly. Estimates of the Man, His Character and His Life's Work," *The Real Estate Record and Builders' Guide*, 43 (May 18, 1889): supplement.

Johnson, Alvin S., *Pioneer's Progress, An Autobiography* (New York, 1952).

Leuchtenburg, William E., ed., *The New Nationalism* (Englewood Cliffs, N.J., 1961).

Lindeman, Eduard C., "A Man of Wisdom," *NR*, 63 (July 16, 1930): 263–65.

Littell, Philip, "A Look at Cornish," *Independent*, 74 (June 5, 1913): 1297–98.

————, "As a Friend," *NR*, 63 (July 16, 1930): 243–45.

Arthur S. Link et al., eds., *The Papers of Woodrow Wilson* (Princeton, 1966–).

Lippmann, Walter, *Drift and Mastery: An Attempt to Diagnose the Current Unrest* (New York, 1914).

————, "Notes for a Biography," *NR*, 63 (July 16, 1930): 250–52.

————, "An Open Mind: William James," *Everybody's Magazine*, 32 (December, 1910): 800–801.

————, *A Preface to Politics* (New York, 1913).

Lovett, Robert Morss, *All Our Years* (New York, 1948).

———, "Herbert Croly" *Harvard Class of 1890, Fiftieth Anniversary (Report IX), 1930–1940* (Norwood, Mass., 1940): 112–14.

———, "Herbert Croly's Contribution to American Life," *NR*, 63 (July 16, 1930): 245–46.

Luhan, Mabel Dodge, *Movers and Shakers* (New York, 1936).

Matthews, T. S., *Name and Address, An Autobiography* (New York, 1960).

———, "One Generation to Another," *NR*, 63 (July 16, 1930): 270–71.

Morison, Elting E., et al., eds., *The Letters of Theodore Roosevelt* (Cambridge, Mass., 1951–1954), 8 vols.

Morse, Caroline M., ed., *Memories of Jane Cunningham Croly, "Jennie June"* (New York, 1904).

Norris, George W., *Fighting Liberal: The Autobiography of George W. Norris* (New York, 1945).

Palmer, George Herbert, *The Autobiography of a Philosopher* (Boston, 1930).

Phillips, Harlan B., ed., *Felix Frankfurter Reminisces* (New York, 1960).

Pinchot, Amos R. E., *History of the Progressive Party, 1912–1916* (New York, 1958 edition).

Pinchot, Gifford, *Breaking New Ground* (New York, 1947).

Platt, Charles, "Herbert Croly and Architecture," *NR*, 63 (July 16, 1930): 257.

Richberg, Donald, *My Hero: The Indiscreet Memoirs of an Eventful but Unheroic Life* (New York, 1954).

Robinson, James Harvey, "The New School," *School and Society*, 11 (January 31, 1920): 129–32.

Ross, Edward A., *Seventy Years of It* (New York, 1936).

Royce, Josiah, *California from the Conquest in 1846 to the Second Vigilance Committee in San Francisco: A Study of American Character* (Boston, 1886).

———, *The Problem of Christianity* (New York, 1913).

———, *The Religious Aspect of Philosophy* (New York, 1885).

Santayana, George, "A Brief History of My Opinions," in Erwin Edman, ed., *The Philosophy of Santayana* (New York, 1942): 1–21.

———, *Character and Opinion in the United States . . .* (New York, 1920).

———, *Persons and Places* (New York, 1944–1953), 3 vols.

Shotwell, James T., *At the Paris Peace Conference* (New York, 1937).

———, *The Autobiography of James T. Shotwell* (Indianapolis, 1961).

Soule, George, "Herbert Croly," *Encyclopedia of the Social Sciences* (New York, 1931): 6, 603.

———, "Herbert Croly's Liberalism," *NR*, 63 (July 16, 1930): 253–57.

Steffens, Lincoln, *The Autobiography of Lincoln Steffens* (New York, 1931).

Stimson, Henry L., and McGeorge Bundy, *On Active Service in Peace and War* (New York, 1947).

Sweet, Clinton W., "David Goodman Croly," *The Real Estate Record and Builders' Guide*, 43 (May 4, 1889): 613–14.

Trachtenberg, Alan, ed., *Memoirs of Waldo Frank* (Amherst, Mass., 1973).

Urofsky, Melvin I., and David W. Levy, eds., *The Letters of Louis D. Brandeis* (Albany, 1971–1978), 5 vols.

Villard, Oswald Garrison, *Fighting Years: Memoirs of a Liberal Editor* (New York, 1939).

———, "Herbert Croly," *Dictionary of American Biography* (New York, 1944): supplement 1, 209–10.

Weyl, Walter E., *The New Democracy* (New York, 1912).

White, William Allen, *The Autobiography of William Allen White* (New York, 1946).

Wilson, Edmund, "H. C.," *NR*, 63 (July 16, 1930): 266–68.

Wilson, Elena, ed., *Edmund Wilson: Letters on Literature and Politics* (New York, 1977).

Secondary Works

Aaron, Daniel, *Men of Good Hope: A Story of American Progressives* (New York, 1951).

Andrews, Wayne, *Architecture, Ambition and Americans: A Social History of American Architecture* (New York, 1955).

Atwood, William H., "Pathfinders of American Liberalism: The Story of the *New Republic*" (unpublished Bachelor's essay, Princeton University, 1941).

Baker, Liva, *Felix Frankfurter* (New York, 1969).

Bannister, Robert C., *Social Darwinism: Science and Myth in Anglo-American Social Thought* (Philadelphia, 1979).

Benson, Lee, *Turner and Beard: American Historical Writing Reconsidered* (New York, 1960).

Bernstein, Melvin H., *John Jay Chapman* (New York, 1964).

Blair, Karen J., *The Clubwoman as Feminist: True Womanhood Redefined, 1868–1914* (New York, 1980).

Bloch, J. M., "The Rise of the *New York World* During the Civil

War Decade" (unpublished Ph.D. dissertation, Harvard University, 1941).

Blum, John M., *The Republican Roosevelt* (Cambridge, Mass., 1954).

Bode, Carl, "Columbia's Carnal Bed," *American Quarterly*, 15 (1963): 52–64.

Bolquerin, M. James, "An Investigation of the Contributions of David, Jane, and Herbert Croly to American Life—With Emphasis on the Influence of the Father on the Son" (unpublished M.A. thesis, University of Missouri, 1948).

Borning, Bernard C., *The Political and Social Thought of Charles A. Beard* (Seattle, 1962).

Bourke, Paul F., "The Status of Politics, 1909–1919: *The New Republic*, Randolph Bourne and Van Wyck Brooks," *Journal of American Studies*, 8 (1974): 171–208.

Brooks, Van Wyck, *The Confident Years, 1885–1915* (New York, 1952).

————, introduction, to Brooks, ed., *The History of a Literary Radical and Other Papers by Randolph Bourne* (New York, 1956).

Buenker, John D., John C. Burnham, and Robert M. Crunden, *Progressivism* (Cambridge, Mass., 1977).

Buranelli, Vincent, *Josiah Royce* (New York, 1964).

Burchard, John, and Albert Bush-Brown, *The Architecture of America: A Social and Cultural History* (Boston, 1961).

Chalmers, David M., *The Social and Political Ideas of the Muckrakers* (New York, 1964).

Chamberlain, John, "Croly and the American Future," *NR*, 101 (November 8, 1939): 33–35.

————, *Farewell to Reform: The Rise, Life and Decay of the Progressive Mind in America* (New York, 1932).

Chapman, William, "Herbert Croly's *The Promise of American Life*," *South Atlantic Quarterly*, 59 (1960): 543–55.

Child, William H., *History of the Town of Cornish, New Hampshire, with Genealogical Record* (Concord, N.H., 1910), 2 vols.

Cominos, Peter T., "Late-Victorian Sexual Respectability and the Social System," *International Review of Social History*, 9 (1963): 18–48.

Commager, Henry Steele, *The American Mind: An Interpretation of American Thought and Character Since the 1880s* (New Haven, 1950).

Cott, Nancy F., *The Bonds of Womanhood: "Woman's Sphere" in New England, 1780–1835* (New Haven, 1977).

Curti, Merle, *The Growth of American Thought* (New York, 1964 edition).

————, *The Roots of American Loyalty* (New York, 1946).

Curti, Merle, *The Social Ideas of American Educators* (New York, 1935).

Degler, Carl, *At Odds: Women and the Family in America from the Revolution to the Present* (New York, 1980).

Dexter, Byron, "Herbert Croly and *The Promise of American Life*," *Political Science Quarterly*, 70 (1955): 197–218.

Diggins, John P., *Mussolini and Fascism: The View from America* (Princeton, 1972).

Dykhuizen, George, *The Life and Mind of John Dewey* (Carbondale, Ill., 1973).

Ellwood, Robert S., Jr., *Alternative Altars: Unconventional and Eastern Spiritualism in America* (Chicago, 1979).

Filene, Peter, "An Obituary for the 'Progressive Movement,' " *American Quarterly*, 22 (1970): 20–34.

Filler, Louis, *Crusaders for American Liberalism* (New York, 1939).

———, *Randolph Bourne* (Washington, D. C., 1943).

Fine, Sidney, *Laissez-Faire and the General Welfare State: A Study of Conflict in American Thought, 1865-1901* (Ann Arbor, 1956).

Forcey, Charles, "Croly and Nationalism," *NR*, 131 (November 22, 1954): 17–22.

———, *The Crossroads of Liberalism: Croly, Weyl, Lippmann and the Progressive Era, 1900–1925* (New York, 1961).

———, introduction, to HC, *PAL* (New York, 1963 edition): vii–xxii.

———, introduction, to Walter E. Weyl, *The New Democracy* (New York, 1964 edition): vii–xix.

Garraty, John A., *Right Hand Man: The Life of George W. Perkins* (New York: 1957).

Gelfand, Lawrence E., *The Inquiry: American Preparations for Peace, 1917–1919* (New Haven, 1963).

Girvetz, Harry, *From Wealth to Welfare: The Evolution of Liberalism* (Stanford, 1950).

Goldman, Eric F., *Rendezvous with Destiny: A History of Modern American Reform* (New York, 1952).

Haber, Samuel, *Efficiency and Uplift. Scientific Management and the Progressive Era, 1890–1920* (Chicago, 1964).

Hale, Nathan J., *Freud and the Americans: The Beginnings of Psychoanalysis in the United States, 1876–1917* (New York, 1971).

Hansen, Olaf, introduction, to Hansen, ed., *The Radical Will* (New York, 1977): 17–62.

Harbaugh, William H., *Power and Responsibility: The Life and Times of Theodore Roosevelt* (New York, 1961).

Harris, Barbara J., *Beyond Her Sphere: Women and the Professions in American History* (Westport, Conn., 1978).

Hawkins, Hugh, *Between Harvard and America: The Educational Leadership of Charles W. Eliot* (New York, 1972).

Hawkins, Richmond L., *Auguste Comte and the United States (1816–1853)* (Cambridge, Mass., 1936).

———, *Positivism in the United States (1853–1861)* (Cambridge, Mass., 1938).

Hays, Samuel P., *The Response to Industrialism, 1885–1914* (Chicago, 1957).

Hicks, Granville, *John Reed: The Making of a Revolutionary* (New York, 1936).

Higham, John, "The Rise of American Intellectual History," *American Historical Review*, 56 (1951): 453–71.

Hofstadter, Richard, *The Age of Reform: From Bryan to FDR* (New York, 1960).

———, "Beard and the Constitution: The History of an Idea," *American Quarterly*, 2 (1950): 195–213.

———, *Social Darwinism in American Thought, 1860–1915* (Philadelphia, 1944).

Howgate, George W., *George Santayana* (Philadelphia, 1938).

Hughes, H. Stuart, *Consciousness and Society: The Reorientation of European Social Thought, 1890–1930* (New York, 1958).

Humes, D. Joy, *Oswald Garrison Villard, Liberal of the 1920s* (Syracuse, 1960).

Jordy, William H., and Ralph Coe, introduction, to Montgomery Schuyler, *American Architecture and Other Writings* (Cambridge, Mass., 1961): 1–89.

Kaplan, Sidney, "The Miscegenation Issue in the Election of 1864," *Journal of Negro History*, 34 (1949): 274–343.

Karier, Clarence, "Making the World Safe for Democracy: An Historical Critique of John Dewey's Pragmatic Liberal Philosophy in the Warfare State," *Educational Theory*, 27 (1977): 12–47.

Kern, Stephen, "Explosive Intimacy: Psychodynamics of the Victorian Family," *History of Childhood Quarterly*, 1 (1974): 437–61.

Kohn, Hans, *American Nationalism: An Interpretative Essay* (New York, 1957).

Kraus, Michael, *The Writing of American History* (Norman, Okla., 1953).

Kuklick, Bruce, *The Rise of American Philosophy: Cambridge, Massachusetts, 1860–1930* (New Haven, 1977).

Lasch, Christopher, *American Liberals and the Russian Revolution* (New York, 1962).

———, "Herbert Croly's America," *New York Review of Books*, 4 (July 1, 1965): 18–19.

———, *The New Radicalism in America (1889–1963): The Intellectual as a Social Type* (New York, 1964).

Leuchtenburg, William E., introduction, to Leuchtenburg, ed., *The New Nationalism* (Englewood Cliffs, N.J., 1961).

———, introduction, to Walter Lippmann, *Drift and Mastery* (Englewood Cliffs, N.J., 1961 edition).

———, "Progressivism and Imperialism: The Progressive Movement and American Foreign Policy, 1898–1916," *Mississippi Valley Historical Review*, 39 (1952): 483–504.

Link, Arthur S., *American Epoch: A History of the United States Since the 1890s* (New York, 1963 edition).

———, "What Happened to the Progressive Movement in the 1920s," *American Historical Review*, 64 (1959): 833–51.

———, *Wilson: The New Freedom* (Princeton, 1956).

———, *Wilson: The Struggle for Neutrality, 1914–1915* (Princeton, 1960).

———, *Wilson: Confusions and Crises, 1915–1916* (Princeton, 1964).

———, *Wilson: Campaigns for Progressivism and Peace, 1916–1917* (Princeton, 1965).

MacKay, Kenneth C., *The Progressive Movement of 1924* (New York, 1947).

May, Henry F., *The End of American Innocence: A Study of the First Years of Our Own Time, 1912–1917* (New York, 1959).

Mason, Alpheus T., *Brandeis: A Free Man's Life* (New York, 1956 edition).

Mazlich, Bruce, *James and John Stuart Mill: Father and Son in the Nineteenth Century* (New York, 1975).

McJimsey, George T., *Genteel Partisan: Manton Marble, 1834–1917* (Ames, Iowa, 1971).

Mills, C. Wright, *Sociology and Pragmatism: The Higher Learning in America* (New York, 1964).

Morgan, H. Wayne, *Unity and Culture: The United States 1877–1900* (Harmondsworth, England, 1971).

Morison, Samuel Eliot, *The Development of Harvard University Since the Inauguration of President Eliot, 1869–1929* (Cambridge, Mass., 1929).

Mott, Frank Luther, *A History of American Magazines* (Cambridge, Mass., 1968), 5 vols.

Mowry, George E., *The Era of Theodore Roosevelt and the Birth of Modern America* (New York, 1962).

Murray, Robert K., *The Red Scare: A Study in National Hysteria* (Minneapolis, 1955).

Neuchterlein, James A., "The Dream of Scientific Liberalism. *The New Republic* and American Progressive Thought, 1914–1920," *Review of Politics*, 42 (1980): 167–90.

Nevius, Blake, *Robert Herrick: The Development of a Novelist* (Berkeley, 1962).

Noble, David, "Herbert Croly and American Progressive Thought," *Western Political Quarterly*, 7 (1954): 537–53.

————, *The Paradox of Progressive Thought* (Minneapolis, 1958).

Nye, Russel B., *Midwestern Progressive Politics: A Historical Study of Its Origins and Development, 1870–1950* (East Lansing, 1951).

Osgood, Robert E., *Ideals and Self-Interest in American Foreign Relations: The Great Transformation of the Twentieth Century* (Chicago, 1953).

Parrish, Michael, *Felix Frankfurter and His Times: The Reform Years* (New York, 1982).

Paul, Sherman, *Randolph Bourne* (Minneapolis, 1966).

Perry, Ralph Barton, *The Thought and Character of William James* (Boston, 1935), 2 vols.

Peterson, H. C., and Gilbert Fite, *Opponents of War, 1917–1918* (Madison, Wis., 1957).

Peterson Merrill D., *The Jeffersonian Image in the American Mind* (New York, 1960).

Pivar, David J., *The Purity Crusade: Sexual Morality and Social Control, 1868–1900* (Westport, Conn., 1973).

Rand, Benjamin, "Philosophical Instruction in Harvard University from 1636 to 1906," *Harvard Graduates' Magazine*, 37 (1928–1929): 29–47, 188–200, 296–311.

Resek, Carl, introduction, to Randolph Bourne, *War and the Intellectuals* (New York, 1964).

Schlesinger, Arthur M., Jr., "Croly and 'The Promise of American Life,' " *NR*, 152 (May 8, 1965): 17–22.

————, introduction, to HC, *PAL* (Cambridge, Mass., 1965 edition).

Schlesinger, Elizabeth B., "The Nineteenth Century Woman's Dilemma and Jennie June," *New York History*, 42 (October 1961): 365–79.

Semonche, John E., *Ray Stannard Baker: A Quest for Democracy in Modern America, 1870–1918* (Chapel Hill, N.C., 1969).

Simon, Walter M., *European Positivism in the Nineteenth Century: An Essay in Intellectual History* (Ithaca, 1963).

Steel, Ronald, *Walter Lippmann and the American Century* (Boston, 1980).

Strout, Cushing, *The Pragmatic Revolt in American History: Carl Becker and Charles Beard* (New Haven, 1958).

Susman, Warren, "The Useless Past: American Intellectuals and the Frontier Thesis: 1910–1930," *Bucknell Review*, 11 (1963): 1–20.

Swanberg, W. A., *Whitney Father, Whitney Heiress* (New York, 1980).

Thayer, H. S., *Meaning and Action: A Critical History of Pragmatism* (Indianapolis, 1968).

Turner, Steven Jay, "The New Education in *The New Republic* Magazine: 1914–1930" (unpublished D.Ed. dissertation, University of Oklahoma, 1983).

Urofsky, Melvin I., "Wilson, Brandeis and the Trust Issue, 1912–1914," *Mid-America*, 49 (1967): 3–28.

Vevier, Charles, *The United States and China, 1906–1913: A Study of Finance and Diplomacy* (New Brunswick, N.J., 1955).

Wade, Hugh Mason, *A Brief History of Cornish, 1763–1974* (Hanover, N.H., 1976).

Webb, James, *The Harmonious Circle: The Lives and Work of G. I. Gurdjieff, P. D. Ouspensky and Their Followers* (New York, 1980).

White, Morton, *Social Thought in America: The Revolt Against Formalism* (New York, 1949).

Wiebe, Robert H., *The Search for Order, 1877–1920* (New York, 1967).

Wiener, Philip P., *Evolution and the Founders of Pragmatism* (Cambridge, Mass., 1949).

Wilson, R. Jackson, *In Quest of Community: Social Philosophy in the United States, 1860–1920* (New York, 1968).

Wirth Arthur G., *John Dewey as Educator: His Design for Work in Education (1894–1904)* (New York, 1966).

Wood, Ann D., " 'The Scribbling Women' and Fanny Fern: Why Women Wrote," *American Quarterly*, 23 (1971): 3–24.

Wood, Mary I., *The History of the General Federation of Women's Clubs for the First Twenty-two Years of Its Organization* (New York, 1912).

Wright, Benjamin F., *Five Public Philosophies of Walter Lippmann* (Austin, Texas, 1973).

Wyllie, Irvin G., *The Self-Made Man in America: The Myth of Rags to Riches* (New Brunswick, N.J., 1954).

INDEX

Aaron, Daniel, 135
Abbot, Francis E., 65
Adams, Charles F., 303
Adams, Henry, 53–54, 57, 96, 103, 303–304
Addams, Jane, 254, 283
Aiken, Conrad, 212, 280
Alden, Cynthia W., 6
"An American Farmer," 93
American Magazine, 141, 159
American Political Science Review, 172
American Union Against Militarism, 251
Anderson, Margaret, 296
Andrews, John B., 212
Angell, Norman, 212, 223, 233, 245, 247–48, 253, 268
"Appeal to the President," 229
Arabic, 225
Architectural Record, 75–76, 84–94, 125
"Art and Life," 76
"At the Parting of the Ways," 133
Atherton, Gertrude, 93, 103, 212
Auguste Comte and Positivism, 36
autobiographical fragment, 3n, 29, 123, 301–302

Baker, George P., 48
Baker, Newton D., 244
Baker, Ray Stannard, 134, 138–39, 212, 247–48, 256, 264
Baldwin, Roger, 256
Barnes, Harry Elmer, 270, 280
Bartlett, William, 12
Bastiat, Frédéric, 58
Beard, Charles A., 103, 180, 209, 212, 268–71, 280
Becker, Carl, 140
Beesly, E. S., 58
Beffel, John N., 286
Bellamy, Edward, 127
Bergson, Henri, 68, 194
Berkeley, George, 59

Beveridge, Albert J., 160, 255
Bliven, Bruce, 278–79, 281, 286, 300
Bocher, Ferdinand, 56–57
Bode, Carl, 16
The Bookman, 132
Bourne, Randolph, 194, 209–211, 214, 259–62, 265–67, 273, 281
Bowen, Francis, 49
Boynton, Percy, 212
Brailsford, H. N., 212, 219, 223
Brandeis, Louis D., 82, 96, 103, 155–60, 187–88, 203, 211, 238, 256, 264–65, 274, 277, 282, 307
The Breach in Civilization, 203n, 290–93, 305
Bridges, J. H., 15, 58, 62
Briggs, LeBaron R., 48, 57
Brooks, John Graham, 212
Brooks, Phillips, 55
Brooks, Van Wyck, 210, 212, 260
Brown, Rollo, 66
Bruere, Robert, 271
Brush, George, 79
Bryan, William Jennings, xii, 103, 111, 122, 129–30, 160
Bryant, William Cullen, 12
Bryce, James, 103, 132–33
Burgess, John W., 105
Burke, Kenneth, 296
Burleson, Albert S., 251–54
Butler, Joseph, 64

Cannon, Joseph B., 151
Catholic World, 257
Chamberlain, John, 135
Channing, Edward, 105
Chapman, John Jay, 47–48, 51–52, 81, 200–201, 211
Chase, Stuart, 279
Chicago Evening Post, 196
Child, Francis J., 48
Christensen, Parley P., 275
Christian Way of Life Committee, 294

Churchill, Winston, 79, 93, 268
Claudel, Paul, 212
Clayton Antitrust Act, 237
Cleveland, Grover, 46, 186
Cleveland Leader, 141, 144–46
Cohen, Morris R., 212, 280
Colby, Frank, 212
Cole, Arthur C., 147
Collier, Robert, 188
Collier's Weekly, 187–88, 216, 255–56
Colton, Arthur, 132
Colum, Padraic, 212
Columbia University, 269–70
Committee for Immigrants in America, 268
Committee of Forty-Eight, 283
Comte, Auguste (and positivism), xv, 15, 22–25, 28–42, 54, 58–60, 62–63, 66–69, 78, 91, 119–20, 124, 131, 140, 158, 180–82, 290, 292–93, 304–305
Conference for Progressive Political Action, 283
Congreve, Richard, 15, 58
Constitution of 1787, 41, 98, 103, 163–64, 172, 177–78, 180–81, 235–36
Coolidge, Calvin, 282–84, 288, 299
Copeland, Charles T., 49
Cornish, New Hampshire, 71, 79–80, 156, 160, 197, 215, 245n, 269, 299–300
Cortissoz, Royal, 122–23
Corwin, Edward S., 212
Cours de Philosophie Positive, 29–32
Cowley, Malcolm, 197, 204, 280, 289
Cox, James, 275
Cox, Kenyon, 79
Crane, Charles R., 188
Crane, Hart, 296
Creel, George, 212, 251–53
Crèvecoeur, J. Hector St. John, 93, 123
Croly, Alice, 26
Croly, David G., 5, 7, 11–19, 22, 24–27, 36–43, 45–73, 78, 91, 103–104, 118–23, 126–27, 131, 140, 180–81, 212, 215, 267, 303–304
Croly, Elizabeth, 11
Croly, Herbert
    personal characteristics: xi–xiv, 69–71, 278, 287–88, 303–304
    and: Jane Cunningham Croly, 20–

22, 26; David Goodman Croly, xv, 26–29, 45–46, 57–64, 119–23; Auguste Comte, xv, 28–29, 58–61, 119–20, 181, 292–93; Religion of Humanity, 3–4, 65–67, 293; early education, 43–44; Harvard College, 44–46, 56–69, 71, 77–78, 80–84, 141; Josiah Royce, 65–66, 125–27; Christianity, 66–67, 289–91, 293–95, 302; *Real Estate Record and Builders' Guide*, 72–75; *Architectural Record*, 75–76, 84–93; marriage, 76–77; Cornish, N. H., 78–80; Theodore Roosevelt, 136–41, 151–61, 239–41; progressivism, 94, 127–31, 150–61, 163–71, 234–37; Louis D. Brandeis, 155–59; Willard and Dorothy Straight, 186–88, 205–209, 276–78; *New Republic*, 187–217, 219–66, 271–74, 278–89; Woodrow Wilson, 162–63, 224, 231–34, 237–39, 243–49, 252–53; pragmatism, 118n, 176–82, 259–62; World War I, 218–32, 249–55, 263–66; Treaty of Versailles, 263–66; New School for Social Research, 269–71; election of 1912, 151–61; of 1916, 241–43; of 1920, 275–76; of 1924, 283–84; of 1928, 284–85; Georges I. Gurdjieff and A. R. Orage, 295–99; final illness and death, 299–300
    views on: American history, 97–109, 163–66, 175; art and architecture, 76, 85–87, 89–93, 124–25; Bruce Bliven, 279; Louis D. Brandeis, 158–59; businessmen and millionaires, 88–89, 106–107; censorship, 250–52; Christianity, 66, 289–94, 304–305; Constitution of 1787, 103, 163–64, 177–78; Croly, David G., 27–29, 122–23; democracy, 98–100, 112–13, 125–26, 163–64, 177–78, 181–82, 302, 306; Democratic party, 111, 142–44, 152, 166, 242–43; division of wealth, 114; federal government, 73–75, 98–100, 113–15, 292; foreign policy, 114, 186–87, 220–21; Georges I. Gurdjieff, 295–99; Mark A. Hanna, 146–50; human nature and regeneration, 115–17, 168–71, 182–84, 304–305; individualism, 74, 97, 100, 115–17, 176; Jeffersonianism v. Hamiltonianism, 73–74, 98–100,

103–104, 110–12, 130–31; labor, 74–
75, 108, 116; Abraham Lincoln, 99–
100; Eduard C. Lindeman, 281; Walter Lippmann, 196, 281; nationalism,
89–91, 98–99, 124–26, 181–82, 306;
A. R. Orage, 296–99; pioneers, 100–
101, 104, 115, 149–50; political
"bosses," 107–108; progressive reform, 94, 109–115, 128–31, 142–46,
159, 164–66, 175–76, 292, 301–302;
prohibition, 282; the promise of
American life, 101–102; Religion of
Humanity, 66–67, 292–93; Republican
party, 122, 142–46, 152–53, 165–66,
242; Theodore Roosevelt, 111–12,
138, 152–55; Josiah Royce, 65; social
education, 168–71, 177–78, 215–16,
269–70; socialism, 74–75, 113–14; sociological laws, 73, 181; specialization, 100–101, 105–109; state and local government, 113, 144, 164; Willard and Dorothy Straight, 200–
201n, 266–67, 276–78; teaching, 82–
83; trusts, 73, 113–14, 156–58; Edmund Wilson, 280; Woodrow Wilson, 162–63, 170–71, 231–32, 242–
43; see also New Republic
  writings: "An American Farmer,"
93; Architectural Record, 76, 84–93;
"Art and Life," 76; autobiographical
fragment, 3n, 29, 123, 301–302; Breach
in Civilization, 290–93, 305; Cleveland
Leader, 144–46; "Democratic Factions
and Insurgent Republicans," 142–44;
"The End of American Isolation,"
220–21, 223; "A Great School of Political Science," 142; "Henry James
and His Countrymen," 93; Houses for
Town or Country, 85; Marcus Alonzo
Hanna, 146–50, 275; "My Aim in The
Promise of American Life," 118; " 'Our
Problems,' " 128; "Pacifism v. Passivism," 221–22; Progressive Democracy,
162–84, 215, 233, 290–91, 305–306;
"The Progressive Voter: He Wants to
Know," 285; The Promise of American
Life, 72, 94–137, 140–42, 144, 148–50,
156, 162, 172, 174–75, 186–87, 197–
98, 215, 220–21, 226, 227n, 278, 290–
91, 293, 305, 307–308; Real Estate Rec-

ord and Builders' Guide, 72–75; "Reli-
gion in Life," 297–98; "A School for
Social Research," 270; "Some Really
Historical Novels," 93; speech on The
New Republic, 216–17; "State Political
Reorganization," 144; Stately Homes in
America, 85; "A Test of Faith in De-
mocracy," 159; "The Two Parties in
1916," 242–43; "Why I Shall Vote for
La Follette," 283–84; Willard Straight,
267, 277–78
Croly, Jane Cunningham, 4–12, 18–26,
  43, 69, 80, 215
Croly, Louise E., 25–27, 76–77, 79, 264,
  297–300
Croly, Minnie, 26
Croly, Patrick, 11
Croly, Vida, 26
Cummings, Edward, 77–78, 81
Cunningham, John, 4–6, 18, 24
Cunningham, Joseph, 4, 24
Cunningham, William, 81

Dana, Charles A., 5
Darwin, Charles (and Darwinism), 15,
  38, 63, 69, 177
Daugherty, Harry, 281
"David, A. C.," 85
Davis, John W., 283–84
Debs, Eugene V., 274, 281
Dell, Floyd, 212, 267
"Democratic Factions and Insurgent Re-
  publicans," 142–44
Democratic party, 42, 110–11, 122, 142–
  43, 152, 154–55, 165–66, 237–38, 242
Demorest's Illustrated Monthly, 5–6
Descartes, René, 59
Desmond, Harry, 85
Deutsch, Babette, 280–86
Dewey, John, 96, 176, 178–79, 181–82,
  210, 212, 219, 246, 254n, 260–62, 270,
  279–80, 286
Dewing, Thomas, 79
Dickens, Charles, 6
Dodge, Mabel, 193, 196, 202
Dos Passos, John, 287
Dreiser, Theodore, 96, 209, 211–12
Drift and Mastery, 171, 194–96
DuBois, W.E.B., 53–54

Dunbar, Charles F., 54, 57–58, 60, 62, 64

Dunne, Finley Peter, 211

Eastman, Max, 212, 251
École Libre des Sciences Politiques, 269
Economic Consequences of the Peace, 279
Edgar, Henry, 22–23
Edwards, Jonathan, xi
Eliot, Charles W., 47–48, 53, 55, 258
Eliot, George, 15
Elmhirst, Dorothy Straight, *see* Dorothy Straight
Elmhirst, Leonard, 277, 285, 300
Ely, Richard T., 77, 96, 127
Emerton, Ephraim, 82
"End of American Isolation," 220–21, 223
Espionage Act, 251
Euripides, 203
Evans, Elizabeth G., 286
Evans, T. C., 6
Everett, Charles C., 61, 64, 81
Everybody's Magazine, 193, 255

F. W. Dodge Corporation, 75, 84
fascism, 307–308
Federal Reserve System, 237
Federal Trade Commission, 173, 234, 237–38
Fichte, Johann G., 51
Fiske, John, 23, 58–59
Fitzgerald, John, 199
Foraker, Joseph B., 149
Forcey, Charles, 27n, 117–18n, 139n, 147, 176, 188n, 243n, 293n
Ford, Ford Madox, 212
Ford, Henry Jones, 172
Fourteen Points, 263, 266
Frank, Leo, 234
Frank, Waldo, 280–81, 284, 295–96, 298–99
Frankfurter, Felix, xii, 26–27, 80, 82–84, 135, 156, 158, 160, 196–98, 213, 218, 256, 268–69, 272, 279, 282–83, 290, 292, 300, 307
The Freeman, 257
Freud, Sigmund, 68–69, 194, 211
Friday, David, 279
Frost, Robert, 212

Fuller, Henry, 79

Gale, Zona, 296
Gates, Lewis E., 48, 81
General Federation of Women's Clubs, 6–7
George, Henry, 54, 60, 123, 129
Ghent, William J., 208, 212
Gilbert and Sullivan, 123
Godkin, E. L., 198
Godkin lectures, 162
Goldman, Eric F., 118n, 130, 135, 138
Gould, Jay, 40
Grant, Robert, 92, 118, 123, 125, 211
"A Great School of Political Science," 142
Greeley, Horace, 16
Gurdjieff, Georges I., 295–99

Hackett, Francis, xiii, 196–97, 199, 203, 205, 214, 222, 239, 263, 272–73, 279
Hall, G. Stanley, 127
Hallowell, Robert, 198–99, 214, 245, 263, 273
Hamilton, Alexander (and Hamiltonianism), 98–99, 103–104, 111–12, 115, 119, 125, 133, 139, 157, 175, 181, 210
Hand, Learned, 27n, 71, 80, 132, 134, 136, 141, 146, 152–54, 156, 158–60, 188n, 196, 201, 208–209, 213, 215, 219, 258, 268–69, 300
Hanna, Daniel R., 146–47, 148n
Hanna, Leonard, 146
Hanna, Mark A., xii, 146–52
Hapgood, Hutchins, 46–47, 61, 70
Hapgood, Norman, 46–47, 51, 56–57, 70, 80, 160, 187–88, 268, 283
Hard, William, 250, 258, 279
Harding, Warren G., 275–76, 281–82, 306
Harper's Weekly, 188, 198, 216, 255, 272–73
Harriman, E. H., 185
Harrison, Frederic, 15, 58
Hart, Albert Bushnell, 212
Harvard College, 44–71, 77–78, 80–84, 141–42
Hays, Samuel P., 135
Hearst, William R., 45, 129
Hearst's Magazine, 255

Hegel, George, 34, 51, 58–59, 63, 65, 67–68, 84, 117–18n
Henderson, Gerard, 279
"Henry James and His Countrymen," 93
Herrick, Robert, 62n, 70, 212, 257, 280
Hewlett, Maurice, 93
Hill, Adams S., 48, 77
Hill, Thomas, 33
History of the Woman's Club Movement in America, 7
Hobson, John A., 212
Hofstadter, Richard, 135
Holmes, Oliver Wendell, Jr., 82, 96, 103, 174, 180, 196, 256–57, 289
Holt, Henry, 210
Hoover, Herbert, 258, 275, 285
House, Edward M., 231, 244–47, 268, 304
Houses for Town or Country, 85
Howard, J. W., 132
Hudson, Frederick, 12
Hughes, Charles Evans, 212, 241–43, 248
Hughes, H. Stuart, 67–68
Hume, David, 59
Hunt, Edward E., 193
Huxley, Thomas, 15

The Independent, 141, 172, 216
"the Inquiry," 244, 248–49, 268
Insurgent movement, 144–46, 151–54, 166. *See also* Progressive party (1912)

Jackson, Andrew (and Jacksonianism), 99, 111, 122, 142, 165, 242
Jackson, Gardner, 286
James, Henry, 93
James, William, 50–52, 55, 57, 59–60, 64, 67–69, 71, 80, 82, 84, 96, 118n, 176, 179, 182, 192, 219
Jefferson, Thomas (and Jeffersonianism), 41–42, 73–74, 98–99, 102–104, 110–13, 115, 119, 122, 125, 130, 133, 142, 145, 170–71, 175, 181, 233, 242
"Jenny June," *see* Jane Cunningham Croly
Jerome, William T., 129
J. H. Morse's School for Boys, 43–44
Johnson, Alvin S., 78, 189n, 199, 208,

210–11, 214, 245, 253, 263, 265, 270–71, 273, 279
Josephson, Matthew, 137n

Kallen, Horace M., 212, 256, 270, 280
Kant, Immanuel, 51, 59
Keating-Owen Child Labor Act, 238
Keller, Helen, 254n
Kellogg, Paul U., 268
Kennan, George, 224
Kent, William, 160
Keynes, John Maynard, 279
King, Clyde, 212
King, William G., 12
Kipling, Rudyard, 139
Kittredge, George L., 48
Kuttner, Alfred B., 211, 214

Labor Research Bureau, 271
La Follette, Robert M., 144, 210, 234, 283–85, 306
The Lamp, 93
Landis, James M., 307
Lane, Franklin K., 160
Langer, William, 280
Lasch, Christopher, 72, 135
Laski, Harold J., 212, 223, 256–57, 269–70, 272, 289
Laughlin, J. Laurence, 60, 62–64, 68
Lazarus, Emma, 79
League of Free Nations Association, 268
Leuchtenburg, William E., 135, 139n
Lewis, Sinclair, 211
Lincoln, Abraham, 13, 99, 103, 111, 122
Lindbergh, Charles A., 282
Lindeman, Eduard C., 281
Link, Arthur S., 135, 245n
Lippmann, Walter, xi, 96, 135, 151, 171, 192–96, 198–99, 202–205, 211, 214, 217–21, 223, 227, 233, 241–42, 244, 245–48, 253, 259, 262–64, 272–73, 275, 281
Littell, Philip, xi, xiv, 71, 80, 160, 197, 202–203, 207–208, 214, 263, 269, 273, 279–80, 286
Littell, Robert, 280
Littré, Maximilien, 15
Lodge, Henry Cabot, 62, 103, 137
London School of Economics, 269
Lovejoy, Arthur O., 212

Lovett, Robert M., xiv, 46–47, 70–71, 81, 135, 265, 279–80, 286, 296
Lowell, Amy, 203–204, 211–12
Lunn, George R., 193
Lusitania, 225, 228

McCarthy, Charles, 256
McClure's Magazine, 255
MacKaye, Percy, 79
McKelway, St. Clair, 17, 25
McKinley, William, 146
McMaster, John B., 105
Macvane, Silas, 57
Mahan, Alfred T., 96–97
Mansfield, Katherine, 295
Marble, Manton, 16
Marcus Alonzo Hanna, 146–50, 275
Martineau, Harriet, 58, 63
Marvin, George, 277
Marx, Karl (and Marxism), 34, 54, 62, 181, 191
Matthews, T. S., xiii, 278, 280, 296
May, Henry F., 135
Meikeljohn, Alexander, 286
Mencken, H. L., 208
Merz, Charles, 272–73, 278
Mill, John Stuart, 24, 35–36, 58–59, 62
Miller, Perry, xi
Miscegenation, 13–14
Mitchell, John, 190
Mitchell, Wesley C., 245, 270
Modern Thinker, 14–15, 23, 212
Monroe Doctrine, 114
Moody, William Vaughn, 70
Mooney, Tom, 281
More, Paul E., 151
Morgan, J. P., 185
Morison, Samuel Eliot, 280
Morris, Gouverneur, 139n
Morrow, James B., 147
Morrow, William, 211
Morse, Caroline, 25
Morse, J. H., 43–44
Mowry, George E., 135
Mumford, Lewis, 212, 280
Münsterberg, Hugo, 52
Murray, Gilbert, 218, 223
"My Aim in *The Promise of American Life*," 118
Myers, George A., 147

The Nation, 132, 172–73, 190–91, 198–99, 216
National Americanization Committee, 268
National Civic Federation Review, 271
Nevinson, Henry, 212
The New Democracy, 190–91
the "New Freedom," 155–56, 162–63, 173, 183, 194–95, 233, 237–38. *See also* Woodrow Wilson
the "New Nationalism," 112, 139–41, 194–95, 216–17, 226, 233, 236–38. *See also* Theodore Roosevelt
The New Republic, xiii, 70, 304–305, 307; origins, 187–217; finances, 187–89, 200–201n, 205–208, 271–72, 276–77; staff, 189–98, 209–14, 272–74, 278–81; offices, 199; luncheons, 199–200; editorial procedures, 202–205; format, 202; reputation, 255–59; circulation, 200–202, 255, 271–72, 288; on domestic issues, 1914–1919, 233–37, 242–43; and Theodore Roosevelt, 216–17, 233, 239–41; and Woodrow Wilson, 231–33, 237–39, 243–48, 263–66; and World War I, 219–33, 249–55, 259–62; and the Treaty of Versailles, 263–66; on domestic issues, 1919–1930, 274–76, 281–87
New School for Social Research, 269–71
New York Daily Graphic, 16
New York Evening Post, 264
New York Globe, 253
New York Times, 172–73, 239, 286
New York Tribune, 257
New York World, 11–16, 123, 272
Nietzsche, Friedrich, 68, 194
Noble, David, 117–18n, 176
Nock, Albert Jay, 257
Norris, Frank, 96
North American Review, 142
Norton, Charles Eliot, 81, 84, 87, 125
Nye, Russel B., 135

Oliver, Frederick S., 103
"On Reading *The New Republic*," 257
Orage, A. R., 296–99, 301
" 'Our Problems,' " 128
The Outlook, 133, 138, 171, 216, 255, 277–78

"Pacifism v. Passivism," 221–22
Palmer, A. Mitchell, 275
Palmer, Alice Freeman, 50
Palmer, George Herbert, 49–50, 52, 55, 57–60, 63–64, 68, 80, 82
Parrish, Maxfield, 79
Patten, Simon, 75, 96, 189–90, 212
Peabody, Francis G., 55, 60
"Peace Without Victory," 230–31
Peirce, Charles Saunders, 127
Percy, Eustace, 160
Perry, Ralph Barton, 212
Pinchot, Amos R. E., 258–59, 296
Pinchot-Ballinger conservation controversy, 151
Platt, Charles A., 70, 79–80, 85–86, 160
Political Science Quarterly, 147, 173
positivism, *see* Auguste Comte and Religion of Humanity
Positivist Primer, 23, 25, 36, 43, 120
Pound, Roscoe, 212, 270
Preface to Politics, 193–95, 211
"Preparedness—A Trojan Horse," 225–26
Progressive Democracy, 162–84, 215, 233, 290–91, 305–306
Progressive party (1912), 154–55, 159–60, 217
Progressive party (1924), 283–84
"The Progressive Voter: He Wants to Know," 285
The Promise of American Life, 72, 94–137, 139–42, 144, 148–50, 156, 162, 172, 174–75, 186–87, 197–98, 215, 220–21, 226, 227n, 278, 290–91, 293, 305, 307–308
"A Punic Peace," 265
Putnam, Emily James, 270

Ratcliffe, S. K., 212, 223
Ravenhill, Margaret, 6
Real Estate Record and Builders' Guide, 14, 17, 41, 64–65, 72–75, 128
The Re-Discovery of America, 281
red scare, 275
Reed, John, 192–93, 196, 198
"Religion in Life," 297–98
Religion of Humanity, 3–4, 22–23, 28, 32–33, 36–37, 40, 60–61, 65–67, 120, 182, 290, 293, 300

Renan, Ernest, 15
Republican party, 42, 54, 110–11, 121–22, 142–46, 151–61, 165–66, 237–38, 242–43
Review of Reviews, 132–33
Rhodes, James Ford, 105, 147
Ricardo, David, 58
Richardson, Henry H., 86
Richberg, Donald, 211–12, 307
Robinson, James Harvey, 212, 254n, 270–71
Rockefeller Foundation, 142
Rockford (Ill.) *Daily News*, 12
Roosevelt, Franklin D., 307
Roosevelt, Theodore, xii, 82, 87, 94, 103, 111–12, 121, 129, 133, 136–41, 144–45, 147, 152–62, 171–72, 175, 184–86, 188, 192, 210, 217–18, 227, 232–34, 239–41, 267, 276, 301, 304
Root, Elihu, 160, 185
Rosenfeld, Paul, 257
Ross, Edward A., 127, 212
Rowell, Chester, 211, 214
Royce, Josiah, 51–52, 56, 59, 63–69, 78, 80, 84, 126–27, 212
Rublee, George, 70, 80, 155, 160, 197, 234, 269
Rudyard, Charlotte, 198, 214
Russell, Bertrand, 280

Sacco and Vanzetti case, 285–88
St. Gaudens, Augustus, 79
Sang, Kugwon, 270n
Santayana, George, 52, 77–78, 80, 82, 84, 87, 117, 125, 132, 192, 212
Saturday Evening Post, 256
Saturday Review (London), 133
Schapiro, J. Salwyn, 173
Schelling, Friedrich, 51
Schiff, Jacob H., 185
Schlesinger, Arthur M., Jr., 118n, 135
"A School of Social Research," 270
Schouler, James, 105
Schuyler, Montgomery, 18
Scopes, John T., 281
Sedgwick, Ellery, 209, 214
Seligman, E.R.A., 75
Seven Arts, 260, 281
Seymour and Blair, 14
Seymour, Horatio, 14, 122

Shaftesbury, Anthony A. C., 63–64
Shaw, Albert, 251
Sherman Antitrust Act, 114, 129
Shipman, Ellen B., 79
Shipman, Louis, 79
Shotwell, James T., 249
Simonds, Frank, 219
Simonson, Lee, 211, 214
Small, Albion W., 176–77
Smith, Adam (and *laissez faire*), 38, 42, 54, 60, 62–63, 65, 73–75, 167, 191, 226
Smith, Alfred E., 284–85, 299, 306
"Some Really Historical Novels," 93
Sorel, Georges, 194
Sorosis, 6, 9
Soule, George, 211, 245, 256, 279
speech on *The New Republic*, 216–17
Spencer, Herbert, 15, 35–36, 58–59, 69
Spinoza, Baruch, 59
"State Political Reorganization," 144
Stately Homes in America, 85
Steffens, Lincoln, 193
Stimson, Henry L., 82, 134–35, 160, 211–12, 242–43, 256
Stokes, Frederick A., 211
Strachey, Lytton, xv
Straight, Dorothy, 76, 186–88, 199, 204–209, 214–16, 233, 267–68, 270–72, 274, 276, 279–81, 284n, 287–88, 297–300
Straight, Willard, 174, 185–89, 198–200, 204–209, 214–16, 222–23, 233, 241–43, 245, 247–50, 258, 266–68, 276, 278, 287
Sullivan, Louis, 87, 90
Survey, 190
Sussex, 229
Sweet, Clinton, 14, 16, 84
Système de Politique Positive, 32–33

Taft, William Howard, 136, 144, 151–54, 160–61
Tarbell, Ida, 246
Tate, Allen, 280
Taussig, Frank W., 54, 60, 62, 64
"A Test of Faith in Democracy," 159
Thomas, Norman, 251, 285
Thompson, William G., 286
Tocqueville, Alexis de, 123

Toksvig, Signe, 273
Toomer, Jean, 296
Treaty of Versailles, 254–55, 263–66, 276, 289, 292
Trowbridge, John, 48
Truth About Love, 15–16, 37
Tugwell, Rexford, 279, 307
Turner, Frederick Jackson, 96, 104
Tweed, William M., 16
"The Two Parties in 1916," 242–43

University Club of New York City, 142
Unleavened Bread, 92, 118, 123, 125
Unpopular Review, 210
Usher, Roland, 219

Vanderbilt, William H., 40
Vaux, Clothilde, 32
Veblen, Thorstein, 96, 254n, 270
Villard, Oswald G., 44, 47–48, 53–54, 70, 72, 77, 188, 233, 251

Wakeman, George, 14n, 22n
Wakeman, Thaddeus B., 22n
Wald, Lillian, 251
Walker, Henry, 79
Wallas, Graham, 192, 194, 212, 218, 270
Walling, William English, 253
Walpole, Hugh, 219
"A War Program for Liberals," 249–50
Ward, Lester Frank, 127
Washington's Farewell Address, 114
Weber, Max, 68
Wells, H. G., 123, 211–12
Wendell, Barrett, 49, 61–62
West, Rebecca, 212, 219
Weyl, Bertha P., 190
Weyl, Walter E., 189–93, 196, 199, 203, 205, 214, 218, 222, 242, 245, 254n, 263, 267
Wharton, Edith, 93
Whig party, 99
White, John, 82
White, William Allen, 96, 148n, 161, 184, 211, 214, 251, 256–57
Whitney, William C., 186
"Why I Shall Vote for La Follette," 283–84
Wiebe, Robert H., 183
Willard Straight, 267, 277–78

Wilson, Edmund, xii–xiii, 3, 273, 280, 286, 289
Wilson, Woodrow, xii, 103, 133, 153–56, 158–60, 162, 170–71, 183, 188, 195, 210, 224–25, 227, 229–34, 237–39, 241–45, 248, 250–52, 255, 263–64, 266, 268, 276, 301
Wolman, Leo, 279, 307
women's club movement, 6–7
Woolens bill, 152

Woolf, Virginia, 280
World Today, 132
World War I, 183–84, 217, 218–33
World's Work, 142
Wright, Frank Lloyd, 90

Young, Stark, 280, 286

Zimmern, Alfred, 212, 223

LIBRARY OF CONGRESS CATALOGING IN PUBLICATION DATA

Levy, David W., 1937–
Herbert Croly of the New republic.

Bibliography: p.   Includes index.
1. Croly, Herbert David, 1869–1930. 2. Social
scientists—United States—Biography. I. Title.
H59.C76L48 1985   300'.924 [B]   84–17768
ISBN 0–691–04725–1